The Cambridge Companion to the Beatles

From *Please Please Me* to *Abbey Road*, this collection of essays tells the fascinating story of the Beatles – the creation of the band, their musical influences, and their cultural significance, with emphasis on their genesis and practices as musicians, songwriters, and recording artists. Through detailed biographical and album analyses, the book uncovers the background of each band member and provides expansive readings of the band's music.

- Traces the group's creative output from their earliest recordings and throughout their career
- Pays particular attention to the social and historical factors which contributed to the creation of the band
- Investigates the Beatles' uniquely enduring musical legacy and cultural power

Clearly organized into three sections, covering Background, Works, and History and Influence, the *Companion* is ideal for course usage, and is also a must-read for all Beatles fans.

The Cambridge Companion to the

BEATLES

. . . .

EDITED BY
Kenneth Womack

CAMBRIDGE
UNIVERSITY PRESS

CAMBRIDGE UNIVERSITY PRESS
Cambridge, New York, Melbourne, Madrid, Cape Town, Singapore, São Paulo, Delhi

Cambridge University Press
The Edinburgh Building, Cambridge CB2 8RU, UK

Published in the United States of America by Cambridge University Press, New York

www.cambridge.org
Information on this title: www.cambridge.org/9780521689762

First published 2009

Printed in the United Kingdom at the University Press, Cambridge

A catalogue record for this publication is available from the British Library

Library of Congress Cataloguing in Publication data
The Cambridge companion to the Beatles / edited by Kenneth Womack.
    p.   cm. – (Cambridge companions to music)
Includes bibliographical references and index.
ISBN 978-0-521-86965-2 (hardback)
1. Beatles.   2. Rock musicians – England.   3. Rock music – History and criticism.
I. Womack, Kenneth.   II. Title.   III. Series.
ML421.B4C33   2009
782.42166092′2 – dc22   2009030744

ISBN 978-0-521-86965-2 hardback
ISBN 978-0-521-68976-2 paperback

For Kenneth E. Zimmerman (1913–2008)

Contents

List of tables [*page* ix]

Notes on contributors [x]

Foreword: I believe in tomorrow: the posthumous life of the Beatles
　　Anthony DeCurtis [xiii]

Acknowledgments [xvii]

Chronology of the Beatles' lives and works [xviii]

Introducing the Beatles　　*Kenneth Womack* [1]

Part I • Background

1　Six boys, six Beatles: the formative years, 1950–1962　　*Dave Laing* [9]

　　Appendix: The repertoire, 1957–1962　[27]

2　The Beatles as recording artists　　*Jerry Zolten* [33]

Part II • Works

3　Rock and roll music　　*Howard Kramer* [65]

4　"Try thinking more": *Rubber Soul* and the Beatles' transformation
　　of pop　　*James M. Decker* [75]

5　Magical mystery tours, and other trips: yellow submarines, newspaper taxis,
　　and the Beatles' psychedelic years　　*Russell Reising and Jim LeBlanc* [90]

6　Revolution　　*Ian Inglis* [112]

7　On their way home: the Beatles in 1969 and 1970　　*Steve Hamelman* [125]

8　Apple Records　　*Bruce Spizer* [142]

9　The solo years　　*Michael Frontani* [153]

10　Any time at all: the Beatles' free phrase rhythms　　*Walter Everett* [183]

Part III • History and influence

11　The Beatles as zeitgeist　　*Sheila Whiteley* [203]

12　Beatles news: product line extensions and the rock
　　canon　　*Gary Burns* [217]

13   "An abstraction, like Christmas": the Beatles for sale and
     for keeps   *John Kimsey*   [230]

     Notes [255]
     Beatles discography, 1962–1970 [286]
     Select bibliography [294]
     Index [311]

Tables

6.1 Major musical sources of *The Beatles* [*page* 122]

10.1 The Beatles' canon on compact disc [184]

10.2 Representative "floaters" in the Beatles' music [189]

11.1 Top lies told by people who grew up in the sixties, seventies, or eighties [204]

Contributors

Gary Burns is Professor of Communication at Northern Illinois University, Editor of the journal *Popular Music and Society*, Executive Secretary of the Midwest Popular Culture Association, and Vice President of the Popular Culture Association and American Culture Association.

James M. Decker is Associate Professor of English at Illinois Central College. He is the author of *Ideology* (2003) and *Henry Miller and Narrative Form: Constructing the Self, Rejecting Modernity* (2005). In addition to contributing numerous articles to such publications as *College Literature* and *Style*, he is editor of *Nexus: The International Henry Miller Journal*.

Anthony DeCurtis is a renowned author and music critic who has written for *Rolling Stone*, the *New York Times*, *Relix*, and a host of other publications. He is the author of *Rocking My Life Away: Writing About Music and Other Matters* (1998) and *In Other Words: Artists Talk About Life and Work* (2005). He teaches in the creative writing program at the University of Pennsylvania.

Walter Everett is Professor of Music and Chair of the Department of Music Theory at the University of Michigan School of Music, Theater, and Dance. He is the author of the two-volume set *The Beatles as Musicians* (1999, 2001) and the editor of the essay collection *Expression in Pop-Rock Music* (1999), and is currently writing a book entitled *The Foundations of Rock from "Blue Suede Shoes" to "Suite: Judy Blue Eyes."*

Michael Frontani is Coordinator of American Studies and Associate Professor in the School of Communications at Elon University, where he teaches courses on film history, film theory, popular music, and mass culture. He is the author of *The Beatles: Image and the Media* (2007), which was selected as a CHOICE Outstanding Academic Title, and numerous essays on popular music, reception, and culture. He is currently working on book-length studies of the Italian American image in American mass consumer society and on American cinema's development and evolution within the context of US culture.

Steve Hamelman is Professor of English at Coastal Carolina University, where he teaches American literature and literary theory. He has written many essays on early American fiction and pop music. He is the author of *But Is It Garbage? On Rock and Trash* (2004), as well as the recipient of *Popular Music and Society*'s R. Serge Denisoff Award.

Ian Inglis is Reader in Popular Music Studies at the University of Northumbria. His doctoral research considered the role of sociological, social-psychological, and cultural theory in explanations of the career of the Beatles. His books include *The Beatles, Popular Music and Society: A Thousand Voices* (2000), *Popular Music and Film* (2003), and *Performance and Popular Music* (2006). He is currently preparing *The Words and Music of George Harrison* for Praeger's *Singer-Songwriter* series.

John Kimsey received his PhD in English from the University of Illinois at Chicago and serves as Associate Professor in DePaul University's School for New Learning. He teaches and writes about modern literature and popular music and has also worked as a professional musician. His writings have appeared in *Sgt. Pepper & the Beatles: It Was Forty Years Ago Today* (2008); *Reading the Beatles: Cultural Studies, Literary Criticism, and the Fab Four* (2006); and the *Journal of Popular Music Studies*, among other publications.

Howard Kramer is the Curatorial Director of the Rock and Roll Hall of Fame and Museum in Cleveland, Ohio. Since joining the museum in 1996, Kramer has curated exhibits on Elvis Presley, the Supremes, Hank Williams, the Doors, Roy Orbison, Tom Petty and the Heartbreakers, the Beach Boys, and many others. His writings have appeared in *Rolling Stone*, the *Cleveland Plain Dealer*, and *Gadfly Magazine*.

Dave Laing is a Visiting Research Fellow at the Institute of Popular Music, University of Liverpool. His books include *The Sound of Our Time* (1970) and *One Chord Wonders* (1985). He is co-editor of *The Faber / Da Capo Companion to Twentieth-Century Popular Music* (1990) and the *Continuum Encyclopaedia of Popular Music of the World* (2002–5).

Jim LeBlanc is Head of Database Management Services at the Cornell University Library, where he has worked since receiving his PhD from Cornell in 1984. In addition to library-related writing and research, his areas of current scholarly interest include popular music, existential phenomenology, and James Joyce studies.

Russell Reising received his BA in Chinese Studies at Miami University and his PhD in American literature from Northwestern University in 1983. He teaches American literature and popular culture at the University of Toledo; he has also been a Fulbright Teaching Fellow at the University of Jyvaskyla in Finland, and a Visiting Fellow in Popular Music Studies at the University of Salford. He has taught, spoken, and published widely on topics in American literature and culture, Japanese literature and culture, popular culture and popular music.

Bruce Spizer is a first-generation Beatles fan and a life-long native of New Orleans, Louisiana. He has an extensive Beatles collection, concentrating primarily on United States and Canadian first-issue records, record promotional items, press kits, and concert posters. A taxman by day, Spizer is a board-certified tax attorney and certified public accountant. A paperback writer by night, he is the author of the critically acclaimed books *The Beatles Records on Vee-Jay, The Beatles' Story on Capitol Records* Parts 1 and 2, *The Beatles on Apple Records, The Beatles Solo on Apple Records*, and *The Beatles Are Coming! The Birth of Beatlemania in America*. His articles on the Beatles are featured regularly in *Beatlology Magazine* and *Beatlefan.*

Sheila Whiteley has written extensively on the Beatles, including chapters in *The Space Between the Notes: Rock and the Counter-Culture* (1992), *Women and Popular Music* (2000), *Mapping the Beat: Popular Music and Contemporary Theory* (1998), *"Every Sound There Is": The Beatles' Revolver and the Transformation of Rock and Roll* (2002), *Reading the Beatles: Cultural Studies, Literary Criticism, and the Fab Four* (2006), *and Sgt. Pepper and the Beatles* (2008).

Kenneth Womack is Professor of English at Penn State University's Altoona College. He serves as Editor of *Interdisciplinary Literary Studies: A Journal of Criticism and Theory* and as Co-Editor (with William Baker) of Oxford University Press's *Year's Work in English Studies*. He is the author or editor of some twenty books, including *Postwar Academic Fiction: Satire, Ethics, Community* (2001), *Key Concepts in Literary Theory* (2002), *Reading the Beatles: Cultural Studies, Literary Criticism, and the Fab Four* (2006), *Postmodern Humanism in Contemporary Literature and Culture: Reconciling the Void* (2006), and *Long and Winding Roads: The Evolving Artistry of the Beatles* (2007).

Jerry Zolten is Associate Professor of Communication Arts and Sciences at Penn State University's Altoona College, where he teaches courses on Communications, American Studies, and Popular Music. He is the producer of CDs by the Fairfield Four and their bass singer Isaac Freeman, co-host with cartoonist Robert Crumb of *Chimpin' the Blues*, a public radio program on the history of early blues, and the author of *Great God A'Mighty! The Dixie Hummingbirds: Celebrating the Rise of Soul Gospel Music* (2002).

Foreword
I believe in tomorrow: the posthumous life of the Beatles

There is no end to the making of many books about the Beatles, obviously –
and I'm not simply talking about this one. The biographies of the band just
get fatter, as do the biographies of its individual members. Critical studies
proliferate. And it's not merely books. Magazine and newspaper articles,
blog posts and tributes of various sorts multiply endlessly. The more we
know the more we need to know.

Not only do the Beatles still seem to be everywhere, but they still seem
to matter so much. Paul McCartney's presence at the Grammy Awards
ceremony amid a host of more contemporary superstars in 2009 elicited
constant comments from the stage, as if being in the presence of a Beatle
titillated even the most jaded celebrities of the music industry. McCartney,
meanwhile, has reincarnated himself as the Fireman and has stormed an
ever-welcoming media, performing in hip contexts and even hosting a
series of "fireside chats" – how perfectly appropriate – on satellite radio.
The tabloid media mark the currents of the sixty-six-year-old cute Beatle's
romantic life with undiminished zeal and glee, and he's given them much
to work with.

John Lennon, of course, remains a figure of enormous regard and significance, both musical and political. References to him dot the pop culture
landscape, while Yoko Ono has become an avatar of the downtown dance
music scene in New York. Martin Scorsese, meanwhile, works on a documentary about the life of George Harrison. Even Ringo's unwillingness
to sign autographs for fans makes international news. *Love*, the Cirque du
Soleil's homage to the Beatles' music, continues to be a long-running hit
in Las Vegas. As I write, the Beatles are soon to have their own version of
the Rock Band video game. The question of when the Beatles' songs will be
available for digital download is one of the biggest unanswered questions
in what remains of the music industry. And, on the academic front, enter-
prising students will soon be able to take a degree in Beatle Studies, a truly
inevitable development.

So what does this all amount to? Let's all agree that the Beatles' music
will last, and deserves to. If that weren't true, I genuinely believe that no
one would care about the band. (Oh, okay, let's simply say "many fewer
people." In the age of the internet, an audience exists for everything.) But
in a turnaround of Gore Vidal's famed comment (about the Cockettes, if
you must know) that sometimes having no talent simply isn't enough, it's

also true that having enormous talent isn't enough to sustain the level of attention that the Beatles have. So what are the reasons for our ongoing fascination with them?

In one sense the Beatles are like a young artist who died tragically before his time. As diverse and experimental as the band's albums are, they serve as sketches that succeeding generations of musicians have set out in one way or another to complete. Robert Fripp once told me in an interview that one of the inspirations for King Crimson was the notion that the Beatles had abandoned their *Sgt. Pepper* period without fully exhausting the musical ideas they had set in motion. It's not hard to think of bands like Radiohead or Wilco in similar terms, picking up on and pursuing directions the Beatles had suggested but never fully defined.

If the Beatles as the inspiration for progressive rock disturbs more than excites you, perhaps the dozens of power-pop bands who learned wit, energy and concision from Beatles songs will please you more. The Beatles, of course, took their own lessons from Buddy Holly, Chuck Berry and Little Richard, but everyone who came after took their cues in how to create smart, melodic rock and roll from the Fab Four. And can enough be said about George Harrison's exploration of Indian music? Singer-songwriters, too, who, needless to say, owe their greatest debt to Bob Dylan, often reference the Beatles. The songs on *Rubber Soul* and *Revolver* rank in importance with Dylan's early records in creating a model for the enigmatic self-examinations that would follow in the decades ahead.

It's often pointed out that, short as it was, the Beatles' career was in some senses ideal. The band never were tempted to hang on past their expiration date, cashing in on their audience's longing for days gone by and creating lucrative, mediocre music. Such a grim result was not their only potential destiny, of course. Dylan, for all of his patchy spots over the past forty years, has demonstrated that it is possible for a rock and roll musician to create vital, important work well into their sixties. Neil Young provides an example of that as well.

But it is much easier for solo artists to accomplish that sort of longevity than it is for bands. The creative and personal balance required to sustain a successful band is so delicate that it's far more remarkable that bands ever manage to stay together than that they break up. For all the dramatic posturing, sniping, business machinations and personal bitterness that characterized the Beatles' split, that old cliché "creative differences" provides as honest an explanation as any other for their estrangement from one another. Probably more honest, in fact. Paul wanted to get back. John wanted to move ahead into uncharted territory with Yoko. George wanted to record his own songs. And Ringo just wanted everyone to get along.

I've written elsewhere about how the Beatles story has the arc of a fairytale with a heartbreaking ending, and that's part of the emotional reason why the story of their rise and fall repeats itself so often. Every time it is told, all of the joy, optimism and sheer fun of the band's early days communicate with exquisite delight. And every time, the ending comes too soon, too soon! And too sad. Lennon spoke of the Beatles' breakup as a divorce, and the band's fans, it turns out, are the children of that split, even when they were born decades after it happened. Everyone who learns to love the Beatles enters their narrative, and travels that not-so-long and winding road with them. Every time you hear the familiar story again, you yearn for a different ending, for something truer to the spirit of the band's music, something more heartening. And, in the end...

I accepted the kind offer to write this Foreword mostly because I never turn down an opportunity to write about the Beatles – my own version, I suppose, of that desire to return to the primal scene of my own intellectual and musical interests to see if somehow, miraculously, the story could end more happily. I read this book with great pleasure, struck both by how consistently deep and substantive it is as well as how eminently readable.

The Beatles have had an extraordinary posthumous life, and it's fair to ask where the band will go from here. Their albums have long been markers on the road of rock music history and literacy. Will the inevitable dismantling of those albums in the digital age diffuse future listeners' understanding of the band's impact? The Beatles, happily, were a great singles band, so it will always remain possible to enjoy their music. But, along with Dylan, the Beatles also shattered the hegemony of the single.

The Beatles, it seems to me, are best understood *in toto*. The early songs benefit from our knowledge of the complexity of the band's later work. The later work's self-consciousness is mitigated by the effortlessness and verve of the early songs. The relative brevity of the band's career enables even non-specialist fans – among whom I number myself – to gain a three-dimensional understanding of the band's music relatively easily.

But how well can the Beatles be understood in bits and pieces – in downloads (legal or not), mashups, and YouTube videos? In some sense that's how young people have been discovering the band for quite some time now. As millions of parents have learned – and as I'm finding out with my own three-year-old daughter – children love the Beatles. It will be quite a while before little Francesca plumbs the depths of *Abbey Road* or the White Album. That said, she loves songs from each and, if she so desires, she will find her way into the full spectrum of the Beatles' music as I first learned about the blues through cover versions of individual songs by the Rolling Stones and the Animals. She'll pick a starting point and go from there.

As I do when I re-encounter the Beatles, Francesca occasionally confounds the past, present, and future. She will use the words "yesterday" and "tomorrow" interchangeably, as a way of saying "not now." "Remember what I told you tomorrow?" she asked recently, trying to remind me of something she had said to me the day before. It struck me as similar to the temporal blurring I feel whenever I enter the world of the Beatles, where my own memories, my experiences with members of the band and their wives and colleagues, and my evolving intellectual comprehension of their music collide with and color one another.

In my case, that's somewhat to do with nostalgia, an occasional sin against the rock critic code that I will admit to, hipsters be damned. As the world of music fragments, fragments and fragments, the Beatles represent a time when the notion of popular music meant something beyond millions of people knowing who you are because you won a singing prize on a TV show. They are the genius-level consensus choice – for kids and hip-hop producers, for boomers and millennial bands, for high-minded critics and casual fans.

When people would ask me in interviews how long I thought the Beatles' music would last, I would routinely answer, "As long as people care about popular music" – never imagining that there might come a time when people didn't. I do remember, as my daughter put it, what the Beatles told me tomorrow, back in the past that would indelibly determine my future. They told me, most importantly, that tomorrow never knows. In that spirit, this book offers an illuminating guide to all readers who are moving forward into the precarious world ahead, bringing the Beatles with them for spiritual nourishment, enriched understanding, necessary insight, and absolute pleasure.

Anthony DeCurtis

Acknowledgments

This volume would not have been completed without the kindness and generosity of a host of friends and colleagues. I am indebted to Vicki Cooper and Becky Jones of Cambridge University Press for their enduring faith in this project. Thanks are also due to Jo Bramwell, Rosina Di Marzo, Alison Powell, Laura Evans, and Oliver Lown for their diligence and professionalism in seeing this volume through production. I am particularly grateful for the skill and efforts of my dedicated staff, including Aaron Heresco, Michele Kennedy, Jacki Mowery, Judy Paul, Annette Smith, Nancy Vogel, and Sheila Evans. I am especially thankful for the guidance and expertise of Jerry Zolten, Howard Kramer, Walter Everett, and Amy Mallory-Kani. Special thanks are due for the encouragement and friendship of Lori J. Bechtel-Wherry, Todd F. Davis, Dinty W. Moore, and James M. Decker. Finally, this volume would not exist, quite literally, were it not for the love and spirit afforded by my wife Jeanine, who makes all things possible.

Kenneth Womack

Chronology of the Beatles' lives and works

1940   **July 7:** Ringo Starr [Richard Starkey] born in Liverpool
     October 9: John Winston Lennon born in Liverpool

1942   **June 18:** James Paul McCartney born in Liverpool

1943   **February 25:** George Harrison born in Liverpool

1957   **July 6:** McCartney meets Lennon after a Quarrymen performance at the Woolton Parish Church garden fete

1958   **February:** Harrison joins Lennon and McCartney as a member of the Quarrymen
     June: the Quarrymen record "That'll Be the Day" and "In Spite of All the Danger" at P. F. Phillips Professional Tape and Disk Record Service in Liverpool

1959   **August 29:** the Quarrymen begin an extensive engagement at Mona Best's Casbah Club in Liverpool
     October: the Quarrymen change their name to Johnny and the Moondogs

1960   **January:** Stu Sutcliffe wins £65 for his prizewinning painting in the John Moores Exhibition; Stu purchases a Höfner bass at Lennon's behest and becomes the Quarrymen's bass guitarist
     May: Alan Williams becomes the manager of Johnny and the Moondogs, who change their name, shortly thereafter, to Long John and the Silver Beetles
     May 18: as the Silver Beetles, the band embarks upon a nine-day Scottish tour in support of Johnny Gentle
     August 12: drummer Pete Best joins the band, which changes its name to the Beatles in advance of its upcoming Hamburg engagement
     August–November: the Beatles perform on the Reeperbahn in Hamburg, first at the Indra Club and later at the Kaiserkeller

1961   **February 9:** the Beatles perform at Liverpool's Cavern Club, eventually becoming the establishment's regular lunchtime act

April–July: the Beatles perform on the Reeperbahn in Hamburg's Top Ten Club; during this period, McCartney replaces Sutcliffe as the band's regular bassist
June: the Beatles record several songs as the Beat Brothers, the backing band for musician Tony Sheridan
November 9: NEMS record-store owner Brian Epstein watches the Beatles perform at the Cavern Club
December 10: Brian Epstein officially becomes the Beatles' manager

1962
January 1: the Beatles audition, unsuccessfully, for Decca Records in London
January 5: "My Bonnie"/"The Saints" by Tony Sheridan and the Beatles released by Polydor
April 10: Sutcliffe dies of a brain hemorrhage in Hamburg
April–May: the Beatles perform at Hamburg's Star-Club
June 6: the Beatles audition at EMI Studios for producer George Martin, who is impressed with their potential, with the exception of Best's drumming ability
August 16: Best is fired from the Beatles
August 18: Starr performs as the Beatles' drummer for the first time
August 23: Lennon marries Cynthia Powell
September 11: the Beatles record "Love Me Do," "Please Please Me," and "P.S. I Love You" at EMI Studios
October 5: "Love Me Do"/"P.S. I Love You" single released by Parlophone; the single reaches no. 17 in the British charts
October: the Beatles return for a brief engagement at Hamburg's Star-Club
October 17: the Beatles' first television appearance on Granada's *People and Places*
November 26: the Beatles complete "Please Please Me" at EMI Studios
December: the Beatles' final engagement at Hamburg's Star Club

1963
January 11: "Please Please Me"/"Ask Me Why" single released by Parlophone. "Please Please Me" reaches the top position in the British charts
January 19: the Beatles appear before a nationally televized audience on *Thank Your Lucky Stars*
February 11: the Beatles record the *Please Please Me* album in a single day's session at EMI Studios

March 22: *Please Please Me* album released by Parlophone

April 11: "From Me to You"/"Thank You Girl" single released by Parlophone

August 23: "She Loves You"/"I'll Get You" single released by Parlophone

October 13: the Beatles perform before a national television audience of some 15 million viewers on the popular British variety show *Val Parnell's Sunday Night at the London Palladium.* Beatlemania is born.

November 22: *With the Beatles* album released by Parlophone

November 29: "I Want to Hold Your Hand"/"This Boy" single released by Parlophone

1964   **February 9:** the Beatles perform on the *Ed Sullivan Show* in New York City to a nationally televized audience of some 74 million viewers

March–April: principal photography for *A Hard Day's Night* feature film

March 20: "Can't Buy Me Love"/"You Can't Do That" single released by Parlophone

June–November: the Beatles' first world tour

July 6: *A Hard Day's Night* premieres at the London Pavilion

July 10: "A Hard Day's Night"/"Things We Said Today" single released by Parlophone

July 10: *A Hard Day's Night* album released by Parlophone

November 4: the Beatles' Royal Variety Command Performance at the Prince of Wales Theatre

November 27: "I Feel Fine"/"She's a Woman" single released by Parlophone

December 4: *Beatles for Sale* album released by Parlophone

December: the Beatles' UK winter tour

1965   **February 11:** Starr marries Maureen Cox

February–May: principal photography for the *Help!* feature film

April 9: "Ticket to Ride"/"Yes It Is" single released by Parlophone

June–July: the Beatles' European tour

July 23: "Help!"/"I'm Down" single released by Parlophone

July 29: *Help!* premieres at the London Pavilion

August 6: *Help!* album released by Parlophone

August: the Beatles' North American tour

August 15: the Beatles perform at Shea Stadium before an audience of some 56,000 fans
August 27: the Beatles meet Elvis Presley
October–November: recording sessions for *Rubber Soul*
October 26: the Beatles receive their MBEs at Buckingham Palace
December 3: "We Can Work it Out"/"Day Tripper" single released by Parlophone
December 3: *Rubber Soul* album released by Parlophone
December: the Beatles' final British tour

1966   **January 21:** Harrison marries Pattie Boyd
April–June: recording sessions for *Revolver*
June 10: "Paperback Writer"/"Rain" single released by Parlophone
June–July: the Beatles' Far East tour
July 29: American magazine *Datebook* republishes Lennon's March 1966 interview in which he proclaims that the Beatles are "more popular than Jesus"
August: the Beatles' final American tour
August 5: "Eleanor Rigby"/"Yellow Submarine" single released by Parlophone
August 5: *Revolver* album released by Parlophone
August 29: the Beatles play at San Francisco's Candlestick Park for their final concert before a paying audience
November 9: Lennon meets Yoko Ono at London's Indica Gallery
November–April: recording sessions for *Sgt. Pepper's Lonely Hearts Club Band*

1967   **February 17:** "Strawberry Fields Forever"/"Penny Lane" single released by Parlophone
June 1: *Sgt. Pepper's Lonely Hearts Club Band* album released by Parlophone
June 25: the Beatles perform "All You Need is Love" on the *Our World* international telecast
July 7: "All You Need is Love"/"Baby You're a Rich Man" single released by Parlophone
August 24: The Beatles meet the Maharishi Mahesh Yogi at the London Hilton

August 27: Brian Epstein is found dead in London from an accidental overdose

September–October: principal photography and recording sessions for the *Magical Mystery Tour* project

November 24: "Hello, Goodbye"/"I Am the Walrus" single released by Parlophone

December 8: *Magical Mystery Tour* EP released by Parlophone

December 26: *Magical Mystery Tour* film televized on the BBC

1968   **February–April:** the Beatles visit the Maharishi's compound at Rishikesh

March 15: "Lady Madonna"/"The Inner Light" single released by Parlophone

May 14: Lennon and McCartney announce the formation of Apple Corps at a New York City press conference

May–October: recording sessions for *The Beatles*

July 17: *Yellow Submarine* cartoon feature premieres at the London Pavilion

August 30: "Hey Jude"/"Revolution" single released by Apple

November 22: *The Beatles* album released by Apple

1969   **January 2:** principal photography for the *Get Back* project commences at Twickenham Studios

January 17: *Yellow Submarine* album released by Apple

January 30: the Beatles' Rooftop Concert at Apple Studios on Savile Row

March 12: McCartney marries Linda Eastman

March 20: Lennon marries Yoko Ono

March 21: Allen Klein appointed as business manager for Apple Corps

April–August: recording sessions for *Abbey Road*

April 11: "Get Back"/"Don't Let Me Down" single released by Apple

May 30: "The Ballad of John and Yoko"/"Old Brown Shoe" single released by Apple

August 22: the Beatles gather at Lennon and Ono's Tittenhurst Park estate for their final photo session

September 26: *Abbey Road* album released by Apple

October 31: "Something"/"Come Together" single released by Apple

1970	**March 6:** "Let It Be"/"You Know My Name (Look Up the Number)" single released by Apple **April 10:** McCartney announces the Beatles' breakup **May 8:** *Let It Be* album released by Apple
1980	**December 8:** Lennon is assassinated in New York City
2001	**November 29:** Harrison dies of cancer in Los Angeles

Introducing the Beatles

KENNETH WOMACK

If the artist could explain in words what he has made, he would not have had to create it.

ALFRED STIEGLITZ

This book is about the Beatles' musical art. It is about the songwriting and recording processes that brought it to fruition, while also studying their recording career as an evolving text that can be interpreted as a body of work. But how, then, do we trace the contours of the Beatles' art? If we understand a work of art to be both the expression or exploration of a creative impulse and the process of creating a material object – whether that object be a novel, a painting, a sculpture, or a song – then we also implicitly recognize the art work to be the result of an indelibly human drive to communicate a set of ideas, to draw upon a sustained sense of aesthetics or ethos in order to establish beauty, and to engage in acts of storytelling in order to generate an emotional reaction. These latter elements enable the art object to function as a symbolic vehicle of cultural expression. If we accept the notion of the Beatles as recording *artists*, how, then, do we define the principal aesthetic and literary-musicological elements that inform John, Paul, George, and Ringo's enduring "body of work"? In order to comprehend their art as the result of a creative synthesis, we must work from a set of principles that assists us in understanding the range of their artistic pursuits as they are made manifest in the recording studio. With the Beatles, there was a genuine sense of wonder – a desire, even, for the primitive feel and muscularity of rock and roll, yet there was also a deeply felt nostalgia that developed throughout their career, a reverence for the awesome weight of the past, and a blunt recognition of the creative possibilities and rewards of authorship.

But we're getting way ahead of ourselves here. Long before Sgt. Pepper taught the band to play – long before the pressures of real life had reached their fever-pitch – there were two boys in love with music, gazing upon a brave new world, and upon each other's imaginations, under the blue suburban skies of a Liverpool churchyard. In many ways, the narrative of the Beatles is – and always will be – their story.

In his classic biography, *James Joyce* (1959), Richard Ellmann observes that his volume "enters Joyce's life to reflect his complex, incessant joining of event and composition." In short, Ellmann seeks to understand "the life of the artist" in order to interpret the great sweep of the novelist's accomplishment (3). As an artistic fusion, the Beatles merit this same depth and scope of treatment. The essayists in this volume trace the group's creative arc from the band's earliest recordings through *Abbey Road* and the twilight of their career. In so doing, it is my sincere hope that the *Cambridge Companion to the Beatles* will reflect the complexity of the Beatles' work, while also communicating the nature and power of their remarkable artistic achievement – both during their heyday and beyond.

In addition to Anthony DeCurtis's prescient Foreword, this anthology features a Beatles chronology, as well as such resources as a "General discography" of the band's UK and US recordings through 1970 and a "Select bibliography" of book-length biographical and critical studies of the Beatles. In the *Companion*'s first section, two contributors address the Beatles' background, including their early years and their emergence as innovative songwriters and recording artists. In "Six boys, six beatles: the formative years, 1950–1962," Dave Laing traces the early years of the Beatles during the late 1950s and early 1960s. Laing takes particular care to demonstrate the future bandmates as express products of the historical process in 1950s-era England. In addition to documenting their passage from childhood and adolescence through young adulthood, Laing examines the musical influences that came together in the personnel of the Quarrymen, Lennon's skiffle group, and the early Beatles. In "The Beatles as recording artists," Jerry Zolten investigates the technological aspects of the group, as well as the role of studio wizardry in the formulation of their art. In addition to discussing the producers and technicians who assisted the Beatles during their studio years, Zolten identifies the key moments of electronic innovation that propelled the band's music to new and uncharted sonic heights. In so doing, Zolten reveals the manner in which the Beatles' art has not only weathered but trumped the music of the ages.

In the *Companion*'s second section, which is devoted to the group's album-length productions, the essayists trace the band's output from *Please Please Me* through their solo careers. Howard Kramer's "Rock and roll music" traces the Beatles' growth from their first album, which they recorded within the space of a single day, through *With the Beatles*. In addition to addressing the recording and release of such landmark singles as "She Loves You" and "I Want to Hold Your Hand," Kramer discusses the manner in which the Beatles consolidated their fame at a breakneck, frenzied speed. Kramer also affords attention to the ways in which the group employed the sounds of "first generation rock and roll" in the gestation of their own innovative musical foundations. In "'Try thinking more': *Rubber Soul* and the Beatles' transformation of pop," James M. Decker examines *Rubber Soul* as the Beatles' "transitional" album, as the long-playing record in which they dispensed with high-octane rock and roll in favor of a new sound that embraces studio technology and the lyricism of pop poetry. Decker devotes considerable emphasis to the group's expanding experimental nature in their work, as well as to their increasing sense of edginess and ambiguity in their music. With the release of *Rubber Soul*, Decker argues, the Beatles began to transcend the creative boundaries of individual tracks in favor of the more nuanced expression inherent in the album as musical construct. In "Magical mystery tours, and other trips: yellow submarines, newspaper taxis, and the Beatles' psychedelic years," Russell Reising and Jim LeBlanc explore the groundbreaking musical accomplishments of the Beatles' psychedelic era from *Revolver* and *Sgt. Pepper's Lonely Hearts Club Band* through the *Magical Mystery Tour* project. Beginning with the spring of 1966, Reising and LeBlanc trace the group's experimentation with psychedelic themes, sounds, and insights in both their words and their music. In so doing, Reising and LeBlanc map out the musical dimension of the Beatles' output during this period, while also identifying the nature of the musical direction that would define their latter efforts in the studio.

Ian Inglis's "Revolution" offers a shrewd reading of the convoluted historical and cultural context inherent in the labyrinthine recording sessions for *The Beatles* (the White Album). Inglis establishes a complex level of acclaim and uncertainty for the Beatles at the dawn of 1968, ranging from the spellbinding success of *Sgt. Pepper* to the critical disdain for *Magical Mystery Tour* – not to mention the traumatizing specter of war and assassination on the international front. Inglis reads the resulting album as a strident contrast with the careful sense of direction and purpose that marked their earlier efforts, with the White Album sporting disunity, fragmentation, and disillusionment as its primary – if not primal – characteristics. In "On their way home: the Beatles in 1969 and 1970," Steve Hamelman provides an expansive analysis of the Beatles' last recordings, including the *Get Back* project and *Abbey Road*. For Hamelman, the group's final spate of music – recorded, for the most part, as the backdrop for the bandmates' impending "divorce" – finds the Beatles reaching new artistic heights in terms of lyricism, and, ironic as it may seem, musical unity. In addition to affording particular attention to the symphonic suite that closes their career, Hamelman addresses the remarkable music synergy that sees the *Get Back* project establishing the musical foundation for the Beatles' swan song on *Abbey Road*. In so doing, writes Hamelman, the band "ends with a benediction ('And in the end, the love you take / Is equal to the love you make') sung sweetly and sincerely to a cushion of strings. The Beatles end the record, their career in fact, with a couplet worthy of Shakespeare." Bruce Spizer's "Apple Records" examines the peculiar role of Apple Corps in the Beatles' history – particularly as a central creative and economic force during their final years as an artistic unit and beyond. In addition to tracing the genesis of Apple from holding company to multi-faceted artistic enterprise, Spizer speculates about the label's influence during the Beatles' solo years. Spizer also identifies the creative and business personalities who piloted the company during its truncated history.

Walter Everett's "Any time at all: the Beatles' free phrase rhythms" explores the bandmates' songwriting proclivities in terms of the rhythmic nature of their music. In this powerful work of musicology, Everett demonstrates that the group's songs are phrase-based in nature, ultimately referencing a vast array of compositions throughout their recording career. As Everett points out, the Beatles' interest in appropriating their music as the vehicle for portraying emotional and interpersonal conflicts serves as the bedrock for their resounding artistic achievement. Michael Frontani's "The solo years" offers one of music criticism's most extensive and thorough examinations of the bandmates' solo output. Drawing upon John, Paul, George, and Ringo's recorded corpus from 1969 through the present, Frontani enumerates the artistic highs and lows of the ex-Beatles' solo careers. Frontani affords special emphasis to the manner in which the former group members both struggle with and venerate their accomplishments as a musical unit during the 1960s.

The *Companion*'s final section, entitled "History and influence," investigates the nature of the band's enduring sociocultural power, as well as the ways in which successive generations have interpreted the Beatles for their own purposes and desires. The essayists in this section also impinge upon the interpersonal, political, and commercial factors that have shaped the group's reception and commodification since their disbandment. In "The Beatles as zeitgeist," Sheila Whiteley examines the band's influence in the 1960s and beyond. Whiteley devotes special attention to the wide-ranging nature of the Beatles' inroads into popular culture in terms of such issues as politics, fashion, commerce, gender, sexuality, and the arts. Whiteley also discusses the manner in which the Beatles' influence spans divergent generations and cultures. In "Beatles news: product line extensions and the rock canon," Gary Burns addresses the evolution of the Beatles as a *bona fide* economic brand. By treating their commercial attainments separately from their critical status as sociocultural icons, Burns identifies the bandmates and their representatives as savvy businessmen who have become increasingly successful during the post-breakup years at promoting their product. Burns argues that the Beatles' remarkably fruitful afterlife is the express result of a deliberate and skillfully marketed product line – a commercial brand that has been every bit as effective as the band's innovative and trendsetting artistic model. Finally, John Kimsey's "'An abstraction, like Christmas': the Beatles for sale and for keeps" offers an extensive study of the internal and external political dynamics that have shaped the

Beatles' reception, repackaging, and self-defining (and, indeed, self-redefining) efforts from 1970 through the present. Kimsey affords considerable attention to such legacy-promoting activities as the *Anthology* series of music and videos released during the 1990s; the calculated release of such albums as *1*, *Let It Be . . . Naked*, and the Capitol Albums; and the recent success of *Love*, the band's Cirque du Soleil venture. In so doing, Kimsey elucidates a marketing strategy that never loses its momentum, that never ceases to produce dividends.

PART ONE

Background

1 Six boys, six Beatles: the formative years, 1950–1962

DAVE LAING

The starting point of critical elaboration is the consciousness of what one really is, and is "knowing thyself" as a product of the historical process to date which has deposited in you an infinity of traces, without leaving an inventory. Therefore it is imperative at the outset to compile such an inventory.[1]   ANTONIO GRAMSCI

Introduction

The chapter deals with the formative years of both the Beatles and the six youths who were group members in the late 1950s and early 1960s, including Stuart Sutcliffe and Pete Best, who left the band in 1961 and 1962 respectively. Although it cannot claim to be a complete inventory (to borrow a term from Gramsci in the quotation above), it is intended to present the boys and the band as products of the historical process in the England of the 1950s through the presentation of some of the "infinity of traces" deposited in them by that historical period.

In this account of the dual formation of the group and the six individuals, I will discuss first the various networks within which the six were enmeshed as children, adolescents and young men: those of the family and social class, of the school and youth culture peer group. The second part of the chapter describes and analyses the musical factors and features that coalesced to form first the Quarrymen skiffle group and then the early Beatles.

The data upon which this chapter is based are drawn from published biographies and autobiographies. These publications are of three types: authorized biographies such as those of Shepherd, Davies, Miles, and the Beatles "themselves";[2] unauthorized biographies such as Goldman's, Connolly's, and Sullivan's psychoanalytical volume;[3] and the memoirs of colleagues, friends, and family such as Epstein, Cynthia Lennon, and Pauline Sutcliffe.[4] The overall quality of this material is uneven, with a number of errors and discrepancies that have confused the general understanding of the early years of the Beatles.[5] A useful corrective to much of this is the testimony of Bill Harry, the editor of the *Mersey Beat* newspaper from 1961. Many of the articles that appeared in the newspaper are available on his website (www.triumphpc.com/mersey-beat).

War babies

The United Kingdom was at war with Germany and its allies between 1939 and 1945. All six boys were born during that conflict. John Lennon, Ringo Starr (Richard Starkey), Pete Best and Stuart Sutcliffe were born in 1940, John and Ringo in Liverpool, Pete in India, and Stuart in Scotland. Paul McCartney and George Harrison were Liverpool-born, in 1942 and 1943 respectively. Although all were infants during the wartime period, the conflict continued to shape British society and culture for at least the first decade of peacetime.

One minor but pertinent index of this was John Lennon's middle name. Until he replaced it with "Ono," John's second forename was Winston, after the British war leader Winston Churchill. It was a permanent reminder of his status as a war baby (the name was also very popular for baby boys in Jamaica, a British colony until 1960) – and there was a set of Churchill's works on display in his aunt Mimi and uncle George's house. This name became something of a minor obsession with John (perhaps because Churchill remained a current political figure until the late 1950s, and regained the post of prime minister from 1951 to 1955). The biographical literature provides three instances. A Beatles' instrumental piece included in a Hamburg set-list was named "Winston's Walk,"[6] and the film *Backbeat* shows John telling an anti-German joke onstage in Hamburg: "My name's John Winston Lennon, Winston after the butcher." Finally, Paul told his biographer of a masturbation session involving several of the Quarrymen in a darkened room. The ritual was for each boy in turn to call out the name of a suitable female sex symbol ("Brigitte Bardot," etc.) but when it was Lennon's turn he deflated the erotic mood by saying, "Winston Churchill." Even the discarding of the name had some anti-imperialist significance, according to Yoko, who told one biographer that John disliked its "implication that he was somehow a subscriber to the spirit of the upper-class British empire and all that."[7]

As a major seaport, Liverpool was one of the main targets of German bombing in the early part of World War II. Paul McCartney's biographer Barry Miles summarized the scale and impact of these air raids:

> From the night of 17 August 1940 until 10 January 1942 there were sixty-eight raids and over five hundred air-raid warnings. Every night thousands of people huddled together in basements and bomb shelters as high-explosive, incendiary and parachute bombs rained down upon the city, killing 2,650, seriously injuring over 2,000 others and leaving much of the city centre in ruins. The dead were buried in mass graves in Anfield cemetery. Over 10,000 of the homes in Liverpool were completely destroyed and over two-thirds of all homes were seriously damaged.[8]

During the war years, the whole country was militarized. Over 5 million men and women served in the armed forces, but none of the six boys lost a close family member in the war, although the bomber pilot father of Eric Griffiths, a founder member of the Quarrymen, did not return from a raid over Germany. Millions more people were mobilized on the "home front." Jim McCartney (Paul's father) was rejected by the armed forces because of defective hearing, but he worked in a munitions factory and was a volunteer fireman at night. Stuart Sutcliffe's father was directed to move from Scotland to Birkenhead on Merseyside to take up a post in the shipyard that was essential for the war effort. In many cities, young children were evacuated to the countryside, although it seems that none of the future Beatles was evacuated from Liverpool.

Even after the air raids had ceased, daily life was subordinated to the war effort, most notably through rationing. Consumption of twelve foodstuffs was placed under restriction in 1940 and 1941.[9] These ranged from meat, butter, and cooking fat to sugar, sweets (candy), and chocolate. In 1940, clothing was rationed and each citizen had an annual number of coupons that could be exchanged in various combinations at clothing stores. The British rock and roll singer Marty Wilde recalled that gray, brown, and black "were all the colours I associate with the war. Almost everything was grey. It wasn't until the Fifties that all colours started to come in clothes."[10]

The depleted state of the British economy meant that rationing was not lifted at the end of World War II. Of the rationed items, only preserves (jams and marmalade) were de-rationed and freely available before 1952. In that year, tea was taken "off ration," but meat, butter, sweets (candy) and chocolate were not de-rationed until the middle of 1954. Clothing coupons remained in force until 1948. There were also severe restrictions on imports from abroad, a decision taken to protect Britain's limited reserves of foreign currency. Among the commodities affected were musical instruments, and it was not possible to import American guitars until the end of the 1950s, when the rock and roll singer Cliff Richard bought one of the first Fender Stratocasters to be seen in Britain for his guitarist, Hank Marvin of the Shadows. The inaccessibility of American instruments in the 1950s meant that the first guitars of aspiring young players were often poorly made imports from continental Europe.

While the wartime army was gradually demobilized after 1945, conscription or National Service was introduced in 1947 for young men. National Service cast a shadow over members of the Beatles until, in 1959, the government announced that National Service would be abolished in 1961, the year in which Ringo, John, Pete and Stu would have become eligible for call-up. The fear of conscription had been enough to prevent Ringo committing himself to a full-time career as a musician with leading Liverpool group Rory Storm and the Hurricanes. When he heard that National Service was to be abolished, his first thought was "'Great, now we can play,' and I left the factory and turned professional with Rory."[11] Paul McCartney went further by hypothesizing that if National Service had not been abolished, and if John, in particular, had been forced to do two years' military service, the Beatles would have split up: "So that was great luck, the government just stopped it in time, allowing us the parting of the waves, and we went through and we had the freedom and the sixties."[12] The band had, in fact, been directly affected in 1960, when a drummer called Norman Chapman, who had played with the Beatles for three weeks, received his conscription papers.[13]

British popular culture was saturated with war stories, humour, and references during the 1950s. Second World War movies, made in both the US and Britain, poured into the cinemas, war stories featured in children's illustrated magazines, and Lennon's favourite radio series, *The Goon Show*, had its roots in the anarchic humour of World War II conscripts.[14]

Family life

In a classic study published in the 1950s, the British sociologist Peter Townshend made a distinction between the immediate family and the extended family. Of the six households in which the boys grew up, all except that of John Lennon conformed to the immediate family model of "one or both parents and their unmarried children living in one household."[15] However, if the model is limited to the ideal type of "both parents" living with their children, only the Harrisons fully qualify. As Peter Brown put it, "George was the only Beatle whose childhood was not marred by divorce [or] death."[16] The position of each household was as follows.

Paul McCartney lived with his father Jim (a cotton salesman), mother Mary (a nurse and midwife), and younger brother Michael, until his mother died in 1956, when he was fourteen. John Lennon lived from the age of five with his childless maternal aunt Mimi and uncle George Smith, owner of a small dairy, who died when John was fifteen. John's father Alfred, a ship's steward, had separated from his mother Julia when John was three, and Julia had given him up to Mimi when she found a new partner, Bobby Dykins, with whom she had two daughters. Julia died in a road accident when John was seventeen. George Harrison lived with his bus driver father Harold, mother Louise, and older siblings Harry, Louise, and Peter. George's mother gave ballroom dancing lessons, and his father was a trade unionist and committee member of a bus workers' social club, where the Beatles (as the Quarrymen) once performed. Ringo Starr, born Richard Starkey, was an only child whose bakery worker father Richard separated from his mother Elsie when he was three. As a child, Ringo spent long periods in hospital with peritonitis and, later, pleurisy. Elsie supported herself and her son through housework and as a barmaid, remarrying when Ringo was fourteen. His stepfather was Harry Graves, a painter and decorator from Romford, near London. Pete Best lived with his Anglo-Indian mother Mona, his grandmother, his boxing promoter father Johnny, and brother Rory. Mona met and married Johnny, who was from a Liverpudlian family, when the latter was serving in the British Army in India. When Pete was fifteen, his parents separated and his father left the family home. His mother later had a child by Neil Aspinall, the Beatles' road manager. Stuart Sutcliffe lived with his father Charles, schoolteacher mother Martha (known as Millie), and sisters Joyce and Pauline. Each of his parents worked away from home for long periods. After his war work, Charles joined the merchant navy as an engineer in 1945. Millie never liked Liverpool and around 1952 she temporarily returned to Scotland to work. She was a member of the Labour Party and an active worker for local Member of Parliament Harold Wilson, who would become Prime Minister in 1964.

These brief family portraits show that only the Harrisons were a nuclear family unaffected by death, divorce, or separation; while the Sutcliffe household was not broken, Stu's sister wrote that with her husband away at sea, Millie "essentially . . . became a single parent."[17] John's adolescence was the most disturbed, by separation from his mother and the deaths of George and Julia.

Townshend defined the extended family as relatives of the immediate family "who live in one, two or more households, usually in a single locality, and who see each other every day, or nearly every day."[18] Townshend derived his definition from a study of a strongly working class district of East London. In the six families of the Beatles, both John and Paul were part of an extended family. In John's case, this principally involved his regular contact with his mother, especially in his teenage years, although Julia and Millie had two other sisters, and Stuart's sister Pauline has written that "one of John's uncles was Paul's English teacher."[19] In the case of the McCartneys, there was a strong link with the family of his paternal uncle, who had played in a band with Paul's father in the 1920s; and Barry Miles writes of "a large extended family of aunts and uncles and cousins"[20] who gave direct support after the death of Paul's mother. In his authorized biography, Paul mentions the Communist husband of a cousin who would regularly visit his father and indulge in political argument.

The existence of an extended family is predicated on the geographical immobility of generations, and five of the six Beatles had roots in Liverpool stretching back for two generations or more. Beyond that point, ancestors of John, Paul, and Ringo have been traced to Ireland, making these three part of the considerable Liverpool Irish community. However, the biographers of George, Ringo, and Pete do not refer to any wider family network within Liverpool. This may imply that none of these lived within an extended family network, or simply that such issues are of no interest to biographers of rock stars. Stuart Sutcliffe had no local extended family, because of the mobility of his parents, who had moved from Edinburgh in Scotland to Merseyside when Stuart was two. Similarly, no local extended family existed on Pete's mother's side of the family, as she was Anglo-Indian.

Two further features of the family background are religious affiliation and social class. While the 1950s was an era when observance of the main Christian religions was in decline in England as a whole, in certain areas it remained a potent force with sectarian connotations. Such affiliations with either Roman Catholicism or Protestantism had been an important component of Liverpool Irish culture, and Paul's mother was an ardent Catholic, as was Stuart's Scottish-born mother. In his contribution to *The Beatles Anthology*, Ringo stated that as a child he "was a Protestant, my mother had been a member of the Orange Lodge,"[21] an indication that this was Ulster Protestantism, a virulent strain of nonconformist Christianity that contrasted with the less intense Anglicanism that led Mimi to send John to the Woolton Sunday school and enrol him in the church choir. Ringo added, in what can be presumed to be a deadpan tone, that in Liverpool the Irish Protestants would "beat up" the Irish Catholics on St Patrick's Day, and the reverse would occur on July 12, "Orangeman's Day."[22]

Biographers and historians have differed widely in their evaluation of the social and economic position of the family of each Beatle. In *Postwar*, a history of Europe since 1945, Tony Judt (an Englishman teaching at New York University) stated confidently that the Beatles "came from the Liverpool working class, with the exception of Paul McCartney who was a notch or two above."[23] Dominic Sandbrook, in his account of the UK in the 1950s, opined that only Ringo "had a genuine claim to working-class origins,"[24] possibly echoing Ian McDonald's comment that "the only working class member of the group was Starr."[25] Sandbrook disqualified George Harrison (the son of a trade unionist and public housing tenant) from the working class because "his childhood had been reasonably comfortable."[26] A third commentator, Paul's authorized biographer Barry Miles, wrote that John was "middle class, the product of a broken home," whereas Paul was "from a warm working-class family."[27]

These striking disagreements serve to confirm Henry Sullivan's observation that "the British class system is slippery,"[28] and his further contention that "Paul's social background belonged in that shadowy area of the British class structure between the working class and the lower middle class"[29] can serve as a general statement about the six Beatles as a whole.

The "slippery" character of the class system is in large part a matter of definition. A Marxist approach based on the relationship of individual economic agents to the "means of production" would distinguish between George Smith and Johnny Best as entrepreneurs or small-business owners and everyone else as employees of various kinds. The official categories of employment used by British government agencies are based on job status. They place professionally qualified workers such as nurses, engineers, and teachers in the lower middle class, above skilled working class occupations such as bus-driving and unskilled work such as that of Elsie Starkey. A third dimension that should be taken into account is the perception of individuals and families of their own position in the social hierarchy and their aspirations for the future. The individual with the greatest awareness in this respect seems to have been John's aunt Mimi, and Sullivan speaks for most commentators when he writes that "Mimi's class ideals were those of the bourgeoisie."[30] Several authors have recounted her initial snobbish disdain for George because of his broad local accent. Mimi's ideals, of course, provided something for John to rebel against.

The boundary between lower middle and working class was extremely porous, not only because individuals or members of different generations of a family could easily move "up" or "down" the social hierarchy, but because in the 1950s members of these adjacent social classes shared a common culture that might be based on religion, politics, or moral schema. This was most emphatically the case for the war baby generation whose middle class and working class members were brought together by changes in the British school system and by the emergence of a youth culture based primarily on music.

School, work, and youth culture

The British secondary school system was radically reorganized by the 1944 Education Act,[31] a meritocratic measure that introduced a tripartite structure in the state school sector of grammar, secondary modern, and technical schools. Access to grammar schools was via success in the "11-plus" examination, taken by all final year primary school students. Primary schooling, from the age of five to eleven, was co-educational (boys and girls together), and often schools were run by religious denominations, Anglican, Roman Catholic, or Jewish.

Across England, the number of children admitted to grammar schools averaged about 30 per cent,[32] although this varied between areas. Paul

McCartney was one of only four out of ninety children at Joseph Williams Primary School to do well enough to be awarded a place at the prestigious Liverpool Institute. Five of the six Beatles passed the 11-plus and entered single-sex grammar schools on Merseyside: Lennon went to Quarry Bank High School, Best to Liverpool Collegiate, McCartney and Harrison to the Liverpool Institute, and Sutcliffe to Prescot Grammar School. Almost inevitably, because of his long absence from primary school through illness, Ringo failed the exam and went to Dingle Vale Secondary Modern school.

Although numerous working class children attended grammar schools, many failed to adapt to the academic environment.[33] Among them were John and George. Both left school early, John to go to art college and George to find work.

Stuart had a parent who had attended grammar school, and he passed the examinations, as eventually did Paul and Pete. All three had plans for further study. Stu attended Liverpool College of Art, where he met John, while Pete and Paul had nascent plans to train as schoolteachers. When the offer was made for the Beatles to play in Hamburg in summer 1960, these plans were put on hold (permanently, as it turned out).

George and Ringo were the only Beatles who ever had paid employment outside music. Ringo had a succession of full-time jobs after leaving secondary modern school with no examination passes. These included working as a delivery boy for British Rail, barman-waiter on the Mersey ferry, and apprentice joiner. While at school, George had a Saturday job as a butcher's delivery boy. After school, he was apprenticed as an electrician at a department store.

According to the biographical literature, Paul was the only Beatle to benefit culturally from the school syllabus. Through his English teacher, Alan Durband, he was introduced to a wide range of poetry and drama, from Shakespeare to Beckett.[34] However, grammar schools and art colleges were also informal incubators of unofficial youth culture as students shared and exchanged new knowledge of music, fashion, films, and books.

In the 1950s the new generation-specific youth cultures existed alongside, and sometimes in tension or conflict with, traditional institutions for the socialization of children. As a young child, John Lennon attended a Church of England Sunday school, was a member of the church choir, and, later, attended a youth club attached to the church. Paul was a Boy Scout, Ringo a Sea Scout, and Stu a member of the Air Training Corps, while George was a motor racing enthusiast, attending the 1955 Aintree Grand Prix. However, none of the future Beatles seems to have been a special fan of either of Liverpool's fanatically supported soccer teams, Liverpool and Everton.

Against that was set the discovery of rock and roll through radio broadcasts and the records discovered by schoolmates. A more directly confrontational practice was the subversion of school uniform through adopting styles of dress associated with the "Teddy boy" subculture.[35] The Liverpool Institute, attended by George and Paul, had a school uniform of black shoes, gray flannel trousers, blazer, white shirt, and tie. George (but not Paul) customized his Teddy boy clothes to wear to school. George's home-made outfit included a cast-off box jacket of his brother's and a pair of flannel trousers whose legs were "drainpiped" or narrowed. He also had a Teddy boy "quiff" hairstyle.[36]

Simon Frith and Howard Horne have documented the important role of local art colleges in disseminating unorthodox ideas and cultural practices, as well as the time and space they provided for artistic (including musical) experimentation.[37] At Liverpool College of Art, John was introduced by Stu and Bill Harry to the work of the American beat generation, and Paul has said that John was a "bohemian Teddy boy" at art college.[38] The Sutcliffe–Harry–Lennon circle occasionally overlapped with a nascent British beat scene,[39] and Royston Ellis, a youthful beat poet,[40] was reportedly backed by John, Paul, and George at a poetry reading in a Liverpool coffee bar. John and Stu also received lurid publicity as beatniks and bohemians in July 1960, when a national newspaper published photographs of their pad at Gambier Terrace under the headline "The Beatnik Horror."[41]

Bill Harry encouraged John's humorous writings, eventually publishing them in 1961 under the pseudonym "Beatcomber" (a pun on the national newspaper humorist Beachcomber) in early issues of Harry's local music paper *Mersey Beat*. John was drawn to comedy performance; he went to see variety shows at Liverpool Empire, starring acts such as Morecambe and Wise, Jimmy James, and Robb Wilton,[42] and he had begun to write poems and nonsense stories influenced by Edward Lear, Stanley Unwin, the Goons, and others at a very early age. When these were published in book form in 1968,[43] Michael Wood described Lennon's humour as mainly composed of jokes that "have already seen good service in most grammar schools in this country."[44]

Early music training and experience

While the rise of rock and roll is often portrayed in terms of a generation gap or clash, each of the six Beatles received encouragement from parents or other relatives in their early musical endeavours. The major exception to this process was John Lennon's Aunt Mimi, who often displayed hostility to his practice sessions and performances with the Quarrymen and the Beatles, although she did buy him a guitar.

Of the future Beatles, only George Harrison and Pete Best had no musical experience prior to the skiffle and rock and roll era. Each of the others received musical training or instruction in the years before 1956. The Sutcliffe children had piano lessons at an early age, and Stuart also sang in a church choir. At the other extreme, Ringo first beat out a rhythm during a hospital therapy session. He maintained his interest on leaving hospital when his stepfather paid for his first drum kit.

In very different ways, both Paul and John came from families with a history of professional music-making, a background that ensured that music would play a role in their early lives. Like Stuart, Paul had piano lessons but also learned harmony from his father, the erstwhile leader of Jim Mac's Jazz Band. Jim's own father had been a brass band player, in the works band of Cope's, a local factory.[45] Paul was given a trumpet for his fourteenth birthday, which he soon swapped for a guitar. He learned how to play left-handed from seeing a picture of Slim Whitman, the American country artist with a big UK following – Whitman had a number one hit in 1955 with "Rose Marie."

His mother, Julia, taught John the banjo. She had learned the instrument from John's father, who had performed in the 1930s as an amateur with his brother. Further back in the Lennon line, John's grandfather Jack had emigrated to the United States with his parents and toured with a professional minstrel troupe before returning to Liverpool, where he died in 1921.

However, what galvanized five of the six future Beatles into intensive musical activity was the example of Lonnie Donegan and his skiffle group. Then, like thousands of other British youths, these skiffle musicians turned to rock and roll.

Skiffle, rock and roll, and the Quarrymen

Skiffle was a curiously British phenomenon. It was played by acoustic, guitar-based groups with rhythm sections consisting of washboards and tea-chest basses. The skiffle repertoire combined (white) American folk songs, both traditional and newly composed (notably by Woody Guthrie), with blues and other material from the African American tradition, learned mostly from the recordings of Leadbelly. Sometimes, British folk tunes or music hall songs were added to the mix. The spark that lit the prairie fire of the skiffle boom in Britain was the success of Lonnie Donegan's recording of Leadbelly's "Rock Island Line." Donegan's version was faster, more febrile and more hoarse than the original. "Rock Island Line" and other releases were hits, and Donegan toured extensively, including playing for a week at the Liverpool Empire theatre in November 1956, where he was seen by several future Beatles. The thirteen-year-old George Harrison got his autograph.[46]

However, skiffle's historical significance was not as a genre of music but as a musical event, one which transformed the instrumental locus of *musica practica*, defined by Roland Barthes in a 1970 essay of the same name as "music one plays" rather than "music one listens to." Barthes wrote that the role of the drawing room piano had been taken by "another public, another repertoire, another instrument (the young generation, vocal music, the guitar)."[47]

In 1957, 250,000 guitars were sold in Britain, compared with an average of 5,000 per year between 1950 and 1955.[48] The guitars were strummed, and the initial skiffle repertoire of songs was shared, by maybe hundreds of skiffle groups throughout Britain.

The prehistory of the Beatles as a band can be traced to the formation of the Quarrymen skiffle group around May 1956. The evolution of the band can be examined in two dimensions; through its changing repertoire and performance style (skiffle to Merseybeat and rock), and through its changing personnel, which transformed its ethos from that of a homosocial friendship group or gang to an equally homosocial professional band whose membership was based primarily on musical skill and compatibility.

The classic ethnographic, participant-observation description of the transformation of a gang into a music group is the article "Beat and Gangs on Merseyside," written by Colin Fletcher, a Merseyside student, and published in the magazine *New Society* in February 1964. Fletcher had been a member of a street gang that was inspired to form its own group by such records as "That'll Be the Day": "What mattered now was not how many boys a gang could muster for a Friday night fight but how well their group played on Saturday night."[49]

Liverpool gangs have a peripheral role in the early history of the Beatles, appearing mainly as menacing forces at dances and concerts where the band played, although Ringo had a closer relationship to a gang in the Dingle, where he grew up.[50] The "gang" from which the Quarrymen emerged was less aggressive, being based on John Lennon's troupe of friends from primary school, whose infamies were limited to stealing candies from the village shop and misbehaving at the church youth club. If they were modeled on any gang, it was William and the Outlaws, heroes of a whimsical series of children's books by Richmal Crompton that were among John's favorite reading as a child.

The nucleus of the Quarrymen consisted of John and two of his gang, Pete Shotton and Eric Griffiths. They recruited another Quarry Bank School boy, Rod Davis, who had attended Sunday school with John and Pete and was a "good" boy who had acquired a banjo, while gang member Len Garry took over the bass from another schoolboy who had not turned up to rehearsals. Another early member, Colin Hanton, was brought into the Quarrymen because he owned a drum kit.

At the beginning the Quarrymen were a wholly typical skiffle group of the 1956–7 period, as were the Rebels, a very short-lived group formed by George Harrison and his gang of school friends. The name Quarrymen connoted an archaic American rural ethos, while containing a Lennonesque pun on the name of his school.

The songs performed by the Quarrymen in their early months included Donegan's hits and those of other skiffle groups.[51] The group's repertoire additionally included "Maggie May," a Liverpool anthem and the only song from this era to be recorded by the Beatles.

I have referred to the Quarrymen as "homosocial," a term used by Eve Kosofsky Sedgwick to describe single-sex affinity groups. These were distinct from homosexual relationships and institutions, although to be homosocial did not preclude an element of sexual contact: "For a man to be a man's man is separated only by an invisible, carefully blurred, always-already-crossed line from being 'interested in men.'"[52]

Many aspects of English society in the 1950s were homosocial in character. Secondary schools were a prime example; there were few integrated grammar or secondary modern schools that admitted both boys and girls. Many employment situations were similarly segregated. In Liverpool, only men worked at the docks or on the transatlantic and other ships. Almost all employees at clerically based companies such as Littlewoods and Vernons, which operated football pools, were women, who checked the betting slips by hand. Vernons, in fact, had a female choir that, in a smaller version, recorded as the Vernons Girls. Many traditional pubs and drinking clubs still had bars that did not admit women.

Both the Quarrymen and the Beatles reflected the homosocial ethos of the era, something emphasized by the occasional threat to their homogeneity by women. Apart from Liverpool singer Cilla Black, no woman performed with the band. Even then, John Lennon betrayed an uneasiness when he "jokingly" referred to her from the stage of the Cavern as "Cyril," a masculine name. Cynthia would later describe the Beatles as "a marriage of four minds, three guitars and a drum."[53] The issue of homosociality was given a twist by the cultural association of singing and musical performance with the female. A very young Lennon said to Pete Shotton: "They say you're a cissy . . . But you're not a cissy, all right? Singing's all right." The occasion was a trip to a secluded spot where the boys would sing out of sight and earshot of others.[54]

Both the nature of the Quarrymen repertoire and its friendship group character underwent major changes during the group's career. From an early stage, its "manager," Nigel Whalley (another of John's gang), described its music on his business card as "Country. Western. Rock 'n' Roll. Skiffle."

The Quarrymen's career as a "pure" skiffle group was therefore brief, to the dissatisfaction of Rod Davis. Rock and roll songs soon came to dominate their repertoire. The first Elvis hit in the UK, "Heartbreak Hotel," came in May 1956, a few months after "Rock Island Line" became a hit, and before the foundation of the group, which probably took place in September or October.[55] John Lennon was an instant Elvis fan and he introduced "Heartbreak Hotel," "Jailhouse Rock," and "Don't Be Cruel."

In the early years, they found songs in various places. A school friend, Mike Hill, played a record by Little Richard to John sometime in 1956 and had to inform John that the singer was black. The following year, Paul and John "went across town" looking for a copy of "Searchin" by the Coasters: "Colin Hanton knew some guy that had it, but we had to get on the bus, do two changes of bus routes . . . So we got the words, and I think we stole the record."[56]

The critical point in the history of the Quarrymen was of course the day John met Paul in July 1957. Paul was already indirectly linked with Lennon's "gang" via his friendship with Ivan Vaughan, a childhood member of the gang who now attended the same school as Paul. Impressed with Paul's musicianship, Ivan now invited him to attend the Quarrymen's performance at the St. Peter's Church, Woolton, garden fete, an event whose musical range included brass band music from the Band of the Cheshire Yeomanry as well as skiffle and rock.

In her memoir of the day of the fete, Lennon's half-sister, Julia Baird, wrote: "We found the *gang*, the group, on the third or fourth lorry [of a procession]."[57] This was the day the Quarrymen began their gradual transformation from an activity of the Lennon gang into a group whose membership was determined mainly by musical skill.

Paul had not been in a skiffle group, though he admired Donegan. By the middle of 1957 he was already a rock and roll aficionado. He and his younger brother Michael listened to broadcasts from Radio Luxembourg in bed.[58] They performed an Everly Brothers song at a Butlins holiday camp talent contest in the summer of 1957, shortly after Paul met John.

At the Woolton fete, Paul was impressed by John's transgression – changing the words of the Dell-Vikings soft rock love song "Come Go with Me" by adding skiffle-type language about a "penitentiary."[59] John, in turn, was impressed by Paul's orthodox musical skills – he knew chords and the "correct" lyrics to Eddie Cochran's song "Twenty Flight Rock."

Paul joined the Quarrymen and played at their occasional gigs during the rest of 1957. The balance of the group changed irrevocably when Paul finally persuaded John to admit George Harrison in the early part of 1958. Still aged only fifteen, George had played occasionally with a local skiffle/rock band, the Les Stewart Quartet, and had auditioned for the Texans, a group led by Alan Caldwell, who, as Rory Storm, would hire Richard Starkey as drummer for the Hurricanes and change his name to the Western-sounding Ringo Starr.

By the end of 1958, the group had been reduced to the trio of John, Paul, and George, plus occasional drummers, a situation that would continue until Pete Best became the permanent drummer in mid-1960. The shift to a fully musician-oriented group was exemplified in the departure of Eric Griffiths. He was asked by the other members to become the bass guitarist, but he didn't want to take on the hire purchase loan needed to buy a guitar and amplifier.

The trio were seen dismissively as a "Bohemian clique" by Johnny Gustafson of the Big 3, a leading Liverpool band of the era. With few paid engagements, John, Paul, George and, occasionally, Len Garry on bass would do acoustic sets at lunchtimes at the art college, playing Buddy Holly and Everly Brothers numbers (often with new, ruder words improvised by John).[60]

Perhaps the most important feature of the early Lennon-McCartney relationship was their determination to write songs as well as perform cover versions of other people's songs. British popular music had no tradition of singers writing their own songs, with the exception of certain comedy or novelty performers from the music hall to George Formby and the Goons. And the Beatles were unique among their Liverpool contemporaries in composing and performing their own material.

John and Paul started trying to co-write in the summer of 1957, soon after they met. They would play truant from art college and the Liverpool Institute to use Paul's house while Jim McCartney was at work. Paul had already composed his first song, "I Lost My Little Girl," which was written shortly after his mother's death. He also occasionally wrote with George; a McCartney-Harrison composition, "In Spite of All the Danger," was included on the group's first privately recorded acetate, with Buddy Holly's "That'll Be the Day."

As already noted, John had been improvising lyrics to existing songs, and this skill was brought to the co-writing sessions. The first successfully composed Lennon-McCartney songs included "One After 909," "Winston's Walk," "Like Dreamers Do," and "Love Me Do"; the last-mentioned was written in 1958 but not recorded and released as the first Beatles single produced by George Martin until four years later.[61]

The final performance of the Quarrymen took place in August 1959 at the opening of the Casbah, a club organized by Mona Best in the basement of her house. All vestiges of skiffle had been sloughed off, and John, Paul, and George were the nucleus of a group with no name.

The Beatles

There is no definite moment at which the Beatles emerged from the Quarrymen like a butterfly from a chrysalis. The group performed as Johnny and the Moondogs at a Manchester talent show in November 1959 (the winners were Ricky and Dave, the stage name of future Hollies members Graham Nash and Allan Clarke). They became the Silver Beetles for an audition for the London-based impresario Larry Parnes and for a subsequent tour of Scotland, backing Parnes's singer Johnny Gentle, in May 1960. Some of the Silver Beetles adopted individual stage names for the Scottish tour: Paul and George were Paul Ramon and Carl Harrison, while Stu Sutcliffe on bass was Stu de Stael, after a famous modern painter. Finally, in this avalanche of names, John and Paul had performed the previous month at Paul's cousin's pub in Caversham, Berkshire, as the Nerk (or Nurk) Twins.[62] The name was taken from a character in John's beloved *Goon Show*.

However, by the time of the first trip to Hamburg in August 1960, "the Beatles" had been definitively adopted as the group name. Most early commentators believed that this name was a tribute to the Crickets, the name of Buddy Holly's group, both crickets and beetles being species of insect. However, anecdotal evidence from interviews and autobiographical sources has suggested that the name was inspired by the film *The Wild One*, where the girlfriends of the motorcycle gang were known as "beetles." Quoted by his authorized biographer, Paul explained how the making of the *Anthology* television series in 1994 led him to investigate the issue and to conclude that the latter explanation was probably correct: "We were actually named after chicks, which I think is fabulous."[63] This androgynous element of the homosocial group was interestingly echoed in the Beatles' fondness for girl group songs such as "Baby It's You" and "Boys" by the Shirelles and "Chains" by the Cookies.[64]

The important period of less than a year between the Manchester talent show and the Hamburg booking saw a step-change in the types of performance given by the group. In place of the occasional paid booking and the art college shows, there were a competition, a tour, and a foreign residency. Each provided a new challenge and test for the nascent Beatles. For the competition and the Parnes audition, the task was to impress judges, not fans. For the tour, the group had to learn how to extend their range to encompass another artist's style and to adjust to alien audiences; they had never before played outside Merseyside.

The Beatles only partly met those challenges, the greatest being the Hamburg residency, first because of the need to solidify the group's membership. While it had been possible to get through the Johnny Gentle tour with a temporary drummer (Tommy Moore), two or more months at a single venue demanded more permanent commitments. To complement the lead guitar of George and the twin rhythm guitars of John and Paul, a permanent drummer and electric bass player were needed.

Stu Sutcliffe had joined as a bass player at the end of 1959. However, his credentials for joining the group were closer to those of the original Quarrymen – personal friendship – than to the quality of musicianship that brought Paul and George into the band. Stu was John's closest art college friend. He was a talented painter but an untried musician. Nevertheless, John persuaded him to spend the money from the sale of a painting exhibited at a Walker Art Gallery event on a new bass guitar, and persuaded the others to accept Stu as a group member. As a potential drummer for Hamburg, the trio successfully approached Pete Best of the Blackjacks, who was already known to them because of the club run by his mother, Mona.

The group spent five months of 1960 playing in Hamburg clubs. The importance of this period for the evolution of the group was threefold: the band learned how to communicate with audiences, they became a wholly integrated unit, and they learned from playing alongside or near an international range of other musicians.

The Beatles were faced with a totally new performance context. They were expected to play, with brief intervals, for up to eight hours a night to foreign (mostly non-English-speaking) audiences, and to prevent the audiences from drifting off to other clubs in the Reeperbahn red light district. After an unsuccessful beginning, they responded to the club owner's instruction to *mach schon* (make a show) by devising dynamic and often comic stage moves, together with elongating three-minute songs using extended solos and repetitive choruses. John claimed with a little exaggeration that "Paul would do [Ray Charles's] 'What'd I Say' for an hour and a half."[65]

The demands of the eight-hour show clarified the onstage relationships between group members, especially in vocal arrangements. According to Paul, they "sang close harmony on the little echo mikes and made a fairly good job of it. It used to sound pretty good, actually."[66] Finally, the group learned much about stagecraft and performance dynamics from other bands and singers on the Reeperbahn. The most notable of these in 1960 was the uninhibited English singer and guitarist Tony Sheridan, but the group was able to observe other leading Liverpool bands, including Rory Storm and the Hurricanes. The Dutch scholar Lutgard Mutsaers has argued that the Beatles were also influenced by "Indorock" groups formed by Indonesian immigrants to the Netherlands, who were prominent on the Hamburg scene in 1960.[67]

The 1960 residency in Hamburg was the first and by far the longest of five stints in Germany.[68] Between and after those trips, the Beatles established themselves as virtually the resident band at the Cavern in Liverpool, playing there 292 times in thirty months between 1961 and 1963.

The sheer quantity of gigs in the two years before the first EMI recordings placed a strain on the Lennon-McCartney songwriting. As this chapter's appendix listing the group's repertoire shows, John and Paul had composed perhaps twenty or thirty songs before the end of 1962, but the Beatles regularly performed only a handful. Their performances were mainly taken up with cover versions. The appendix lists about 150 songs performed at least once by the group in the four years or so before their first hit record. While many of these were hits of the late 1950s and early 1960s by American pop artists and girl groups, about half were "classic" rock and roll numbers learned from the records of Little Richard, Chuck Berry, Elvis Presley, Buddy Holly, and others. Although rock and roll was regarded as outmoded by the mainstream pop industry at the end of the 1950s, it continued to form the backbone of Beatles' performances. Of the sixteen tracks included on the *Rockin' At the Star Club* album recorded in Hamburg in December 1962, ten were rock and roll songs from the mid-1950s.

So when the time came to begin recording for EMI, while every single contained only original songs, the first two albums, *Please Please Me* and *With the Beatles* (both 1963) each contained six cover versions and eight original songs. They had to fight to have their own songs as the A sides of their first and second singles ("Love Me Do" and "Please Please Me"). On both occasions, George Martin was insistent that they record "How Do You Do It?" by an old-school songwriter, Mitch Murray, but he eventually backed down and foisted the song on another Brian Epstein group, Gerry and the Pacemakers. That version reached number one in April 1963, shortly before the third Beatles single, "From Me to You," topped the British charts.

The final phase of the prehistory of the band began with the arrival of Brian Epstein. Musically, the Beatles were already at their peak as composers and performers, but their reach was limited to their devoted audiences in Liverpool and Hamburg. Epstein was to be the catalyst for the process that took them to a national, then global, audience. In brief, he added the haircuts, the suits, and the recording contract.

Brian Epstein's early life and his role in the Beatles' career has been told in his own somewhat unreliable memoir *A Cellarful of Noise*, in numerous

Beatle biographies, and most effectively in *The Brian Epstein Story* by television directors Anthony Wall and the late Debbie Geller. Briefly, he had
trained as an actor in London, but in 1961 he was running the record
department of NEMS, a Liverpool store owned by his family, a pillar of the
local Jewish community. He was taken by one of his staff to see a lunchtime
Cavern show by the Beatles in November 1961.

In little more than a month, Epstein had signed a management contract
with the Beatles. He determined to change their bohemian Teddy boy image
by organizing matching suits and haircuts. Most significantly, he ignored
their live career – which in any case was self-generating between the Hamburg and Liverpool residencies – in favor of seeking a recording deal with a
London-based company.

Epstein did not scruple to use his status as a leading record retailer to seek
auditions for the band. After an unsuccessful attempt to persuade Decca
to sign the Beatles – where he was memorably told that "guitar groups are
out" – he finally linked up with George Martin at EMI's Parlophone label.
The Parlophone audition was successful. The band made their first demo
tape at Abbey Road Studios in June 1962. Martin was not overly impressed
but decided to take a chance and record a single. This was, of course, "Love
Me Do," backed with "P.S. I Love You."

George Martin also insisted that Pete Best's drumming was not good
enough, and encouraged Epstein to replace him. Pete's sacking reverberated
around the Cavern and other Liverpool venues, because for many fans he
was the most popular Beatle. John and Paul determined that Ringo Starr
of Rory Storm and the Hurricanes was the best replacement; they had
known him in Hamburg. They drove to a holiday camp on the English
east coast where the Storm group had a summer residency. Ringo accepted
the job; but, having been sought out for his musicianship, he discovered
he was joining something like a gang, finding the others to be a tight-knit
friendship group with in-jokes.

Finale

On November 26 1962, the Beatles completed the recording of what would
be their second single, "Please Please Me." George Martin told them: "Gentlemen, you've just made your first number one record."[69] The formative
years were at an end.

Appendix: the repertoire, 1957–1962

The following list is the most comprehensive published to date of the songs performed live by the Quarrymen and the Beatles prior to 1963. I have identified over 150 songs covered by the band plus twenty-seven original compositions. The list is probably not definitive: for example, Ian MacDonald plausibly claimed that the group performed some thirty Elvis Presley numbers,[70] but I have found references to only eight. The sources for the list are both written and recorded.[71] One important source of the group's pre-fame repertoire is the many sessions for the BBC between 1962 and 1965.[72] Each of these sessions usually included some cover versions which would have been learned by the band prior to 1963, after which the Beatles did not add any songs by other acts to their live or recorded repertoire.

Pre-1963 recordings were made in Hamburg as backing tracks for Tony Sheridan and Wally (a member of the Hurricanes), plus the Christmas 1962 Star-Club session, later issued commercially by Columbia Records. Earlier in 1962, the Beatles had made audition tapes for Decca and EMI.

In percentage terms, almost half of the list (47 percent) are rock and roll songs, mostly from the 1950s; 14 percent are compositions by group members, although not all of these were performed live; 13 percent of the songs are US pop, mainly from the early 1960s; 10 percent rhythm and blues and early Motown; 6 percent pre-1945 pop songs; 5 percent songs by US girl groups; and the final 5 percent from miscellaneous sources.

Lennon-McCartney compositions

"Ask Me Why"
"Cat's Walk"
"Do You Want to Know a Secret"
"Hello Little Girl"
"Hot as Sun"
"I Call Your Name"
"I Saw Her Standing There"
"I'll Always be in Love with You"
"I'll Follow the Sun"
"Just Fun"
"Keep Looking That Way"
"Like Dreamers Do"
"Looking Glass"
"Love Me Do"
"Love of the Loved"
"Misery"
"One After 909"
"Please Please Me"
"P.S. I Love You"

"Somedays"
"That's My Woman"
"There's a Place"
"Thinking of Linking"
"What Goes On"
"When I'm Sixty Four"
"Winston's Walk"
"Years Roll Along"

US rock and roll
Chuck Berry (14 songs)
"Almost Grown"
"Carol"
"Got to Find My Baby"
"Johnny B. Goode"
"Little Queenie"
"Maybellene"
"Memphis, Tennessee"
"Reelin' and Rockin'"
"Rock and Roll Music"
"Roll Over Beethoven"
"Sweet Little Sixteen"
"Talkin' About You"
"Too Much Monkey Business"
"Vacation Time"

Eddie Cochran (2 songs)
"C'mon Everybody"
"Twenty Flight Rock"

Everly Brothers (6 songs)
"All I Have to Do is Dream"
"Bye Bye Love"
"Cathy's Clown"
"So How Come (No One Loves Me)"
"So Sad"
"Wake Up Little Susie"

Buddy Holly (11 songs)
"Crying, Waiting, Hoping"
"Everyday"
"It's So Easy"
"Mailman, Bring Me No More Blues"
"Maybe Baby"
"Peggy Sue"
"Raining In My Heart"
"Reminiscing"
"That'll Be the Day"

"Think it Over"
"Words of Love"

Little Richard (12 songs)
   "Good Golly Miss Molly"
   "Hey! Hey! Hey! Hey!"
   "Kansas City"
   "Long Tall Sally"
   "Lucille"
   "Miss Ann"
   "Ooh! My Soul"
   "Ready Teddy"
   "Rip it Up"
   "Send Me Some Lovin'"
   "Slippin' and Slidin'"
   "Tutti Frutti"

Carl Perkins (11 songs)
   "Blue Suede Shoes"
   "Boppin' the Blues"
   "Everybody's Trying to Be My Baby"
   "Glad All Over"
   "Gone, Gone, Gone"
   "Honey Don't"
   "Lend Me Your Comb"
   "Matchbox"
   "Sure to Fall (in Love with You)"
   "Tennessee"
   "Your True Love"

Elvis Presley (8 songs)
   "Blue Moon of Kentucky"
   "I Don't Care If the Sun Don't Shine"
   "I Forgot to Remember to Forget"
   "Love Me Tender"
   "Milk Cow Blues"
   "That's All Right (Mama)"
   "That's When Your Heartaches Begin"
   "Wooden Heart"

Larry Williams (6 songs)
   "Bad Boy"
   "Bony Moronie"
   "Dizzy Miss Lizzy"
   "Peaches and Cream"
   "Short Fat Fanny"
   "Slow Down"

Other rock and roll (15 songs)

"Be-Bop-A-Lula" (Gene Vincent)

"Clarabella" (Jodimars)

"Corrine, Corrina" (Ray Peterson and others)

"Guitar Boogie Shuffle" (various, instrumental)

"Mean Woman Blues" (Jerry Lee Lewis and various)

"Move On Down the Line"

"Move Over"

"New Orleans"

"Nothin' Shakin' (but the Leaves on the Trees)" (Eddie Fontaine)

"Raunchy" (Bill Justis instrumental)

"Red Hot" (Billy Riley)

"Red Sails in the Sunset" (Fats Domino)

"Rock-a-Chicka" (Frankie Vaughan)

"Skinnie Minnie" (Bill Haley)

"Whole Lotta Shakin' Going On" (Jerry Lee Lewis)

Rhythm and blues and Motown (18 songs)

"A Shot of Rhythm and Blues" (Arthur Alexander)

"Anna (Go to Him)" (Arthur Alexander)

"Hallelujah, I Love Her So" (Ray Charles)

"I Got A Woman" (Ray Charles)

"If You Gotta Make A Fool of Somebody" (James Ray)

"Leave My Kitten Alone" (Little Willie John)

"Money" (That's What I Want) (Barrett Strong)

"Mr. Moonlight" (Doctor Feelgood and the Interns of Love)

"Searchin'" (Coasters)

"September in the Rain" (Dinah Washington)

"Soldier of Love" (Arthur Alexander)

"Some Other Guy" (Richie Barrett)

"The Hippy Hippy Shake" (Chan Romero)

"Three Cool Cats" (Coasters)

"Twist and Shout" (Isley Brothers)

"What'd I Say" (Ray Charles)

"You Really Got a Hold on Me" (Smokey Robinson)

"Young Blood" (Coasters)

US pop (15 songs)

"Be-Bop Baby" (Ricky Nelson)

"But I Do" (Clarence Henry)

"Don't Ever Change" (Crickets, composed by Goffin and King)

"Dream Baby" (Roy Orbison)

"Dream Lover" (Bobby Darin)

"He'll Have To Go" (Jim Reeves)

"I Got a Feeling" (Ricky Nelson)

"I Just Don't Understand" (Ann Margret)
"Lonesome Tears in My Eyes" (Johnny Burnette)
"Peppermint Twist" (Joey Dee and the Starliters)
"Sharing You" (Bobby Vee, composed by Goffin and King)
"Sheila" (Tommy Roe)
"Take Good Care of My Baby" (Bobby Vee)
"To Know Her is to Love Her" (Teddy Bears)
"Where Have You Been All My Life" (Mann and Weil)

US girl groups (9 songs)

"Baby It's You" (Shirelles)
"Boys" (Shirelles)
"Chains" (Cookies)
"Devil in Her Heart" (Donays, as . . . 'His Heart')
"Keep Your Hands Off My Baby" (Little Eva)
"Mama Said" (Shirelles)
"Please Mr. Postman" (Marvelettes)
"Shimmy Shake" (Orlons)
"Will You Love Me Tomorrow" (Shirelles)

Pre-1945 vaudeville and pop (10 songs)

"Ain't She Sweet"
"Beautiful Dreamer" (Stephen Foster)
"Bésame Mucho" (Coasters version)
"Darktown" (probably Darktown Strutters Ball, US minstrel song)
"Falling in Love Again" (Marlene Dietrich)
"I Remember You" (as by Frank Ifield)
"I'm Gonna Sit Right Down and Cry (Over You)" (?)
"The Sheik of Araby" (rock and roll version by Lou Monte)
"Up a Lazy River" (probably the Bobby Darin version)
"Your Feet's Too Big" (Fats Waller)

Miscellaneous
Stage and film musicals (5 songs)

"A Taste of Honey" (film theme recorded by Lenny Welch)
"Honeymoon Song" (film theme by Mikis Theodorakis)
"Over the Rainbow" (Judy Garland)
"Till There Was You" (from *The Music Man* via Peggy Lee's 1958 version)
"True Love" (from *High Society*, duet by Bing Crosby and Grace Kelly)

UK pop (1 song)

"A Picture of You" (Joe Brown)

Others (8 songs)

"Better Luck Next Time" (provenance unknown)
"Dance in the Streets" (provenance unknown)

"Don't Forbid Me" (provenance unknown)
"My Bonnie" (traditional, sung by Tony Sheridan)
"Nobody but You" (provenance unknown)
"Somebody Help Me" (provenance unknown)
"Swingin' Thing" (provenance unknown)
"You Don't Understand Me" (provenance unknown)

2 The Beatles as recording artists

JERRY ZOLTEN

When the Beatles – John Lennon, Paul McCartney, George Harrison, and Pete Best – recorded their first tracks as professionals in Hamburg, Germany, in June 1961, the "art" of electrical analog recording was essentially as it always had been. Basically, the players positioned themselves in front of microphones and performed as if they were live on stage – except there was no audience. Only present were producers, technicians, other musicians, and onlookers. The performance happened all at once, everyone playing the whole way through and as many times as it took to get it "right." And in the end, it was the producers and technicians, *not* the Beatles, who had control over the final sound, what listeners heard when the record was played.

As to the songs, half the ones the Beatles recorded that day were curiously archaic: "Ain't She Sweet," "My Bonnie," "When the Saints Go Marching In," "Sweet Georgia Brown," all throwbacks to a previous generation, as were, for that matter, the circumstances of the session itself. Pete Best said he was taken aback by the makeshift "studio." "We wondered if we had come to the right place. We had been expecting a recording setup on the grand scale . . . Instead, we found ourselves in an unexciting school gym [actually, Friedrich Elbert Halle] with a massive stage and lots of drapes."[1]

Did those initial recording forays significantly advance the artistry or career of the Beatles? Other than getting a foot in the door, decidedly not, reported Paul and John with characteristic cheekiness in their first ever 1962 radio interview:

> Paul: We made a recording with a fella called Tony Sheridan. We were working in a club called "The Top Ten Club" in Hamburg. And we made a recording with him called, "My Bonnie," which got to number five in the German Hit Parade.
>
> John: Ach Tung!
>
> Paul: (giggles) But it didn't do a thing over here, you know. It wasn't a very good record, but the Germans must've liked it a bit. And we did an instrumental which was released in France on an EP of Tony Sheridan's, which George and John wrote themselves. That wasn't released here. It got one copy. That's all, you know. It didn't do anything.[2]

John Lennon was acerbically candid about it with Beatles biographer Hunter Davies. "When the offer came, we thought it would be easy. The Germans had such shitty records. Ours was bound to be better. We did five of our own numbers, but they didn't like them. They preferred 'My Bonnie Lies Over the Ocean.'"[3]

A year or so later, the Beatles – Ringo Starr now occupying the place of Pete Best – teamed with producer George Martin on a run of LPs that had a profound impact on pop music worldwide. The earliest collaborations, though conventionally recorded, were catchy, smartly arranged pop hits. Then, in a succession of mid-sixties studio-savvy albums that peaked in 1967 with *Sgt. Pepper's Lonely Hearts Club Band*, the Beatles and George Martin entered rarified territory, and in the process played an incisive role in revolutionizing the art of studio recording. Certainly flashes of things to come pre-dated the Beatles, not only in American rhythm and blues and rock and roll, but in earlier genres with a handful of studio wizards pointing the way. So, who were these "wizards" and what exactly did they do? Let's take a sidetrack into the evolution of recording artistry.

"And at the end of the day you had your album"

From the get-go, the technology of recording had a *de facto* impact on music. Essentially, the invention of sound recording by Thomas Edison in the late 1800s introduced an entirely new way to hear music. Before Edison, musical performance – with the exception of reproducing player pianos – could only be experienced "live" and "in person." Recording, both literally and figuratively, "revolutionized" that experience. Back in the 1920s, Louis Armstrong fans hearing him in person for the first time were initially put off because he didn't sound like his records. In the early 1930s, the buxom "shout to the rafters" style of blues diva Bessie Smith was displaced by *sotto voce* Billie Holiday, the latter's success dependent on the microphone to capture and convey her intimate sound. Crooner Bing Crosby, noted his biographer Gary Giddins, "understood the microphone, and that electricity paradoxically makes music more rather than less human; because you don't have to shout, you . . . can now sing in a normal tone of voice."[4] In the days of 78-rpm records, even the duration of a performance – three minutes – was dictated by the limits of how much could fit on a 10-inch shellac disk.

Now jump to the 1950s and early sixties, the era of American rhythm and blues and rock and roll. A number of producers and musicians, some rockers, others not, began experimenting with the "art" of recording. They recognized that rapidly evolving technologies could be used to create sonic realities existent only on recordings. They produced performances that could not, in fact, be duplicated "live" on stage. Small examples surfaced here and there – echo effects achieved through basement and hallway placement of ambient microphones; the double, even triple-track layering of vocal leads; vocal tracks speeded up to mask intonation problems or, with teen idols more good-looking than able to sing, stitched together a phrase at a time to create the illusion of continuous performance. Then, capping it all was Phil Spector, his famous "Wall of Sound" achieved through multi-tracking, mike placement, voices as upfront in the mix as loud orchestras and electric instruments, everything awash in a sea of reverberation. Spector was among the first of a new breed of producer, not merely button-pushing, dial-turning "techies," but co-creators with musicians in the "art" of recording music. In those early days, Phil Spector's studio ingenuity sparked the imaginations of many in the upcoming generation of rock and roll producers and musicians.

One of those was musician, arranger, and lyricist Van Dyke Parks, vision-ary producer/performer and collaborator with Brian Wilson on the ill-fated but three-decades-later triumphant *Smile*, a Beach Boys project that Parks maintains had a more immediate influence on the Beatles' *Sgt. Pepper* (1967) than the more generally acknowledged *Pet Sounds* (1966). On his role as a recording arts revolutionary, Parks labels himself "fair game." In talking about his own awakening to studio possibilities, Parks provided a telling overview of those whose earlier inventiveness influenced both the Beach Boys and the Beatles.

"When I entered this business of recording," said Parks, "my first job in town was in 1963 with 'Bare Necessities,' a song from Disney's *The Jungle Book*." Producers and musicians back then, he says, talked about how a room "sounded," meaning the musical sonority inherent in a recording space. In those days, he adds, "the technology of recording was accelerating greatly and quickly."

> That was with the advent of "close-miking," where an instrument that you would think in a roomful of sax and trumpets and trombones – big band – would not have been heard. But if you put a mike very close . . . their power – the potential for plectrum instruments to be heard above the general roar of full blown instruments – was all a new reality.

Then came a new generation of rockers, studio neophytes, "musicians," says Parks, who "were empowered, politically charged, but generally musically illiterate."

> They didn't come in with charts that were all prepared. They came in with various ideas and generally moved the studio away from the efficiency of a 3-hour session in which maybe three tunes would get done in one or two takes. Dean Martin and Frank Sinatra would say, "That's enough, boys."

Parks offers the example of one track from *Pet Sounds* that cost the Beach Boys more than $62,000 to record and "took a week or even more of procedural layering... And all with the new real estate of multi-track recording... but also some understanding about how microphones captured in an intimate way what had never been featured before."

That "understanding" evolved for Parks and his contemporaries from an appreciation of what their predecessors had done in the studio, minor epiphanies at the time, but later, profoundly utilitarian. "I can remember hearing Spike Jones doing 'Cocktails for Two' in 1948," says Parks.

> And what was interesting to me was that Jones had things like bicycle bells and whoopee cushions. Whatever he wanted. Spike Jones would put the sound very close to a microphone... and I thought that was a phenomenon! I recognized that there was something coming through a speaker that wasn't available in a room when I walked into a concert.

Parks also became aware of mike placement and synchronized multi-track recording through the artistry of Les Paul and Esquivel. Les Paul pioneered the layering of vocal parts and guitar lines. "With 'Lover' by Les Paul and Mary Ford," said Parks, "he did... what they called the 'choir of wire,' these triadic guitar lines..., a special sound that he invented for recording... and once again made a step forward. It was stuff I had never heard before. Absolutely changed my perception."

As did Juan Garcia Esquivel, the "King of Space-Age Pop," billed on his records as simply "Esquivel." Parks heard Esquivel in the early sixties when Parks and older brother Carson came to Los Angeles as the "Steeltown Two" to perform folk music. Though middle-of-the-road in style, Esquivel's experiments with two-track stereo were revolutionary. He recorded two orchestras playing simultaneously in separate studios so that in playback one could be heard coming out on the right, the other on the left. "Esquivel," said Parks, "would put *two* mikes in a piano, and so when a piano did a glissando from the bottom to the top of the keyboard, you would hear it pass like a train from left to right. Very imaginative."[5]

The idea to make studio technology part of music artistry, to consciously apply the medium to the message, flowed from these artists as well as a legion of unnamed rock and roll and rhythm and blues producers. Van Dyke Parks, Brian Wilson, and, of course, George Martin and the Beatles were caught up in the swell.

In the mid-1960s, Brian Wilson, like the Beatles, was enchanted with studio technique. His influential album *Pet Sounds* (1966) was famously characterized as "richly textured, multi-layered, and inventively arranged." *Pet Sounds*, says Wilson, was inspired by the Beatles earlier *Rubber Soul* (1965), affirming the rivalry that existed between the two groups during this peak creative period. On *Pet Sounds*, Wilson supplemented rock and roll's conventional guitar-bass-keyboard-drum with full orchestration and a Spike Jones ragtag of "accordion, theremin, bicycle bells, kazoo, banjo, glockenspiel, and even barking dogs and a Sparklett's water jug," setting the stage for the even more sonically ambitious *Smile*.[6]

Smile was intended as the follow-up to *Pet Sounds*, and writing and recording began in August 1966. The eventual collapse of the project became the stuff of pop music lore, which is why the reimagining and completion of *Smile* by Wilson and Parks in 2004 attracted significant attention . . . and prompted Wilson to comment retrospectively on his then sense of rivalry with the Beatles as well as this about the influence of Phil Spector: "What I learned from Phil Spector," said Wilson, was "to make songs echo . . . to combine piano and guitar to make one sound. Combine horns and strings to make another sound, strings with voices to make a sound. There's all kind of possibilities in the studio."[7]

The Beatles carried forward those same canons, as did Van Dyke Parks on his own solo recording project, *Song Cycle* (1968). The important point here is that for all of them, technology was not evoked merely as gimmick, but rather as application that contributed to the music's ability to convey meaning and provoke emotional response. "When I got into the position of actually . . . being in charge of how studio results appeared on a record," Parks said, "I was absolutely fascinated by it."

> All of those things to me were not just trivial or prosthetic pursuits, but could maybe even bring some emotional value to music in new ways and mean something . . . I plunged right into *Song Cycle* . . . and I went hog wild . . . They should have called it *Song Psycho* . . . In fact, when I took it to the company president, he said, "it's a very nice title . . . but where are the songs?" I forgot to include them!
>
> But I did prove that I was a fanatic, obsessed about studio procedures. I think I did a lot to advance a kind of a sound which would be unavailable in performance, and something different . . . So honestly, I've got to admit I happened to be at the right age at the right time and in the right place to benefit fully from studio technology at the apogee of analog recording. It was the luck of the draw.[8]

As it was for the Beatles. Skip back a few years to October 1962 and their first venture into EMI's London-based Abbey Road studios with George Martin, the result a debut British single, "Love Me Do"/"P.S. I Love You." Though Martin was more impressed with the Beatles' charisma than with their early material,[9] the record was surprisingly a modest hit, enough to merit a follow-up, the second Beatles hit, "Please Please Me"/"Ask Me Why," produced a month later in November.

The UK success of these four original Lennon-McCartney 45-rpm singles prompted the recording of the Beatles' first British $33\frac{1}{3}$ "long-playing" album, *Please Please Me.* The ten additional tracks filling out the album were recorded in a day's time at a marathon session in February 1963, the LP released in March on Parlophone. The Beatles had produced four hit singles and an album in the space of six months.

Almost half of the debut album's tracks – "Anna," "Chains," "Boys," "Baby It's You," "A Taste of Honey," and "Twist and Shout" – were covers of American rock and roll B sides. The new originals were "I Saw Her Standing There," "Misery," "Do You Want to Know a Secret," and "There's a Place." "The whole album only took a day," said Paul McCartney, ". . . so it was amazingly cheap, no-messing, just a massive effort from us . . . We started at ten in the morning and finished at ten at night . . . And at the end of the day you had your album."[10] Back then, though, the technology of analog recording – soundwaves directly imprinted on tape or disk – even at EMI, allowed little creativity beyond the straightforward performance of the songs. Recording machines were two-track stereo, the tape a narrow quarter-inch in width. Once a master was recorded, introducing additional sound required a second recording machine.

Beatles session engineer Geoff Emerick recalled from those days George Martin wanting handclaps added to a completed track. "Because the song had been recorded directly to a two-track tape . . . this was accomplished . . . by loading a blank reel of tape on a second machine and putting it in record while the first machine played back, essentially making a copy of the original tape, along with the overdub."[11] In other words, as one or more of the Beatles clapped along to a playback of the master track, those claps along with the master track were newly recorded on to the second machine, resulting in a revised master with clapping now interpolated into the mix. This was typically the extent of studio artistry in the early days. George Harrison offered a tidy summary in 1965:

> Right from the beginning when we started recording, we'd just record in one take. You know, things like "Twist and Shout" and "I Saw Her Standing There," which were all on our first album in England – we just turned the recorder on. We got a sound balance in the studio – just put the tape on and did it like that. So we never did any of this overdubbing or adding orchestras or anything like that.[12]

"Four-track . . . made the studios into much more of a workshop"

In late 1963 and continuing through 1964, the Beatles use of studio technology evolved as they developed a second album and gained access to four-track recording. In the process, they became increasingly aware of the growing disparity between what they did in the studio and what they could perform on stage. Said George Harrison, "It's only recently where we've been using a bit of overdub stuff. We've added things like tambourine, which you don't notice, you know. Because we still like to think we can get basically the same sound on stage."[13] With each session, though, the Beatles progressed beyond a point where they could replicate on stage what the public heard on record.

By late 1963, the Beatles were a phenomenon in Britain, but barely a whisper in America. EMI's UK strategy was cautious, namely: release a single, gauge response, release a timely follow-up, and then if warranted – which it always was – produce an entire album. The smashing success of *Please Please Me* motivated EMI to move ahead with slightly more aggression.

In the summer and fall of that year, the Beatles exhaustively toured Great Britain as they worked up songs for a second album. On Thursday, October 17, they went to Abbey Road to record incidental material in addition to a new single. The strategy was to keep the Beatles in the public eye until a second album could be released. That single – "I Want to Hold Your Hand"/"This Boy" – hit enormously in the UK. Four months later, in January 1964, "I Want to Hold Your Hand," released in the US on Capitol with "I Saw Her Standing There" on the flipside, at last broke the Beatles into the American Top Ten.

The real significance of "I Want to Hold Your Hand," however, was that it was the first to be recorded with four-track technology. The session was a milestone in the group's studio artistry, Beatles chronicler Mark Lewisohn calling it "the dawn of a new era for the Beatles at Abbey Road." Production possibilities were amplified exponentially overnight and changed how the Beatles made records. "The luxury of working in four-track instead of two-track," reflected Geoff Emerick, "gave . . . a great deal more control over balance of the instruments." And indeed, stereo separation, especially between bass and rhythm guitar, brought a new dimensionality to the Beatles' recorded sound. In a short time, the production team established what would become a standard "general approach" to recording the Beatles; the specific procedure being, said Emerick, to "put drums and bass on one track, combine Lennon's and Harrison's guitars on another, and then put the vocals on a third track. The fourth track was the 'catch-all' track for whatever sweetening George Martin wanted to add – handclaps, harmonica, keyboard, guitar solo, whatever."[14]

Interestingly, EMI had four-track recording capability from the start, but label execs thought the Beatles too "lowbrow" to warrant access. Only success on a grand scale opened the doors to optimum facility. After "I Want to Hold Your Hand," says Geoff Emerick, the Beatles "always recorded in multi-track. Four-track all the way through to the White Album, eight-track afterward. Apparently," said Emerick, "the bigwigs at EMI had decided that the band had now earned sufficient monies for the label – many millions of pounds, for sure – to be afforded the same honor as 'serious' musicians, none of whom, I'm sure, brought in even a fraction of the income the Beatles did."[15]

One enormous ramification of four-track was that recording no longer had to take place in real time. Performances could now be created in layers, bits and pieces assembled and adjusted post-session. "With four-track," said Beatles technical engineer Ken Townsend, "one could do a basic rhythm track and then add on vocals and whatever else later. It made the studios into much more of a workshop."[16] Now, for example, John Lennon could sing and then afterwards lay a harmonica track over his own voice, or, with instrumental tracks complete, a Beatle could come in anytime to re-record a guitar part, experiment with an instrumental effect, or improve upon a vocal lead or harmony. In the end, a finished recording was, like a film montage, a splicing together and overlay of carefully selected "takes" to create the final master.

The second album, in the UK titled *With the Beatles*, was released in November 1963 with advance orders of 300,000. Most Beatles fans likely never noticed the differences in four-track recording. The most obvious changes were in the double-tracking of lead vocals, notably John Lennon on "It Won't Be Long" and "Not a Second Time," Paul McCartney on "All My Loving," and George Harrison on "Don't Bother Me" and the Chuck Berry cover, "Roll Over Beethoven." The net effect was an appealing "fattening" of the vocals, somehow livelier from the millisecond space that separated the two vocal tracks. A noticeable bit of unreality occurs in John Lennon's cover of the Marvelettes' "Please Mister Postman." Lennon is recorded harmonizing with himself, and can be heard on the last syllable of "delivah the let-tah, the sooner the bet-tah" overlapping as he comes in with the first word of the next verse. A telling glimpse behind the technical curtain *en route* to greater studio complexities to come.

Following the release of *With the Beatles* – issued by Capitol in the USA in modified form as *Meet the Beatles* – the group toured the UK as they also developed material for future recordings, the desired optimum, two LPs per year. In early 1964, the Beatles were focused on the soundtrack to *A Hard Day's Night*, their first movie. Though the film and soundtrack LP premiered in the UK in July, to drum up excitement for the project, some tracks were issued earlier as singles. Case in point: "Can't Buy Me Love," recorded in one session in late January and released about five months before the film. Advance orders topped a million, the record charting worldwide and at number one in America the week of April 4, 1964.

The recording of "Can't Buy Me Love" is an excellent example of Beatles studio craft in that phase of their career. "Remarkably," writes Mark Lewisohn, "the song was recorded from start to finish in just four takes." Each take introduced changes, the first, reports Lewisohn, with a "very bluesy" McCartney vocal lead, and Lennon and Harrison on backup vocal harmonies. "Take two," says Lewisohn, "was much the same, but take three switches to the style they were eventually to use." On take three, McCartney's vocal shifts from blues to rock and the Lennon/Harrison backups disappear altogether. Then, in a fourth take – still subject to later remixes – were added "a vocal overdub by Paul and a lead guitar overdub by George." His double-tracked guitar lead was positioned in the mix to cut across both stereo channels. "In what was probably under one hour's work the Beatles had started, altered, and completed one of their biggest selling songs. It was to be typical of their industry throughout the year."[17]

"Can't Buy Me Love," however, required an additional tweak before it was truly complete. A "technical problem" was discovered in post-production, reported Geoff Emerick, the cause likely an incorrect spooling of the master tape following the session. "The tape," said Emerick, "had a ripple in it resulting in the intermittent loss of treble on Ringo's hi-hat cymbal." With pressure to release and the Beatles unavailable on tour, Emerick, George Martin, and future Pink Floyd producer Norman Smith took emergency action. "Norman headed down into the studio to overdub a hastily set-up hi-hat onto a few bars of the song while I recorded him . . . Thanks to Norman's considerable skills as a drummer, the repair was made quickly and seamlessly, and I doubt if even the Beatles themselves ever realized that their performance had been surreptitiously augmented."[18]

"No one heard us, not even ourselves"

Between 1964 and 1966, the Beatles maintained their maddening pace of writing, recording, and now "acting." They turned out twenty hit singles, a second film, *Help!*, and four smashing UK albums, *Beatles For Sale*, *Help!*, *Rubber Soul*, and *Revolver*, each released in varying forms worldwide. The Beatles were now stars on the international stage, the penultimate rock and roll band, the ones to emulate and to beat. In America, competition came from Bob Dylan and "folk rock," the Beach Boys and the California sound, and Motown and southern soul. Also in the Beatles' wake came the "British Invasion," spearheaded by the blues-oriented Rolling Stones, the Animals, the Who, the Yardbirds with Eric Clapton, and Them, and on the lighter side, the Dave Clark Five, the Hollies, Herman's Hermits, Gerry and the Pacemakers, the Troggs, and Peter and Gordon.

During this period, the Beatles extended their touring internationally, including the market they most wanted to conquer, the United States. Concerts in the US were staged at mega-venues, the audiences enormous and so fired up and at such a distance that any artistic connection was impossible. Their performances, quite simply, could not be heard, obliterated in the mass hysteria of "Beatlemania." For the Beatles, touring became increasingly excruciating.

The first of four US tours was brief, two weeks in February, 1964, the Beatles playing the Coliseum in Washington DC and Carnegie Hall in New York City. More important to their American success, however, were their appearances on *The Ed Sullivan Show*. Over 73 million viewers tuned in on February 9 and watched as teenage fans in a studio audience of more than 700 screamed, jumped, and went wild as the Beatles performed. The close-miked television broadcast provided home viewers a better hearing than those actually in the studio.

There would be three more Beatles tours in the USA between 1964 and 1966, the music consistently drowned out by relentlessly screaming Beatlemaniacs. "That's the . . . great truth," said Ringo Starr. "No one heard us, not even ourselves. I found it very hard . . . I couldn't do any [drum] fills . . . I'm just there . . . to hold it together somehow . . . and the timing usually went all to cock. And that's why we were bad players."[19]

The summer tour of 1964 covered thirty-two shows in thirty-four days. More than 17,000 attended the first concert at San Francisco's Cow Palace; the performance was stopped twice because of fans pelting the Beatles with jelly beans, a reckless show of affection in response to George Harrison's remark that Ringo had been stealing his "jelly babies." The tour played most major American cities, the venues convention centers, arenas, or stadiums, the crowds ranging from 14,000 to more than 20,000.

The tours of 1965 and 1966 followed essentially the same pattern, except that on this go-round the venues were exclusively baseball stadiums and the chaos exponentially more unsettling.

The August 15, 1965 New York Shea Stadium concert, 55,600 attending, was memorable, having been filmed for American television. *En route* to Portland, Oregon, a plane engine caught fire. That night, Beach Boys Mike Love and Carl Wilson visited backstage. At tour's end in late August, the Beatles stayed for a few days in a rented Los Angeles mansion and met with the King, Elvis Presley.

The Beatles' 1966 tour of America was their last tour ever. The exceptionally turbulent year drove the Beatles permanently away from live performance and towards a sequestered life in the studio where they would take recording art to new heights. John Lennon's offhand remark that the Beatles were now more popular than Jesus spawned hate mail and death threats.

Capitol Records released *Yesterday and Today*, an album pieced together for American consumption from a mishmash of UK singles and tracks culled from *Rubber Soul* and *Revolver*. The album cover sparked public outrage with its picture of the Beatles in butcher aprons surrounded by slabs of bloody meat and disembodied baby doll heads, George Harrison's upraised middle finger, judging from the expression on his face, hidden from view inside one of them. In explaining the album's recall, Capitol press liaison Ron Tepper said the cover was intended as "'pop art' satire." John Lennon called it a protest over Capitol's crass repackaging of the British albums, a "butchering" of their artistic integrity, as far as the Beatles were concerned.[20]

In July, the Beatles were literally pummeled in the Philippines *en route* to and in the airport, having inadvertently offended the family of President Marcos by failing to show at the palace for a special pre-concert gathering.[21] In America, fans disrupted the Cleveland Municipal Stadium concert by rushing the stage. The Beatles were rattled in Memphis by Ku-Klux-Klan threats over the "Jesus" remark, and momentarily feared for their lives at the pop-pop-popping of firecrackers. In Cincinnati, they were pressured but refused to play during a lightning storm at an outdoor concert. The final tour date was August 29 at San Francisco's Candlestick Park. The Beatles drove up from Los Angeles, where they had stayed a few days in a rented Beverly Hills mansion.

At the time, Brian Wilson and Van Dyke Parks were immersed in the *Smile* project at Armen Steiner's "Eight-Track Studios" on the southwest corner of Yucca and Argyle. Parks tells of two Beatles, which two he doesn't say, visiting the studio. "It's always seemed probable to me," says Parks, "that this was arranged through Derek Taylor." The visit was prompted by a desire to sample what rival Brian Wilson was working at, but also to check out the eight-track recording machine, a light-year jump from the four-track the Beatles had been using at Abbey Road. "It was the only one in town at first," and what they heard, says Parks, were the "*Smile* master tapes, unmixed." "Neither Brian nor I were there. It was a surreptitious act of British aggression," Parks adds, now able to joke about it with the distance of time. "We heard about it from an assistant engineer at the studio and didn't take it well." Parks maintains that "*Sgt. Pepper* was a direct result of what they heard from the *Smile* tapes."[22]

"We could . . . create any fantasy"

Eight-track technology was not available to the Beatles at Abbey Road for two more years, with the recording of "Hey Jude" in August 1968. And while the Beatles' brush with *Smile* may have nudged them toward the idea of a "concept" album, the more probable result was a rededication to the direction the Beatles, as evidenced by *Rubber Soul* (1965) and *Revolver* (1966), had already boldly taken, if anything reaffirming their established recording aesthetic.

Whatever the case, the important point here is that the Beatles elected to trade strife on the road for life within Abbey Road. "Everyone thought we toured for years," said Ringo Starr, "but we didn't . . . We'd finished touring in '66 to go into the studio where we could hear each other . . . and create any fantasy that came out of anybody's brain."[23] Abbey Road became a haven for studio creativity, shelter from the chaos of "Beatlemania." "Some of the best stuff we did," said George Harrison, "was when we stopped touring and spent a lot of time in the studio . . . I think *that* was some of the best music."[24]

And it was. The Beatles' coming of age as recording artists was stunningly realized on the two progressively innovative albums *Rubber Soul* and *Revolver*, which coincided with their last two years of touring.

The title *Rubber Soul*, suggests Mark Lewisohn – a play on the term "plastic soul" used by black musicians at the time as a dig at Mick Jagger's derivative performance style – had been particularly difficult. At that juncture, Lennon and McCartney had no ready-made songs, and the time frame for release was stressfully short. "John and Paul, really for the first time in their lives," said Mark Lewisohn, "had to force themselves to come up with more than a dozen new songs." Recording began in October of 1965 with a UK album release date set three months later in December.[25] Nonetheless, the songs – "Drive My Car," "Norwegian Wood (This Bird Has Flown)," "You Won't See Me," "Nowhere Man," "Think For Yourself," "The Word," "Michelle," "What Goes On," "Girl," "I'm Looking Through You," "In My Life," "Wait," "If I Needed Someone," and "Run For Your Life" – were appealing, several outstanding.

Rubber Soul also marked a giant step ahead in the Beatles' studio artistry, beyond anything they had done before. Though deadlines loomed, sessions were longer. Said Paul McCartney at the time: "D'you know the longest session we ever did in the studios? It was for the *Rubber Soul* album. It went on from five in the evening till half-past six the next day. It was tough but we had to do it. We do a lot of longer sessions now than we used to, because I suppose we're far more interested in our sound."[26]

As for the recording artistry of *Rubber Soul*, there were the now standard overdubs, vocal and instrumental overlays, and departures from "real time" performance. John Lennon's "In My Life," for example, went without a middle section until one was created and patched in four days later.[27] There were new sonic ingredients and textures, as in close-miked solo acoustic guitar, Lennon's sensuous intake of breath on "Girl," Hammond organ, electric piano, harmonium, and, on "Norwegian Wood," traditional Indian sitar, tabla, and, on a scrapped take, finger cymbals. Studio techs also constructed a fuzz box, "controlled distortion," said engineer Ken Townsend, effectively applied to McCartney's bass in "Think For Yourself." *Rubber Soul*, said George Martin, "was the first album to present a new, growing Beatles to the world. For the first time we began to think of albums as art on their own, as complete entities."[28]

With the next album, *Revolver*, the Beatles moved even further into rarified territory, what Lewisohn described as a "*quantum jump* into not merely tomorrow but sometime next week."[29] Paul McCartney predicted that "it would be the best we've ever done. Every track on the LP," he said, "has something special . . . George wanted to get his Indian stuff on the record, I wanted to do some electronic things. And John even had a song [Tomorrow Never Knows] in which his inspiration was *The Tibetan Book of the Dead*."[30] Indeed, there were the blithely spirited: "Good Day Sunshine," "And Your Bird Can Sing," "Taxman," "I Want to Tell You," "Got To Get You into My Life," "Doctor Robert"; the somberly introspective: "Eleanor Rigby," "I'm Only Sleeping," "For No One," "Here, There and Everywhere"; the exotic: "Love You To," "Tomorrow Never Knows"; and the fantastical "Yellow Submarine."

Studio technique abounded, and functioned as an instrument itself, wholly integrated into the art of the music. Tracks featured string sections, orchestral horns, backwards lead guitar, "Dopplerized" vocals and guitars fed through a revolving Leslie organ speaker, "jangle box" electronic guitar effects, Indian musicians only, no Beatles playing at all (on "Love You To"), and the illusion of spatial location achieved through stereo imaging, that is, the placement of sound in varying degrees and at different points along the virtual stereo arc.

Revolver also incorporated sonic abstractions created by saturating sections of tape with sound overlays to the point of non-recognition. The tapes were then "looped" to play back unendingly. Each Beatle had a home tape recorder rigged for such experimentation, which was how, for example, the strident seagull-like squawking on "Tomorrow Never Knows" was achieved. In actuality, the sounds were a tape loop of distorted guitar strums stacked in overlay and played backwards.[31]

The "Yellow Submarine" session was characterized by Geoff Emerick as having a "marijuana-influenced" Marx Brothers atmosphere. Microphones, both ambient and individual, were placed around the room to capture input from "raucous" guests, who included Marianne Faithful, Rolling Stones Mick Jagger and Brian Jones, and George Harrison's wife Patti. "The entire EMI collection of percussion instruments and sound effects boxes," says Emerick, "was strewn all over the studio, with people grabbing bells and whistles and gongs at random. To simulate the sound of a submarine submerging, John grabbed a straw and began blowing bubbles into a glass." At one point, Lennon tried the failed experiment of singing into a tiny condom-wrapped microphone submersed in a water-filled milk bottle. The finished "Yellow Submarine" incorporated echo-chambered ad-libs, clanking chains, sound effects from the EMI record library, and the *pièce de résistance*, a *non sequitur* Sousa-style marching brass band plunked down in place of an intended guitar solo. To avoid the delay of negotiating a royalty for the pre-existing brass band track, George Martin instructed Emerick to record it on tape, chop the tape into pieces, and then splice it back together randomly for insertion into the song. It was "unrecognizable enough," says Emerick, "that EMI was never sued by the original copyright holder of the song."[32]

"*Revolver*," said Mark Lewisohn, "is a pop masterpiece . . . the album which, by common consent, shows the Beatles at the peak of their creativity, welding very strong, economical but lyrically incisive song material with brave studio experimentation."[33] The *Revolver* sessions also yielded two tracks not on the album but released two months before as a single. "Paperback Writer" and "Rain" introduced technological artistic elements that became standard Beatles fare.

"Paperback Writer" was innovative in its use of echo through electronic delay as well as in boosting Paul McCartney's bass sound. "'Paperback Writer,'" says George Martin, "was the first time that we have had echo on a Beatles track." "You know," said George Harrison, "'Paperback writer, writer, writer . . .'"[34] McCartney, meanwhile, "had long been complaining that the bass on the Beatles records wasn't as loud or as full as on the American records he so loved," said Geoff Emerick. McCartney wanted the pumping front-and-center sound of southern soul and Motown. To get it, he switched from his usual Hofner bass to a Rickenbacker. Then, instead of the usual method of miking the bass amp speaker, Emerick rewired a large studio loudspeaker, in effect reversing its function from sound emitter to sound receptor, transforming the loudspeaker into a giant microphone. Placed in front of McCartney's amp speaker, it captured and boosted his bass sound like never before.[35]

"Rain," a composition with the feel of an Indian raga, marked the Beatles' first use of variable speed recording and backwards sound. A variable speed recording machine was rigged to slow down or speed up on command. The "unusual sonic texture" of "Rain" was accomplished, says Emerick, "by having the band play the backing track at a really fast tempo while I recorded them on a sped up tape machine. When we slowed the tape back down to normal speed, the music played back at the desired tempo, but with a radically different tonal quality."[36]

Backwards sound, on the other hand, came about by chance. "In those days," said John Lennon, "we used to take a seven-and-a-half-inch tape cut of a track home and, by the next night, arrange what we were going to put on top of it."

> I went home and I was out of my mind, stoned, because we had been working till five in the morning. I . . . stuck the tape on . . . backwards and played "Rain" and it came out backwards . . . and I was thinking, "Wow, this is fantastic." So, the next day I went in and said, "What about the end of the song? Why don't we have the whole of the song again, you know, backwards?" We didn't do that, but we just laid my voice track and guitar track over the last half-minute backwards. You can hear it at the end. It sounds as if I'm singing Indian.[37]

In effect, *Revolver* distanced the Beatles impossibly from what they could perform on stage. Commenting at the time, George Harrison said, "If we get to . . . doing some of the things on our LP on stage . . . I suppose we'll go on with a couple of tape recorders."[38] That, of course, never happened. *Revolver* was released in August 1966, a week before the start of the final American tour. Other than a straight performance of "Paperback Writer," their then hit single, the Beatles performed not one song from *Revolver*. They had fully transitioned to the irreproducible.

"There were no creative boundaries"

The enormous critical and commercial success of *Rubber Soul* and *Revolver* endowed the Beatles with confidence to continue experimenting, to trust their instincts completely. Even before a post-*Revolver* album was conceived, Lennon and McCartney were articulating the recording philosophy that would inform *Sgt. Pepper*. As to what a future album might contain, John Lennon told the *New Musical Express*: "Literally anything. Electronic music, jokes":

> One thing's for sure – the next LP is going to be very different. We wanted to have it so that there was no space between the tracks – just continuous . . . Paul and I are very keen on this electronic music. You make it clinking a couple of glasses together or with bleeps from the radio, then you loop the tape to repeat the noises at intervals. Some people build up whole symphonies from it.[39]

In the midst of the *Revolver* sessions, McCartney revealed himself to be on the same wavelength. "I've stopped regarding things as 'way-out' anymore."

I've stopped thinking that anything is weird or different. There'll always be people about, like that Andy Warhol in the States . . . who makes great long films of people just sleeping. Nothin' weird anymore. We sit down and write, or go into the recording studios, and we just see what comes up . . . I keep my eyes open and I see what's going on around me. Anyone can learn if they look. I mean, nowadays I'm interested in the electronic music of people like Berlo [Luciano Berio] and Stockhaussens [Karlheinz Stockhausen], who's great. It opens your eyes and ears . . . I, for one, am sick of doing sounds that people can claim to have heard before.[40]

These attitudes set the tone for what most critics regard as the pinnacle of the Beatles' work as recording artists, *Sgt. Pepper's Lonely Hearts Club Band*. Recording began in late November 1966, almost four months after the last American tour date and the release of *Revolver*. At this juncture, the Beatles had proven their mettle, earned the right to do as they wished, break rules, and move in any musical direction. And, indeed, *Sgt. Pepper* was that kind of album. Yes, it was a "concept" album – of sorts – the songs "bookended" between two versions of the title track, all in the context of a concert presented by the Beatles' arcane *alter ego*, Sgt. Pepper's Lonely Hearts Club Band. "It was going to be an album of another band that wasn't us," said Paul McCartney. "We were going to call ourselves something else, and just imagine all the time that it wasn't us playing this album" – a mind game that freed the Beatles to break from all prior conceptions of who they were.[41] "Because we knew that the Beatles wouldn't ever have to play the songs live," said Geoff Emerick, "there were no creative boundaries."[42]

On *Sgt. Pepper*, the Beatles indulged every creative impulse that came to mind. If there *was* a unifying theme, it was that stature afforded them the freedom to sound exactly as they pleased – which they did. The sonic assemblage included a battery of keyboards including piano, Hammond organ, harpsichord, harmonium, and Mellotron. There were also orchestral brass and horns, violins, harp, and cellos; chimes, calliope, glockenspiel; and sampled applause, laughter, crowds, and animal noise.

Lyrical content was slice-of-life, portraiture, evocative, mystical, psychedelic, and even at times, as George Harrison once put it, "fruity." Songs passed by as vignettes, the album an abstract canvas of a Beatles vision of the world, not only through literal meaning, but through the sweep of sound, sonic textures, breaks from songwriting convention, themes lifted from newspaper stories, a child's drawing, a Corn Flakes advertisement, a parking ticket from a meter maid, a circus poster, visions from an acid trip. *Sgt. Pepper* was a pastiche of swirling timbres, like a Van Gogh painting and perhaps no less a masterpiece, or at least a shot at trying to create something that would endure. There is studio artistry at every turn in *Sgt. Pepper*, far more, really, than can be covered in a book chapter, though some highlights can certainly be explored.

John Lennon's "Strawberry Fields Forever" was the starting point, though in the end not making it on to the album. George Martin explained that Beatles manager Brian Epstein, nervous that between projects "The Beatles were slipping . . . wanted another single out that was going to be a blockbuster."[43] "Strawberry Fields Forever" got the nod. As sonically radical as anything the Beatles had ever done, recording it set the tone and aesthetic that distinguished *Sgt. Pepper*.

At the heart of the track's sonic texture was the Mellotron, a wave-of-the-future keyboard programmed to imitate other instruments or sounds, a conceptual forerunner of the Moog synthesizer. As Geoff Emerick described it: "Each key triggered a tape loop of a real instrument playing the equivalent note . . . You could have flutes, strings, or choir at the touch of a button. Some of the keys were even set up to trigger complete prerecorded rhythm sections or musical phrases instead of single notes."[44] The flute-like pump organ that colors "Strawberry Fields Forever" was worked out and performed by Paul McCartney.

Another measure of studio wizardry was required to complete the track. The "Strawberry Fields Forever" we hear is actually stitched together from two versions in differing keys. John Lennon wrestled for weeks over which of the various takes he preferred, finally settling on the first half of one and the second half of another. "Even though the two takes John wanted . . . were recorded a week apart," said Geoff Emerick, " . . . the keys . . . were only a semi-tone apart – and the tempos were fairly close. After some trial-and-error experimentation, I discovered that by speeding up the playback of the first take and slowing down the playback of the second, I could get them to match in both pitch and tempo."[45]

Also contributing to the track's otherworldly quality were backwards cymbals, plucked piano, sitar, and an Indian instrument called the sword-mandel. "Strawberry Fields Forever" closed with an unusual reprieve, a sort of "freak-out" replay in reverse. The reprieve was notable, however, for another reason. Recording took place around the time of American Thanksgiving, and there was studio chatter about "turkey and all the trimmings." Lennon got a kick out of inserting *non sequitur* absurdities into the mix, and so in the reprieve's trail-off, he utters, "Cranberry sauce." Some of the more obsessed Beatles fans, convinced there were secret messages buried within the groove, Rorschached the phrase into "Paul is dead," the rumor lingering for years. Such was the public's fixation, denied seeing the Beatles in person, manifesting a Beatlemania of the imagination.[46] John Lennon capped it perfectly. "'Cranberry sauce.' That's all I said. Some people like ping-pong, other people like digging over graves. Some people will do anything rather than be here now."[47]

The *Sgt. Pepper* sessions continued on into December with two tracks, "When I'm Sixty Four," from the early days jamming at the Cavern, and "Penny Lane," a nostalgic reimagining of the old neighborhood in Liverpool: "Just reliving childhood," said John Lennon.[48] There was nothing remarkably unusual in the recording beyond McCartney's request for orchestral horns on "Penny Lane," most notably a high-pitched piccolo trumpet that caught his ear in a television broadcast of a Bach Brandenburg Concerto. Also at McCartney's insistence, in spite of an incredulous George Martin, "When I'm Sixty Four" was speeded up by at least a half-pitch to give it a more "youthful" sound.[49]

"When I'm Sixty Four" found a place on the finished LP, while "Penny Lane," an ideal thematic foil to "Strawberry Fields Forever," did not, destined instead to be paired with that track as Brain Epstein's desired single. The year had come to a close, and with a solid start, said George Martin, "we all went home for Christmas."[50] Recording resumed in mid-January after a holiday break. Meantime, the "Strawberry Fields Forever"/"Penny Lane" single, though disappointingly never reaching number one, broke into the US Top Ten in March three months prior to the release of *Sgt. Pepper*.

All told, *Sgt. Pepper*, at a cost of £50,000 (equivalent in 1967 to about $138,000), took an unprecedented (for the Beatles) six months to complete.[51] "I must confess,' said George Martin, "as it was getting longer and longer into the album, and more and more avant-garde, I was beginning to wonder whether we were being . . . over the top, and . . . maybe pretentious. There was a slight niggle of worry. I thought, 'Is the public ready for this yet?'" Said Geoff Emerick, "We were getting a bit overwhelmed, I mean, it was just that we couldn't see it ever coming to an end."[52] But of course it did, and when all was said and done, *Sgt. Pepper*, recording completed in April 1967, released in the UK on June 1 and in the US on June 2, was a showcase of studio artistry and innovation, shaking up how rock and roll would from then on be recorded. "When the Beatles unleashed *Sgt. Pepper's Lonely Hearts Club Band*," read the editorial kickoff to *Mojo* magazine's 2007 article celebrating the fortieth anniversary of the album's release, "they blew the finest minds of their generation and changed all music forever."[53]

"We don't want it to sound like a guitar"

Electronic innovation was intrinsic to *Sgt. Pepper's* aesthetic. Surprisingly, given the complexity of the production, four-track was still the core means of recording. Music or sound was recorded across each of four tracks, the levels mixed and then reduced down to a single master track, the process repeated until all four tracks were full and deemed complete. The trouble with repeated dubbing down, however, was a build-up of distracting resid- ual noise. To rectify that, *Sgt. Pepper* was recorded using recently developed Dolby Noise Reduction. Artistically, the benefit was an enabling of more complex overlay along with a new clarity in the recorded sound. The Beatles also made liberal use of electronic effects such as "phasing" and "flanging." Related to echo, these effects arose out of the subtle variants in tempo and pitch between slightly out-of-synch playbacks of the same track, achiev- ing what Geoff Emerick called "a sweeping *swoosh*."[54] The overall texture of "Being for the Benefit of Mr. Kite!" relies on phasing, whereas George Harrison's guitar solo is flanged on "Fixing a Hole." ADT, or "Artificial Double Tracking" was another important electronic innovation. Devel- oped by engineer Ken Townsend, ADT, by automatically doubling vocals or instrumentals, eliminated the tedious process of performing the same part twice.[55] Finally, there was the "direct lining" of McCartney's bass, plugging the instrument directly into the recording console as opposed to placing a microphone in front of his bass amp speaker. "I think direct injection," said Ken Townsend, "was probably used on Beatles sessions for the first time anywhere in the world."[56]

The net effect of electronic dabbling was that it made the conventional sound unconventional. Nothing, in fact, was real. Lead vocals, certainly recognizable as individual Beatles, came at us ethereally, or from a distance, or somehow thicker, or submersed in something we couldn't quite put a finger on. Background voices were sped up or slowed down, reverberated, equalized, electronically altered one way or another to impart a preter- natural quality. Engineer Richard Lush recalls Lennon saying: "I want to sound different today, nothing like I sounded yesterday."[57] "John and Paul's attitude," says Geoff Emerick, " . . . was 'we're going to play guitar, but we don't want it to sound like a guitar; we're going to play piano, but we don't want it to sound like piano.'"[58]

If this all has a psychedelic ring to it, that is entirely accurate. Listen to the shifting textures of John Lennon's voice on "Lucy in the Sky with Diamonds," the tinkling otherworldly keyboard, the flanged guitar running parallel to the lead vocal. "Lucy" used variable speed more than any other track on the album. Lyrics also reinforced the euphoric feel. Lennon says the images were drawn from Lewis Carroll's *Alice in Wonderland*. "It was Alice in the boat."

> She is buying an egg and it turns into Humpty Dumpty. The woman serving
> in the shop turns into a sheep and the next minute they are rowing in a
> rowing boat somewhere and I was visualizing that. There was also the image
> of the female who would someday come save me . . . a "girl with
> kaleidoscope eyes" who would come out of the sky.[59]

Lennon always insisted that any connection between "Lucy in the Sky with Diamonds" and LSD was purely coincidental. "My son Julian came in one day with a picture he painted about a school friend of his named Lucy. He had sketched in some stars in the sky and called it 'Lucy in the Sky with Diamonds.' Simple."[60] And yet not so simple. Even taking Lennon at his word, the overall "dayglow" aesthetic of *Sgt. Pepper* without doubt reflected a generation's chemically inspired perceptual realignment. Nonetheless, the artistic strategy was entirely sober and deliberate, the goal being to create a surreal vision through sound. The resulting work could not be performed on stage, but existed only in the bubble of the studio; could not be experienced "live" by a mass audience, but only through turntable spin and a trip through an electronic speaker.

The scenes in *Sgt. Pepper* were set with inserted cheers, applause, rooster crows, stampeding menagerie – or through swirling sound, as on "Being for the Benefit of Mr. Kite!," lyrics lifted literally from a poster for "Pablo Fanque's Circus Royal." "John had said he wanted to 'smell the sawdust on the floor,' wanted to taste the atmosphere of the circus," said George Martin. "I said to him, 'What we need is a calliope . . . steam whistles played by a keyboard."[61] There were none to be found, so Martin and his team created a fairground in the studio.

> I knew we needed a backwash, a general mush of sound, like if you go to a fairground, shut your eyes and listen: rifle shots, hurdy-gurdy noises, people shouting and – way in the distance, just a tremendous chaotic sound. So I got hold of old calliope tapes, playing "Stars and Stripes Forever" and other Sousa marches, chopped the tapes up into small sections and had Geoff Emerick throw them up in the air, re-assembling them at random.[62]

Apparently, this was a frequent technique on *Sgt. Pepper*. The album's finale – a sonic orgasm, a bit of nonsense, and a treat for the dogs – was, up to that point in time, unprecedented in rock history. The closing track was "A Day in the Life," a juxtaposing of John Lennon's glib newspaper cutout lines – "a lucky man who made the grade," "4,000 holes in Blackburn, Lancashire," "the English army had just won the war," "I'd love to turn you on" – and Paul McCartney's out-of-breath working man who "had a smoke" and "went into a dream." It was McCartney's idea to end with an orchestral build-up. Lennon's directive was: "I want it to be like a musical orgasm."[63] Forty classical musicians were assembled, their sound aggrandized by recording the orchestra four times, once on each of the four tracks, with an ultimate mix-down to a single master. Geoff Emerick oversaw the recording, carefully adjusting the volume controls "to get the crescendo of the orchestra just right."

George Martin created a twenty-four-bar score with measured instruc-
tions. "At the very beginning," says Martin, "I put into the musical score the
lowest note each instrument could play, ending with an E-major chord."

> And at the beginning of each of the 24 bars I put a note showing roughly
> where they should be at that point. Then I had to instruct them. "We're
> going to start very very quietly and end up very very loud. We're to start very
> low in pitch and end up very high. You've got to make your own way up
> there, as slide-y as possible so that the clarinets slurp, trombones gliss,
> violins slide without fingering any notes. And whatever you do, don't listen
> to the fellow next to you because I don't want you to be doing the same
> thing." Of course they all looked at me as though I was mad.[64]

"The orchestra just couldn't understand what George was talking about,"
says Geoff Emerick, "or why they were being paid to go from one note to
another in 24 bars. It didn't make any sense to them because they were all
classically trained."[65] Nonetheless, the massive rumbling crescendo came
off as planned, followed immediately by a "Ta-Da-a-a-a!" in the form of a
crashing E-major piano chord, John, Paul, Ringo, and Mal Evans at three
pianos all hitting the keys at the same moment, loud pedals full open, the
final chord lingering for forty seconds. Still, Sgt. Pepper was not ended.

"They were all thrilled with what they heard," said Geoff Emerick,
"but John and Paul felt that they wanted something additional to end the
album . . . John had read somewhere that dogs could hear higher frequencies
than humans could, and requested that a supersonic tone be placed at the
end to give them something to listen to." A 15-kilocycle tone was patched
in, yet still the Beatles wanted more. John Lennon said: "[Let's] put on some
gobbledygook, then bifurcate it, splange it, and loop it." "He always loved the
sound of nonsense words," says Emerick. "To George Martin's amusement,
the four Beatles endorsed the idea wholeheartedly and raced down to the
studio while Richard hurriedly put up a couple of microphones."

> They looned about for five minutes or so, saying whatever came to mind as I
> recorded them on a two-track machine. When I played the tape back for
> them, John identified a few seconds that he particularly liked – it consisted
> primarily of Paul repeating the words "Never needed any other way" for no
> particular reason while the others chattered away in the background – which
> I duly made into a loop, then flew into the ending. And with that, *Sgt.
> Pepper's Lonely Hearts Club Band* was done.[66]

A high-water mark in recording artistry, *Sgt. Pepper* was released in both
mono and stereo versions, the two mixes markedly different. The Beatles
took part in and approved the mono mix, while the stereo mix was created by
Emerick and his team without their input. Hardcore fans maintain that the
mono is *Sgt. Pepper* as the Beatles intended. Following the album's release,

though, the critical quibbling was not about the preferred mix, but rather about the Beatles themselves. A critic for the British *Daily Mail* wrote: "It's now around four years since the Beatles happened, and . . . the Beatles have changed completely . . . They have isolated themselves, not only personally, but also musically. They have become contemplative, secretive, exclusive and excluded."[67]

Most fans, and especially fellow musicians, however, found the album eye-opening, exciting, and the wave of the future. The Beatles had graduated from wanting to hold hands to blowing out minds. At the *Sgt. Pepper* release party, George Harrison said: "People are very, very aware of what's going on around them nowadays. They think for themselves and I don't think we can ever be accused of under-estimating the intelligence of our fans." Added John Lennon: "The people who have bought our records in the past must realize that we couldn't go on making the same type forever. We must change and I believe those people know this."[68]

"The break-up of the Beatles can be heard"

The Beatles carried forward the studio artistry of *Sgt. Pepper* to the projects that marked the last years of their existence as a unified group. No question, the Beatles and their creative team were the right people at the right place and time, like Brian Wilson and the Beach Boys, perfectly catching the wave of advancing recording technology. When all was said and done, though, the Beatles emerged with a broader, more enduring body of work, a goodly portion of that post-*Sgt. Pepper*.

Immediately following *Sgt. Pepper* was *Magical Mystery Tour* (1967), the album pieced together by Capitol for the US market from the soundtrack of a BBC-filmed television production and collected singles including "Strawberry Fields Forever" and "Penny Lane." Pictured on the cover were the Beatles in the funny fuzzy animal costumes they wore for the TV show. "I Am the Walrus" was the TV tie-in track, the lyrics nonsensical with sonic exotica that included a children's choir and snippets of radio programs recorded directly into the sound console. "One track," said John Lennon, "was live BBC Radio – Shakespeare or something – I just fed in whatever lines came in."[69] The most memorable song on the album was "All You Need is Love," composed especially for a satellite broadcast viewed worldwide by more than 200 million on June 25, 1967. The Beatles recorded a rhythm track earlier that day, and, with invited friends and a small orchestra, played and sang along to it during the live broadcast. With post-production adjustments, the resulting single was an international hit by mid-July.

The first album release on the Beatles' own Apple label came in November 1968 with the double LP titled *The Beatles*, called by fans the White Album because of its plain white covers. The album's thirty tracks, most written during the Beatles' stay in India with the Maharishi Mahesh Yogi, ranged from brilliant to throwaway to (in the view of some critics) nearly incomprehensible. More than on any previous album, the lyrics and sonic characteristics revealed the Beatles not so much as a unified group but as distinct entities. Discerning listeners sensed fractures in the façade. "The break-up of the Beatles can be heard on the double-album," said John Lennon, "... on which, I thought that every track sounded as if it came from an individual Beatle."[70]

John Lennon offered poignancy in "Julia," cynical comment in "Happiness is a Warm Gun" and "Revolution," and a rollicking Chuck Berry-style send-up of the Beach Boys in "Back in the USSR." Paul McCartney provided cartoon-ish character sketches in "The Continuing Story of Bungalow Bill" and "Rocky Raccoon," acoustic guitar gems in "Mother Nature's Son" and "Blackbird," and screaming Little Richard intensity in "Helter Skelter," a song unfortunately linked to Charles Manson, who claimed it as inspiration for the brutal 1969 Tate/LaBianca murders.

The White Album also signals the emergence of George Harrison as an "A" songwriter, with four tracks including the ethereal "Long, Long, Long" and, with Eric Clapton on lead guitar, "While My Guitar Gently Weeps," one of the all-time Beatles favorites. Ringo Starr delivered on his own "Don't Pass Me By," and as the album's closing lullaby came John Lennon's tongue-in-cheek but nonetheless charming "Good Night." It should be noted that Ringo Starr, frustrated by growing tensions between band members, left the group in the midst of recording. "We're doing this album," Starr said in 1976, "and I'm getting weird – saying to me-self, 'I've gotta leave this band. It's not working,' ... and I went away for two weeks. [Laughs] ... And then I got a telegram from John saying, 'Great drums' on the tracks we'd done. And I came back and it was great, 'cuz George had set up all these flowers all over the studio saying welcome home."[71]

Two of the tracks on the double White Album are pure studio indulgence, one the shortest, the other the longest. Paul McCartney's "Why Don't We Do It in the Road" clocked in at one minute and forty-two seconds, a foretaste of his solo career with McCartney singing and playing all the instruments, no studio tricks beyond that. John Lennon's "Revolution 9," on the other hand, was total artifice, an abstruse eight-minute-plus pastiche of electronica. "Altogether, 154 entries from at least 45 sources."[72] "Revolution 9" was totally about studio as instrument, the track a collage of tape loops and effects: a "faceless voice" uttering "Number Nine, Number Nine"; George Martin saying: "Geoff, put the red light on"; sampled orchestral dubs from

"A Day in the Life"; backwards-played bits and pieces of choir, symphony, opera, and Lennon on Mellotron. Paul McCartney did not contribute, but George Harrison did, he and Lennon lying on the floor "saying strange things like 'the Watusi' and 'the Twist'" and "reading out bizarre lines of prose" as Yoko Ono hummed "at a very high pitch."[73]

"Revolution 9" drew the fire of critics upon the album's release. The *New Musical Express* called the track "a pretentious piece of old codswallop which is nothing more than a long, long collection of noises and sounds seemingly dedicated towards the expanding sale of Aspros [a headache remedy]."[74] John Lennon's cool rebuttal was simply that "I imposed 'Revolution 9' on *The Beatles* for all the people who just want to hear the beat all the time."[75]

"I hope we passed the audition"

In the final two years before the last work on a Beatles track at Abbey Road on April 2, 1970, four LPs would be released. An emotionally difficult time for the Beatles, the period was marked by increasing tensions exacerbated by Yoko Ono's interjection into the creative process as well as by business issues that surfaced in the wake of manager Brian Epstein's death in 1967. None of it was helped by the fact that the Beatles had now gone three years without the personal affirmation that comes only from direct contact with people through live performance. All of these troubling elements were reflected in the direction and tone of the Beatles' remaining studio work.

Yellow Submarine came out in January 1969, a recasting of that title track as plot inspiration for a film depicting the Beatles as animated characters and ending with actual performance footage. The film was welcomed by fans hungry for any sort of visual experience of the Beatles, affirmation that they were still working as a team. The soundtrack LP offered one side of appealing B tracks supplemented with "All You Need is Love," and a flipside of instrumentals recorded for the film by George Martin and orchestra.

Three final albums would come while the Beatles were still intact: *Abbey Road* (September 1969), their last collaboration in that studio; *Hey Jude* (February 1970), a collection of UK singles packaged for US release; and *Get Back*, a derailed effort to simplify, ultimately retitled and released as *Let It Be* (May 1970).

Abbey Road, recorded in July and August of 1969 and regarded by many, including Ringo Starr, as the Beatles' best, was the first to be released.[76] The title was a tip of the hat to the studio that nurtured their evolution as recording artists. This was the album that showed the Beatles crossing Abbey Road, Paul McCartney barefoot, adding fuel to the absurdly persistent rumor that he was dead. The greater irony of *Abbey Road*, however, is that it was released before *Hey Jude* and *Let It Be*, when in fact most of its tracks were recorded after the tracks on those albums. Given that and the intention here to focus on recording artistry, these albums are best reckoned with in order of recording rather than of release.

Hey Jude was essentially another of Capitol's cobbling together for the US market of UK singles. The salient track was, of course, "Hey Jude." Otherwise, the album was a collection of unusually disparate singles. "Can't Buy Me Love" and "I Should Have Known Better" dated from 1964, "Paperback Writer" and "Rain" from 1966.

"Lady Madonna" was a more recent standout, a 1968 hit single and the last Beatles issue on either Parlophone or Capitol. The track was a straightforward Paul McCartney rock and roll performance in the mold of the 1956 British hit "Bad Penny Blues." Beyond the four-man saxophone section, fuzzed guitar, and doubled piano, the only other studio artifice was what sounded like muted trumpets. "In actual fact," said Ringo Starr, "it's just John and Paul sort of humming through their [cupped] hands into the mike . . . It sounded great, so we decided to use it."[77]

The title track, "Hey Jude," also recorded in 1968, was the Beatles' first use of eight-track technology. With "Revolution" as the flip, "Hey Jude" was the debut single on Apple. Originally titled "Hey Jules," the song was written by Paul McCartney for John Lennon's son Julian, grappling at the time with his parents' divorce. McCartney recorded the base track at the piano singing as he played. Later, a forty-piece orchestra was dubbed in. "We also got them singing on the end," said George Martin, and though "I don't think they liked doing it very much," the song "became one of the biggest single sellers that we ever had."[78]

Abbey Road at the time did not yet have eight-track capability. "Hey Jude" was rehearsed there, but recorded and mixed at Trident Studios, which did have eight-track. In playback at Abbey Road, however, the track sounded flawed. "Obviously," recounted Geoff Emerick, "something at Trident had been misaligned and the only hope of salvaging the mix was to whack on massive amounts of treble equalization . . . Eventually we got it to sound pretty good, although the track still didn't have the kind of in-your-face presence that characterizes most Beatles recordings done at Abbey Road."[79]

The most compelling feature of "Hey Jude" as a recording is its unconventional arrangement, a daring seven-minutes-plus long, nearly half of it a fade-out that never fades, as much a "hook" as the song's primary verses. "It certainly was the longest single we had made at the time," said George Martin.[80] Or, for that matter, *anyone* had made. "We liked the end," said Paul McCartney. "We liked it going on . . . The DJs can always fade it down if they want to. If you get fed up with it, you can always turn it over."[81]

Following the release of the "Hey Jude"/"Revolution" single, John, Paul, George, and Ringo moved on to an album conceived as the Beatles pared down, a full-circle return to rock and roll basics – voices, drums, bass, rhythm and lead guitar. No overdubs, technicalities, or backwards anything. The studio proceedings were to be filmed for television broadcast, with the working title, *Get Back*. Recording began on January 2, 1969 and culminated on January 30 with the news-making concert staged on the rooftop of the Beatles' Savile Row offices, John Lennon famously remarking at the close, "I hope we passed the audition."[82]

Sidestepping the minutia of the Beatles unraveling during this period, suffice it to say that tracks for the new stripped-down album were recorded in the group's own studios at Apple headquarters and in live performance during the rooftop concert. As events transpired, though, *Get Back*, the LP, never made it to record stores. The Beatles' new adviser, Allen Klein, with profit in mind, wanted a 35-mm cinematic film in place of the TV broadcast as well as studio rather than live rooftop recordings.[83] There were additional commercial considerations as well, but the main thrust was that the album was delayed. Only two tracks, "Get Back" and "Don't Let Me Down," were released to the public in the form of a single in April 1969.

The evolution of "Get Back," the song, was lengthy, numerous recordings made over a few months' time, some live, others in studio. The finished version was ultimately created by Paul McCartney and producer/engineer Glyn Johns from the eleventh of fourteen studio takes and a seamlessly tacked on coda from the third live rooftop performance.[84] Glyn Johns would put together a finished *Get Back* album true to the original stripped-down intentions of the Beatles, but his efforts were rejected. The album eventually saw light a year later, but in modified form and with a new producer. More on that in a moment, but first, *Abbey Road*, a homecoming of sorts and a white flag in the midst of the battle that *Get Back* had turned out to be.

Abbey Road was a return to the "home" studio, a last opportunity, as it turned out, to work in house with George Martin, Geoff Emerick, and some from the old team. There were, however, changes at Abbey Road. One, noted Emerick, was the switch from outmoded glowing tube electronics to transistorized components. The new mixing console, for instance, lacked the warmth of the old tube model in how it captured the Beatles' sound. George Harrison was troubled "that there was less body in the guitar sound," and Ringo Starr "was playing as hard as ever, but you didn't hear the same impact."[85]

Another change this time around was more human than technical. John Lennon and Yoko Ono had been in an automobile accident as the sessions were starting. The others worked for a time without Lennon, but he seemed discouragingly disengaged when he at last arrived. To compound matters,

Lennon had a bed placed in the studio for the recuperating Yoko Ono, a microphone positioned overhead so her artistic suggestions could be heard. "I'd spent nearly seven years of my life in recording studios," said Emerick, "and I thought I'd seen it all . . . but this took the cake."[86]

With all the distractions, tensions, and technicalities, *Abbey Road* still emerged as rich with memorable tracks, two of them George Harrison's best work with the Beatles. The first, a standalone from side one, is "Something," a gorgeous love song of unusual texture and structure. Harrison performed his own vocals, drums, and piano on the initial demo. Three months and several discarded versions later in May, 1969, the core master take was recorded with Paul and Ringo on bass and drums respectively, John Lennon on guitar, George Harrison on guitar played through a rotating Leslie organ speaker, and American R&B artist Billy Preston on piano. Aside from his musicianship, Harrison invited Preston because his presence tended to dampen the other Beatles' bickering. With strings dubbed into the final mix, the track was deemed complete in August.

The most compelling aspect of *Abbey Road* was the second-side roller-coaster ride, aptly described by author Ken Womack as "Lennon and McCartney's ultimate vehicle for their nostalgic journey to a comparatively genial, untarnished past."[87] Ten songs – some just beyond a minute – and one an afterthought, pass by in a cyclorama of sound, tempo, and mood. Listeners come away with a sense that they have somehow experienced the whole dynamic sweep of the Beatles' career in twenty-one brief minutes. The effect derived from pure studio artistry, not merely by how songs were recorded, but from careful sequencing and interfacing that never provided the listener with a moment to break away from the action. In this regard, *Abbey Road* is a crowning studio achievement.

The side soars from the start with the second of George Harrison's masterpieces, "Here Comes the Sun," an optimistic message of clearing sky and light, a clever construction of major chords and brightly picked acoustic guitar. With McCartney on bass and Starr on drums, Harrison otherwise carries the show, performing vocals, guitars, harmonium, and Moog synthesizer, the recently invented keyboard instrument that used computers to simulate instrumental sounds and beyond. The final sonic texture of the song was enriched by an overdubbed seventeen-piece orchestra.[88]

Next came John Lennon's sultry "Because," an impressionistic piece inspired by the chords of Beethoven's "Moonlight Sonata" sequenced in reverse. John, Paul, and George sing in close harmony, George Martin on harpsichord, and George Harrison programming and performing on Moog synthesizer.[89]

Here began the stepping-off point, Paul McCartney's "You Never Give Me Your Money," a linkage of four short and distinct themes, serving as a platform that segues into John Lennon's regal "Sun King," the recording replete with Romance languages, chirping crickets, and ethereal harmony. The pace builds in momentum, four songs of just over a minute to less than two in unbroken succession before resolving into "Carry That Weight," a rousing orchestral piece, the lyrics seeming to speak at once of both the Beatles' burden of staying together and the listeners' need to brace up for a time when the Beatles would be no more. There is a brief reprise of "You Never Give Me Your Money" before a return to the main theme and then a skillful break from tempo as the track transitions into the semi-finale, "The End."

That two-minute four-second track encapsulates all that made the Beatles great. Screaming vocals, a hard-driving beat, the first ever Ringo Starr drum solo, a sampling of searing lead guitar solos from John, Paul, and George, and, in the end, the mellow side, Paul McCartney's lead vocal buoyed by John Lennon's multi-tracked backup harmony, the words shining through most of all. "And in the end, the love you take is equal to the love you make." A somber farewell until ameliorated by Paul McCartney's twenty-three-second afterthought, "Her Majesty," as if the Beatles had left the stage and, when the show seemed irretrievably over, his smiling face peaked out briefly from behind a side curtain – and then he's gone. The Beatles all attended the August 20, 1969 session during which the final *Abbey Road* mix and running order sequence were fixed. "It was the last time," writes Mark Lewisohn, "that they were together inside the recording studio where they had changed the face of popular music."[90] And, I would add, how it was recorded.

Yes, it's true, there was one more album to follow, the retooled *Get Back*, now titled *Let It Be.* The Beatles, long gone from the project, brought in legendary producer Phil Spector to finish the album. Spector, though admired, was difficult to work with in the studio as he heavy-handedly imposed his own vision on the Beatles' work, the concept of "stripped-down" lost in the mix. Spector, critics would say, overzealously added orchestral and choir overdubs as well as his trademark reverb. Geoff Emerick described Spector barking commands at veteran Abbey Road engineers and screaming at musicians: "You'll do what I tell you to do, and you'll like it!" As musicians rehearsed "The Long and Winding Road," Emerick recalls that Spector "turned around and said . . . loudly enough for us all to hear, 'I hope Paul likes this, because I've changed the chords . . . ' Spector was not just remixing the Beatles' music, he was actually *altering* it."[91]

Let It Be and the theatrical film that coincided with its release in May 1970 were well enough received by both critics and the public, a number of songs being first-tier Beatles fare. "Two of Us," a personal favorite, conjured up the good karma that had been the hallmark of the Lennon-McCartney partnership. Three of the album's best songs shine out from the shadow cast by Phil Spector's imposing "Wall of Sound." John Lennon's "All Across the Universe," originally a simple recording, was now overdubbed with a thirty-five-piece orchestra and fourteen-voice choir. "Let It Be," Paul McCartney's piano-accompanied gospel-tinged hymn, was now supplemented with brass and cellos. "The Long and Winding Road" was framed unflatteringly by orchestral overdubs and a choir that sounded disengaged from the emotion in McCartney's performance. This is not to diminish Phil Spector, because his groundbreaking work as a producer was perfectly suited to his own projects. He simply wasn't the right fit for the Beatles at that point in time. If anything, putting the artistic studio decisions in the hands of an outsider, even one of Phil Spector's stature, served only to reveal how brilliant George Martin, the Beatles, and their in-house creative team were in developing the body of studio work that transformed how pop music was recorded.

The Beatles had made a decision to cut themselves off from the sustenance of live performance in exchange for the freedom that came with isolation in the studio. By doing so, they positioned themselves to revolutionize the art of recording, and that is what they did, for evermore defining what it truly meant to be a recording artist. Perhaps it is too obvious or trite to say, but in the end, all the Beatles really did need was love. They told us so. And since they could no longer find it among themselves, they went their separate ways to find it, each on his own.

PART TWO

Works

3 Rock and roll music

HOWARD KRAMER

George Martin, in many ways, birthed the Beatles as we know them. We know them through their records, not their performances. They arrived on his step as a nightclub-hardened beat group with virtually no studio experience and, under his tutelage, they became the musical group that personified the studio as an instrument. The Beatles' first three long-playing records, *Please Please Me*, *With the Beatles*, and *A Hard Day's Night*, were a short ramp leading up to a colossal cultural shift. Astonishingly, they were all recorded and released in a twenty-two-month period. To examine those cornerstone recordings, we must first see how they arrived there.

The first experience any of the Beatles had with recording was in 1958, when the Quarrymen, with John Lennon, Paul McCartney, George Harrison, Colin Hanton, and Duff Lowe, cut a shellac disc of two songs at a home studio in Liverpool. One was Buddy Holly and the Crickets' "That'll Be the Day," a highly appropriate choice considering Holly's pervasive influence on the band. The other was "In Spite of All the Danger," a McCartney-Harrison composition characterized by McCartney as "very influenced by Elvis."[1] To the participants, the event had a magical feel, as they now could return to their homes and play an actual performance of their own. Still, a professional studio seemed an unattainable dream, and they were barely beyond being just a scruffy little skiffle group.

The evolution of the Quarrymen into the Beatles was a path forged on the streets and in the rank nightclubs of Hamburg, Germany. As Lennon said, "I grew up in Hamburg, not Liverpool." During the Beatles' second stay in Hamburg, they were recruited by independent producer Bert Kaempfert, who would have a substantial career of his own, to back fellow English performer Tony Sheridan. The Beatles and Sheridan were appearing together at the Top Ten Club. The results were musically unspectacular. Sheridan's vocal performance is a pale amalgam of Elvis Presley, Jack Scott, and Gene Vincent. The Beatles' instrumental backing shows competence, but little more. During the sessions, the Beatles cut a few songs not featuring Sheridan, the well-worn chestnut "Ain't She Sweet," sung by Lennon, and another original instrumental, "Cry for a Shadow." When the record of "My Bonnie" was released, Sheridan got top billing, and the Beatles were renamed the Beat Brothers. It was very anticlimactic for the Beatles.

The Kaempfert sessions, however, resulted in a profound event in the Beatles' career. Legend has it that on October 28, 1961, a young man named Raymond Jones came into NEMS Music Store in Liverpool and asked its proprietor, Brian Epstein, if they had "My Bonnie" by the Beatles in stock. Within two weeks, Epstein witnessed the Beatles for the first time, and was managing them by December. His goal was to procure a recording contract. As the proprietor of a successful record shop, and possessed of a well-groomed manner, Epstein could open doors for his new clients. In 1961, there were, essentially, four major record companies in England: EMI, Pye, Philips, and Decca. Epstein arranged for the Beatles to audition for Decca Records in London on January 1, 1962.

The Beatles' session at Decca began at 11:00 a.m. There is little evidence to suggest the session lasted much longer than the combined duration of the fifteen songs. John Lennon recalled: "We virtually recorded our Cavern show, with a few omissions."[2] As in their live performances, and typical of many of the groups on their circuit, the Beatles covered a wide spectrum of material: R&B ("Money [That's What I Want]," "Three Cool Cats"), standards ("Bésame Mucho," "The Sheik of Araby") show tunes ("Till There Was You") and rock and roll ("Memphis," "Crying, Waiting, Hoping"). Three Lennon-McCartney compositions ("Hello Little Girl," "Love of the Loved," "Like Dreamers Do") were also performed. The resulting recording is not much more than a mere transcription of the event. Decca certainly had no incentive to make it more than that. Essentially, the Beatles set up their gear and the engineer rolled tape. There were no overdubs and the only effect used is a uniform echo. You can hear a nervous tightening in all of their voices. The playing is steady and tight, but clipped. Epstein had high hopes that the originals would be recognized as a sign of the Beatles' exceptional talent. The previous two years of near constant performing made the foursome, with Pete Best still on drums, a respectable unit, but Decca was unimpressed. They passed on the group.

Despite this disappointment, Epstein was allowed by Decca to use the tape to shop the band. Pye soon declined to sign the Beatles, too. Epstein's confidence, as well as the band's, was wavering. Epstein continued to beat a path between Liverpool and London. A series of fortunate events placed Epstein in a meeting with Parlophone Records' label head, George Martin.

The Beatles passed the audition with George Martin and Parlophone. That session, June 1962, yielded only confirmation that Martin was willing to take a shot at the group. Later, he recalled saying: "I've got nothing to lose."[3] I could go on and on with the minutiae of historical details, but the key thing here is the Beatles got the break they desperately needed. George Martin certainly found the band that changed the fortunes of his label (and all of Great Britain, for that matter). But what he didn't yet know was that he was about to begin the most seamless and symbiotic artist–producer relationship in the history of recorded music.

At the time, an artist's success was based entirely on the sale of singles. Martin's first choice for a single was "How Do You Do It," a song by Mitch Murray and Barry Mason that had been on Martin's desk for several months. In the June audition, the Beatles recorded "Love Me Do." After they signed, Martin pitched the group "How Do You Do It" and they dutifully learned and recorded the song in their first fully fledged Abbey Road session on September 4, 1962. They also cut "Love Me Do," this time with Ringo Starr on drums, replacing Pete Best, who had been fired three weeks earlier. Martin and his lieutenant, Ron Richards, heard potential in "Love Me Do," but were not convinced. The following week, the Beatles, with session drummer Andy White behind the kit and Starr on tambourine, cut a usable master. Martin conceded to the Beatles, and their own composition became their debut single. "Love Me Do"/"P.S. I Love You" was released on October 5.

It's a misconception that the Beatles' first release wasn't much of a hit. The peak of "Love Me Do" at number seventeen was a solid foothold for the band. It had an eighteen-week chart run that was mirrored by their follow-up single, "Please Please Me." Cut while "Love Me Do" was climbing the charts, "Please Please Me," with its upbeat R&B tempo and sweet harmonica hook, started life as a mid-tempo song in the Roy Orbison mold. George Martin's advice to bring up the tempo yielded the group's first chart-topper.

In between the sessions with Martin, the Beatles were working virtually every day, with two gigs in one day a common event. The day before the September 4 session, they played a lunchtime set at their hometown club, the Cavern, and an evening show in Widnes, Lancashire. The day after the session, they were back at the Cavern. This pace continued unabated for the next four years. As the Beatles' successes mounted, the level of pressure related to their performances, writing, and recording grew exponentially.

"Please Please Me" shone a light on a new type of pop group in Britain. The record business was still running on a decades-old business model predicated on a hierarchy of song, publisher, record company, and performer. Songwriters wrote the material on contract to publishers. The publishers then pushed the song to record companies and producers who could match the song with a performer. The publisher was the main money-generator and beneficiary through the licensing and royalty income. A song could, and often did, have several competing versions vying for the public's attention. The one that hit would also be a boon to the particular label that released it. As for the artists, they were lucky to be paid at all. Prior to the Beatles, pop/rock music in the UK adhered to a tight formula; bands had a named lead singer with a backing band (Cliff Richard and the Shadows,

Shane Fenton and the Fentones) that often performed steps in unison, or a lead singer with a dynamic stage name (Billy Fury, Marty Wilde, Adam Faith). Impresario Larry Parnes, who had passed on the Beatles early in their career, managed many of the latter. Both of these types of performers were just another extension of the old model, beholden to publishers and producers for material. The Beatles were self-contained in the truest sense. They wrote and performed their own music and, by design, did not stick one sole member into the limelight.

With two hit singles to their credit, the Beatles now had to create an album. George Martin said: "I asked them what they had that we could record quickly, and the answer was their stage act."[4] It was finely honed and well rehearsed. A session was scheduled for Monday, February 11, 1963. As Mark Lewisohn, in his essential book *The Complete Beatles Recording Sessions*, wrote of this day: "There can scarcely have been 585 more productive minutes in the history of recorded music."[5] It is a bold yet undeniable statement. Between 10:00 a.m. and 10:45 p.m., the Beatles cut thirteen songs, twelve of which, along with "Please Please Me" and its B side "Ask Me Why," became their entire first long-playing record.

Released in the first week of April 1963, *Please Please Me* promptly installed itself at number one and remained in the album charts for seventy weeks. Oddly enough, the album bore a resemblance to the Beatles' Decca audition. It contained R&B ("Twist and Shout," "Chains") pop ("A Taste of Honey") and original rock and roll.

The addition of those McCartney/Lennon originals (as they were billed on the record) changed the landscape dramatically. The eight originals on *Please Please Me*, compared to the three found on the Decca audition, reveal significant artistic growth. Kicking off the record was "I Saw Her Standing There," a fiery original rocker. This track served as a declaration that there should be no question about the legitimacy of the Beatles. "I Saw Her Standing There" was a *bona fide* rock and roll song, joining the rare company of "Move It" by Cliff Richard and the Shadows and "Shakin' All Over" by Johnny Kidd and the Pirates as genuine UK rock songs. It sounded like it could have been stolen from a Little Richard Specialty Records session.

The Beatles' influences were on clear display throughout the LP. "Misery" and "There's a Place" blend Everly Brothers-type harmonies with a nod to Brill Building composition. The Brill Building is further evident in the two Shirelles covers, "Boys" and "Baby It's You," and the Cookies' "Chains." John Lennon's vocals on the sublime country soul of Arthur Alexander's "Anna (Go To Him)" are a touchstone for virtually everything he ever recorded afterward. Add to that his throat-shredding performance on the Isley Brothers' "Twist and Shout" and Lennon arrives on the scene as one of the most promising white rock vocalists. Considering that Lennon was suffering from a terrible cold and sore throat, that February day only amplifies its greatness.

Released less than three weeks after *Please Please Me* came the Beatles' third single. Curiously, it was not included on their debut LP. Then again, they were still operating in a world where the single was king. Written on the back of a tour bus while on the road supporting Helen Shapiro and recorded on March 5, 1963, "From Me to You" became the tipping point for the band. The complete session, which surfaced on a bootleg CD in 1994, shows the group running through several takes of the song, complete with Lennon's directions to McCartney to "keep right in with your harmonies." "From Me to You" wasn't a revelatory piece of music. Like its predecessors, it had ringing guitars, vocal harmonies, and a great harmonica hook. This time, however, the Beatles had a feverishly growing audience, and "From Me to You" hit number one on May 4 and remained there for seven weeks. *Please Please Me* followed it to number one on the album chart the following week and remained there for an astounding thirty weeks.

In addition to their tireless live performance schedule, the Beatles had to cut dedicated live sessions of their songs for the BBC to play achieve airplay. It's hard for today's radio audiences to conceive, but in the UK in 1963 most music performances had to be sourced from live sessions. This was a negotiated contract point with the musicians' union to ensure that the broadcasting of records would not take jobs from musicians. Furthermore, pop music, under the name of light programs, was only one small part of the programming spectrum found at the BBC. The biggest pop music program, *Saturday Club*, could have more than 3 million listeners, nearly 7 percent of England's population. A single appearance could make a career; repeated appearances practically ensured it. The power was very similar to the hold the Grand Ole Opry had on country music in the USA. Between April 4 and May 21, 1963, the Beatles recorded no fewer than six different versions of "From Me to You" for broadcast on various BBC programs. With the explosion of Beatlemania, the Beatles actually began hosting their own BBC program, *Pop Go the Beatles*, in June 1963. The sessions for those broadcasts remained officially unreleased until 1994's *Live at the BBC*. For those who wish to hear what the Beatles sounded like as a performing unit, this is the record to play.

The Beatles' star had risen and became fixed at the pinnacle of the UK entertainment world. Conventional wisdom would dictate that they had no place to go but down. Nothing could be more wrong. In August, the Beatles dropped the musical equivalent of the atom bomb. (It wouldn't be the last time that would happen.) "She Loves You" is practically viral in its catchiness. With its explosive tom-tom drum roll and exuberant opening chorus, complete with the indelible "Yeah, yeah, yeah" vocal hook, "She

Loves You" was an unstoppable juggernaut. It spent a total of six weeks at number one and became a hit in several European countries and Australia. "She Loves You" became the biggest-selling single in UK history until 1977, when it was displaced by Paul McCartney's "Mull of Kintyre."

The Beatles had no real competition at this point. Elvis Presley, the first rock and roll deity, was ensconced in Hollywood making mediocre films, and Presley's contemporaries had mostly fallen away in various ignominious ways. The Beatles' immediate predecessors, such as Cliff Richard, seemed irrelevant by comparison (although Richard did maintain a very successful career for decades). The machine of Liverpool-based groups also managed by Brian Epstein, such as Gerry and the Pacemakers, Brian Poole and the Tremeloes, and Billy J. Kramer and the Dakotas, were also topping the UK charts, but the Beatles were different. They had more than charisma. They possessed the type of magnetism that made Presley a revolution seven years prior, only multiplied by a factor of four. And where Presley had shrouded his ambition in his polite Southern son persona, the Beatles were openly ambitious. John Lennon often rallied his bandmates by asking, "Where are we going, boys?" "To the toppermost of the poppermost, Johnny!!" they replied. It wasn't a joke. In February 1963, *New Musical Express* ran a page on the Beatles in which they each filled out answers to a questionnaire. It asked for their personal statistics, likes, and hobbies. In the category of "Professional ambition," John Lennon answered, "To be rich and famous."

The task of a second album was at hand. Success brought with it the luxury of more time to record. For *With the Beatles*, the group spread out the recording sessions to seven days over the course of four months. Luxury is a relative term, as the group continued to work virtually every day either in performance, in session for the BBC, or making television appearances. (They also bade farewell to their hometown haunt of the Cavern on August 3 after nearly 300 appearances there.)

With the Beatles contained eight new originals, including George Harrison's first solo composition, "Don't Bother Me." The six non-originals heavily favored contemporary American rhythm and blues, notably three from the blossoming Motown stable. The Beatles hadn't quite shaken show tunes, and included "Till There Was You" from *The Music Man*, a song they had performed at their Decca audition. Again, it was the Lennon-McCartney originals that set them apart. Pick any tune: "Hold Me Tight," "It Won't Be Long," or "All My Loving" are all joyous and steady rocking songs with fantastically emotive lead vocals and harmonies, sharp guitars, and swinging drums. Even Ringo's spotlight, "I Wanna Be Your Man," a song initially given to the Rolling Stones and thought by Lennon and McCartney to be substandard, was a kicking rave-up awash with tremolo-laden guitars. If "She Loves You" was a statement about the pop craftsmanship abilities of the Beatles and the Lennon-McCartney team, *With the Beatles* said there was a lot more where that came from. *With the Beatles* did not need the inclusion of "She Loves You" to make it a hit. It entered the album chart on December 7, posted itself at number one for twenty-one weeks, and was the best-selling album of 1963.

EMI, the parent corporation of Parlophone, was suddenly awash with money. They acted as any self-respecting, profit-driven record company would in that situation; they immediately saw repackaging opportunities with the Beatles' limited output. Between July and November, EMI released three EPs, four-song, 7-inch extended play records, of existing hits and album tracks. Why release a record only once when you can release and sell it twice?

No discussion of *With the Beatles* can be contemplated without considering the album cover. On *Please Please Me*, the band assembled above the entrance to EMI's Manchester Square headquarters, where photographer Angus McBean framed the four Beatles in color as vibrant and youthful extensions of the contemporary architecture, a new band for a new era in Britain. They were smiling, besuited and clean cut, if you excuse Ringo's Teddy boy hair. The cover of *With the Beatles* created an iconography comparable only to Alfred Wertheimer's 1956 photos of Elvis Presley. Like Wertheimer's photos, it was stark yet filled with energy. It was shot by photographer Robert Freeman in black and white at the Palace Court Hotel in Bournemouth, the Beatles posing tightly in black turtlenecks with the light from a window half illuminating their still and fixed facial expressions. It's dark and nearly brooding, but the image transmits a message that change is here. Rock and roll is not dead. The eyes of the four are deep and knowing. The millions who bought this record, and its North American equivalent, understood. This image permitted all who connected with it to declare: "This is new. This is mine. This is not like what came before." If the visual wasn't enough of a cultural demarcation, *With the Beatles* was released on November 22, 1963, the day John F. Kennedy was assassinated.

Beatlemania was in full-blown effect in England. The Beatles sometimes had to dress as policemen to sneak into theatres where they performed. Hordes of screaming fans drowned out the meager PA systems of the day, leaving the Beatles to lipread one another just to follow a song in performance. Outside of the UK, they were the hottest thing throughout Scandinavia and Australia. In the United States, the birthplace of the Beatles' musical heroes, they were virtually unknown. Capitol Records, EMI's partner in the USA, passed on the Beatles, and their first few records were released on a smattering of independent labels. Frustrated with the lack of cooperation, Brian Epstein called Capitol Records president, Alan Livingston, and convinced him to release the records. As this chapter must restrict itself to the first three UK albums, I highly recommend any and all of Bruce Spizer's books to those who wish to learn more about the Beatles' records in America.

Hard on the heels of *With the Beatles* came yet another irresistible free-standing single. One might say that the Beatles could have put out a record of them making animal noises and it would have hit number one, just based on the mass hysteria enveloping them. Whether that is true or not, the Beatles dropped yet another indelible piece of pop perfection. Britain's *New Musical Express* described "I Want to Hold Your Hand" as "repetitious almost to the point of hypnosis . . . [a] power-packer disc." Perhaps the venerable music magazine was looking for an excuse to account for the Beatles' hold on the public. Cut in October during the recording of *With the Beatles*, "I Want to Hold Your Hand" rocketed to number one for a five-week run as 1963 closed.

The session for "I Want to Hold Your Hand" also marked the first time the Beatles cut a session with a four-track recorder. Despite the fact that this technology had been in use in the US for several years, EMI was slow to adopt it. Once it was done, though, the Beatles took to it immediately. With the additional tracks available, overdubbing became easier and allowed for a more expansive sonic canvas. In the next four years, the Beatles' mastery of this medium would be revealed.

The new year saw Beatlemania reach an unstoppable pitch around the world. As they became an international commodity, the Beatles expanded their touring. In January 1964, they were in residency at the Paris Olympia, supporting French singer Sylvie Vartan and American singer-guitarist Trini Lopez. Odeon Records, EMI's licensee in Germany, felt that the only way to sell large quantities of records there was for the Beatles to sing in German. The session at EMI's Pathé Marconi studios was meant to cut German-language versions of "I Want to Hold Your Hand" and "She Loves You." After they cut "Komm, Gib Mir Diene Hand" and "Sie Lieb Dich," ample time remained to record another Lennon-McCartney original, "Can't Buy Me Love." It was the only session recorded by the Beatles outside of the UK.

To fill the time between singles, EMI continued to release EPs. "All My Loving," a track from *With the Beatles* so strong that Paul McCartney opened his shows on his 2002 US tour with it, was coupled with "Money (That's What I Want)" and the now thrice-released "Ask Me Why" and "P.S. I Love You."

It opens with a cold-start vocal, and immediately the Beatles are off to the races. "Can't Buy Me Love" is yet another gem steeped in first-generation rock and roll. The subject of money and riches has a strong tradition in all pop music, and "Can't Buy Me Love" fitted the bill like an answer record to the Drifters' classic "Money Honey." In light of the Beatles' immense popularity and imminent wealth, it also possesses the makings of a classic British "piss-take," at least one with self-deprecating overtones. "Can't Buy Me Love" spent three weeks at number one and was the UK's best-selling single of 1964.

If a three-week run at number one for "Can't Buy Me Love" seems puny by comparison to previous hits, there is a solid economic reason. Although the Beatles were firmly seated at the mountaintop of pop music in 1964, in their wake came a flood of performers who now jockeyed with the Fab Four for chart-toppers. By the end of 1964, the list of fellow British bands to bag a number one hit reads like a *Who's Who* of British rock: the Dave Clark Five, the Animals, the Rolling Stones, Manfred Mann, the Kinks, and Herman's Hermits. So complete was British domination that only two American acts, Roy Orbison and the Supremes, hit the top in 1964. On the album side of the business, the Beatles' dominance was nearly complete. Their albums clocked a total of forty weeks at number one that year.

Another EP hit the streets in June 1964. The *Long Tall Sally* EP was full of covers of American songs and one original. "I Call Your Name" was a castoff that Lennon gave to Billy J. Kramer and the Dakotas a year earlier, but had now deemed worthy of recording. The covers of Carl Perkins, Larry Williams, and Little Richard were straight from the Beatles' stage repertoire.

The path from the top of the charts to the silver screen was well worn when the Beatles cut their four-picture deal with United Artists. The first film was *A Hard Day's Night*, a black and white "documentary" of a couple of days in the life of the Beatles. Written by Alun Owen and directed by Richard Lester, it proved to be a splendid platform for the group and a remarkably enduring film. The film was shot over March and April with recording sessions spread out between February and June.

The soundtrack marked the first time a Beatles album comprised entirely Lennon-McCartney compositions, thirteen in total, and *A Hard Day's Night* shows them truly blossoming as songwriters. There was collaboration, but the die was cast with the primary songwriter taking lead vocals. In his *New Musical Express* review of July 3, 1963, Allan Evans wrote: "I don't think this album has the uninhibited joyous drive of the former Beatles' LPs, but it is still way out ahead of rivals." While there is no question that the Beatles had no creative rivals, Evans's perception of a lack of joy missed a key point. In the face of inconceivable tumult, they found a way to grow, both as individuals and as artists. Two songs in particular, McCartney's "Things We Said Today" and Lennon's "I'll Be Back," ring slightly of melancholy but point to a style that would develop into the songs that filled *Rubber Soul* eighteen months later. Released on July 10, 1964, *A Hard Day's Night* sat at number one for twenty-one consecutive weeks. It was displaced by *Beatles For Sale.*

We look back now and see a lifetime of work. In truth, the Beatles would be over and done as a working group in little more than five years from this point. Their first two years as a recording entity were frenzied and prolific, and truly changed much of the world. This was merely the first step.

4 "Try thinking more": *Rubber Soul* and the Beatles' transformation of pop

JAMES M. DECKER

The new songs had no humility. They pushed past the veil and opened a window into the darkness and climbed through it with a knife in their teeth. . . . They were beautiful songs, full of places and textures – flesh, velvet, concrete, city towers, desert sand, snakes, violence, wet glands, childhood, the pure wings of night insects. Anything you could think of was there, and you could move through it as if it were an endless series of rooms and passages full of visions and adventures. And even if it was about killing and dying – that was just another place to go.

MARY GAITSKILL, *VERONICA*[1]

While Mary Gaitskill's character Alison Owen does not refer to the Beatles in the above epigraph, the musical and lyrical range of what she deems the "new songs" owes a tremendous debt to the group from Liverpool. While some early pop artists, such as Chuck Berry, had occasionally explored topics other than puppy love, teen angst, and the exuberance of youth,[2] serious considerations of subjects beyond this terrain fell mainly to performers in the traditional and folk genres, and few ever reached the level of "visions and adventures." Indeed, had a few brave souls forayed into this uncharted territory, the audience might have taunted them off the stage. Starting with *A Hard Day's Night*, however, and reaching fruition in *Rubber Soul* and *Revolver*, the Beatles crossed a thematic threshold that would both inspire their pop contemporaries and develop an audience ready for songs about more than hand-holding and whispered secrets. It is no coincidence that *Rubber Soul* took its narrative cues more from folk crossovers such as Bob Dylan and the Byrds than from the Beatles' pop cohorts. Sonically the influences were numerous, from the soul alluded to in the album's title to country and western and Indian sitar music.[3]

Remarkably, while critics inevitably cite *Rubber Soul* as the Beatles' "transitional" album, the shift from successful pop act to unparalleled masters of the studio took but three years.[4] Ultimately, the demarcation between Beatlemania and the studio years proves an arbitrary one, for from the beginning the Beatles, especially John Lennon, showed a lyrical uneasiness with their expected subject matter. In numerous songs – such as "Misery" (1963), "Not a Second Time" (1963), "Little Child" (1963), and "Tell Me Why" (1964) – love's anxiety and pain burst through among the paeans to love's gleaming rewards.[5] For the early Beatles, the dark vulnerability of Roy Orbison battles with the sunny, sexualized confidence of Little Richard. In

1965, however, a combination of their narcotic tourism, distaste for grueling concert schedules, broader experiences and reading, increased fascination with studio technology, and, above all, economic power allowed the former approach to dominate. With *Rubber Soul*, the Beatles' propensity to experiment – always strong – gelled, particularly with respect to a dissatisfaction with transparent lyrics. The alternation between positive and negative relationships that marked the movement between their earlier songs now often appeared *within* individual tracks, creating an ambiguity relatively unheard of in pop songs – but lauded in poetry. The Beatles coupled their lyrical transformation with a stronger awareness of the studio's possibilities for transcending the raw energy of quickly recorded songs such as "I Saw Her Standing There" and "It Won't Be Long," and for drawing from a more nuanced palette of sounds. In *Revolver* and beyond, the Beatles pressed forward, delving into the creative *process* with even more zeal, having learned much from the *Rubber Soul* sessions.[6] Pushing their lyrics beyond the thematic boundaries of any previous pop artist, the Beatles later took on such heady concepts as hallucinogenic consciousness and alienation, while at the same time their sonic demands pressed their engineers literally to invent new technology. Another important testament to the Beatles' commitment to a new sound on *Rubber Soul* is that, for the first time, no covers appeared. In a business where careers were measured in months, the Beatles were old hands, and on *Rubber Soul* they proved that they did not merely intend to rehash yesterday's aesthetic to an audience that bored quickly.

A glance at the Beatles' 1964 partial itinerary[7] captures but a fraction of the frenzy, exhilaration, and exhaustion felt by the group during their triumphant march across the globe. Between concert trips to the United States and Australia – among many other countries – the Beatles appeared on countless television and radio programs, recorded two albums, and acted in *A Hard Day's Night*. By 1965, however, the music itself was generally lost in the din of publicity and thousands of screaming teens, and one might find it perfectly logical if the Beatles had abandoned any pretense of producing a quality product and simply rode out the wave of fame until the crowds found a new Greatest Thing. The cycle of musical popularity and obscurity, of boom and bust, long pre-dated the rock era, and few would have dared to speculate that the Beatles would survive the demand for a fresh face. Even Elvis had faded, after all. The Beatles, though, never created songs out of complacency,[8] perhaps owing to the complicated relationship between Lennon and McCartney, and discovered in the studio both an outlet for their creative energies and a haven from the constant demands on their time. Working on their craft, ironically, became their escape from *selling* their product, and as the Beatles looked around Abbey studios and started paying attention to how George Martin produced their songs, they discovered that they, too, could contribute. As Lennon recalled, "*Rubber Soul* was a matter of having experienced the recording studio; having grown musically as well, but [getting] the knowledge of the place, of the studio. We were more precise about making the album, that's all, and we took over the cover and everything."[9] Having survived their rites of passage, the initiated Beatles seized their autonomy and would henceforth become not the passive instruments of the studio's magic but the active wavers of the wand. McCartney put it succinctly: "We'd had our cute period and now it was time to expand."[10]

Expand they did. While externally less radical a break with tradition than *Revolver*, *Rubber Soul* lays the necessary groundwork for the Beatles' more explicit attempts at questioning the pop hegemony of idealized love. Although some compliment the Beatles for being "ahead of their time," the group's consistent popularity somewhat belies that characterization. Typically, *avant-garde* artists lack a wide audience and measure their impact more in terms of historical influence. The Velvet Underground, for instance, failed to chart a single top forty hit, yet the group's infusion of jarring instrumentation and sordid lyrics inspired numerous bands that would achieve a far higher degree of popular acclaim once audiences were better prepared. In the Beatles' case, however, Brian Epstein's publicity juggernaut ensured both an audience receptive to the Beatles' "brand" and one that would be sorely disappointed were the Beatles' expansion an overly dramatic one.[11] Too many bewildering changes, however intellectually stimulating to the Beatles, would estrange the base and result in poor word-of-mouth publicity.[12] Theodor Adorno refers to this phenomenon as "the rupture between autonomous production and the public."[13] For Adorno, the angry confusion that can result from an audience's rejection of experimentation that pursues novelty to the exclusion of conventional procedures finds its roots in the "alienation of production from consumption," which ultimately "has its specific basis in this necessity of consumer consciousness to refer back to an intellectual and social situation in which everything that goes beyond the given realities, every revelation of their contradictions, amounts to a threat."[14] Beholden to their label, the Beatles still lacked the autonomy to abandon the mature conventions of pop in favor of emergent techniques. However, by advancing incrementally, the band supplied consumers with the referential signposts that Adorno deems a prerequisite for a non-producer to comprehend or "recognize" the music.[15] In Mark Lewisohn's words, *Rubber Soul* acts as a "very necessary platform between the class pop music of *Help!* and the experimental ideas of *Revolver*."[16] Beyond the marketing impact, the Beatle's *Rubber Soul* spurred on competitors such as Brian Wilson, Pete Townshend, and Ray Davies to experiment with similar methods.

Rubber Soul opens with "Drive My Car," a hard-charging rocker that with its bouncy "beep beep" vocals outwardly resembles the band's earlier output. Entranced by the tune's immediate, if ametrical,[17] sonic hook, casual listeners – which included most in the Beatles' audience – might not have at first noticed the subtle shift in the narrative dynamic marked by the song's first line. Musically, moreover, Tim Riley notes that the song's beat "has a new freedom to it."[18] In singing "Asked a girl what she wanted to be," the Beatles reveal a lyrical perspective that moves away from the more solipsistic pop ethos of earlier songs such as "I Want to Hold Your Hand," "Not a Second Time," and even "Ticket to Ride." In these earlier songs, the Beatles almost universally objectify the narrator's lover and focus on how love or its dissolution makes him feel (or, alternatively, how the narrator believes he can make her feel). "Drive My Car," by contrast, establishes a dialogue in which the female announces *her* dreams and desires – desires that include thinly veiled sexual urges ("you can drive my car"; "I can show you a better time") but not necessarily love ("maybe I'll love you"). No longer the central attraction, the male narrator functions now as a way station of sorts: "You can do something in between." Love, while still present as an idealized state that the female may withhold, fades to the background, as the lover expresses her true design to "be famous, a star of the screen." The cosmopolitan narrator, far from put off by this cynical attitude, fully participates in the transaction, not pledging, as in "Love Me Do," to be true, but stating that his "prospects are good" and that he "could start right away." The lack of a car, rather than a male companion – whether the narrator or not – is the impetus behind the materialistic "girl's" heartbreak. The male cares little that his paramour wants to call the shots or that she lacks the symbol of her would-be superiority – so long as his sexual appetites are satisfied, and the repeated lines that close the song suggest they are. In fact, a more complex process of reification may be taking place, one in which the boy appears to acknowledge the girl's subjectivity but in actuality exploits her need for control and fame for his own more immediate wishes: he lets her think that the lack of commitment is *her* idea, yet he is perfectly willing to accede to a one-dimensional relationship and betrays no sign of emasculation.[19] Hiding in plain sight, the Beatles' innovative approach to lyrics enables more passive fans to enjoy the song (perhaps even mishearing "baby, I love you" for "maybe I'll love you"), while more active listeners may marvel at the subversion of the most basic tenet of the pop ethos: the idealization of the love relationship. The disjunction between the catchy harmony and the cynical lyrics – reminiscent of Bertolt Brecht's *Threepenny Opera* – allows the Beatles to smuggle in their new aesthetic, as it were. In "Drive My Car," the Beatles evince ambivalence toward their erstwhile subject matter and a new willingness to take lyrical and musical chances.

"Norwegian Wood (This Bird Has Flown)" continues *Rubber Soul*'s interrogation of sexual ambiguities. With Harrison's inaugural effort on the sitar, the song anticipates the more radical instrumentation of *Revolver* and later albums. Fusing the sitar's eastern flavor with crisp, unhurried guitar lines and understated percussion and bass, "Norwegian Wood" bathes its listeners in a nostalgic melody that again contrasts with the lyrical narrative, which, while contemplative, does not contain a longing for the past but rather reveals an acrimonious memory. As with many of the tracks on *Rubber Soul*, "Norwegian Wood" reinterprets a familiar theme, in this case the loss of "love" (well represented in earlier songs such as "Don't Bother Me" and "Misery"), providing listeners with security yet challenging those inclined to acknowledge the limitations of the standard treatment. In earlier efforts such as "I Call Your Name," the narrator, while undeniably hurt and even confused, recalls an idealized moment of love, a time of perfect emotional synthesis, the absence of which results in agony. In "Norwegian Wood," however, such harmony never existed, and alienation and wasted potential take its place. Lennon's lyrics – about one of his affairs – echo the muddled sense of power in "Drive My Car" and reflect the group's more mature analysis of interpersonal relationships: "I once had a girl / Or should I say / She once had me." In fact, neither party "has" the other – emotionally or sexually – and the entire memory casts the scene as an elaborate deception stemming from jaded self-interest. Subverting the hand-holding innocence of the Beatles' initial phase, the "bird" takes the narrator back to her place, an action likely to be viewed, whether in working-class Liverpool or posh London, as a clear sign of sexual intent, particularly after she asks the narrator to stay. The Norwegian wood serves a dual purpose, both as a symbol of how empty small talk ("Isn't it good / Norwegian wood?") may serve as a prelude to emotionally meaningless sex and of the counterfeit quality of the relationship: McCartney notes that the fashionable-sounding wood is in fact "cheap pine."[20] The prospective lover is particularly cryptic in telling the narrator "to sit anywhere" despite the fact that "there wasn't a chair." Looking back, the narrator detects a false note similar to the "daytripper" who takes one "half the way there," yet at the time the narrator himself is predatory and willing to read the signifiers as he sees fit: "Biding my time / Drinking her wine." Clearly, the narrator is willing to put up with the "bird's" nonsense so long as the night culminates as he expects with sex, an expectation heightened by her declaration that "It's time for bed." Perhaps indicating more of a struggle than the song reveals, thirteen seconds of instrumentation ensue before the would-be lover reveals that "she worked in the morning and started to laugh." The first clause indicates that the narrator's plans for sexual conquest will come to naught, while the latter demonstrates that the woman knows perfectly well what the narrator expected and that she derides him for the assumption. Humiliated, the narrator "crawled off to sleep in the bath," only to awake to an empty house – "This bird has flown." McCartney remembers that he added the final sequence in which the narrator "lit a fire" and ironically asks, "Isn't it good / Norwegian wood?" He further avers that the narrator turns arsonist, that the fire was not in a fireplace but in the apartment itself. Such an interpretation, if on the level,[21] makes the relaxed instrumentation even more jolting, as such a hostile reaction to sexual rebuff is mystifying. The anger that such a response reveals is undoubtedly disproportionate, even psychopathic, and it poses the question why the narrator would not have stormed out at 2 a.m. Perhaps – replayed endlessly – the humiliation leads the narrator to insert within his memory an empowering fantasy in place of the mundane reality of leaving the flat. In any event, with "Norwegian Wood (This Bird Has Flown)," the Beatles move pop music to stunning new territory, away from lyrics ripe for parody by the likes of Steve Allen and toward the poetic or, as Riley puts it, the "allusive."[22]

In contrast, "You Won't See Me," while making some musical strides, owes far more in terms of narrative to the Beatlemania phase than to the "more surreal" (in McCartney's words) tactics of other songs on the album.[23] Walter Everett rightly points out that the tune's "sterile, manufactured sheen" feels out of place on *Rubber Soul*, an album that consciously moved away from slick pop formulas.[24] The generic quality of the song is borne out in the lyrics, which stake out narrative terrain similar to "No Reply," with a frustrated lover apostrophizing the object of his affections and gently indicating that he would continue the relationship despite being done wrong – though in both cases the girl fails to hear the plea.[25] In both songs, attempts to phone are fruitless, with parents' (presumably) running interference in "No Reply" and a busy line sounding in "You Won't See Me." In the former song, a rival is seen walking "hand in hand" with the lover, but in the latter the engaged line perhaps only hints that the paramour has found another. In both songs, moreover, the self-centered narrator laments that he might die. "No Reply" takes the direct approach ("I nearly died"), while "You Won't See Me" prefers a more oblique reference ("I just can't go on"). Neither song attempts to comprehend the other person's position, preferring instead to wallow in self-pity. In short, "You Won't See Me," while a serviceable tune in the pop tradition, fails to measure up to the strides made by nearly every other song on *Rubber Soul*.

In sharp distinction, "Nowhere Man" broke much thematic ground, offering a critique of social detachment and apathy. Indeed, Kenneth Womack calls the song's protagonist "the band's first genuinely literary character."[26] More than any other track on the album, "Nowhere Man" breaks the unstated rules for pop content. Love, cars, parental constraints –

"Nowhere Man" leaves these commonplaces behind and explores what the philosopher Michael Fraenkel termed "the law of function," a state wherein individuals resemble machines more than "conscious spiritual organisms."[27] The Nowhere Man lacks existential curiosity, "Doesn't have a point of view." Rather, this figure weaves "Nowhere plans for nobody," moving zombie-like (Fraenkel equated the state to death-in-life) through motions intended to accomplish no more than feeding his belly and placing a roof over his head. The higher functions on Maslow's hierarchy are blithely ignored, a dangerous strategy in the post-Gulf of Tonkin 1960s: "Just sees what he wants to see." This phenomenon, the song notes, might stem from the bounty of Western civilization, which allows citizens to ignore world events even as they benefit from them: "Isn't he a bit like you and me?" Breaking the third wall, this last question appeals directly to the readers and forces them to pay attention in a way that even the more complex relationship songs on *Rubber Soul* fail to achieve. The narrator (really narrators, as multiple voices sing the words) ponders whether the Nowhere Man can empathize with his fellows, wondering, "Can you see me at all?" While the song threatens to wither in despair, Lennon's lyrics avoid this by pleading with the anti-hero to "please listen" and connect with humanity, for only then will he "know what [he's] missing." While he does not employ the word, Lennon is clearly talking about Love, not in the limited sense that the Beatles used it in prior songs, but as "the underlying theme to the universe," as he glossed the primary subject of *Rubber Soul*.[28] The Nowhere Man, perhaps, loves himself, but more likely he has more in common with Fraenkel's machine, performing an anonymous function in an anonymous corporation. The narrators call on him to Love, to transcend his own material needs and to search out both Truth and the rest of the world. Only empathy and Love can save the Nowhere Man from pure emptiness and the law of function. If fans had failed to see the Beatles' transformation on the first two songs on *Rubber Soul*, they could hardly fail to do so on the fourth, particularly given its release as a single in the United States.

With Harrison's "Think for Yourself," the group ostensibly returns to familiar thematic ground. Rather than the dialogue of "Drive My Car," the song offers another of the band's dramatic monologues directed at a voiceless love interest. However, the message of "Think for Yourself" differs strikingly from "Not a Second Time" or "Do You Want to Know a Secret?" in that it presents a rejection of the paramour's offers of intimacy and "all the good things" that it entails. The relationship presented here appears much more complex, and the narrator advances a more sophisticated perspective: "good things" might be tempting but false. "Lies" that perhaps once would have appealed are now unmasked as the product of fantasy. The (former, one supposes) lover's suggestion that if "we close our eyes" pleasurable events will follow fails to convince the narrator and leads him to distance himself: "I won't be there with you." On one level, the narrator might simply be expressing a dissatisfaction with previous phases of the relationship – broken promises, perhaps, or unacceptable behavior on the part of the lover. However, the injunction to "think for yourself" indicates a more expanded consciousness on the part of the narrator, possibly to the point of rejecting the traditional "good things" attendant to a marriage (career, family, materialism, etc.) in favor of a spiritually aware existence. For the narrator, the love interest here reveals an uncritical acceptance of collective values that, more often than not, lead not to fairytale endings but "misery" for the participants. An "opaque" mind unwittingly participates in a master narrative designed to strip one of individual identity in exchange for meaningless baubles. The narrator holds out some hope, though, with his comment that "the future still looks good / and you've got time to rectify / all the things that you should." Critical thinking – asking questions skeptical of the love-as-fairytale model – can steer one clear of the "ruins of the life" that the lover currently cherishes. The narrator clearly rejects his lover's ethos and "won't be there" to witness the disillusionment he feels inevitable, yet he leaves her with advice to "try thinking more." Harrison and the Beatles have thus raised the stakes from the naïve idealism of hand-holding to the recognition that life offers more possibilities to those who would actively pursue an expanded consciousness – a theme that they will plumb even further in *Revolver*. Combined with what Devin McKinney calls the song's "piercingly, gratingly *wrong*" sound, the track provides the "distressing and confused" qualities that Adorno views as driving the "critical impulse" of music that would successfully challenge convention.[29] An album filled with such shock would no doubt have disaffected those comfortable with the pop formula, but when juxtaposed with songs such as "You Won't See Me," the innovations seem less drastic, less visible, yet they still help cultivate a "new" audience that may, when listening to the more technically and narratologically advanced *Revolver*, refer backward (*à la* Adorno) and sense the "equivalency" that aids comprehension.[30]

The escape from wretchedness that Harrison offers in "Think for Yourself" appears more explicitly in the album's next song, "The Word." While the former song provides a methodology, independent thinking, the latter offers a philosophy stripped to its minimalist essence. Riley reminds readers that while the song's "message has grown trite . . . it tapped an attitude that was then enlisting activists in the civil rights and antiwar causes."[31] A singular love song, "The Word" only nominally, if at all, directs its attentions to a specific love interest. Superficially, one might suppose that the narrator is calling on a paramour to acknowledge that their relationship is indeed based on love. In being "like me," this interpretation holds that the narrator desires that his partner view the relationship far more seriously than she has hitherto. However, the balance of the lyrics scuttles such a reading as overly simplistic. In "The Word," the Beatles offer the first of their songs about Love, the concept, rather than love, the specific act. In a world full of hatred and violence, the simple act of love can offer "sunshine." Self-reflexively commenting on the Beatles' earlier corpus, perhaps, the narrator indicates that "In the beginning I misunderstood / But now I've got it, the word is good." Love here is presented as a spiritual idea, an attitude that moves one closer to God. With proselytizing zeal, the narrator-prophet joyously counsels his listeners (as opposed to the single listener of the dramatic monologues) to "spread the word" that will set them "free" in contrast to the opaque mental prison outlined in "Think for Yourself." The Truth is so simple and so profound that both the "good and the bad books" reveal it, but one must be aware and receptive of Love in order to see the "light." Love is "just the way," however. That is, spiritual enlightenment portends far more than the typical conceptions of love might suggest. The song's repeated final lines transform the word into a mantra, a method of attaining higher consciousness: "Say the word love / Say the word love / Say the word love / Say the word love." If one can transcend the communal baggage associated with love-as-fetish – the "misunderstood" vision the Beatles advance in their early work – then one might experience the ecstasy of true Love and scale divine heights.

The album's next two songs illustrate *Rubber Soul*'s "transitional" status well. The metaphysics of songs such as "Nowhere Man" and "The Word" are counterbalanced by lighter, more traditional narrative fare such as "Michelle" and "What Goes On," helping to move the audience slowly to the more challenging themes and music presented in albums such as *Revolver* and *Abbey Road*. While the songs, especially "Michelle," make advances musically and in terms of tone, lyrically they lack the sophistication of "Norwegian Wood" and "Think for Yourself." "Michelle" returns to the dramatic monologue, and while it does acknowledge the ineffable nature of love ("I'm hoping you will know what I mean"), it nevertheless expresses desire in straightforward terms: "I want you, I want you, I want you." These echo, though employing McCartney's new more nostalgic tone (first achieved in "Yesterday" and perhaps perfected in "Eleanor Rigby"), earlier communications of desire in songs such as "Do You Want to Know a Secret" ("You'll never know how much I really love you"), and even the doubt revealed in the far more aggressive "I Should Have Known Better" ("If this is love, you've got to give me more"). The song does, however, differ in that it seems far less positive about the definition of love than earlier ones (the narrator assumes, however, that, French or not, Michelle will have little difficulty grasping the concept: "the only words that I know you'll understand"), but lyrically it offers little beyond the bare statement of that uncertainty, and it even returns to the concept of possession ("*ma* belle"; "what you mean to *me*") ironically interrogated in "Drive My Car" and "Norwegian Wood." The Beatles make up for this deficit via their sentimental orchestration and the plaintive, wistful tone of the vocals, what Everett calls "wondrous tonal motions" and "complexities of mode mixture."[32] The presentation creates the effect of something *more* existing within the narrator – the ineffable quality mentioned above – an emotional truth that he is unable to define. In concert, the music and the vocal expression provide the song a gravitas unearned by the lyrics themselves, yet the familiar referent of the narrative allows listeners to absorb the complexities of the music in a fluid way.

"What Goes On," like "Michelle," represents a retrograde achievement lyrically, and Womack asserts that "it is . . . quite arguably the weakest and most incongruous track on the album."[33] A reiteration of the angst-ridden theme present in the Beatles' music since "Please Please Me," "I Call Your Name," and "This Boy," the tune expresses vexation and confusion over a "girl's" infidelity. As in many such songs, and in contrast to the awareness of "Drive My Car," "What Goes On" employs an interrogative method, asking for clarification and placing blame for the relationship's demise squarely on the lover's shoulders: "What goes on in your mind? / What goes on in your heart? / You are tearing me apart." The suggestion that the girl tells a "lie" is unsupported by the narrative, which itself offers a viable alternative: that the other boy and the lover were, indeed, merely walking as no more than friends. The narrator's paranoia, though, admits of no other possibility than cheating, and his narrative reconstruction of the event offers little evidence apart from "I saw him with you." The latent insecurities of the narrator bubble to the surface ("I was blind") and finally burst into hyperbole: "Did you mean to break my heart and watch me die?" The narrator makes no attempt at self-analysis as in "Norwegian Wood," and he fails to grow from the experience. Lyrically formulaic and musically plain (though perhaps the "country" feel is offered as an arch parody of the lyrics), "What Goes On" anchors the Beatles in the very tradition that they are exploding during many other moments on *Rubber Soul*.

On the surface, "Girl" shares similarities with "What Goes On." Chief among these is the (ostensible) rejected-lover paradigm and the lack of understanding on the part of the narrator. Nevertheless, in "Girl," the Beatles handle the material in a far different way and take the subgenre to its limits by using questions not to convey confusion and frustration but as a more sophisticated environmental explanation for the lover's behavior. Additionally, here the girl "came to stay": in an ironic twist, the narrator, while similar to those of "What Goes On" and its ilk, cannot reject a woman who, while not apparently cheating, fails to live up to her rhetoric ("she promises the earth to me and I believe her"). The monologue is directed, moreover, not at the girl but at an existential "anybody": this is a lonely plea for understanding and empathy. As in "Drive My Car," the relationship presented here is far more complicated than the love-equals-bliss / rejection-equals-pain prescription offered in earlier songs. The girl torments the narrator, yet he does not "regret a single day." Pain and pleasure are muddled, inseparable in the narrator, and while he recognizes his lover's use of emotional manipulation, he cannot resist it: "When I think of all the times I tried to leave her / She will turn to me and start to cry." Unlike the speaker in "What Goes On," the narrator here has specific grievances ("She's the kind of girl / Who puts you down when friends are there"), and he questions not her but himself: "After all this time I don't know why." Rather than interrogating the lover, the speaker uses questions to theorize about her behavior and the nature of domestic roles: "Was she told when she was younger that pain would lead to pleasure? / Did she understand it when they said / That a man must break his back to earn his day of leisure?" The Beatles reveal a class consciousness here as well as a notion of internalized environmental stimuli – even if those stimuli are processed in a faulty way. The death alluded to here ("Will she still believe it when he's dead?") is far different than the exaggerated pain indicated by the speaker of "What Goes On" in that it refers not to angst and frustration but to physical stress *endured* by a man intent on pleasing his woman but incapable of doing so. The subtle interrelational dynamic presented here reflects yet again the more sophisticated ideas being employed covertly in the guise of a traditional pop format.

"I'm Looking through You," although not as philosophical as "Think for Yourself" explores a similar thematic landscape. As with "Girl" and other of *Rubber Soul*'s more experimental songs, "I'm Looking Through You" takes one of the Beatles' common subgenres – in this case the "confrontation" song as represented by "You Can't Do That" and "Not a Second Time" – and heightens the level of discourse, despite using what Riley calls a "cast of clichés."[34] While in the aforementioned songs an aggressive speaker masks his vulnerabilities by taking a "no nonsense" approach to infidelity, in "I'm Looking Through You" the narrator is more concerned with contemplating the nature of mental growth and its effects on love. Although the narrator does confront the lover (and in a typically humiliating way), he notes that his perception of the woman has transformed: "where did you go?" The difference, moreover, is not physical but mental: "you're not the same." Quickly, however, listeners recognize that the change has taken place within the *narrator* rather than the lover, for while her "voice is soothing . . . the words aren't clear." After a nod to the traditional model ("tell me why you did not treat me right"), the speaker observes that "Love has a nasty habit of disappearing overnight," a phenomenon that he attributes to the ex-lover's lack of perception: "You're thinking of me the same old way." Clearly, the narrator has grown, yet the woman has failed to keep up. Her inability to change costs her the relationship, much as the woman in "Think For Yourself" is chastised for her stunted mental capacity. Unlike the latter song, however, the narrative is not markedly distinct from the subgenre's norms, and a passive listener could easily miss the more sophisticated narrative approach.

As with many of the songs on *Rubber Soul*, "In My Life" adopts a nostalgic tone; however, the narrator qualifies his longing for the past with a recognition of the dynamic nature of the present and of his love for his partner. Anticipating "Strawberry Fields Forever" and "Penny Lane," the song initially situates itself within a positive (though far less specific) memory of past places, friends, and lovers. The narrator notes that he has "loved them all," and observes, but not bitterly, of the places (though, significantly, not the people) that "some have changed / Some forever, not for better." After establishing the importance of these people and places, however, the narrator reveals his true subject, his comment to his lover that "no one compares" with her and that an uncritical, ideal view of the past is not possible in relation to his feelings toward the newness of love. His notion of "love as something new" here denotes not a simple novelty but an evolutionary experience that contrast greatly with the lack of change perceived in "I'm Looking Through You." While his past is significant, "these memories lose their meaning" when juxtaposed to the vibrant nature of a maturing love. The love interest, like those in earlier songs, is paramount, yet unlike the more one-dimensional figures of "Thank You Girl" or "And I Love Her," the world of love is not hermetically sealed. The narrator has outside interests, can juggle multiple memories, yet he also recognizes that he'll love his woman "more" than he can others competing for his attention. In the earlier, naïve songs, the possibility of other lovers does not exist, while in this more mature, complex universe, the narrator is not overcompensating for any fear that the "ideal" won't be achieved. Further adding to the song's narrative complexity is what McKinney labels the "explicit foretaste of death within its loving remembrance of things past."[35] Love is here viewed within the narrator's life cycle rather than as an all-encompassing preoccupation.

While not nearly as emotionally self-actualized as his counterpart in "In My Life," the speaker of "Wait" also differs positively from those of earlier songs, although the record itself betrays more similarities to earlier efforts than to *Rubber Soul*'s best tracks. A "reconciliation" song, "Wait" suggests a turbulent, passion-filled relationship, but the lack of concrete details harms the narrative significantly. Nevertheless, the narrator does not rely on a strategy of braggadocio and threats (as in "Run for Your Life"), but rather emphasizes a fresh start: "We'll forget the tears we cried." Unlike a similar song, "You Like Me Too Much," the speaker is not willing to admit fault, but rather emphasizes the reciprocal nature of the relationship: "I've been good, as good as I can be / And if you do, I'll trust in you." The trust, thus, is not unconditional as with the naïve/idealist subject positions in earlier songs. The speaker also recognizes and encourages the autonomy of his lover: "But if your heart breaks, don't wait, turn me away." Despite these nuances, however, the song fails to address the core issues that led to the initial breakup (though perhaps the speaker's infidelity is intimated by the phrase "as good as I can be") and does not attain the strength of "Norwegian Wood," "Girl," or "Think For Yourself." It simply lacks specificity. As Womack writes, "the song simply doesn't go anywhere."[36] The lack of musical innovation, moreover, cannot rescue it, as is the case with "Michelle," from accusations of triviality.

"If I Needed Someone," as with *Rubber Soul*'s other weaker tracks, does reveal some narrative strides, yet it also shares more in common with the Beatles' earlier phase than it does with their later triumphs. Like "Wait," the song avoids the layered narrative details of "Nowhere Man," "Drive My Car," and other of the album's most innovative texts. Despite this, however, the song does offer a counter-narrative to the more traditional pop idealism of the Beatles' earlier efforts. The speaker, ensconced in a fulfilling relationship, rejects an overture from another love interest, but he does so in a way that ironically diminishes his love with what Sheila Whiteley views as "a sense of cynicism" and disillusionment.[37] In earlier songs, love is unquestionably "forever," and even spurned lovers emphasize betrayal rather than a true loss of love. Here, however, the narrator reveals a curious indifference to the ideal of eternal love: "If I had more time to spend / Then I guess I'd be with you my friend." The casualness of the "I guess" portends something far different from the inevitability of love as signified in songs such as "Thank You Girl" or "And I Love Her." Further, despite the narrator's protest that he is "too much in love," he calls on his admirer to "Carve [her] number on [his] wall," hardly an act of loyalty to his present love. He compounds this emotional infidelity by declaring that if at a future date he "needed someone," he might call her. Temporal dilemmas, rather than any notion of eternal love, seem at issue here, and the speaker cynically mentions that had the woman "come some other day / . . . it might not have been like this." Effectually, he suggests that the "love" is not ideal but dependent solely on chronological circumstances. He never unequivocally denies that he could "love" the interested party despite his involvement with another. The scenario lacks context, though, and listeners cannot as readily visualize the scene as they can with "Norwegian Wood" or "Girl." While sonically the song is relatively conventional, its cynicism is unexpected, although again a more passive listener might view the track as yet another Beatles' love song.

Rubber Soul concludes with either one of the album's most conventional tracks or with a sly attempt at innovation. At first blush, "Run For Your Life" appears to be the bitter final act of the drama initiated in "You Can't Do That," an earlier song wherein the narrator threatens his loquacious lover and declares that he'll "go out of [his] mind." In the sequel, the threat is far more specific and deadly: "I'd rather see you dead, little girl / Than to be with another man." Many of the Beatles' songs – particularly those penned mainly by Lennon – reveal a misogynistic streak, and this composition is clearly the most overt, with its depictions of ownership ("little girl") and control ("I can't spend my whole life trying / Just to make you toe the line") as well as the obvious violence. The sheer over-the-top nature of the reaction in relation to the (unspecified) infraction, however, might look forward to the Beatles' later use of parody (see "Why Don't We Do It in the Road" or "Baby You're a Rich Man," for example). It is conceivable that the Beatles are in fact mocking their earlier efforts, here stripping any romantic pretense from the lyrics. Lennon remarked that he nicked the central violent image from Elvis Presley's "Baby Let's Play House," further opening up the door for an interpretation involving parody.[38] Nevertheless, such a reading may be too generous and dependent on contextualization. After all, the narrator sings "Let this be a sermon / I mean everything I said." The song may simply be a thuggish anomaly that looks backward rather than forward and poses an odd choice as the culminating track on an album wherein the Beatles consciously treated the entire recording process as artistic venture.[39]

Such lyrics as those found on "Run For Your Life" and "Wait" remain problematic on an album filled with gems such as "Norwegian Wood" and "Nowhere Man." Of course, with multiple songwriters, it's illogical to expect identical growth, and one must place *Rubber Soul* within its context as follow-up to *Help!*, an album that had a few innovative songs, such as "Yesterday" and "You've Got to Hide Your Love Away," coexisting with many more conventional ones such as "The Night Before" and "Another Girl." *Rubber Soul* both changes the ratio and adds further complexities, both musically (daring instrumentation, technological self-awareness) and narratologically (expanded thematic range, concrete characterization). Arguably, however, by retaining vestiges of their earlier aesthetic, the Beatles were able to earn concessions from both George Martin and his superiors. A sharper break – one that altogether rejected the expected pop conventions – might have outpaced the majority of the audience and set up not *Revolver* and *Sgt. Pepper's Lonely Hearts Club Band*, but a reprimand and a quick retreat to the proven formula, the "pre-given and pre-accepted" structure that Adorno cites as characteristic of popular music.[40] With just enough similarities to recognizable generic archetypes to avoid audience-driven charges of incomprehensibility and betrayal, *Rubber Soul* smuggles in a variety of techniques hitherto unexplored in popular music and incrementally teaches a sizable element of the audience both to be cognizant of more flexible definitions of pop music and to *desire* and *expect* them as well. Within months of the Beatles' inaugural efforts on *Rubber Soul,* other groups, such as the Kinks, Love, and Jefferson Airplane, to name but a few, would be regularly experimenting with techniques unheard of – save on some of the Beatles' own earlier records – in the pop realm before December 1965. The "new songs" indeed "pushed past the veil" and revealed an unlimited potential.

5 Magical mystery tours, and other trips: yellow submarines, newspaper taxis, and the Beatles' psychedelic years

RUSSELL REISING AND JIM LeBLANC

The day of the LSD experience often becomes a dramatic and easily discernible landmark in the development of individual artists. STANISLAV GROF[1]

One evening in April of 1965, Beatles George Harrison and John Lennon, along with George's fiancée Pattie Boyd, and John's wife Cynthia, dined with John Riley, a prominent dentist in London.[2] Their host secretly slipped LSD-laced sugar cubes into the after-dinner coffees, and so began a night filled with bouts of intense sensory excitement.[3] Lennon later exhorted listeners to "take a drink from [the] special cup" of a physician named "Doctor Robert," a song on which dreamy, seemingly floating vocal harmonies declared: "well, well, well, you're feeling fine," quite likely commemorating the quaffing of their first and subsequent magic cups.[4] In August of that same year, Harrison and Lennon again took LSD; this time, Ringo Starr joined in, as did actor Peter Fonda. As Harrison sat poolside, struggling somewhat with the effects of the drug, Fonda related a story from his youth in which he nearly died from blood loss. "I know what it's like to be dead," he stated. Lennon, perhaps in an effort to free the group from the morbid impact of Fonda's story, retorted: "Who put all that shit in your head?"[5] Lennon memorialized this event in "She Said She Said," a track on which he changed the sex of his interlocutor and related that: "She said I know what it's like to be dead . . . / I said who put all those things in your head." On yet another early LSD trip, Lennon distilled his reading of *The Psychedelic Experience*, Tim Leary, Ralph Metzner, and Richard Alpert's reworking of *The Tibetan Book of the Dead* into a guide for those seeking spiritual enlightenment via the psychedelic journey, into the powerful initial verse ("Turn off your mind, relax and float downstream . . . It is not dying")[6] of the groundbreaking "Tomorrow Never Knows." The Beatles recorded all three of these compositions in the spring of 1966, a time that marks the band's initial infusion of psychedelic themes, sounds, and insights into their music. This chapter examines first, the experimental musical dimension of the Beatles' output during their psychedelic phase, and second, important themes representative of their lyrics.

Tuned in and turned on: psychedelia and the 1960s

LSD advocate Timothy Leary's first encounter with *Sgt. Pepper's Lonely Hearts Club Band*[7] registers the immediate impact of the Beatles' work:

> One hot sunny day Rosemary and I wandered down to the main camp [at the infamous Millbrook estate] and I found the entire community gathered around a battery-operated record player. We joined them to listen for the first time to *Sergeant* [*sic*] *Pepper's Lonely Hearts Club Band*, a creation that probably best symbolized the so-called Summer of Love. The album was a most influential media statement about multiple realities and became an instant drug-culture classic.[8]

Leary reveals his ongoing fascination with the album by structuring much of *High Priest* (1968), an experimental chronicle of his LSD experiences, around his punning responses to Beatles' lyrics. Focusing on *Sgt. Pepper*, Leary celebrates his own explorations, trials, and tribulations in Beatlesque lyrical play, some even echoing Lennon's bold poetry in songs like "I Am the Walrus." After comparing his pre-LSD life in which he was "an anonymous institutional employee who drove to work each morning ... drove home each night and drank martinis" to being "trapped in a dark room," Leary draws on the first line from "A Day in the Life" to showcase how his first dose of LSD propelled him into a state of reborn psychedelic illumination: "Woke up, fell out of dead." Being an infamous celebrity under increasing media and legal scrutiny, he strikes back at his detractors, altering Lennon's opening lines to "I led the news today oh joy ... And though the views was rather mad ..." And, in one other memorable variation, Leary plays on his own famous dictum: "Tune in, turn on, drop out" with "I'd ove turned you on,"[9] signaling his partnership with the Beatles' own "I'd love to turn you on."

Aside from some ineffable fusion between music and listener, what makes music "psychedelic"? The term stems from the Greek *psyche*, meaning "spirit," and *delos*, meaning "revealed"; thus "psychedelic" equals something like "mind-manifesting." It appears for the first time in an exchange between Dr. Humphrey Osmond and Aldous Huxley in 1957; Huxley sent Osmond the following couplet:

> To make this trivial world sublime,
> Take half a Gramme of phanerothyme.

Not satisfied with Huxley's cumbersome term, Osmond responded with what became the countercultural coinage:

> To fathom Hell or soar angelic,
> Just take a pinch of psychedelic.[10]

After synthesizing a batch of LSD-25 (the twenty-fifth variation in his experiments with lysergic acid, while searching for a cure for migraines) on April 16, 1943, and handling (and thereby absorbing) the crystalline compound, Swiss chemist Albert Hofmann experienced "an uninterrupted stream of fantastic images of extraordinary plasticity and vividness and accompanied by an intense kaleidoscopic play of colors."[11] Users might perceive halos and auras surrounding objects, and people and things often seem to shimmer or actually move about, even when stable, leaving visual "trails" or "afterimages." These effects are prone to change quite abruptly in conjunction with modifications in the environmental, social, or emotional atmosphere of the user's situation. Thoughts can flow unusually freely and dreamily, and LSD users often turn reflectively inward. Users may lose their notion of personal identity as their sense of self merges with the world around them, and both time and space are commonly distorted.[12]

Acoustically, these otherwise visual and psychological effects manifest themselves synesthetically in musical forms that rock critic Jim DeRogatis calls "sonic clues." Among these aural psychedelic effects and their musical equivalents, DeRogatis lists the "buzz" with which inanimate objects seem to tremble with energy; the apparent fusion of self with the world ("life flows on within you and without you," as Harrison writes in "Within You Without You"), including its sounds; distortion of time through drifting or abruptly changing tempos; dreamy, circular, or sustained and droning melodies and harmonics; alterations of instrumental and vocal sounds; reverb, echoes, and tape delays that convey an expanded sense of space; and multi-layered mixes that give recordings a heavily textured sound.[13] Similarly, Sheila Whiteley coined the term "psychedelic coding" for the ways in which different styles of progressive rock share techniques that convey a musical equivalent of hallucinogenic experience:

> These include the manipulation of timbre (blurred, bright, overlapping), upward movement (and its comparison with psychedelic flight), harmonies (lurching, oscillating), rhythms (regular, irregular), relationships (foreground, background) and collages which provide a point of comparison with more conventionalized, i.e., normal treatment.[14]

The Wikipedia entry for "psychedelic music" refers to its sonic showcasing of "a wildly colourful palette" and a "magic carpet of sound." John Lennon himself told George Martin that he wished to "smell the sawdust" and wanted the music to "swirl" in "Being for the Benefit of Mr. Kite!"[15] Perhaps this "otherworldly" element in certain instances of Western rock music, especially in the LSD-conscious youth counterculture of the mid- to late 1960s, best characterizes a recording as psychedelic.

The Beatles were not the first rock group to showcase the impact of LSD; their major psychedelic recordings date from the time of LSD's criminalization and its subsequent underground flourishing. Many important psychedelic recordings pre-date *Revolver*. Both the Yardbirds ("Heart Full of Soul") and the Kinks ("See My Friends") experimented with psychedelically evocative sitars and sitar-like sounds in 1965, even prior to George Harrison's use of the instrument on "Norwegian Wood." The Byrds released "Eight Miles High" in 1965, and songs such as Bob Dylan's "Visions of Johanna," Love's "7 and 7 Is," the Beach Boys' "Good Vibrations," and the groundbreaking album *The Psychedelic Sounds of the 13th Floor Elevators*, all appeared in 1966. The Doors' "The Crystal Ship," Moby Grape's "Omaha," and the Jefferson Airplane's *Surrealistic Pillow* beat *Sgt. Pepper* to the shelves in 1967. As Big Brother and the Holding Company guitarist Sam Andrew remarked, it was with the release of *Revolver* that he and other members of the San Francisco music scene "realized that the Beatles had definitely come 'on board.'"[16]

Revolver: the Beatles go psychedelic

Revolver singlehandedly made Beatlemania irrelevant.[17]

The Beatles entered EMI's Studio 3 on April 6, 1966, to begin a project that would revolutionize pop music. During the preceding several weeks, Harrison had intensified his study of Indian music, which he had begun the previous year. Paul McCartney had become an integral part of the "underground" *avant-garde* culture of swinging London and studied the work of experimental composers Luciano Berio and Karlheinz Stockhausen. Lennon had languished at his Weybridge estate throughout much of the winter, though he had also begun to take a greater interest in politics, as well as more LSD.[18] It was chiefly Lennon who introduced psychedelic currents into the Beatles' work, although, as we shall see, Harrison's interest in South Asian sounds and McCartney's dabbling in *musique concrète* had an impact as well.

Lennon brought to that session the outline for an ambitiously "trippy" song to be based on *The Psychedelic Experience*. Lennon's lyrics encouraged listeners to set aside their egos ("Lay down all thought, surrender to the void") and turn inward ("That you may see the meaning of within"). Originally designated "Mark I" (indicating the band's awareness of the pioneering nature of the piece),[19] "Tomorrow Never Knows" is essentially a chant backed by a relentless C-major chord, a static harmony sustained principally by a tamboura played by Harrison, along with tape loops of dense sound that stay strangely in key. Lennon's vocal provides little harmonic variation outside of a passing intonation of B♭ in the fifth measure of each verse (repeated in the coda), accompanied by a ♭VII chord on an organ, which enters the instrumental mix seemingly just for this moment. This sonic droning suggests the meditative state of the psychedelic experience, and the lyrical references to mental relaxation, along with overt invitations to synesthesia and oneiric thought in the line "But listen to the color of your dreams," intensify the effect. The drug "buzz" is invoked not only through Harrison's humming tamboura, but by Starr's compressed and limited drums, which sound full, but peculiarly dulled. Moreover, Starr's accompaniment throughout the piece consists of a kind of stumbling march, providing a bit of temporal disruption, in which the first accent of each bar falls on the measure's first beat and the second stress occurs in the second half of the measure's third quarter, double sixteenth notes in stuttering pre-emption of the normal rhythmic emphasis on the second backbeat – hardly a classic rock and roll gesture.[20]

The new electronic tools at the band's disposal, developed and deployed brilliantly by George Martin and engineer Geoff Emerick, contributed greatly to the innovative psychedelic ambience that would characterize the Beatles' recordings throughout 1966 and 1967. For example, John Lennon wished "to sound like the Dalai Lama chanting from a mountaintop" on "Tomorrow Never Knows." To produce this effect in the studio, the EMI recording staff piped the singer's vocals through a rotating Leslie speaker wired to a Hammond organ.[21] The resulting sonic swirling creates a sense of distance that expands the vocal space of the track, first heard after the song's instrumental break, beginning with "That love is all and love is everyone" in the fourth verse and continuing to the end of the song. Moreover, in the instrumental break we hear the first instance of backward recording, as what was originally a bluesy, C-minor guitar solo played by Harrison is reversed, an effect that not only clips certain notes sharply, but injects the otherwise Western flavor of the song with an Asian feel. A fuzz box and a Leslie speaker enhance the sound of this backward solo. Finally, there are the tape loops. That night McCartney created five "little symphonies" on his home Brennell tape machine. By removing the erase tape heads and recording over and over on the same tape, he supersaturated the sound, giving "Tomorrow Never Knows" its electronic density and otherworldly seagull-like cries, adding an acoustic sureality to the composition.[22] The completed piece showcases nearly all the elements of musical psychedelia that the band employed on its next three albums and that rock musicians have continued exploring.

A review of the psychedelic content of some other Beatles compositions recorded between April and June reveals the extent to which "Tomorrow

Never Knows" informed the rest of the Beatles' work that spring, beginning with the single recorded just a few days after the sessions began. "Paperback Writer," McCartney's A side, is not particularly psychedelic, influenced more by the harmonies on the Beach Boys' recently released *Pet Sounds.* Many Beatles scholars, however, consider the so-called B side of the single, Lennon's "Rain" as the band's first psychedelic record, released on May 23 in the USA and June 10 in the UK.[23] The track is full of technical innovations: limiters, compressors, Leslie speakers, tapes played backwards, and a new trick – vari-speed recording in which Lennon's guitar and Starr's drums were taped faster than what is heard on the final version of the piece and Lennon's vocal was taped slower, then speeded up for the final mix. Everett remarks that the electronically slowed drums and rhythm guitar introduce "a subtle but rich tone of queasy hesitation that could be likened to the nausea of an acid trip" and Lennon's speeded-up vocal reflects the "brilliant iridescence of an acid-streaked sunshine."[24] And the backward vocal that closes the piece became the first instance of reversed recording released to the public.

The theme of "Rain" – rain or shine, the weather makes no difference; "it's just a state of mind" – registers the inwardness of psychedelic experience. As in "Within You Without You," which laments "people who hide themselves behind a wall of illusion" and "never glimpse the truth," "Rain" targets one of the most common subjects of psychedelic criticism: "squares" – those afraid of life and who, as a result, isolate themselves from authentic experience, a situation represented in the song by the meteorological image of rain. Exposing their strategies of avoidance (hiding from rain *and* the sun), Lennon's lyrics suggest the most drastic diagnosis of such escapism: "they might as well be dead," and, as the reversed lyrics at the song's conclusion suggest, such people have it all backwards. The Beatles "don't mind" what kind of weather the day brings because, from their psychedelic perspective, "it's just a state of mind," and "the weather's fine," regardless of rain or shine, a perspective they insist on with lines like "I can show you, I can show you" and "can you hear me, can you hear me," the doubling of each phrase indicating the degree of certainty and the insistence they feel. Jimi Hendrix would later compose his own praise of rainy days for *Electric Ladyland*'s "Rainy Day Dream Away," intoning: "Rainy day, rain all day / Ain't no use in gettin' uptight . . . Lay back and dream on a rainy day."

The first side of the 1966 album *Revolver* (released on August 5 in the UK and August 8 in the USA) opens with Harrison's "Taxman," in which the singer's compressed voice counts off a mysterious (and metrically misleading) "one-two-three-four-one-two" with off-mike studio buzz behind him. The vaguely Indian tones of McCartney's distorted guitar solos, one immediately after the bridge and one in the song's fade-out, add psychedelic flavor to the piece.[25] Sonically, McCartney's "Eleanor Rigby" is hardly psychedelic, though its minimal harmonic variation and the Leslie speaker used for the singer's backing counter-melody in the last refrain reinforce the reflective mood of the piece. Lennon's "I'm Only Sleeping" features an intensely psychedelic sound, echoing "Rain" and anticipating "Tomorrow Never Knows" thematically and musically. As in "Rain," the instrumental parts were recorded higher and Lennon's vocals lower than what we hear in the finished piece. As in both "Tomorrow Never Knows" and "Rain," the band used reversed taping in "I'm Only Sleeping" – this time, with two of Harrison's overdubbed guitar parts, which first appear in the fifth measure of the second verse and intensify in the coda.[26]

The Indian instrumentation in Harrison's "Love You To," especially its languid opening strums, transports a Western audience to a world that is ancient and exotic. The lack of a clearly measured tempo in the song's overture sets musical and, in this particular context, spiritual time adrift – until the tune kicks into gear and the singer observes that "Each day just goes so fast" and "A lifetime is so short." The song's sparse chord structure, consisting of only I and ♭VII (as in "Tomorrow Never Knows"), adds a meditative harmonic coloring to the drone of the tamboura.[27] Except for the relaxed, time-bending tempo of the introduction, there are no overt psychedelic elements in McCartney's "Here, There and Everywhere." McCartney's lush ballad almost seems out of place on the otherwise experimental *Revolver*, but, perhaps because of this, adds to the record's overall atmospheric diversity, another hallmark of psychedelic albums. So too may McCartney's "Yellow Submarine," if it weren't for the band's incorporation of vari-speed technique for the instruments and vocals, echoing off-mike shouting by Lennon, and a panoply of clinking and rattling sound effects made by everyone who happened to be in the studio in the wee hours of June 1, 1966.[28] "She Said She Said," the track that concludes the A side of the *Revolver* LP, is another Lennon composition with an inward-looking, metaphysical theme. More than just acid talk, however, "She Said She Said" also approximates musically several typical effects of the drug. As Everett observes, Lennon's speeded-up vocal, Starr's frequent use of the crash cymbal, and Harrison's distorted lead guitar intensify "the vividness of [musical] colors and glow of light" on this track. The shift from 4/4 to 3/4 meter in the bridge – a move to another "time," both in terms of musical rhythm and the thematic evocation of childhood memories – "may suggest the mystical, dreamlike changes in perceptions of environment and time experienced among the subjective effects of LSD."[29] Harrison's occasional repetition of Lennon's vocal line at a measure's remove creates acoustic reverberations or "trails." Moreover, "the droning cyclical I – ♭VII – IV – I harmonic pattern is a further type of repetition that may be related to the timeless quality of both an LSD trip and the mantra-based meditation in Indian practice."[30]

Sgt. Pepper and *Magical Mystery Tour*: the Beatles go over the top

> JOHN: Where are we going, fellas?
> OTHER BEATLES: To the toppermost of the poppermost![31]

Though their next album, *Sgt. Pepper's Lonely Hearts Club Band*, was significantly more popular, critics have since gradually begun to acknowledge the importance of *Revolver* as the most significant advance in the Beatles' work.[32] In any case, most critics and fans agree that the Beatles reached their creative apogee at some point between the spring of 1966 and the spring of 1967 and that the band's innovative impact, the overall quality of their work, and the Beatles' influence on contemporary and later generations of rock musicians began to decline thereafter – that is, with the summer and fall singles of 1967 and with *Magical Mystery Tour*. Once again, a remarkable single previewed the themes and sounds of the forthcoming album. In December 1966, after another substantial break during which the Beatles rested or pursued individual projects, the band began work on a song that reflected memories from Lennon's childhood, "Strawberry Fields Forever." The opening electronic, flute-like melody, played by McCartney on a Mellotron, assures us that the band had not abandoned its preoccupation with psychedelic sounds and themes. In "Strawberry Fields," they continued to push EMI's four-track recording technology to its limit through tape reductions and numerous overdubs. In addition to the Mellotron, Harrison brought the exotic sound of a reverb-heavy svaramandal to the recording, and Martin and Emerick perfected the vari-speed technique to such a point that they were able to splice recordings from two separate takes in two different keys (!) by slowing down one take and speeding up the other (the splice occurs approximately 60 seconds into the song).[33]

The pervasive lyrical theme of dreams versus reality indicates that Lennon had not abandoned the introspective quest begun in "Tomorrow Never Knows" and his other compositions for *Revolver*. "Being for the Benefit of Mr. Kite!," for example, filters actual circus poster copy through the Beatles' whirlwind of sounds, taking on a dreamlike (perhaps nightmarish) quality as a result. McCartney's "Penny Lane" is another song derived from childhood memories of Liverpool, and, as in Lennon's composition, McCartney toys with the everyday reality of his images – the pretty, poppy-selling nurse who "feels as if she's in a play" and "is anyway," for example. In "Penny Lane," the composer sought a "clean sound" (in contrast to

Lennon's murky tones),[34] though to achieve this aim Martin and Emerick used the vari-speed technique to speed up McCartney's vocal, giving his delivery the sharp iridescence heard on the final recording. Lennon plays limited and slowed-down congas on the piece, and the heavy, electronically enhanced reverberation of one of the song's four pianos adds a "stylized foggy" tone to the chorus and the piece's final chord.[35]

A single glance at Peter Blake's cover art for *Sgt. Pepper's Lonely Hearts Club Band* alerts the listener to the fact that the enclosed record will be heavily psychedelic. Although the conceits meant to characterize this album and the Beatles' next collection of songs (the surrogate band in *Pepper* and the mystery tour in *Magical Mystery Tour*) were essentially McCartney's ideas,[36] the most psychedelic compositions during this period, as was the case with *Revolver*, came from Harrison and Lennon – though a certain amount of electronic wizardry was applied to McCartney's "Getting Better" and "Fixing a Hole," and to perhaps his most psychedelic effort ever, "Lovely Rita." Lennon's "Lucy in the Sky with Diamonds," "Being for the Benefit of Mr. Kite!" and "Good Morning Good Morning," along with Harrison's "Within You Without You" represent the tracks of greatest psychedelic interest on the album – apart, of course, from "A Day in the Life."

Even before the final touches had been added to *Sgt. Pepper*, McCartney had the idea for the band's next project: a film inspired by Ken Kesey and the Merry Pranksters' psychedelic bus trip across the United States. Songs for this film, along with material destined for the psychedelic cartoon *Yellow Submarine*, were recorded throughout 1967. As early as February, in fact, the band completed Harrison's "Only a Northern Song," a reject from *Sgt. Pepper* that the Beatles later handed over for use in *Yellow Submarine*. In May, they recorded another of Harrison's compositions, "It's All Too Much," also used for *Yellow Submarine*. The dense layering, with overdubs and tape loops, lends both songs a psychedelic flavor. Harrison based his "It's All Too Much" on "realizations that appeared during and after some LSD experiences, which were later confirmed in meditation."[37] "All You Need Is Love" was written for performance in *Our World*. Backing its subsequent release as a single was the Lennon-McCartney collaboration, "Baby You're a Rich Man," featuring Lennon on the clavioline, an unusual double reed instrument which introduced Indian melodic colors to the piece, and McCartney on piano, taped backwards for parts of the third verse.

In their music for *Magical Mystery Tour*, the Beatles continued to incorporate psychedelic themes and effects, without introducing any strikingly new sounds or innovations to their musical catalog. The chorus of the title song, in fact, uses the same I–♭III–IV–I chord progression that we hear in the title track of *Sgt. Pepper's Lonely Hearts Club Band.* The Beatles also incorporate a Leslie speaker for Harrison's lead guitar, a tape loop of bus and traffic sounds, and speeded-up backing vocals and trumpets into this piece.[38] The vari-speed technique is also used in McCartney's "The Fool on the Hill" (to speed up the chattering bird-like sounds heard at the very end of the song) and "Hello, Goodbye" (to speed up the lead vocal, giving them the "clean" sound the composer often strove to achieve during this period).[39] The band uses a droning organ and reversed backing vocals in Harrison's "Blue Jay Way" and, as Everett points out, the song's "unusual Lydian scale altered with an occasional ♭3" gives the melody an Indian quality.[40]

In late 1967 and early 1968, the Beatles once again turned to solo projects and began organizational work for Apple Corps, Ltd., their doomed multimedia business venture. In February, 1968, the four set off for a retreat with the Maharishi Mahesh Yogi in India, whom they had met the previous August in the UK. When they returned, fully stocked with new material, Lennon, McCartney, and Harrison began to work much more independently of one another in the studio, ultimately sacrificing the cohesive sound of the band's earlier work. In retrospect, then, the Beatles clearly peaked during their psychedelic period, having fully transformed themselves from the tight rock and roll band of the Hamburg years into a group who embraced, echoed, and shaped the *Zeitgeist* of the early to mid-1960s better than other composers and performers of that era, and finally into masters of the recording studio, who produced a body of psychedelic work that has stood for decades as the epitome of pop music innovation and influence.

LSD and the Beatles' peak

> We must always remember to thank the CIA and the Army for LSD . . . They invented LSD to control people and what they did was give us freedom.[41]

In addition to the extensive use of electronic gadgetry and effects, the Beatles turned to more reflective and occasionally surreal lyrical content during this period. It's almost a cliché to trace the Beatles' development from "I Want to Hold Your Hand" to "I'd love to turn you on." Psychedelic lyricism did, in fact, generate a vision infinitely more interested in matters of the intellect, the spirit, ecstatic merging, hallucinatory clarity, meditative innerness, even the fate of the species, than surfing or stolen kisses in souped-up hot rods. They no longer asked coy questions like "Do You Want to Know a Secret"; rather they recorded communiqués and directives. Beginning with tracks like "I Want to Tell You," "Rain," and "Within You Without You," the Beatles adopted an urgent tone, intent on channeling some essential knowledge, the psychological and/or philosophical epiphanies of LSD experiences, to an increasingly turned-on fan base: "I want to tell you / My head is filled with things to say." As Czech LSD researcher Dr. Stanislav Grof characterizes this phenomenon:

> In addition, an increasing number of reports seemed to suggest that sometimes a single administration of LSD could have a deep influence on the personality structure of the subject, his or her hierarchy of values, basic attitudes, and entire life style. The changes were so dramatic that they were compared with psychological conversions.[42]

In some respects, British psychiatrist and LSD pioneer R. D. Laing set the tone for such imperatives in the "Bird of Paradise" conclusion to his revolutionary *The Politics of Experience*, published in January 1967. Laing echoes Timothy Leary and anticipates "A Day in the Life" as he concludes that volume: "If I could turn you on, if I could drive you out of your wretched mind, if I could tell you, I would let you know."[43] In his autobiography, discussed earlier, Leary registers such thinking with the following plays on "Sgt. Pepper's Lonely Hearts Club Band":

> So may I introduce to you . . .
> The fact you've known for all these years . . .
> He don't really want to top the show
> But I thought that you might like to know
> That the singer's going to write a wrong.[44]

Laing and Leary advance the idea, common among enthusiasts, that the LSD experience granted the user a new take on reality, one capable of revealing facts and righting the wrongs perpetrated by a culture inured to bourgeois values and ordinary perceptions. Indeed, it is this dimension of the psychedelic experience that characterizes some of the Beatles' most psychedelic pronouncements of this phase. The Kaleidoscope's "I Found Out" is a representative example of this subgenre: "I found out without a doubt what it's all about / And now I know in my soul just where to go." As in McCartney's "Got to Get You Into My Life" and its emphatic horns and vocals, absolute certainty expressed with rhetorical hyperbole usually characterizes such songs.

Indeed, the Beatles "want to tell" us something new, something urgent, and, in so doing, set the stage for an important subgenre of psychedelic music, that of the messianic pronouncement. They articulate similar modes of social criticism throughout their psychedelic phase, either bemoaning or exposing "all the lonely people" ("Eleanor Rigby"), those who make "me feel like I've never been born" (She Said She Said"), those who fill them "up with [their] rules" ("It's Getting Better"), and those who need to stare at traffic fatalities and to count the "holes in Blackburn, Lancashire" ("A Day in the Life"). In "I'm Only Sleeping," Lennon bemoans the lives of those "Running everywhere at such a speed" and beseeches them not to "spoil [his] day" with the frantic pace at which they live their lives, a line of reasoning he returns to in the first line of "Tomorrow Never Knows": "Turn off your mind, *relax*, and float downstream" (emphasis added). McCartney mounts this same critique in *Sgt. Pepper's Lonely Hearts Club Band*, when, in "Fixing a Hole," he lashes out at the "silly people" who run around and worry him and whom he doesn't let "get past [his] door." This rejection of haste and the frantic pace of ordinary life, along with a vision of bemused equanimity, partially reflects the growing influence of Asian forms of spirituality on psychedelic culture generally.

The Beatles' critique of materialism also reflects the psychedelic vision of society. Of course, such a critique pre-dates psychedelic culture, ranging from the biblical "It is easier for a camel to pass through the eye of a needle, than for a rich man to enter the kingdom of God" (Matthew 19:24) to Henry David Thoreau's condemnations of those entrapped in materialism and leading lives of "quiet desperation." The Beatles and many groups after them returned to these notions with new levels of intensity and seriousness, fueled in large part by their LSD experiences. Aside from "Taxman," which, paradoxically, bewails the tax burden of increasingly rich rock stars, the Beatles consistently dismantle the premises and effects of materialism, examining its many facets. In "Love You To," Harrison offers to "make love to you" as an alternative to being screwed in the ground and having one's head filled with "things." Harrison's notion of being screwed in the ground can also be taken not only to suggest the colloquial "being screwed," or even symbolic burial, but to indicate that being screwed into the muck of earthly existence inhibits one's quest for transcendence. *Revolver*'s "Yellow Submarine" picks up on the same theme in its anti-materialist tone. The crew lives "a life of ease" because everyone has "all [they] need," but such desires are fulfilled not by money or goods, but rather by the simple "sky of blue and sea of green." The song's exuberant chorus testifies to the simple pleasures of brotherhood, exotic adventure, and an appreciation of nature, the latter of which also characterizes "Good Day Sunshine" and its own melodic embrace of a beautiful day.

In "And Your Bird Can Sing" the Beatles counter various symbols of consumeristic pleasure with simple directness. The song's antagonist might have everything and might have seen everything ("You say you've seen seven wonders"), but eventually, the Beatles suggest, "your prized possessions start to wear you down." Moreover, even in the midst of the affluence suggested by the song, the one who has all and who has seen all can neither see nor hear the song's "me," a diminishment of whatever satisfaction the other might have. The lines "But you don't get me," "But you can't see me," and "But you can't hear me" each follow some claim to "richness," and are all doubled ("But you can't see me, you can't see me," etc.), intensifying the existential poverty. The Beatles return to this critique in "Baby You're a Rich Man," with its repeated lines "You keep all your money in a big brown bag inside a zoo / What a thing to do," mocking the lunacy and perhaps even subhuman nature of such crude hoarding behaviors. "She's Leaving Home," in which the young woman's parents, even in the midst of their sorrow, expose their absolute conviction in the power of money and things, expresses this critique quite movingly. The parents can't imagine their daughter leaving so affluent a home, a perspective made more absurd by virtue of the dialogical dramatization of the girl's actions and the parents' lament:

> She (we gave her most of our lives)
> Is leaving (sacrificed most of our lives)
> Home (we gave her everything money could buy)

That song's final punning of "buy" with "bye" highlights the dead end of materialism and the values of a generation that has outlived its relevance, a sense of obsolescence conveyed by the elegance of the musical score for harp and string quartet. The sound is beautiful, to be sure, and certainly an appropriate contribution to *Sgt. Pepper*'s kaleidoscopic pallet, but hardly in touch with the musical adventurism of the album or the iconic Carnaby Street ethos. It represents the parents' point of view, one of loss and confusion.

Psychedelic journeys within and without

> "I was alone, I took a ride
> I didn't know what I would find there"   "Got to Get You Into My Life"

With "Yellow Submarine" (the song and the film), the Beatles introduce a new and important thematic element into their work of the psychedelic era. In fact, one of the differences between the group's earlier work and that of the psychedelic phase can be glimpsed in their songs about psychedelic "tripping," represented as various forms of traveling, from the literal to fantastical images of hallucinatory vividness and strangeness. The Beatles evolve from songs like "Drive My Car" and "Ticket to Ride," and lines like "I been told when a boy kiss a girl / Take a trip around the world" ("Boys"), to compositions like "Tomorrow Never Knows," "Lucy in the Sky with Diamonds," "Magical Mystery Tour," the soaring instrumental

"Flying," and, later, "Across the Universe," all of which feature varieties of psychedelic "tripping." Both "Tomorrow Never Knows" and "Lucy in the Sky with Diamonds" recount ventures into introspective realms, often with epiphanic results. "Tomorrow Never Knows" begins, of course, with Lennon's paraphrase of Leary, Metzner, and Alpert's psychedelic manual, "Turn off your mind, relax, and float upstream," an odd invocation considering the song has almost no movement, lyrically or musically. "Lucy in the Sky with Diamonds" opens with the directive to "Picture yourself in a boat on a river / With tangerine trees and marmalade skies" and adds even stranger modes of transportation like "newspaper taxis" and train stations where "plasticine porters with looking glass ties" tote your luggage. Such attention to vivid detail also characterizes many LSD test subjects. One such account in Sidney Cohen's *The Beyond Within* anticipates the Beatles' work in "Lucy": "Time. Each second separated by infinity. The Camera has stopped, and the world is caught in a silly snapshot pose."[45] In fact, the rainbow of psychedelic travel possibilities in "Lucy" (all only "pictured" in one's head to begin with), along with its multi-colored visual tableaux ("kaleidoscope eyes," "tangerine trees," and "marmalade skies") do suggest something akin to postcards sent home from a psychedelic journey. Moreover, the effects of Lennon's voice in "Lucy" suggest that of a seductive guide on an otherworldly excursion. The sound is technically enhanced using vari-speed and echo, producing at times a "helium-light" delivery,[46] as well as dreamily floating emphasis on the word "Ah" and the phrase "incredibly high." Such an alluring presentation looks forward to Miss Wendy Winters, the sexy tour hostess from the film *Magical Mystery Tour*, and the lyrics also reference the street slang of an LSD dealer as a "travel agent," providing the potential tripper with a chemical passport to one's inner latitudes. Such rhetoric also commonly characterized the liner notes and promotional copy for the marketing of psychedelic albums. Consider the following tantalizer for Rotary Connection's first album: "Turn yourself on with a diamond needle . . . travel with us in your favorite color."[47]

In even their most ordinary realizations of the idea, the Beatles imagine traveling via forms of transportation that strain at literal credibility, though yellow submarines, after all, may not have been so unusual. Hollywood heartthrob Cary Grant rode in a pink one in the 1959 film *Operation Petticoat*, made during his own extensive LSD psychotherapeutic regimen that included over sixty LSD therapy sessions.[48] Ringo, of course, sings about alternative lives of joy and natural beauty all experienced communally from the ocean depths. Later psychedelic artists expanded on the motif in songs like the Doors' "Crystal Ship," the Beach Boys' "Sloop John B," Jimi Hendrix's "1983, A Merman I Should Turn to Be," and Yes's monumental

Tales from Topographic Oceans. All these songs, like the sound of waves in Otis Redding's "Dock of the Bay," exploit the fluidity and strangeness of oceanic voyaging, and, as in "Rain," watery immersions of all sorts, as appropriate metaphors for the LSD experience. As George sings, "life *flows* on within you and without you."

Expressing the psychedelic motif of metaphorical journeying, the Beatles take numerous "trips" with yellow submarines, newspaper taxis, and magical mystery tours. Albert Hofmann's famous ride home on his white bicycle after discovering LSD-25 set the tone for numerous musical celebrations of traveling (or "tripping") and its resulting inner transformations. The Byrds' "Eight Miles High," Pink Floyd's "Interstellar Overdrive," the Rolling Stones' "10,000 Light Years from Home," Kaleidoscope's "Flight from Ashiya," Steppenwolf's "Magic Carpet Ride," the 13th Floor Elevators' "Roller Coaster," and the Mirror's "Faster than Light" all pay tribute to the psychedelic inner journey, as do Jimi Hendrix's travels by dragonfly and on eagles' wings ("Spanish Castle Magic" and "Voodoo Child"). Of course, their "Magical Mystery Tour" guaranteed "the trip of a lifetime" to anyone who joined them on their bus tour through the English countryside. The travel agent at that film's beginning notes: "When a man buys a ticket for a magical mystery tour, he knows what to expect. We guarantee him the trip of a lifetime, and that's just what he gets."[49] The motif also forms the basis of the criticism of the "beautiful people" mocked in "Baby You're a Rich Man," those who have traveled only "as far as the eye can see" and, when they arrived, saw "nothing that doesn't show," both indicating the limitations of their conventionalism.

The Beatles also approach "the trip" as a way of traveling through time. As Paul sings, "Penny Lane is in my ears and in my eyes"; in other words, like "rain," a state of mind. "Eleanor Rigby," and, to a lesser extent, the later "She's Leaving Home" take us back to the classical ambiences of an earlier era by virtue of their string arrangements (they are also two of the four songs on which no Beatle plays an instrument); and "Love You To," "Within You Without You," and 1968's "The Inner Light" all sample Asian sounds of great antiquity, almost like stepping back through time and space. Like *Revolver*'s "She Said She Said," "Strawberry Fields" and "Penny Lane" represent nostalgic visitations to moments and places of childhood innocence or strangeness, with quirky bankers and firemen occupying landscapes where, as John Lennon sang, "nothing is real." Moreover, even the disturbing images and bizarre sonic effects of "Being for the Benefit of Mr. Kite!" don't obscure the song's focus on a traditional family entertainment from a bygone day, albeit one reimagined as a place where "everything is surreal." Such time traveling becomes a staple of psychedelic lyricism, and figures prominently in Pink Floyd's corpus and in such classics as Neil Young's "Sugar

Mountain" and Donovan's "Atlantis." Psychedelia also renewed interest in traditional English folk music, especially in groups such as Pentangle, Fairport Convention, Lindisfarne, and the experimental Incredible String Band. This trippy nostalgia is invoked through suggestions of mysticism and antiquity: lush, exotic harmonies, and instrumentation (which often dabbled in Asian exoticism with tablas and sitar sounds). Beatles tunes like the campy "Your Mother Should Know," "Octopus's Garden," and "Oh! Darling," with their samplings of earlier musical styles, round out the most common themes of psychedelic nostalgia. We could, of course, regard the entire *Sgt. Pepper's Lonely Hearts Club Band* concept, the narrative tenor of the animated film *Yellow Submarine,* and the general silliness of the *Magical Mystery Tour* escapades (including the Bonzo Dog Band's performance of the archly ironic and anachronistic "Death Cab for Cutie" in the cabaret scene) as being in this category as well. The Beatles add complexity and wit to this ensemble of songs by having their guru-like figure, "The Fool on the Hill" who, though "well on his way" with his "head in a cloud," paradoxically spends his life "sitting perfectly still." In a contemporary expansion of this theme, the most musically and visually thrilling segment of the Cirque du Soleil's 2006 production *Love,* a dazzling tribute to the music and legacy of the Beatles (imagined by George Harrison and produced by Sir George Martin and son, Giles Martin), "mashes" together "Within You Without You" with "Tomorrow Never Knows" and features a group of children in nightgowns sitting on a bed that appears to be flying through the theater until the bed disappears and the billowing, white, cloud-like fabric on which they had been traveling disappears into the stage in a tornadic swirl. *That* is psychedelic.

Psychedelic music frequently complements such versions of thematic traveling through space and/or time by experimenting with notions of time through unexpectedly shifting meters and noddingly relaxed pacing (*tempo rubato*), as well as electronically slowed or accelerated recording techniques. Fourteen of the forty-four tracks recorded and released during the Beatles' psychedelic period (including those new numbers included on the *Yellow Submarine* soundtrack in 1968), or some 30 percent of this material, manifest one of these metric characteristics, and, as we've already noted, the Beatles were fond of the EMI engineers' experimentation with vari-speed. Cam Cloud suggests that "the passage of time seems to slow down tremendously when under the influence of acid.... At the peak of a very powerful trip it may seem as if time has come to a complete stop, plunging the tripper into a timeless, eternal realm."[50] And, as one of the subjects interviewed for Cohen's still influential study, *The Beyond Within,* puts it, "Centuries were lived, yet the minute hand of the watch barely moved. My Rorschach took 200 light years, the longest on record."[51]

Harrison tugs at the limits of this phenomenon in his "Blue Jay Way." The composition's repetitious refrain of "please don't be long . . . don't be long" is saturated with artificial double tracking, or ADT (in which double-tracked vocals are presented just a touch out of sync), reversed tapes, and phasing, those modes of electronic psychedelic rhetoric that seem to stretch and bend the very fabric of time into a web of anguished expectation. Harrison's sonic experiments plumb the nature of time itself, offering, in the process, aural approximations of the subjective experience of duration.

Although the hallucinogenic imagery of Lennon's "I Am the Walrus" doesn't deal expressly with time, the musicality of the number's treatment of time is dark and threatening. Madow and Sobul have remarked that the "slow, methodical . . . cello seeps like molasses into the right channel, miring us in a slow swirling ooze."[52] The surreal lyrics of "Walrus" give further evidence of the composer's interest during this period both in nonsensical wordplay and in reflective questioning of one's own identity (recalling "She Said She Said" and "Strawberry Fields Forever"), possibly a symptom of drug-induced paranoia, given the sinister coloring of this track. Extensive tape reduction to accommodate multiple dubs, along with Lennon's distorted vocal, are among the sonic clues that give this piece its psychedelic sound – not to mention the unusual melodic and harmonic progressions in the song.[53]

And in the end, "All You Need is Love"

The sentiments and celebrations of the "summer of love" pervade the rhetoric of the era, and new possibilities for the power of love blossomed across Europe and North America. Ranging from the desperate and loveless landscapes of "Taxman," "Eleanor Rigby," and "A Day in the Life" to the anthemic tribute of "All You Need is Love," the Beatles explore the many faces of love, few of them resembling devotionals to the possibilities of love imagined earlier in the rock era, in which drive-in movies, back seats of cars, and lovers panting "I Think We're Alone Now" defined the genre. For the Beatles and for millions of others, love and LSD went hand in hand during the late 1960s. At the same time that the Beatles were recording *Revolver* and *Sgt. Pepper's Lonely Hearts Club Band*, pseudo-sociological studies like *The Sexual Paradise of LSD* (1967) and *LSD on Campus* (1966) provided lurid accounts of LSD-fueled orgies and rampant sexual experimentation; and an entire subgenre of pornographic fiction emerged, churning out titles like *Sex Happy Hippie* ("Take a trip with Trippy, the sex happy hippie!") (1968).[54] The now infamous G. Gordon Liddy, then a prosecutor in Duchess County, New York, and his task force of sheriff's deputies, staked out Timothy Leary's communal Millbrook estate, having heard that "at Leary's lair the panties were dropping as fast as the acid."[55] When, early one morning in 1966, their binoculars detected a film being shown within the mansion, they decided to raid it, fully expecting to discover "a citadel of smut as well as a den of dopers." They were crushed to discover a group of relaxed people enjoying a waterfall projected on the wall.[56] Not that LSD and sex didn't prove an explosive combination, but this unconventional "love fest" sets the tone for the ways the Beatles (and much psychedelic music) examine, and usually celebrate, love.

Many of the songs of the psychedelic era investigate individuals, their thoughts and conditions: "I'm Only Sleeping," "I Want to Tell You," "Tomorrow Never Knows," "Fixing a Hole," "A Day in the Life," and others. Conventional love songs still punctuate the repertoire, such as "Good Day Sunshine," songs of lost love, like "For No One," and even the tense overtures of on-the-make songs like "Lovely Rita." Other love songs, however, strain at the genre's conventions. Both "With a Little Help from My Friends" and "When I'm Sixty-Four" address being loved and accepted in a slightly whimsical way, but both also insinuate an undercurrent of insecurity. The singer echoes the Jefferson Airplane's "Somebody to Love" when he responds to questions like "What do I do when my love is away" with answers like "I just need somebody to love" and "I want somebody to love." Rather than depending intensely on one person, though, the songs emphasize a communal sense of getting help from one's friends, a sentiment first expressed in "Yellow Submarine," with its lyrical celebration that "And our friends are all on board / Many more of them live next door" and the satiated assurance that "Everyone of us has all we need." In fact, the joyously repeated "We all live in a yellow submarine" simultaneously affirms life and communal love. Even the gerontological domestic idyll suggested by "When I'm Sixty-Four" hints at the insecurities of aging with a loved one. The speaker genuinely wonders if "she" will need him and feed him when he's old, and he reminds her that he might come in "handy mending a fuse," quite possibly an allusion to maintaining their "fusion" as a happy couple.

More consistent with the tradition of psychedelic lyricism, the Beatles also penned songs in which love figures more as metaphorical or symbolic union, not necessarily of two people romantically involved. While the "you" in "Got to Get You Into My Life" suggests that McCartney is writing just another "silly love song," the song's introductory quatrain introduces an entirely different possibility. McCartney and Lennon recalled that "Got to Get You Into My Life" was a tribute to McCartney's early drug experiences, but they differ on whether the "you" in the song refers to marijuana or LSD.[57]

> I was alone, I took a ride
> I didn't know what I would find there
> Another road where maybe I could see
> Maybe another kind of mind there.

Indeed, this "ride" taken with the possibility of finding "another kind of mind" comports nicely with other songs in which the hypothetical "she" of the poem is actually a drug-induced ecstasy, Eric Burdon and the Animals' "Girl Named Sandoz," with Sandoz referring to the Swiss pharmaceutical company that manufactured LSD-25 rather than a woman, being a noteworthy examples. So, the dazzling beauty of the hypothetical "girl" in the songs actually refers to the hallucinatory effects of psychedelic experience.

Along these same lines, several of the Beatles' most engaging and far-reaching "love" songs, especially those penned by George Harrison, address the concept/emotion from a spiritual and philosophical perspective. While the singer of "Love You To" does express willingness to "make love to you," the lyrics focus more on love as a way of life, a redemption from the frenzy of daily living, a sentiment returned to in Lennon's "I'm Only Sleeping" ("Running everywhere at such a speed / Till they find there's no need") and McCartney's "Fixing a Hole" ("Silly people run around they worry me"). "Each day just goes so fast," the singer bemoans, and "A lifetime is so short," certainly beyond any material or commercial value. In addition to these existential pressures, other active, more sinister, problems face us:

> There's people standing round
> Who screw you in the ground
> They'll fill your head with all the things you see.

Like the lovers in Bruce Cockburn's "Lovers in a Dangerous Time," these are two people against a hostile world, and all they can do is "make love all day long" and "make love singing songs," their only recourse in an otherwise loveless and chaotic world.

Harrison's "Within You Without You" returns to the issues of "Love You To," and expresses the new extent of his Hindu-influenced thinking. Equally critical of illusions of the material world and celebratory of psychedelic visions of love, "Within You Without You" begins with a meditation on separateness and alienation ("We were talking about the space between us all"). Harrison drives deeper into the implications of and solutions to such a state. The symptoms of detachment and illusion are living behind a veil, having one's love go cold, and an obsession with materialism. The solution, "all you need," we might say, is love, variously imagined, most powerfully as a cosmic force.

> We were talking about the love we all could share when we find it
> To try our best to hold it there with our love
> With our love we could save the world.

The song's title and reassuring refrain, that "life flows on within you and without you," is another way of conceptualizing love, the life force whose circulation fuses self with others, self with cosmos, self with redemption. Harrison's later "Long, Long, Long" is probably the epitome of this genre, fusing and confusing, as it does, the plausible love for a woman with what Ian MacDonald beautifully refers to as a "touching token of exhausted, relieved, reconciliation with God."[58]

We find the most hyperbolic tributes to love in "Tomorrow Never Knows" and, of course, "All You Need is Love." In fact, the three albums we're considering begin with the sterility of "Taxman" and "Eleanor Rigby," only to end with the affirmations of "All You Need is Love," perhaps representing the most significant "trip" the Beatles ever took. On June 25, 1967, just weeks after the release of *Sgt. Pepper's Lonely Hearts Club Band*, the live broadcast of the Beatles and many famous friends singing "All You Need is Love" in the first ever global live television link reached an estimated 350 million people in twenty-six countries, the largest television audience up to that date in history. As the culmination of the Beatles' explicitly psychedelic phase, the song is remarkably conventional (except for the verses in 7/4 meter) and almost anachronistic, compared to the experimental and bracing instrumentation and electronic effects that characterize *Revolver*, *Sgt. Pepper's Lonely Hearts Club Band*, and *Magical Mystery Tour*. Known, of course, for its refrain, "All You Need is Love" advances the most hyperbolic and insistent message in the entire Beatles corpus. It is a song of extreme statements; nothing is tempered or modulated.

> There's *nothing* you can do that can't be done.
> *Nothing* you can sing that can't be sung
> *Nothing* you can say but you can learn how to play the game.
> It's easy.[59]

"Nothings," "no ones," "nowheres," "alls," "all togethers," and "everybodys" pervade the song, culminating in the final reversals of "All you need is love" and "love is all you need." Given the drift of the anti-materialist message common to the Beatles' psychedelic recordings, we might even guess that the many "nothings" in the song also suggest that happiness and love depend on "no thing," rather than the material comforts provided by the parents of "She's Leaving Home" and criticized in "And Your Bird Can Sing," "Within You Without You," "Baby You're a Rich Man," and more. Ironic, to be sure, coming from the increasingly rich and powerful Beatles, but a message fully consistent with the spiritual and psychedelic values they had all been cultivating during the years of 1966 and 1967, and a fitting coda to the lines of thought initiated on *Revolver*. As Lennon sings in "Tomorrow Never Knows," anticipating Harrison's lyrics to "Within You Without You" and "All You Need is Love," "Love is all and love is everyone / It is knowing, it is knowing." Taken together, then, love is life, love is knowing, love can save the world. Of course, Lennon's conclusion to *Revolver* begins with his paraphrase of lines from Leary's *Psychedelic Manual*, lines and a book which figure in one of the most beautiful scenes from the annals of psychedelic history, one that recontextualizes the psychedelic engagement with love in a non-sexual way.

The Beatles' tribute to love registers much of the optimism of the "love generation" and the so-called "Summer of Love," of course, but it also echoes in rhetoric and emotion one of the most beautiful stories in psychedelic history, one also prepared for by their own "Tomorrow Never Knows" and its source, Timothy Leary's *Psychedelic Manual*, based on the *Tibetan Book of the Dead*, guidebooks for transitioning into symbolic and literal rebirths respectively. On November 22, 1963, LSD pioneer and eminent theoretician, Aldous Huxley, lay on his deathbed, succumbing to cancer of the throat. At Huxley's request, his wife, Laura, injected him with 250 mg of LSD. She reports that, almost immediately, an "immense expression of complete bliss and love" come over the dying writer's face, and she whispered to him:

> Light and free you let go, darling, forward and up . . . you are going toward the light . . . . You are going toward a greater love than you have ever known. You are going toward the best, the greatest love, and it is easy . . . and you are doing it so beautifully.[60]

Another equally remarkable account, Malden Grange Bishop's autobiography, appropriately titled *The Discovery of Love: A Psychedelic Experience with LSD-25*, documents how an ordinary, middle-aged businessman has his entire conception of love transformed by a single experience. When looking at photos of his wife during his trip, Bishop perceives that "there was a bright, radiant glow about Anniel's face. I had never seen it so clearly before. She was filled with love, yet she was waiting for me to give the signal to let her come in with her great love. I was overwhelmed."[61] Bishop concludes his exploration of love with the following tribute, which anticipates all of the Beatles' (and many of Motown's) celebrations of love by half a decade:

> Love is the most powerful force in the universe. There is no problem love cannot solve. There is no mountain too high, no stone too hard. Love is the only force which can save mankind from the inevitable destruction of hate. There can be no thermonuclear war where there is love. There can be no

poverty where there is love. There can be no lines of color, of creed, of nationality where there is love. There can be no misery, filth, hate, pain where there is love. This is all so simple, so plain, that it seems incredible that man in this so-called modern age of the 20th Century does not understand it.[62]

The Beatles' songs capture precisely these assurances, this gentleness, this absolute embrace of love, light, and transcendence in their own lyrics, especially through sheer repetition (recall the similarly repetitious mantra whispered by Laura Huxley to her dying husband). "All," "everybody," "all together now": these and other affirmations of communal purpose and psychedelic certitude anchor much of the spirit of the era. As Bishop might have said, "All You Need is Love"! And as the Beatles sang near their own end:

And in the end, the love you take
Is equal to the love you make.

6 Revolution

IAN INGLIS

After five years of uninterrupted success, in which their achievements as composers, recording artists, and performers had attracted unprecedented levels of attention and acclaim, the Beatles entered 1968 in somewhat uncertain mood. Delighted with the critical impact of *Sgt. Pepper*, confused by the consequences of Brian Epstein's death, startled at the overwhelmingly negative reactions to *Magical Mystery Tour*, and separated through their growing involvements in a number of (often film-related) projects,[1] the group – for the first time in their career – seemed to have temporarily mislaid the sense of direction and purpose that had previously distinguished it. This lack of unity gradually became so apparent that it became the defining characteristic of the Beatles' music throughout 1968.

While it was always true that historical and cultural conditions helped to implicitly shape the Beatles' output, the dramatic and divisive events of 1968 created a political context of fragmentation, argument, disunity, confrontation, and disillusionment, which inevitably – and explicitly – found its way into their music. These events included US escalation of the war in Vietnam, following the Tet Offensive launched by the Viet Cong at the start of the year; Czechoslovakia's election of Alexander Dubček as its leader, and its subsequent invasion by the Soviet Union; the assassinations of Martin Luther King and Robert Kennedy; the increasing numbers of student-led demonstrations, rallies, and occupations across Europe; the violent police response to protests at the Democrat convention in Chicago; Irish Catholic marches leading to street battles in Londonderry and military intervention in Northern Ireland; Conservative MP Enoch Powell's "river of blood" speech and the focus on anti-immigration policies to which it led; the punitive response to the iconic black power salute given by 200-meter medalists Tommie Smith and John Carlos at the Mexico Olympics; and the election of Richard Nixon as US President. Far from being seen as unconnected incidents, these and other events were widely regarded as constituents of a cultural shift through which challenges to the established order were no longer tolerated, as they had been earlier in the decade, but were met by a determined resistance to maintain (or reclaim) lost ground:

> By the eventful year of 1968, this phase of exhaustion and loss of momentum, this "fading into reality" of the collective dreams of the fifties

and sixties, this rightward swing and the beginnings of transition to a different age, could be seen all over the world . . . The speed with which, in just a few years, the American Dream, the most powerful image of the twentieth century, had collapsed into nightmare, had left the world quite stunned . . . By 1968 there were many other examples of disillusionment overtaking the dreams which had been so conspicuous over the previous decade.[2]

It was equally true, of course, that the Beatles' own experiences, circumstances, and emotions frequently and inevitably colored their songs. In 1968, there were four specific and significant developments which impacted on the personal context of their music. The first (partly to fill the vacuum caused by Epstein's death) was the formal creation, in January, of Apple, the group's own recording, management, and production company. Second, in February the group decamped to India, for several weeks' intensive tuition in transcendental meditation at the Maharishi Mahesh Yogi's ashram in Rishikesh. Third, John Lennon left his wife, Cynthia, for the Japanese conceptual artist Yoko Ono. Fourth, Paul McCartney's five-year romance with actress Jane Asher ended, shortly after he met New York photographer and future wife, Linda Eastman.

The unforeseen combination of their disrupted personal lives and a turbulent political climate effectively shaped much of the music created by the Beatles throughout the year. Moreover, it raised the prospect of a future in which the four Beatles themselves might not continue as a group. At the start of the year, this was nothing more than a remote possibility; by the end of the year, it had become, for many observers, a probability.

Preparation: *Yellow Submarine*

In 1963, United Artists had contracted with Brian Epstein to produce three Beatles films. *A Hard Day's Night* and *Help!* (both directed by Richard Lester) had been hugely successful, but by 1967 the Beatles, reluctant to submit themselves to the demands of movie-making and largely unimpressed by the potential scripts they had been offered, were unwilling to agree to United Artists' demands for the promised third film. The solution, negotiated between Brian Epstein and Al Brodax (producer of the US television cartoon series *The Beatles*) was that the group could fulfill their obligation by cooperating in the production of a full-length cartoon inspired by the lyrics of "Yellow Submarine." Dismayed by the prospect, the group distanced themselves from the project, refused to supply any new music, and offered only previously rejected songs for the soundtrack. These were George Harrison's "It's All Too Much" and "Only A Northern Song,"

Paul McCartney's "All Together Now" (all recorded during the *Sgt. Pepper* sessions in April–May 1967), and John Lennon's "Hey Bulldog" (recorded in February 1968).

All four songs were dismissed, by critics and by the Beatles themselves, as trivial and unimportant examples of their music. The two compositions by Harrison have been described, respectively, as "little more than formless shrieking"[3] and "a self-indulgent dirge . . . quickly set aside and forgotten."[4] In its obvious haste to reproduce "the repetitive chant of a children's game,"[5] the nursery-rhyme-based "All Together Now" showed little attention to either words or music; and John Lennon remarked, "I knocked off 'Hey Bulldog' . . . it's a good sounding record that means nothing."[6]

Given such adverse comments and the group's transparent lack of interest in the film and its music, it was ironic that, after viewing some early footage, they were impressed enough to agree to appear in its final scene; and following the positive response to its release in July 1968,[7] they engaged in a reappraisal of its merits, thereby allowing themselves to be rather more associated with its unexpected, and enduring, status:

> The film is a masterpiece and it has opened up new and undreamed of horizons for animation. It bears seeing several times for its content to be fully appreciated, and it has given such an impetus to the full-length animation cinema that it is already a classic.[8]

As a result, the music was also reassessed, so much so that the songs came to be identified as early and influential examples of contemporary musical genres: psychedelia ("All Together Now"), blues-based rock ("Hey Bulldog"), heavy metal ("It's All Too Much"), and electronic ("Only a Northern Song"). However, when the soundtrack album was released (on the group's Apple label) in January of the following year (by which time critical scrutiny had switched to the group's double album, *The Beatles*, released in November 1968), it was noticeable that some of the initial apprehension about the project still persisted: uniquely, *Yellow Submarine*'s sleeve notes, written by the Beatles' press agent, Derek Taylor, said nothing about the music it contained, but reproduced, in full, a review of *The Beatles* that had appeared in the *Observer*. His explanation that he "wanted the people who bought the *Yellow Submarine* album to buy and enjoy the really wonderful *The Beatles* album"[9] was seen by many as a tacit admission by the group that it remained less than satisfied by its musical contributions. As a result, *Yellow Submarine* occupied, and continues to occupy, a curious and somewhat uneasy position in the group's musical history.

Evolution: "Lady Madonna" to "Hey Jude"

Much of the Beatles' impact in 1963 and 1964 was achieved through their remarkable sequence of successful hit singles (eight, from "Love Me Do" in October 1962 to "I Feel Fine" in November 1964). By 1968, the configurations of popular music had been transformed (largely as a result of the Beatles themselves) and two related trajectories had emerged – pop (built around singles) and rock (built around albums). However, there still existed a huge demand for Beatles singles, particularly in the USA, which the group was loath to ignore; and a week-long session in February at the Abbey Road studios produced four new songs, from which its next single would be selected.

"Lady Madonna," written and sung by Paul McCartney, was a stated attempt by the group to mimic the boogie style of New Orleans rock and roll, popularized by Fats Domino in the 1950s. Utilizing the same piano riff that had introduced jazz trumpeter Humphrey Lyttleton's "Bad Penny Blues" (also, coincidentally, produced by George Martin) in 1956, the song fused traditional musical forms with an unexpected, contemporary lyric that paid tribute to the plight of the working woman. As McCartney acknowledged, it was a deliberate exercise:

> "Lady Madonna" was me sitting down at the piano trying to write a bluesy boogie-woogie thing. I got my left hand doing an arpeggio thing with the chord, an ascending boogie-woogie left hand, then a descending right hand. I always liked that, the juxtaposition of a line going down meeting a line going up.[10]

Although "Lady Madonna" was chosen as the A side of the next single, the inclusion of George Harrison's "The Inner Light" on the B side was perhaps the more significant decision, breaking as it did the group's exclusive reliance on Lennon-McCartney compositions on both sides of its singles. Harrison had created the song's instrumental track a few weeks earlier with various Indian musicians at EMI's studios in Bombay, during his recording of the film score for *Wonderwall*. The lyrics were adapted from Juan Mascaro's translation of a poem in Lao-Tse's *Tao Te Ching*. As with "Lady Madonna," it was the extraordinary synthesis of separate musical and lyrical traditions (in this case, Indian instrumentation, Chinese philosophy, and Western popular music) that distinguished the song. Harrison was well aware that its innovative structure might deter traditional pop audiences – "I think the song went unnoticed by most people because I was getting a bit 'out of it' as far as Western popular music was concerned"[11] – and its appearance on the single was a bold and unequivocal indication of the ways in which the Beatles were confronting conventional assumptions about their responsibilities as musicians.

The other two songs were compositions by John Lennon. "Hey Bulldog," as discussed above, was immediately discarded until it was used to complete the allocation of new tracks for *Yellow Submarine*; it also has the distinction of being the song most quickly recorded by the Beatles after their decision, in August 1966, to stop touring in order to concentrate on studio work. That it took less than ten hours from start to finish says much about the group's estimation of its relative importance. Lennon described the other song, "Across the Universe," as one over which he had little control, and whose origins were more magical than musical:

> I was lying next to my first wife in bed . . . she'd gone to sleep and I'd kept hearing these words over and over, flowing like an endless stream . . . I don't know where it came from . . . such an extraordinary meter and I can never repeat it! It's not a matter of craftsmanship; it wrote itself. It drove me out of bed . . . I went downstairs and I couldn't get to sleep until I put it on paper.[12]

It is, without doubt, one of Lennon's and the Beatles' loveliest melodies and most thoughtful lyrics; Mellers noted how "the flux of the visible universe – evoked in the beautiful poem – is timelessly stilled in a sublimation of folk and country-western music."[13] It was, therefore, puzzling that the song was not released until December 1969, when it was included on a compilation charity album, *No One's Gonna Change Our World*, for the World Wildlife Fund; and it did not appear on a Beatles' album until *Let It Be* in May 1970.

Although Apple had been established at the start of the year, the "Lady Madonna"/"The Inner Light" single was released, in March, on the Parlophone label. To publicly launch the new label (its other artists included James Taylor, Jackie Lomax, and Mary Hopkin) in August, the Beatles determined that their next single should be especially memorable. While visiting Cynthia Lennon and her son Julian, following the collapse of the Lennons' marriage in May, Paul McCartney had begun to incorporate his reaction to their situation into a broader songwriting strategy:

> I started with the idea "Hey Jules," which was Julian, don't make it bad, take a sad song and make it better. Hey, try and deal with this terrible thing . . . And I got this idea for a song, "Hey Jude," and made up a few little things so I had the idea by the time I got there. I changed it to "Jude" because I thought that sounded a bit better.[14]

But while its inspiration was unusual, it was the song's construction that attracted more interest. At a time when the typical single was rarely longer than two or three minutes in length, the seven minutes and eleven seconds of "Hey Jude" (including a four-minute closing chorus) were quite exceptional, and, like so much of the Beatles' music, provided models which others were quick to follow.[15] "Hey Jude" also became the Beatles' biggest-selling single.

On the B side of the record was the first of three tracks bearing the title "Revolution" that the group would record that year. Written by John Lennon, it signaled his frustration and resentment at the Beatles' commercial obligation to avoid overt political comment. Envious of Bob Dylan's ability to engage in meaningful contemporary debates in song, Lennon's politicization had accelerated since his relationship with Yoko Ono, and the death of Brian Epstein had removed the last serious restraint on his desire to participate in "serious" forms of discourse. These factors, set alongside the student protests sweeping Europe and the emergence of a counterculture fighting for the withdrawal of US troops from Vietnam, encouraged Lennon to write, and the Beatles to record, the group's first explicitly political song, as he later explained:

> I wanted it out as a single: as a statement of the Beatles' position on Vietnam and the Beatles' position on revolution. For years, on the Beatles' tours, Brian Epstein had stopped us from saying anything about Vietnam or the war. And he wouldn't allow questions about it. But on one of the last tours, I said, "I am going to answer about the war. We can't ignore it." I *absolutely* wanted the Beatles to say something about the war.[16]

What the Beatles did say about the war was rather confusing, as the lyrics ranged across endorsements and denials of violence as a legitimate tactic, veered between the merits of political and personal change, and failed to identify any specific ideological solution. The sense of confusion was added to by the instrumental combination of two distorted lead guitars and an unusually heavy drum track, which emphasized the atmosphere of discord and friction both musically and contextually.

What the song also demonstrated was the astonishing evolution in the personal and professional career of the group over the previous twelve months. The contrast between the married family man calmly reassuring audiences that "love is all you need" through the Summer of Love, and the adulterous political activist screaming of the necessity to "change the world" in the Year of the Barricades, could not have been better exemplified than it was here.

Revolution: *The Beatles*

Within weeks of its release in November 1968, the double album *The Beatles* had been unofficially, but effectively, re-christened as The White Album, the name derived from its plain, all-white cover, designed by Richard Hamilton. Regarded by some as the group's finest,[17] it was certainly the longest, containing more than ninety minutes of music, mostly written during the weeks in Rishikesh earlier in the year. It was recorded over a four-month period from June to early October, but its significance was not limited to, or even concentrated on, its musical properties. The tensions and interactions between three distinct, yet related, components – narrative, aesthetic, and musical – gave *The Beatles* an immediate momentum and lasting reputation.

Narrative

Lennon, McCartney, and Harrison had each returned from Rishikesh with several new songs that they were keen to record. However, the fact that they were largely individual compositions rather than collaborative efforts led to intense competition for their inclusion on the new album. Since their withdrawal from live performance, they were no longer able to rely on their participation in a demanding touring schedule to bind them together as colleagues; instead, they became competitors. In addition, the increasing number of invitations and opportunities to engage in solo projects through 1968 (including McCartney's work as record producer for Mary Hopkin, the Bonzo Dog Band and the Black Dyke Mills Band; Harrison's musical collaborations with Cream and Jackie Lomax; and Lennon's adaptation of *In His Own Write* for the National Theatre and his *You Are Here* exhibition at London's Robert Fraser Gallery) and the lack of agreement when they did engage in shared projects (such as the visit to India, when one by one the Beatles became suspicious of the Maharishi Mahesh Yogi's motives, leaving George Harrison as the only remaining follower) further undermined any sense of common purpose. Given the personal upheavals and professional reorientations in which the four were involved, it was hardly surprising that there was an absence of agreement about, and throughout, the making of *The Beatles*. In this respect, *The Beatles* was not an album by the Beatles, but a collection of thirty separate songs by four performers who happened (for the time being, at least) to be members of the same group, but who showed little willingness to cooperate with one another. George Harrison recognized the change in emphasis at that time:

> There was also a lot more individual stuff and, for the first time, people were accepting that it *was* individual. I remember having three studios operating at the same time: Paul was doing some overdubs in one, John was in another, and I was recording some horns or something in a third ... What else do you do when you've got so many songs and you want to get rid of them so that you can write more? There was a lot of ego in the band, and there were a lot of songs that maybe should have been elbowed.[18]

But whatever hostility might have been created by musical disagreements and rivalries, the unease was significantly compounded by the constant presence of Yoko Ono during the recording sessions. From the beginning of their career, the Beatles had vigorously enforced a policy that excluded any and all outsiders from the recording studio: the presence of girlfriends and wives, family and friends, even manager Brian Epstein, was strictly prohibited in order to allow the group, and producer George Martin, to concentrate uninterruptedly on its music.[19] Lennon's unilateral decision to encourage Ono's attendance at every session, even providing a bed for her in the studio, was unsurprisingly seen by McCartney, Harrison, and Starr, not only as a personal affront, but also as an explicit abandonment of their consensual work ethos. And while they may have been prepared to tolerate this as a temporary, if bizarre, inconvenience, the fact that she was invited to contribute musically to "The Continuing Story of Bungalow Bill" and "Revolution 9" was a serious and lasting blow to the unity the four had long shared. Indeed, this was re-emphasized later in the year by the release of John Lennon and Yoko Ono's *Two Virgins* album, and by their participation in BBC's *The Rolling Stones Rock 'n' Roll Circus*, in which they performed songs (including "Yer Blues") as members of an impromptu group with Eric Clapton, Mitch Mitchell, and Keith Richards.

As the recording of *The Beatles* progressed, it became increasingly evident that the group's arguments were far more than local disagreements, but reflected fundamental and evident divisions of approach and ambition: "To a man, the staff working with the group inside Abbey Road confirm this. The sessions were becoming tangibly tense and fraught, and tempers were being lost more easily and more frequently than ever before."[20] In mid-July, studio engineer Geoff Emerick, who had worked with the Beatles since 1963, departed in response to the group's incessant quarrels. And when, in August, McCartney's criticism of Ringo Starr's contribution to "Back in the USSR" led the drummer to walk out, it was perceived by many to be an unavoidable outcome of the sessions' personal and professional turmoil, as Starr admitted:

> I felt I was playing like shit. And those three were really getting on. I had this feeling that nobody loved me. I felt horrible. So I said to myself, "What am I doing here? Those three are getting along so well and I'm not even playing well." That was madness, so I went away on holiday to sort things out. I don't know, maybe I was just paranoid. To play in a band you have to trust each other.[21]

He allowed himself to be persuaded to return two weeks later, but the fact that one of the four had (albeit temporarily) left the group signaled a decisive moment in the history of the Beatles, as was confirmed by John Lennon:

> After Brian [Epstein] died we collapsed. We broke up then. We made the double album, the set . . . it's like if you took each track off and gave it all mine and all George's . . . it was just me and a backing group, Paul and a backing group . . . and I enjoyed it, but we broke up then.[22]

The photographs and drawings of Yoko Ono that were included on the album's lyric sheet, and the formal, printed acknowledgment to Linda Eastman (who had taken many of the photographs), were the final confirmation that with the album, the Beatles had engaged in a radical restructuring of obligations and relationships, whose repercussions would govern much, if not all, of their future careers.

Aesthetic

The Beatles divided critics more than any other of the group's albums; but this division was less to do with disagreements about quality than with confusions about the aesthetics, or cultures, of the album itself. On the one hand, it was described as "unsurpassed . . . seamless gear changes and bomb bursts of jaw-dropping brilliance";[23] "unquestionably glorious . . . a rich tapestry of musical textures";[24] and "a musical outpouring of overwhelming quantity, richness and diversity."[25]

On the other hand, it was seen as "something of a failure . . . it consisted of rough sketches of songs";[26] "without the necessary spark to lift many of the songs out of the ordinary . . . a collection of bits and pieces";[27] and "songs or song fragments [that] reeked of the argument and self-indulgence that had gone into their making."[28] Whether positive or negative, all assessments of *The Beatles* drew attention to its fragmentary aesthetic. However, while some complained about the lack of a coherent style, others recognized this as the album's *raison d'être*.

In fact, *The Beatles* has been designated as popular music's first post-modern album.[29] Within postmodern theory and practice, it has become axiomatic that the only certainty is that there are no longer any certainties, and, in this respect, the album was an early example of the rejection of constant principles, determination to transgress and combine creative codes, and repudiation of familiar systems of classification that characterized artistic production in the last decades of the twentieth century. The strategies utilized by the Beatles included bricolage (multiple quotation from earlier styles and periods), fragmentation (paradox, contradiction, incongruity), pastiche (imitation of another work, artist, or genre), parody (imitation for comic or satirical effect), reflexivity (self-conscious reference or attribution to itself), plurality (the absence of a single preferred reading), irony (the deliberate juxtaposition of meaning), exaggeration (abnormal enlargement or intensification), anti-representation (the deflection of attempts to define "reality"), and meta-art (the admission that all art is constructed). In its design, production, and execution, *The Beatles* employed all these elements (many of which had been present in much of the group's previous work) to fashion a contemporary text whose music(s) described the present, recalled the past, and anticipated the future.

The full significance of these tendencies was often overlooked, even by those who drew attention to them. Kozinn's comment that the album was "a fascinating compendium of compositional and performance styles that shows how wide-ranging the Beatles' musical imaginations were,"[30] and O'Grady's observation that "aside from a frequent preoccupation with satire and irony of various kinds, the album fails to demonstrate any particular theme or conceptual reference point,"[31] were incomplete in that the features they identified were seen as interesting and incidental rather than definitive. The culture of postmodernism may have constituted a new and unfamiliar trajectory in 1968, but it was one which the Beatles were well positioned to embrace and exploit:

> By employing the disruptive aesthetics of postmodern art, the White Album calls attention away from itself as a source of meaning and instead clears a space where readers can engage the issues of what popular music is and what role it plays. It does not hold up a unified, understandable, interpretable theme, but blurs any possible theme, making it impossible to grasp its essential motivation . . . The album deconstructs itself, pop music, the Beatles themselves, and their own musical history.[32]

Music

While its extraordinary compilation of musical styles and inflections made the album impossible to classify as a coherent whole, there were, nevertheless, sufficient principal musical constituents within each song to permit the tentative and broad categorizations set out in Table 6.1. These classifications can only be indicative, since many of the songs contained elements drawn from different genres, presented startling combinations of tempo and delivery, and blurred boundaries between past and present musical approaches. Paul McCartney revealed that this was quite intentional, when he explained: "We felt it was time to step back because that is what we wanted to do. You can still make good music without going forward."[33]

Nowhere was this better demonstrated than in the four rock and roll-based songs; just as "Lady Madonna" had been inspired by the compositions and vocal style of Fats Domino, so McCartney's "Birthday," "Helter Skelter," "Why Don't We Do It in the Road," and Lennon's "Everybody's Got Something to Hide Except Me and My Monkey" reproduced the insistent rhythms, vocal shrieks, and alliterative and onomatopoeic lyrics of two more of the group's early mentors, Little Richard and Larry Williams. While

Table 6.1 *Major musical sources of* The Beatles

Folk	Blackbird; I Will; Mother Nature's Son
Rock	Savoy Truffle; While My Guitar Gently Weeps; I'm So Tired
Rock and Roll	Why Don't We Do It in the Road; Birthday; Everybody's Got Something to Hide Except Me and My Monkey; Helter Skelter
Ska	Ob-La-Di Ob-La-Da
Psychedelia	Glass Onion; Sexy Sadie
Vaudeville	Martha My Dear; Honey Pie
Country	Don't Pass Me By; Rocky Raccoon
Doo-Wop	Happiness Is a Warm Gun; Revolution 1
Ballad	Long Long Long; Julia
Rhythm and Blues	Back in the USSR
Avant Garde	Revolution 9
Blues	Yer Blues
Nursery Rhyme	Dear Prudence; The Continuing Story of Bungalow Bill; Piggies; Cry Baby Cry; Good Night
Miscellaneous	Wild Honey Pie

those songs derived from the group's adolescence in the 1950s, there was a set of five – "Cry Baby Cry," "Piggies," "The Continuing Story of Bungalow Bill," "Dear Prudence," and "Good Night" – whose origins lay in the memories of their childhoods in the 1940s. McCartney's perennial liking for the legacy of vaudeville and music hall, and for its reinterpretation by Fred Astaire in his stage and screen musicals of the 1930s, was evidenced in "Martha My Dear" and "Honey Pie"; and "Rocky Raccoon" and "Don't Pass Me By" (the first composition of Ringo Starr) revisited the traditions of the country ballad.

But while these songs generally recalled past musical styles, their specific creation often lay in current and spontaneous events. "Helter Skelter" was a deliberate attempt to surpass the renowned volume and excitement of the Who; "Dear Prudence" was written for one of their Rishikesh companions, Prudence Farrow; "Martha My Dear" was about McCartney's Old English sheepdog, Martha; "Good Night" was composed as a lullaby for Lennon's son Julian; and "Sexy Sadie" chronicled the group's disillusionment with the Maharishi Mahesh Yogi. Musically and lyrically, the album was thus able to incorporate past and present concerns not only between songs but also within them.

No less important was the contribution of specific friends and peers to several of the songs. The West Coast harmony vocals on "Back in the USSR" were added to the track following the group's association with Beach Boy Mike Love at Rishikesh; "Rocky Raccoon" was also written in Rishikesh, with the assistance of the British folk singer-songwriter Donovan; "Revolution 9" was a joint attempt by Lennon and Ono to translate her *avant-garde* art into *avant-garde* music; and the lead guitar on "While My Guitar Gently Weeps" was played by Eric Clapton, who was invited by George Harrison in order to provide a distinctive guitar solo and as a mark of their growing friendship.

Following the largely positive reaction to "Revolution", the group were able to use several of the album's songs to refer – directly or indirectly – to the broader political context. "Back in the USSR" was an oblique comment on the continuing Cold War and Russian occupation of Czechoslovakia; "Blackbird" was a response to the ongoing racial tensions in the USA; "Happiness is a Warm Gun" was inspired by the spiraling gun culture in the same country; and "Piggies" was a savage attack on the corporate greed of contemporary capitalism. And finally, two songs were intensely personal statements that revealed much about their authors: "Long Long Long" was "a yearning, beautiful song... an oasis of calm and faith"[34] recording the happiness that came with George Harrison's discovery of God; and "Julia" (with lyrics adapted from Kahlil Gibran's *Sand and Foam*) was John Lennon's song to his dead mother, which managed to "evoke through music a language that is deeper than words."[35]

Although double albums were still comparatively rare, *The Beatles* was not popular music's first,[36] and there were doubts about its sales potential. In addition, George Martin was reluctant to release so much of the group's music at one time, especially given his lack of enthusiasm about some of the songs. However, his objections were overruled by the Beatles' absolute and unanimous insistence that their music should be presented in its entirety, and *The Beatles* became the group's biggest-selling album.

Redirection

Although 1968 brought with it an exceptional twelve months of political revolution, professional reconstruction, and personal reorientation, the Beatles had by no means resolved these issues by the end of the year. The repercussions of Lennon's controversial relationship with Yoko Ono, McCartney's decisive involvement with Linda Eastman, Harrison's deepening interest in Eastern religion, Starr's feelings of despondency, and their *de facto* managerless state were only magnified by the failure of Apple to meet its original objectives: "By the fall of 1968 Apple was slowly rotting away, losing a reported £20,000 a week from gross mismanagement and employee pilfering."[37]

As the year closed with no satisfactory resolution to these problems and differences in sight (and with the emergence of new difficulties, following Lennon's arrest and conviction in October for possession of cannabis), it was apparent that the direction along which the Beatles had traveled for the previous several years was no longer viable. The temporary uncertainty present at the start of the year seemed to have relentlessly spiraled into a permanent discomfort. While the diversity of the music they produced in 1968 indicated a number of plausible alternative trajectories, both individual and collective, the absence of any common agreement about preferred destinations had created a sense of distance and unease within the group, whose outcome could not be predicted.

7 On their way home: the Beatles in 1969 and 1970

STEVE HAMELMAN

Given the high amount of magnificent music the Beatles recorded in 1969, it may surprise millions of casual listeners to learn that aside from a few numbers, all of the official tracks from the band's last full year – including classics such as "Let It Be," "Get Back," "The Long and Winding Road," "Come Together," "Across the Universe," "Something," "Don't Let Me Down," and the medley on side two of *Abbey Road* – were created to the tune of four once inseparable friends going through an ugly divorce. Most of the tracks belie sessions where egos were so wounded by the slightest offense, whether real or imagined, that only in patches did the Fab Four function with a unified vision and in a collaborative spirit. *Abbey Road* and *Let It Be*, along with "The Ballad of John and Yoko" and three B sides, were made amid spats, sulks, shouting matches, temporary alliances, simmering jealousies, and many sessions with one or more of the Beatles absent. "Given these circumstances," writes Walter Everett, "it is somewhat remarkable that *Abbey Road* is universally recognized as a coherent demonstration of inspired composition, impeccable vocal and instrumental ensemble, and clean and cleverly colorful engineering."[1] And while *Let It Be* may not possess the polish of *Abbey Road*, many listeners prefer it for that very reason. Shining through the ramshackle and at times poorly performed and indifferently recorded pieces are melodies, harmonies, and grooves as addictive as any in the Beatles' canon. So artful were the Beatles, and so blessed with good material, that evidence of internecine strife is concealed on *Abbey Road*, the band's attempt in mid-1969 to end its career with one last masterpiece, and *Let It Be*, the band's attempt in early 1969 (but released in 1970) to "get back" to its musical roots as the boys commenced the final phase of disintegration.

Discontent had begun infecting their ranks as early as 1967 – the year that Brian Epstein died, that Paul's "Hello Goodbye" was chosen as the A side to John's B side "I Am the Walrus" (a decision Everett calls "one more nail in the Beatles' coffin"),[2] and that Paul saddled the others with *Magical Mystery Tour*, a popular and critical disaster. Discord flared up in 1968 during work on *The Beatles*, and in 1969 conflict dogged them from first day to last. On January 2, 1969, they arrived at Twickenham Film Studios in London to film rehearsals for a documentary movie and a come-back televised concert (the location causing heated debate) at the end of the month-long rehearsals, and record an album named *Get Back* – all in all, a Paul-devised project that, after much argument and delay, became the album *Let It Be*. Almost exactly one year later, on January 4, 1970, at Abbey Road/EMI Studios, Paul, George, and Ringo convened the Beatles' last recording session (John was on vacation in Denmark).[3] The intervening twelve months saw four musicians who had altered the history of popular culture vacillating between a pinnacle of creative collaboration and a nadir of disintegrative self-absorption.

The business of breaking up

Like almost everything else in their career, the Beatles' breakup was another unique chapter in rock and roll history. Evidence of its singularity lies mainly in the music they made in 1969. Of equal note, however, is the excruciating indecisiveness they brought to the act of dissolution.

The end came and went several times in 1969. On January 10, George quit the band for a few days following a showdown with John during the *Get Back* rehearsals at Twickenham.[4] Doug Sulpy and Ray Schweighhardt wonder how the band held together at all through these fractious sessions, noting among other impasses the dialog on January 13, when "the Beatles [were] nearer to breaking up than they had ever been before."[5] Philip Norman states that "the Beatles ceased to exist"[6] on the afternoon of September 12, 1969, when John was invited to play at a festival in Toronto. He boarded a plane the next day with a makeshift Plastic Ono Band, which, as the ensuing live album testifies, gave a pedestrian performance. But it was in a business meeting within days of his return from the gig that Lennon declared he was "divorcing" the other Beatles.[7] His decision was hushed up for half a year, when on April 10, 1970, Paul trumped his former partner's card by feeding the breakup scoop to the media via the inclusion of an insert inside advance press copies of his first solo album, *McCartney*.[8] To secure his artistic freedom from the Beatles' management, Paul filed suit to dissolve the partnership on December 31, 1970, the band's business affairs went into receivership on March 12, 1971, and the band formally "ceased to exist" on January 9, 1975. Clearly, the Beatles were incapable of ending it all in one fell swoop, spending most of 1969 either back-stabbing one another or courting new muses and pursuing new whims, ultimately enhancing their stature by recording music of a quality impressive even in relation to their previous peerless work.

For a full appreciation of this peerless work, one must look briefly at modern and postmodern aesthetics. New Critics in the 1940s preached that it was a mistake to read authorial intention into works of literary art. Structuralists and poststructuralists of the 1960s through 1980s took this dictum of "the intentional fallacy" – no one is fully aware of an author's intentions, the author included, which is why in the act of interpretation all intention must be discounted – to the next extreme. They argued that the existence of an autonomous author in absolute command of the signifiers (lines of verse, musical notations, swabs of paint) comprising a text was an axiom of humanistic ideology holding that transcendent meaning is encoded in literature and other means of artistic communication. Despite falling into disfavor with the rise of multicultural, political, and context-based theories in the 1990s, the legacy of formalism, structuralism, and poststructuralism lingers sufficiently to bedevil critics who seek to establish definite correspondences between a given text and the details of a given creator's life at the time of composition.

No matter how intriguing from a theoretical standpoint, the Beatles music of 1969 shatters the New Critics' argument that private intentions matter not at all in the analysis of texts made public, and it renders untenable all arguments that the Author (and the reader's burden of having to tease out the unmediated origins of a given text) died *c.* 1968.[9] In fact, there can be little intelligent discussion of *Abbey Road* and *Let It Be* without awareness of their biographical background. The songs that ended up on these two disks, as well as "The Ballad of John and Yoko" and "Don't Let Me Down," illuminate the Beatles' personal affairs in ways that "Do You Want to Know a Secret," "I Want to Hold Your Hand," "When I Get Home," "Eight Days a Week," "Getting Better," "Day Tripper," and dozens more do not. Many tracks from 1969 teem with melancholy and nostalgia, some drip with sarcasm, and others sound the depths of insecurity, loneliness, and desire. In all cases, the composer's thoughts and feelings are transmuted into original and timeless music by the other three Beatles.[10] Since few if any of the tunes from 1969 lack biographical overtones or reference points, the critic is obligated to throw the precepts of postmodern aesthetics to the wind, touching on both particular and universal aspects of the band's music.[11]

What, then, was on their minds in 1969? What caused such close companions to belittle and betray one another at almost every opportunity? Why did they abandon the *Get Back* concert-film project, stew in their discontent for a few months, pursue solo interests, pool their resources for the common good by regrouping for *Abbey Road*, and then, more decisively than before, go their separate ways at last?

Throughout 1969 the Beatles as single musical corpus was being drawn and quartered by internal and external forces too potent for each Beatle to resist. Yoko Ono, soon to be joined by Allen Klein, was pulling – *had been* pulling since mid-1968 – John out of one socket. Abetting Lennon's withdrawal from the Beatles were, in no particular order, his fury at the others for their rudeness to Yoko (whom he married on March 20, 1969); his resentment toward Paul for everything from refusing to record "Cold Turkey" in fall 1969 to Paul's having become the dominant creative force and *de facto* leader of the band; his addiction to heroin, the cause of mental and emotional instability; his infatuation with experimental and political rock; and the paranoia that seemed to be his primary state of mind.[12] Yanking Paul was a combination of the need to perform live; his relationship with Linda Eastman (whom he met in May 1968 and married on March 12, 1969); mounting impatience with John, George, and Ringo's indifference to and/or hostility toward the Beatles as a working unit with a viable future; and the allure of getting away from it all at his farmhouse in Scotland. George felt frustration at having his new compositions bypassed time and time again. "Isn't It a Pity," "All Things Must Pass," and "Let It Down" (all destined for epic treatment on 1970's *All Things Must Pass*) were introduced and shelved at Twickenham. George, moreover, was further alienated by Paul's micromanaging and John's venom in the studio (or worse, his tolerance of Yoko's intrusiveness). Finally, Ringo seemed to be reading the band's doom in the tea-leaves: he began to gravitate toward a career in both film (his role in *The Magic Christian* got under way in March 1969) and solo albums (he began recording *Sentimental Journey* in October). After ten-plus years together, these four friends and fellow musicians were ripe to go their own ways artistically, politically, and personally.

Of preeminent concern to all of them, however, was money – that is, the chaos at Apple Corps. In a January 1969 issue of *Disc and Music Echo*, John made public Apple's tattered state, lamenting that "if it carries on like this, all of us will be broke in the next six months."[13] Started in December 1967 as a combination of tax shelter and utopian business model, Apple was already a losing cause by the time its records division was established at 3 Savile Row, London, in July 1968. First came the boutique, purveyors of psychedelic clothing and apparel to London hipsters. Apple quickly branched out into record, publicity, film, electronics, and publishing divisions. From day one, sponging, shoplifting, and incompetence characterized Apple's daily operations. The boutique closed for good in a sensational public giveaway of its inventory in July 1968 after a mere eight cash-draining months. While the other divisions went about tanking, Apple Records fared better. Its first single was the worldwide hit "Hey Jude" (October 1968), and its roster included (the Beatles aside) the Iveys (Badfinger), Mary Hopkin, James Taylor, and the Modern Jazz Quartet. But the relative success of Apple Records would not be enough to stop the slide of the Beatles into bankruptcy.

Enter Allen Klein. Stereotypically "New York" in his antagonistic manner, Klein had by the mid-sixties become manager of several British Invasion bands, the Rolling Stones chief among them. In late 1968, with Apple falling to pieces in step with the group's loss of direction, Klein's long-standing ambition to manage the Beatles was now within reach. He began to insinuate himself into the Beatles' inner circle by meeting with John in January 1969. Swayed by the lawyer's style and strategic plan, John endorsed Klein, and Ringo and George soon followed his cue. In the meantime, Paul had come to terms with Linda Eastman's brother John and father Lee of the New York firm Eastman and Eastman. A three-to-one battle shaped up. Apple was foundering, and the imminent takeover of the Beatles' first management company, NEMS (which deducted 25 percent of the band's income before sending the rest on to Apple, where the income was further diminished), intensified the need to act quickly. Klein and the Eastmans assumed different duties – business manager and general counsel of Apple, respectively[14] – to fend off the Beatles' financial foes, but in the end the Beatles lost their bid for NEMS.

Klein was undeterred. A campaign of intimidation helped him gain some concessions from Triumph Investment Trust, victor in the NEMS contest. More wrangling remained over Dick James's sale of his 23 percent share (compared to the Beatles' 31 percent) of Northern Songs, the Beatles' publishing company, to Associated Television Corporation (ATV), which, commanding 35 percent, moved to gain majority share in the company, in effect foreclosing the Beatles' chance to control their own music. Klein came close to beating ATV until an off-color remark by John, leveled at the businessmen besieging the band, helped to send Klein's allies to ATV's side, thereby scotching weeks of negotiation and clinching the Beatles' loss of their own profitable songbook.[15]

Klein's management contract was signed in early May – three for, one (Paul) against: enough, however, to put Klein in charge of Apple. He proceeded to purge the offices and operations at 3 Savile Row of all excess. No one was safe from the New Yorker's swift, sharp axe. Despite turmoil at Apple that would last well into the next year, the four Beatles, in addition to doing solo, session, and production work with new and established names, made sporadic group-related visits to the studio. According to Mark Lewisohn's log for April and May,[16] they nailed Harrison's ferocious B side "Old Brown Shoe" and hammered out arrangements for some songs to be perfected within the next few months on *Abbey Road*. Distraction and rancor notwithstanding, the Fab Four's impetus to create was not exhausted; their genius was yet to reach full flood.

Klein persevered. He was determined to renegotiate contracts with EMI and Capitol Records, largely, observers inclined to cynicism would note, to collect a 20 percent commission per the contract signed on May 8 by all the Beatles save Paul (insisting 15 percent was reasonable, he marveled that his bandmates "were completely besotted with this guy").[17] By September

1969, with a majority holding of Northern Songs now in ATV's grasp, the indefatigable manager had delivered on his promise to rid Apple Corps of deadbeats and cost overruns. Moreover, he had pressured Capitol Records in North America to raise his clients' royalties to a dazzling 25 percent of retail.[18] Ironically, on the September day that the Beatles gathered to sign the sweet new deal, Lennon broke up the band. With the Capitol coup barely in place and another assault on ATV in the works, Klein advised the boys that leaking news of their split would weaken his bargaining position against legal teams conspiring to milk every last shilling out of rock music's biggest cash cow. The Beatles complied with the cover-up until Paul, enraged by the band's demand that he postpone the April 1970 release of *McCartney* in favor of *Let It Be*, forged ahead with the first solo Beatle masterpiece, beating out George's *All Things Must Pass* and John's *Plastic Ono Band* by seven and eight months, respectively.[19]

The art of making music

No matter how battered and bruised by the collapse of empire, image, and friendship, the band limped toward death singing like the swans of ancient fable, sweetly, beautifully, of their own demise. "There's no success like failure," Bob Dylan had sung in 1965, "and failure's no success at all" – unless you were the Beatles. Unimaginably gifted, they wrested marvelous songs from the jaws of their abject failure as friends and business partners. As musicians, each one channeled the negativity needed to break free from what had become a claustrophobic collective into music as fine as anything else recorded in rock history.

In late 1968, the Beatles decided to make a record stripped of artifice and technical trickery. Psychedelia and baroque pop were fast becoming obsolete.[20] Roots-based records were popping up all around them – Dylan's *John Wesley Harding* (1967), the Rolling Stones' *Beggars Banquet* (1968), the Byrds' *Sweetheart of the Rodeo* (1969; the Byrds had already covered Goffin-King's "Goin' Back" in 1968), Fairport Convention's *Liege and Lief* (1969), and, of most interest to George Harrison (in November 1968 he had jammed with the Band and Dylan in upstate New York), the Band's *Music from Big Pink* and *The Band* (1968, 1969).

Between January 2 and 31, 1969, first at Twickenham Studios and then at Apple's basement studio, the Beatles taped scores of covers (mostly tunes played in their formative years in Liverpool and Hamburg) and multiple takes of a few dozen originals. Twelve of these cuts would see life fifteen months later on *Let It Be*. So checkered were the recording and production of this simultaneously penultimate (second-to-last recorded) and ultimate (last released) album that *Let It Be* sounds both scrappy and scrapped. Beset by "old hostilities," the men creating it were now, according to Mark Lewisohn, "just a tired, jaded rock group going through the motions."[21] Lennon later confided: "We couldn't get into it. And we put down a few tracks and nobody was in it at all . . . it just was a dreadful, dreadful feeling in Twickenham."[22]

And yet something clicked when push came to shove. In Tim Riley's view, *Let It Be*'s

> patched history looks worse on paper than it sounds on vinyl. The band's mood is more centered than it is on the "White Album," and sharing the formulative process of writing with their audience is open and intriguing; *Let It Be* doesn't play parodic games or manipulate images of public identity. Beneath Spector's uninspired textures a group is at work, and . . . the Beatles' distinctive joy in playing together remains palpable.[23]

Backing up this view is the testimony of several members of the film crew who found the sessions lively and fun.[24] The tapes also reveal plenty of rip-'em-up takes punctuated by jokes and laughter. Still, a tentative air hangs over *Let It Be*, a malaise of mismatched motives, a haggard nonchalance. Keeping in mind the gigantic inventory of bootlegs derived from unreleased material, a huge cache of stolen session tapes recovered in 2003, and 2003's revised version of the record, *Let It Be . . . Naked*, Steve Matteo correctly avers that *Let It Be* "remains an inconclusive and unfinished work."[25]

The album would have been even more "unfinished" had the band not deserted Twickenham for the warmer confines of Apple Studios on January 15. First, however, there was an inconvenient wrinkle regarding machinery. Apple Corps employee "Magic" Alex Mardas was a self-proclaimed electronics wizard who had persuaded the band to bankroll a seventy-two-track recording console encased in a state-of-the-art studio housed in Apple's basement. Upon first inspection, George Martin declared Mardas's console of *sixteen* unworkable channels a disaster, on a par with the badly wired and baffled room, and had it torn out at once, hauling in gear from EMI. Things got even better when, thanks to George Harrison's initiative, the band hooked the services of veteran rhythm and blues keyboardist Billy Preston. He began jamming with the band on the afternoon of January 22, their first day back to *Get Back*. Improvement in mood and music was immediate partly because the Beatles behaved well for their guest but also because the stress-inducing plan to cap off the rehearsals with a live show, either at London's Roundhouse Theatre, a Tunisian amphitheater, a stretch of the Sahara Desert, or on the deck of a ship, was ditched. Instead, the band brought it all back home: on January 30, the Beatles (with Billy Preston) put on a forty-two-minute show, their last ever, in front of about twenty technicians, associates, and friends on the rooftop of 3 Savile Row.

Sound engineer Glyn Johns's work on *Get Back* began in earnest in March when Paul and John, burdening Johns with thirty hours of live and studio performance, instructed him to make an album. This left John and Yoko free to play the part of peace diplomats at two "bed-ins" with musical accompaniment, most famously June's "Give Peace a Chance," taped in a Montreal hotel with bedside celebrities chiming in. The couple also gave the world *Unfinished Music, No. 2: Life with the Lions* on the same day, May 9, that George released his meditations on the Moog synthesizer, *Electronic Sound* – the only two disks issued on Apple's experimental imprint Zapple. While John and Yoko indulged in feedback, sound effects, and random frequencies, and George explored the weird beauty of first-generation electronica, Ringo had been filming *The Magic Christian* from March to May. Paul's portfolio in 1969 lists producing, playing, and/or writing for Jackie Lomax, Mary Hopkin, and Steve Miller (drums, bass, vocal on Miller's "My Dark Hour" in May 1969).

For the band proper, the spring's main commercial product was not the album *Get Back* but the single "Get Back"/"Don't Let Me Down" (April 11) – Paul's apostrophe to John, nudging him to return to the Beatles' nest, and John's apostrophe to Yoko and/or some other addiction construed as first love and last.[26] On another day in April, Lennon and McCartney buried their hatchets to bang out John's narrative of his marital adventures, "The Ballad of John and Yoko," paired with "Old Brown Shoe" for release on May 30. Eager to tape the A side even though Ringo and George were unavailable, John played guitars while Paul handled drums, bass, piano, and shakers. Listeners spellbound by this "ballad's" propulsion, singalongability, and audacity might find it hard to fathom that for months John and Paul had been fighting a legal and musical war.[27] The manic shuffle "Old Brown Shoe," as well, showed the whole band in blistering form, with Paul's slithery bass triplets triggering Ringo's rolls and George's slide-lines, the smoking groove bolstered by Paul's syncopated piano and George's lethal vocal about "escaping from this zoo" of duality through the power of love.

Abbey Road

May and June came and went. Despite having a cover photograph (later used on *The Beatles 1967–1970*), there was still no consensus on *Get Back* except that it was not good enough to go out. The Beatles did, however, retain enough common sense and self-worth to rally behind McCartney's idea that, with George Martin back where *he* once belonged at the producer's helm, the Beatles should make one more album. Martin, believing *Get Back* had done in the Beatles, was taken aback by the proposal but agreed to it "only if you [the band] let me produce it the way we used to."[28] Martin was especially concerned about John. At this juncture Lennon may have been at a personal low, but he was game for one last masterpiece, as were the others.[29] And so, reviving thirteen originals from the January sessions that were not in the can for the future *Let It Be*, and conjuring up killer cuts like "Come Together" and "Here Comes the Sun," the Beatles worked throughout July and August on 1969's topping achievement.

Martin's condition notwithstanding, there was drama. John arrived, with Yoko in tow, on July 9, nine days late because of a car crash requiring hospitalization in Scotland. To everyone's astonishment, a big bed for Yoko, convalescent *and* pregnant, was installed in the studio, a microphone within her reach. Stifling their exasperation at this spectacle, the other Fabs plugged on. The level of their collegiality has been the subject of debate ever since. At one extreme is Ian MacDonald's harsh verdict: "Basically a set of solo performances, *Abbey Road* was largely put together by the group in isolation from one another and in an atmosphere veering from cold tolerance to childish violence. Lennon twice argued savagely with McCartney, at one point taking a less-than-peaceful swing at his wife Linda."[30] Yet George Martin testified that "everybody worked frightfully well."[31]

The truth lies somewhere within the slender crack that divides thesis and antithesis. *Abbey Road*, after all, is a synthesis of opposites, the mystery of dialectics solved in sound: John's rock aggression offset by Paul's pop suavity; George's transcendent sensibility grounded by Ringo's earthy tom-tom rolls;[32] the band's impending disintegration veiled by its temporary and tentative unity; the miscellany of self-standing numbers (John's preference) on side one mirrored by the suite-like medleys (Paul's innovation, resisted by John) on side two – side one ending with Lennon's long, rhythmically intricate, gut-wrenching confession "I Want You (She's So Heavy)" cut short in the midst of its consummation into pure white whoosh, and side two ending with McCartney's acoustic bagatelle "Her Majesty" cut short in the midst of its irreverent poke at England's queen.

To say the album's kick-off cut, "Come Together," is derivative because Timothy Leary coined the title's phrase for a political campaign and Chuck Berry spawned the riff and opening line is like saying Shakespeare's *Hamlet* is derivative because the Bard reconceived an earlier *Hamlet* by Thomas Kyd. "Come Together" leaves any debts to Leary and Berry far behind. Boasting the funkiest rhythm track in the entire Fab catalogue, the tune's surreal lyrics burst with images – "He got joo-joo eyeball," "Hold you in his armchair you can feel his disease" – that tease listeners with glimpses into the composer's narcotic ("shoot me") and erotic ("come together,"

"Ono sideboard") dysfunctionalism. But that the lyrics say nothing definite about either of these dysfunctions is one of the tune's strengths. The Beatles' resident revolutionary implies in this *tour de* poetry and groove that interpretation is the most democratic privilege of all. With John bouncing back from his springtime peevishness, Paul and Ringo respond by *laying it down* for his rock and roll word-gumbo. Ringo delivers dead on time through the blend of hi-hat/snare triplets at the top of each verse with, everywhere else, a four-beat tom/snare tattoo anchored by a dry bass drum figure. Humming between high and low registers, Paul's bass coils around John's voice like a vine encircling a swaying limb in a steamy swamp.[33]

In "Come Together," Paul may have set a new high for rock bass playing; the next song, "Something," meets if not exceeds that high. Dating back to late 1968, Harrison's "Something," tinkered with in January and April, was brought to fruition in mid-July. Universally celebrated as a masterpiece commensurate with the best Lennon-McCartney compositions, it is worth noting, as most sources do, that Frank Sinatra called "Something" the greatest love song in half a century. The real value of this compliment, noted by no one, lies in the fact that Sinatra had once called rock and roll "the most brutal, ugly, desperate, vicious form of expression it has been my misfortune to hear."[34]And "Something" *is* rock and roll: behind Paul's contrapuntal bass lines (too busy, allegedly, for George) and George's gorgeous guitar/vocal are Ringo's immovable backbeat and varied tom-tom fills, as urgent as anything he pounded out for spectators in the Cavern or Star Club.

Next up, "Maxwell's Silver Hammer," Paul's so-called "vaudeville" number, is frequently maligned; yet is it all that different from "Your Mother Should Know" or "When I'm Sixty-Four"?[35] To some ears, this silly little tale about Joan, Teacher, Judge, and Maxwell defines McCartney's fundamental triteness; to other ears, the song is as delightful, and surely no more silly, than Ringo's "Octopus's Garden," which incorporates sound effects with equally charming results. Never mentioned is that dynamically, each of these numbers, separated by Paul's 12/8 pop-blues "Oh! Darling" (more Fats Domino style than John Lennon substance), makes sense placed, as some songs had to be, within the long shadow of gravity and grace cast by "Come Together" and "Something," and in advance of *Abbey Road*'s longest and only harrowing number, "I Want You (She's So Heavy)." At the very least, Paul's tune provides comic relief while Ringo's tune, despite being the utopian fantasy he imagined after quitting the Beatles for a week or two in 1968, need not engage listeners on anything resembling a serious personal level. The fact that children invariably love both songs says much about their underrated qualities.

On the other hand, children would likely be upset by the varying time signatures and scorching lyrics of "I Want You (She's So Heavy)." On this eight-minute cry of love, John Lennon no longer screens his insecurity behind the pop art of "I'm a Loser" or "Help!", no longer feels compelled to "hide his love away," instead distilling his agony into twelve pleading words set to a manic-depressive score. Paul's bass, prominent again, both hooks into and tugs away from melody and groove; Ringo tumbles around his new calfskin tom heads and jabs into the ride cymbal's bell; George feeds starving John sweet and sharp guitar lines; Billy Preston unleashes cascading organ chords; and John does the rest – guitars, voice, and Moog synthesizer with wind generator, cranked louder and louder during the song's two-minute run up to, and off, the cliff of silence.[36]

And that was how *Abbey Road* was going to end until August 20, the last time all four Beatles were together in a studio. On that fateful day the side-two medleys previously recorded were synchronized into place. Lennon had lobbied against the medley concept, to no avail. "Everybody praises the album so much," he said eleven years later, "but none of the songs had anything to do with each other, no thread at all, only the fact that we stuck them together."[37] One could argue, however, that beautiful and consistent sound is a thread unto itself. There is also the fact that at least three songs – "Here Comes the Sun," "You Never Give Me Your Money" (only "your funny paper," moans Paul, buried in legal documents), and "Carry That Weight" – echo the business battles of the spring. Another one, the lush "Sun King," revisits "Here Comes the Sun," while "Golden Slumbers," Paul's collaboration with Elizabethan lyricist Thomas Dekker (Paul stumbled upon the sheet music of Dekker's "Golden Slumbers" at the piano at his father's house), segues organically into "Carry That Weight," which itself quotes "You Never Give Me Your Money," whose theme of freedom ("Oh that magic feeling, nowhere to go") and escape ("Soon we'll be away from here, / Step on the gas and wipe that tear away") reconnects it to the vernal optimism of "Here Comes the Sun." These tunes are from the same weave, the same cloth, and, *contra* Lennon, the second side's other numbers are neither more nor less interrelated than the songs on either side of, say, *Help!* or *Beatles for Sale*.

The provenance of "Here Comes the Sun," side one's opener, is well documented. George Harrison in Eric Clapton's garden relaxing from the strain of business, guitar in hand, penned a joyful tune, his second instant classic on *Abbey Road*. Foreshadowing seventies mellow rock but without the simpering qualities of its average practitioner, "Here Comes the Sun" interweaves delicate guitars with mellifluous Moog flourishes, catchy verses, chorus, and bridge, and, again, Ringo's tom-rich coloration. The uniqueness of John's "Because" lies in, first, the Beethoven-inspired melody (a variation on the "Moonlight" sonata) plucked by George Martin on harpsichord and, second, the "nine-man choir"[38] comprising John, Paul, and George, triply overdubbed. EMI sound engineer Geoff Emerick cites "Because" as an example of group harmony at the *Abbey Road* sessions,[39] as was the recording of the serene "Sun King" and its mate, the swaying "Mean Mr. Mustard": "They pulled it off – it really was a group effort, and all four Beatles played with energy and enthusiasm, each making his own unique contribution to the sound and arrangement."[40]

Resurrected from the January sessions, "Polythene Pam," modeled partly on a Fab fan from days of yore, pulses madly, as if the mere memory of this "attractively built" girl could make male hormones rage; and "She Came In Through the Bathroom Window," from 1968, at once chugs, thanks to Ringo's percussive attack, and glides, thanks to the call-response of Paul's chiming guitar, through three verses filled with clever phrases ("But now she sucks her thumb and wanders / By the banks of her own lagoon") and two choruses. Attaining climax, these two erotic rockers leave "Golden Slumbers" and "Carry That Weight" to march toward the "The End," which encompasses the polarity at the heart of the Beatles: rock and roll earthiness and spiritual vision. Ringo's first and last drum solo (fifteen seconds long, cymbal-less) leads up to a white-hot guitar battle. Emerick again: "For the hour or so that it took them to play those solos, all the bad blood, all the fighting, all the crap that had gone down between the three former friends was forgotten. John, Paul, and George looked like they had gone back in time, like they were kids again, playing together for the sheer enjoyment of it."[41] "The End" ends with a benediction ("And in the end, the love you take / Is equal to the love you make") sung sweetly and sincerely to a cushion of strings. The Beatles end the record, their career in fact, with a couplet worthy of Shakespeare.

But then *Abbey Road* ends a second time. "Her Majesty" is a twenty-three second fragment plucked from between "Mean Mr. Mustard" and "Polythene Pam." Paul had ordered the fragment to be thrown away; an engineer bound by EMI policy instead spliced it at the end of the master tape. Upon hearing "Her Majesty" jump out unexpectedly after a twenty-second silence following "The End," Paul was delighted, and thus "Her Majesty" stayed put. Meaning nothing, it says everything about the Beatles' irreverence, sense of timing, sense of scale, trust in accident, and faith in the listener to get the joke at the end of a career-long hard day's night.

Let It Be

Between the release of *Abbey Road* in September 1969 and the release of *Let It Be* in May 1970, there were two singles by the Plastic Ono Band

and two by the Beatles. October's "Cold Turkey" (cut by Lennon, Ono, Starr, Eric Clapton, and Klaus Voormann) depicted Lennon's struggle with heroin withdrawal.[42] In January 1970, Lennon, now backed by Harrison, Preston, Voormann, and Alan White, with Phil Spector producing, cranked out "Instant Karma." "Something"/"Come Together" was issued in October 1969, and "Let It Be" came out in March 1970, backed with the splendid lounge act parody that had been kicking around since 1967, "You Know My Name (Look Up the Number)."

Not until early January 1970 did the band return to *Get Back*, now named *Let It Be*, the soundtrack for the film that would open in New York City on May 13, 1970. By this time Paul was secretly recording his first solo album under everyone's noses and Ringo was wrapping up *Sentimental Journey*. Unhappy with Glyn Johns's latest labors on *Let It Be*, John and George hired Phil Spector to finish the album once and for all. Released on May 8, *Let It Be* was a mishmash of the back to basics aesthetic and Spector's Wall of Sound mannerisms. It retained, as links between tunes, snippets of dialogue cobbled together by Johns from the studio sessions and rooftop concert. In the space of two weeks Spector remixed, re-edited, and re-sequenced the album. Before it was pressed and distributed, Paul objected – too late to do any good – to the orchestral and choral embellishments that Spector, without the composer's permission, had foisted upon "The Long and Winding Road." Also scored for orchestra were "Across the Universe," a favorite Lennon track bearing the scars of previous studio manipulations, and "I Me Mine," originally ninety-four seconds in length, almost doubled through Spector's ingenuity, and then made even bigger with strings and brass. But this was only the beginning of the criticism. Lennon and Harrison, both hiring Spector to produce their initial post-Beatles work, may have been able to stomach his meddlings, but McCartney was disgusted, as were legions of critics and fans.

Blaming Spector for ruining *Let It Be* is like blaming Yoko for breaking up the Beatles. Both figures are default scapegoats for those who cannot accept certain realities of life or art. Granted, Spector gussied up Paul's greatest, starkest study of nostalgia, "The Long and Winding Road," yet that Spectorized song *did* go to number one in America, and "Let It Be" also topped the charts. As John Lennon noted after the fact, albeit with some exaggeration, the producer "was given the shittiest load of badly recorded shit with a lousy feeling to it ever, and he made something out of it. He did a great job."[43] Indeed, with the passage of time, the *New Musical Express*'s barb in 1970 that *Let It Be* was "a cheapskate epitaph, a cardboard tombstone, a sad and tatty end"[44] is hard to countenance. Had the reviewer, Alan Smith, complained that the record was tentative, arbitrarily sequenced, rough around the edges, and somewhat eccentrically produced, he would have been closer to the truth, which is that *Let It Be* was (and is) indeed all those things – but much more too. It is a posthumous collection of delectable and nourishing scraps tossed away from the table by four banqueters tired of pretending to enjoy one another's company at a gloomy, dyspeptic feast. Cheapskate? No: the Beatles fried their nerves in its making. Cardboard? Not even close: it croons, howls, chirps, screams, laughs, cries, whispers, and rocks. Tatty? Hardly: "Let It Be," "The Long and Winding Road," and "Get Back," the global hits, sound more philosophical than tatty, and these songs are not necessarily the album's high points.

In McCartney's "Two of Us," George's wish that the Beatles could make music on the order of the Band is realized. In a manner that can only be called "laid back" but without the term's pejorative shading, Paul pulls off the neat trick of writing a billet doux to Linda in the verse and an open letter to John in the six-bar bridge. Paul sings of "chasing paper, getting nowhere" with Linda, and to John he reflects, "You and I have memories, longer than the road that stretches out ahead." As he and "you" make their "way back home," Paul posits another identity for "you": every member of the audience. "Goodbye," the *sotto*-spoken last word in the fade-out, sets the valedictory mood for the rest of the album, just as it embraces with typical Beatles generosity every fan who has traveled so far for so many years with the band. We are all on the same road home somewhere, suggests Paul, twisting nostalgia into a sentiment close to happy closure and hope.

The entropy oozing out of the three-beat measures of "Dig a Pony" imparts a mixture of charm and puzzlement to what creeps along like a waltz tuned to a junkie's verbal ramble – until the junkie "comes clean," as it were, crying out, "All I want is you / Everything has got to be just like you want it to." Lines such as "You can syndicate any boat you row," or his swipe at the Rolling Stones, "I roll a stoney, / Well, you can imitate everyone you know," are as intriguing as any ever concocted by Lennon, which is not to suggest they can lay claim to coherence. In the next song, however, they can. "Across the Universe" finds Spector taking the basic elements (John's voice and guitar) from a version taped in February 1968 and drenching them in strings and female chorale. But the ballad survives this makeover because its main draw is some of John's best poetry, sung without irony or agitation, rare for Lennon in 1969. "Images of broken light . . . dance before me like a million eyes," "Limitless undying love . . . shines around me like a million suns," he sings, two poignant verses among many rounded out by the refrain "Nothing's going to change my world."

Next, "I Me Mine" has George licking the wounds of ego ("All through the day, I me mine") in a smart little rocker employing burning guitars, full-bore drums, and urgent organ in a face-off between 12/8 time and a head-blasting shuffle. While the informal – some would say slipshod – nature of the *Let It Be* enterprise is evoked in the snatches of dialogue heard between most of the album's twelve tunes, "Dig It" and "Maggie May" are other benchmarks of the record's poetics of improvisation. "Maggie May" conjures up the unusual image of the Beatles as buskers. In Liverpudlian dialect, John and Paul slap out this forty-second portrait of a street-crawler. At forty-nine seconds, "Dig It" was whittled down from a twelve-minute jam churning beneath and around Lennon's associative wordplay.[45] Separating these two exempla of extemporaneity is the majestic "Let It Be."[46] To summon the courage to push past the collapse of his band, which happened to be the greatest in history, and to muster the strength needed to keep his head held high as lawyers *and* best friend John Lennon closed in on him tooth and claw, Paul invoked for guidance the spirit of his long-deceased mother Mary McCartney. Glorious melody notwithstanding, the miracle of "Let It Be" is that it lacks self-pity or cheap sentiment. "I" is the only pronoun Paul has at his disposal; but the "I" in the opening clause – "When I find myself in times of trouble" – identifies much more than he himself; it is the universal "I" channeled through the voice of the Beatle most sympathetic to the suffering of his fellow human beings. This is why "Let It Be" is not a pity-party for Paul McCartney. He knows that to "let it be" is to "let go," to accept every manifestation and facet of loss, and, as Emily Dickinson suggested, to do that is the hardest thing a person ever has to do.[47] At once simple and profound, comparable to Mozart's "Sonata Facile" or a late painting by Mark Rothko, "Let It Be" is both medium and message of courage and compassion.

Side two more than holds its own with such sublimity. "I've Got a Feeling" and "One After 909" (rooftop concert takes) are sublime after their own fashion. The first number is a conflation of two half-songs, one each by John and Paul (whose lead vocal returns him, for sheer intensity, to "Hey Jude" territory), laced together with Harrison guitar lines that prove he was not afraid of getting back to rock and roll. "One After 909," composed by two pre-Beatle teens in 1957, is another minor miracle: Paul's bad-boy bass pumps time, dallying with Preston's electric piano and Harrison's Telecaster. George fills the holes between the singers' grunts and shouts with needle-like licks, and his sixteen-bar lead rips holes in the physics of sound. The vocals of John and Paul rip too, as if they were back shredding their throats in front of drunken sailors in the fifth set on a Saturday night in Hamburg.

"The Long and Winding Road" retards the impending end, as does the surpassingly ironic "For You Blue," a twelve-bar blues, one of the few recorded by the Fabs. But finally *Get Back / Let It Be* reaches its arbitrary end. Beginning life as an improvisation on January 14, 1969, "Get Back" was finished by the 26th of that month and later underwent two surgeries, one that added a fade-out coda to the single version, and one, the album version, that tacked on John's quip at the end of the rooftop concert where he expresses hope that the group "passed the audition." Ringo's snare and bass nail down the tune's anapestic rhythm, John and Billy Preston trade funky eight-bar solos, and Paul, as if to memorialize his latter-day role as coach, camp-director, manager, and headmaster of the band, does not ask but tells a certain Jo Jo to "get back to where you once belonged." If it is easy to see John in Jo Jo, it is not easy to see "sweet Loretta Martin" in anyone else in the Beatles' camp. It is wise, therefore, not to read too much into Paul at his inconsequential best: "All the girls around her say she's got it coming, / But she gets it while she can."

Let It Be . . . Naked

The epilogue to the saga of *Let It Be* is short but not particularly sweet. The movie came and went in 1970; postmodern audiences have been denied a DVD with restored footage, cleaned-up audio-visual, and extras. But Paul was determined to undo wrongs done to the music itself. At last the world would get the album the Beatles intended to make in January 1969.

Bearing the adjective "naked," the resulting 2003 edition struck many listeners as a lateral move at best. Absent from the remastered and re-sequenced program are "Maggie May" and "Dig It." Present is the fine rooftop take of "Don't Let Me Down." The biggest change in the new disc is the erasure of Phil Spector's orchestration from "The Long and Winding Road," "I Me Mine," and "Across the Universe," and of Glyn Johns's between-song banterings. In striking at the enemy (Spector) with the Pro-Tools technology at their command, however, McCartney's production team also laid low the Beatles' less culpable, less offensive ally (Johns – although to be fair, Spector did splice much of the convivial chatter into the 1970 album). With the *audio verité* dimension wiped clean, *Let It Be . . . Naked* comes to the consumer nestled in digital excelsior. Yes, the music is punchier, with increased clarity, but more than a trifle dry, listless, and, worst of all, redundant. Definitive versions of "The Long and Winding Road" and "I Me Mine" grace 1996's *Anthology 3*, and nothing could surpass the 1970 masters of "One After 909," "I've Got a Feeling," "Two of Us," and "Get Back." Consequently, fans long familiar with the slap-happiness of "Maggie May," the persiflage of John and Paul, and the idiosyncrasies of Phil Spector may be disconcerted by *Naked*'s relative sterility.

A step ahead must be measured by the deficiencies that the past factors into the present. Instead of restoring truth extracted from miles of tape used in January 1969, *Let It Be . . . Naked* reinforces a myth of closure. *Let It Be* is far from done. And though we know it never can be complete, we do expect the final attempt at a final artifact to present a much bigger chunk of the reams of music rehearsed in January 1969, much more dialogue,[48] some bonus video footage, maybe even a booklet of plates from Ethan Russell's book of photographs packaged with the original LP. Until some, most, or all of these things can be effected by any creative forces left at Apple/EMI, Beatle-lovers will have to let it – their dream for an album at peace with its initial potential – be.

8 Apple Records

BRUCE SPIZER

We've got this thing called Apple, which is going to be records, films, and electronics, which all tie up. JOHN LENNON

In mid-May 1968, John Lennon and Paul McCartney flew to New York to announce the Beatles' latest venture, Apple. After holding interviews in their hotel suite with *Time*, *Newsweek*, *Business Week*, and *Forbes* magazines and conducting a press conference, the two Beatles appeared on NBC-TV's *Tonight Show* on May 14. While viewers may have naïvely hoped the pair would perform, John and Paul were there to talk business.

John explained that their accountant had told them that they could give their money to the government or do something with it. "So we decided to play businessmen for a bit, because we've got to run our own affairs now. So we've got this thing called Apple, which is going to be records, films, and electronics, which all tie up. And to make a sort of an umbrella so people who want to make films about . . . grass . . . don't have to get on their knees in an office, you know, begging for a break. We'll try and do it like that. That's the idea. I mean we'll find out what happens, but that's what we're trying to do."

Lennon's remarks summarize how Apple came about and why the Beatles were becoming businessmen. The company was not created for Utopian reasons. It was formed to shelter the Beatles' sizable income from British taxes. Dating back to the spring of 1967, the Beatles had been meeting regularly with their advisers to discuss ways of spending their money to defer immediate recognition of income. Although initially involved in common tax shelters such as real estate, the group rejected additional investments in traditional businesses before entering into an area suggested by Paul – music publishing. McCartney, who had received several hefty royalty checks generated by the numerous performances of songs in the Lennon-McCartney catalog, was well aware of the money to be made in publishing hit songs. He and the other Beatles envisioned the development of new song-writing talent while increasing their wealth. With their attention shifting away from traditional investments, it was only natural for their plans to include other areas that interested them, such as music, film, and electronics. As for the Beatles running their own affairs, this was necessitated by the death of manager Brian Epstein in August, 1967.

John and Paul told the TV audience what their Apple company planned to do. It was to be a place where people with talent could go, rather than begging for a break from big business. Paul explained: "Big companies are so big that if you're little and good it takes you like sixty years to make it. And so people miss out on these little good people." John provided a metaphor based on fellow Beatle George Harrison saying he was "sick of being told to keep out of the park." According to Lennon, "That's what it's all about, you know. We're trying to make a park for people to come in and do what they want." So that explained what the Beatles were trying to do. It wouldn't take long for the Beatles to "find out what happens." But on that idealistic evening in May 1968, it sounded like a noble venture that the Beatles could pull off. After all, they were the Beatles.

The first public appearance of the Apple name had come nearly one year earlier, in June 1967, with the release of *Sgt. Pepper's Lonely Hearts Club Band.* The back of the album's elaborate jacket contains the following credit: "Cover by MC Productions and The Apple." This obscure reference went largely unnoticed, giving no hint of what the Beatles were up to or that they would soon be operating as Apple.

The Apple name resurfaced five months later in November, 1967, with *Magical Mystery Tour.* An Apple logo, surrounded by the phrase "apple presents," appears above the group's name on the inside gatefold covers to the British EP and the American album. Once again, fans were left in the dark about the meaning of the Apple.

The *Magical Mystery Tour* film, which first appeared on December 26, 1967, on the BBC, was the first Apple project. The movie was shot in segments without the benefit of a script during September through November 1967. Although the film was brutally panned by the critics and described at the time as the Beatles' first major failure, it is now regarded as an interesting period piece depicting the freewheeling spirit of the sixties.

Rather than bringing in experienced businessmen, the Beatles hired trusted friends to run Apple. Long-time Beatles road manager Neil Aspinall was named managing director. Alistair Taylor, who had been involved in the group's day-to-day logistics as an assistant to manager Brian Epstein, was brought in to serve as Apple's general manager. Another former Epstein employee, Terry Doran, was hired to head Apple Music Publishing.

The first songwriter signed to Apple Music Publishing was George Alexander. He and three other musicians formed a band, which John Lennon named Grapefruit in recognition of a poetry book by Yoko Ono. As Apple had not yet established its record division at that time, the group had to look elsewhere to obtain a recording contract, signing with EMI's Stateside subsidiary in the UK and Equinox in the USA. Although the Beatles participated in the group's promotion, Grapefruit failed to make an impact in either market, being limited to a number twenty-one British hit with its debut single, *Dear Delilah.* Apple Music Publishing signed other songwriters, including Jackie Lomax, who would soon become an Apple recording artist.

The Beatles' venture into electronics was entrusted to a twenty-seven-year-old Greek television repairman, Alexis Mardas. John was impressed by the self-proclaimed electronic genius and madcap inventor, naming him "Magic Alex." He was constantly coming up with ideas, though few of his projects ever proved practical. Magic Alex claimed he could invent a force field that would cause a house to hover above the ground. He demonstrated wallpaper that could serve as a stereo system's speakers. He created a device that enabled a person to reach another person by phone merely by saying the individual's name. This was an early form of voice-recognition technology. Although Apple Electronics patented eight of his inventions, none ever went into production.

The Beatles' faith in Magic Alex led the group to have him design what was to be the ultimate recording studio. It was to have a seventy-two-track recorder at a time when sixteen tracks was state of the art, with most modern studios being limited to eight. When the Beatles first attempted to use his studio in the basement of their Apple headquarters, they found it to be a total disaster and had to bring in a mobile recording unit from EMI Studios.

Apple also ventured briefly into the retail clothing business by opening up a boutique on Baker Street. The bulk of the clothing was designed by a trio of Dutch fashion designers who joined up with a British publicist and called themselves The Fool. The boutique was run without any business controls, enabling employees to raid the cash registers. Customers came by to look at the beautiful clothes and the beautiful people, browse, and shoplift. The fashion designers' freewheeling spirit and spending also contributed to the store losing nearly half a million dollars (about £167,000) in its first six months. The Beatles, realizing that they had been made fools of by The Fool, shut the store down and invited the public to attend one last free-for-all orgy of legal shoplifting.

Having set up film, publishing, electronics, and retail divisions, the Beatles finally turned their attention to what they did best – making records. Apple Records was set up with the same idealistic philosophy as the rest of Apple. It would discover and develop new talent. The Beatles also hoped that their musician friends would come to Apple when their existing contracts with other labels expired.

Apple hired Ron Kass, an American who headed Liberty Records' British operations, as president of Apple Records. Paul McCartney brought in Peter

Asher, who was the brother of Paul's former girlfriend Jane Asher, and had gained fame in the mid-sixties as half of Peter and Gordon, to serve as head of Apple's A&R (artist and repertoire) department. His job was to discover and develop recording artists for the label. His first major signing was James Taylor. At the request of the Beatles, Capitol Records executive Ken Mansfield was given the title of US manager of Apple Records.

Rather than hire an expensive conventional ad agency, Paul decided he could fashion a campaign to launch Apple Records. His concept was to show a one-man band who would be touted as an Apple success story. The ad showed Alistair Taylor sitting on a stool with a bass drum strapped on his back. He wore a harmonica around his neck and strummed a guitar. He was surrounded by a microphone, tape recorder, washboard, and brass instruments. The ad explained that the man had sent a tape, picture, and letter to Apple. To drive home the point that his doing so paid off and to encourage others to submit their music to Apple, the ad concluded with, "This man now owns a Bentley!"

The ad ran in several music magazines and was distributed as a handbill poster throughout London. Apple received over 400 tapes in two weeks and hundreds more during the next few months. While this unique way of searching for new talent fitted well within the free spirit of Apple, it was not productive. According to Peter Asher, "None of it was much good unfortunately. Out of the myriad of tapes we got in the mail, we didn't sign anyone."

Because the Beatles were under contract to EMI and Capitol, the group were unable to sign a recording agreement with their own company, Apple. However, EMI and Capitol agreed to press the group's records with Apple labels. EMI and Capitol also entered into agreements to manufacture and distribute Apple product.

The first four Apple singles were released simultaneously in late August 1968. In Britain, Apple prepared an elaborate press kit containing the discs, pictures of the artists, bios, and descriptions of the music. It came in a box titled "Our First Four," and was distributed to British radio stations and members of the press. In the USA, Capitol assembled a press kit with equivalent but different-looking contents. It was housed in a glossy cream-colored folder with a large green Apple logo on its front side. While Apple in London hand-delivered copies of "Our First Four" to the Queen and the Prime Minister, Capitol did not send a copy of the press kit to the White House.

The main item of interest of the first four Apple releases was the new Beatles single, "Hey Jude"/"Revolution," which topped both the UK and American charts for several weeks. "Hey Jude" was a glorious singalong by

Paul that clocked in at seven minutes eleven seconds at a time when the average pop tune was two to three minutes long. "Revolution" was an all-out rocker with distorted guitars and relevant lyrics sung by John. Future releases on Apple by the Beatles included the White Album, *Get Back, Abbey Road* and *Let It Be.*

The other three initial releases epitomized the free spirit of Apple and its quest to discover and develop talent. The artists ranged from an eighteen-year-old female Welsh folksinger to a veteran Liverpool rocker and a band founded in 1855.

Mary Hopkin was signed to Apple after supermodel Twiggy told Paul McCartney of Hopkin's talent shortly after the young folk singer appeared on the British talent show *Opportunity Knocks.* For her debut single, McCartney selected a Lithuanian folk song adopted by American Gene Raskin, "Those Were the Days." Paul produced the single, giving it an orchestral backing that was bouncy, moving and nostalgic. Although its running time of five minutes five seconds was well in excess of the length of other singles of its day (except the new Beatles disc), the song topped the British charts and peaked at number two in the States, unable to move past the Beatles' "Hey Jude."

Jackie Lomax is a Liverpool native who sang lead and played bass in the Undertakers, a group that had shared the bill with the Beatles in the early sixties. After his group broke up, Lomax signed a management contract with Brian Epstein and released a single under the name Lomax Alliance. His first Apple single was produced by George Harrison, who wrote the A side, "Sour Milk Sea." The song was recorded in June 1968, with an all-star cast featuring Lomax on lead vocals and rhythm guitar, Harrison on rhythm guitar, Paul McCartney on bass, Ringo on drums, Eric Clapton on lead guitar, Nicky Hopkin on keyboards, and Eddie Clayton on conga drums. Although a great rock single, the disc was overshadowed by "Hey Jude" and "Those Were the Days" and did not chart.

The Black Dyke Mills Band is a brass band formed in the village of Queensbury, Yorkshire, England, in 1855. The group was sponsored by John Foster and Sons, Ltd. In 1968, the group consisted of twenty-seven members plus a percussion section. In 1967 they had won the National Championship Band of Great Britain award for the seventh time since 1945. Their single, which was produced by Paul, consisted of "Thingumybob," a theme song written by Paul for a TV show, and a brass band version of the Beatles hit "Yellow Submarine." The record baffled radio programmers and did not chart.

The euphoria of setting up a record company initially prompted Paul to take a very active role with Apple artists. In addition to participating in all four of the label's first releases, McCartney guided the career of Mary Hopkin by selecting the songs for, and producing, her first album, *Post Card*, and by writing and producing her follow-up single, "Goodbye." He also played bass and guitar on several of her songs. Paul further assisted Jackie Lomax by producing his recording of the Coasters' "Thumbin' a Ride." McCartney was also very active in the early recordings of the pop rock band Badfinger. He wrote, produced, and played piano on the hit "Come and Get It" and co-produced two other songs, "Carry On Till Tomorrow" and "Rock of All Ages," also playing piano on the latter track. Paul played bass on James Taylor's first single, "Carolina in My Mind."

After Allen Klein took over the company's management in 1969, Paul limited his involvement with Apple to the release of his own records. His first solo album, *McCartney*, was one of the first rock albums to feature a musician playing all of the instruments. After completing his second album, *Ram*, Paul put together a new band, Wings, which included his wife, Linda, on keyboards and vocals. Paul McCartney and Wings released several successful singles and albums for Apple, including "My Love," "Live and Let Die" and "Band on the Run."

Shortly after his return from the New York media blitz announcing Apple to the world, John became involved with Yoko Ono. He took advantage of Apple's free spirit by releasing a series of experimental albums with Yoko, including the notorious *Unfinished Music No. 1: Two Virgins*, which features a black and white full frontal nude photograph of John and Yoko on its cover. Beginning with the release of "Give Peace a Chance" in the summer of 1969, John released a series of singles credited to the Plastic Ono Band. The concept of the band was that it had no fixed membership. Apple's press agent, Derek Taylor, wrote: "The band may be the property of Apple, but it also belongs to everyone because what it represents is freedom, freedom for performers to be themselves, taking no heed of who they are or what they look like or where they have been or what their music is supposed to be . . . It could be anything." Its ever-changing line-up would later include George Harrison, Ringo Starr, Eric Clapton, Klaus Voormann, Nicky Hopkins, and Jim Keltner.

John's first true solo album, *John Lennon/Plastic Ono Band*, was a stark-sounding collection of personal songs covering such difficult topics as the pain of being abandoned by his father and mother, his mother's death, and his loss of faith in popular icons, including the Beatles. No artist has every bared his soul more than John did. The teen angst of grunge music pales by comparison. His second solo album, *Imagine*, was an easier listen. Although the toughness was still present in some of the songs, there were also themes of optimism and the exuberant joy of love. John described it as "commercial with no compromise" and "*Plastic Ono* with chocolate coating." The album's title track remains a classic call for world peace. His later solo work contained some great songs, but did not equal the brilliance of the first two albums.

While the other Beatles often participated in recording sessions by Apple artists, John did so only if the project involved Yoko. He produced or co-produced her early recordings, played on many of the songs, and assembled musicians such as Eric Clapton, Klaus Voormann, and Ringo Starr to play on the tracks. Yoko became one of the more prolific Apple artists. In addition to sharing five albums with John and having seven of her songs appear on the B sides to Plastic Ono Band singles, she released four solo albums and four solo singles.

Lennon was responsible for two very diverse signings by Apple. John Tavener was a classical musician and composer. He recorded two albums for the label, including 1970's *The Whale*, which was recorded at the Church of St. John the Evangelist in London. Ringo attended the sessions and contributed voices and percussion. Lennon also gave thumbs up to a tape by a band containing a reggae arrangement of his "Give Peace a Chance." The group, which was named the Hot Chocolate Band by Mavis Smith of Apple's press office, was led by Jamaican singer Errol Brown and Trinidadian Tony Wilson. When their Apple single did not chart, the group left the label, became associated with producer Mickie Most, shortened their name to Hot Chocolate, and scored three top ten hits in America.

Shortly after John and Yoko moved to New York in late May 1971, they ran into political activists Jerry Rubin and David Peel; the latter was also a streetwise musician. John arranged for Peel to sign with Apple, and co-produced, with Yoko, his album *The Pope Smokes Dope*. Through Peel, John became familiar with Elephant's Memory, a New York bar band that John used to back him on his highly political album *Some Time in New York City*. After completion of that album, John and Yoko produced an album by the group for Apple.

George Harrison, who often had to fight to get the Beatles to record his songs, enjoyed the freedom given to him under Apple. His soundtrack recording for the film *Wonderwall* was one of the first projects developed for Apple. Recorded in London, and Bombay, India, during November 1967 through January 1968, the album features both rock and Indian musicians. Harrison made his score a "mini-anthology of Indian music" because he "wanted to help turn the public on to Indian music." In addition to Indian chants, drones, and ragas, the album also contains rockers, majestic pop songs, and cowboy music. It was one of the first albums released in the genre now known as world music.

George's second project for Apple was even more unconventional. *Electronic Sound* consists of two long selections of sounds generated by a Moog synthesizer, an electronic keyboard instrument. One composition is full of snapping and hissing sounds and wind and other noises. The other contains wind sound effects, sustained notes, reverberating notes, and random noises. The record posed the question, "If a Beatle released an album and nobody played it, would it still make an electronic sound?" Harrison's experience with the Moog synthesizer would lead to more practical applications during the recording of the Beatles album *Abbey Road*.

After the Beatles broke up, George recorded four studio albums for Apple. The first, *All Things Must Pass*, contains several songs that George auditioned for the Beatles during the group's January 1969 *Get Back* sessions. The album topped the US charts for several weeks and peaked at number four in the UK.

George produced several discs for Apple artists. In addition to writing and producing Jackie Lomax's first single, "Sour Milk Sea," he produced Lomax's first album, *Is This What You Want*. After bringing in Billy Preston to record with the Beatles during the *Get Back* sessions, Harrison arranged for Apple to buy out Preston's Capitol contract. He produced Preston's first album, *That's the Way God Planned It*, which features a stellar cast of musicians, including Harrison, Eric Clapton, Ginger Baker, Keith Richards, Klaus Voormann, and Ringo. George co-produced Preston's second Apple LP, *Encouraging Words*, utilizing several of the musicians who took part in the *All Things Must Pass* sessions. The album contains Preston's versions of George's *My Sweet Lord* and *All Things Must Pass*, as well as one track co-written by the pair, *Sing One for the Lord*.

At Harrison's request, Apple signed American rhythm and blues singer/songwriter Doris Troy, who had sung backup vocals on, and co-written songs for, Billy Preston's second Apple LP. George produced and co-wrote her first Apple single, "Ain't That Cute," and was actively involved in her *Doris Troy* album, co-writing a few songs and lining up the musicians from his *All Things Must Pass* sessions.

George's fascination with Indian music and the Hare Krishna movement prompted him to bring the London branch of the Radha Krishna Temple to Apple. Harrison produced, and added harmonium, guitar, and bass to, a pair of traditional Krishna chants, *Hare Krishna Mantra* and *Prayer to Spiritual Masters*. The former became a surprise number twelve hit in Britain. The group's follow-up single, *Govinda*, was even better, but stalled at twenty-six on the UK charts. Harrison produced a few more tracks to flesh out an album.

In June 1971, George worked with sitar master Ravi Shankar on the soundtrack to *Raga*, an Apple Films documentary on Shankar. He also produced a single for Shankar. It was during this time that Shankar approached George about organizing a benefit concert for the refugee children of Bangladesh. The ensuing event, "the Concert for Bangladesh," was the first large-scale benefit concert, pre-dating Live Aid by fourteen years. Harrison put together an all-star band featuring himself, Eric Clapton, Billy Preston, Leon Russell, Ringo Starr, and other veteran musicians and singers. The concerts raised nearly $250,000, with proceeds from the film of the event and the soundtrack album adding to the cause.

Harrison produced four tracks for Badfinger's third album, *Straight Up*, before bowing out to organize the Concert for Bangladesh. He played guitar on two of the tracks, including the hit single "Day After Day." George also served as producer for Lon and Derek Van Eaton's single "Sweet Music."

Harrison's use of Phil Spector as co-producer of his *All Things Must Pass* and *Bangladesh* albums led to him co-producing some tracks with Spector's then wife, Ronnie, who gained fame in the sixties as the lead singer of the Ronettes of "Be My Baby" fame. Her recording of Harrison's "Try Some, Buy Some" was issued as a single.

Ringo's first project for Apple was *Sentimental Journey*, an album of standards from the twenties, thirties, forties, and early fifties. One of the tracks, "Star Dust," was arranged by Paul. At the time the disc was recorded during 1969 and 1970, the idea of a rock star doing an album of pop standards was unheard of. Thirteen years later, Linda Ronstadt shifted gears and released the first of her three albums of standards arranged by Nelson Riddle. Aging rockers such as Bryan Ferry, Boz Scaggs, and Rod Stewart have belatedly jumped on the big band wagon. Ringo was way ahead of the curve, releasing his collection of standards before his thirtieth birthday at a time when big band songs weren't cool.

Ringo's second album was another specialty project: a collection of country and western tunes recorded in Nashville and titled *Beaucoups of Blues*. During his tenure with the Beatles, Ringo sang lead on country and western songs such as Carl Perkins's "Honey Don't" and Buck Owens's "Act Naturally." One of his original compositions, "Don't Pass Me By," has a distinct country feel, complete with prominent fiddle. As was the case with his first album, *Beaucoups of Blues* had difficulty finding an audience as most Beatles fans were not ready for an entire LP of country and western, and fans of country music were unlikely to buy an album from an ex-Beatle.

After issuing albums of standards and country and western tunes, Ringo finally released a rock and roll record, "It Don't Come Easy." The song was written by Ringo, with substantial, but uncredited, assistance from George Harrison, who also produced the single. The disc was a substantial hit in both the UK and the USA. His second single, "Back Off Boogaloo," was written by Ringo and produced by George, who also played the track's stinging slide guitar.

Much to everyone's surprise, Ringo kept churning out the hits. His self-titled *Ringo* LP produced three hit singles in the USA (only two singles were released in the UK), including "Photograph," which was co-written by Ringo and George. John and Paul also contributed songs to the LP. John's "I Am the Greatest" was a near Beatles reunion featuring John, George, Ringo, Billy Preston, and Klaus Voormann. Although not as successful as its predecessor, Ringo's next LP, *Goodnight Vienna*, also gave birth to three more US hit singles for Ringo. John Lennon wrote and played on the title track and gave Ringo his arrangement of the Platters' hit "Only You."

Although Ringo did not write songs for other Apple artists or produce any sessions for others, he played drums on records by Jackie Lomax, Billy Preston, Doris Troy, Yoko Ono, Lon and Derek Van Eaton, and John Tavener. He also arranged for Apple to sign singer/songwriter Chris Hodge after hearing his demo of "We're On Our Way."

Although the Beatles played a significant role in recruiting Apple artists, some were brought in by others. Ron Kass, who served as president of Apple Records until being fired by Allen Klein, signed the Modern Jazz Quartet away from Atlantic Records. The group recorded two albums for Apple before returning to Atlantic. Peter Asher signed folk singer James Taylor to Apple and produced his debut album, *James Taylor*.

Apple's Tony King was impressed by a tape sent to him by the Sundown Playboys, a band from Lake Charles, Louisiana. Apple released a single pairing two Cajun songs (sung in a French dialect as spoken by Acadian immigrants living in Louisiana) written by guitarist Daryl Higginbotham: "Saturday Night Special" and "Valse de Soleil" ("Sundown Waltz"). Although Apple worked hard to obtain radio airplay for the disc, it did not chart. Authentic roots music had yet to gain interest in 1972.

Although Apple issued records by twenty non-Beatle artists, by the end of 1973 the label was nothing more than an outlet for solo Beatle releases. The trend began with the introduction of Allen Klein, who alienated Paul from participating in Apple and who focused on Apple's most profitable artists – John, Paul, George, and Ringo.

The final release of the first Apple era was George's "This Guitar (Can't Keep From Crying)," which was issued in the USA on December 8, 1975, and in the UK on February 6, 1976. The disc became the first single by an ex-Beatle to fail to chart in either country. It was a sad end and a far cry from the success of Apple's first release, "Hey Jude." But in between there had been some great moments of music. Apple's free-spirit approach had fostered the release of a diverse batch of records that included pop rock, rock and roll, big band standards, brass bands, jazz, classical, Indian ragas, Krishna chants, rhythm and blues, gospel, country, folk, experimental, electronic, and Cajun hoedowns.

Although John became sidetracked and never followed up on his vision of Apple, his mission statement proved quite prophetic: "We've got this thing called Apple, which is going to be records, films and electronics, which all tie up." And it came to be that music, video and electronic computers, cell phones and personal listening and viewing devices are intertwined in a way that John could only have imagined.

9 The solo years

MICHAEL FRONTANI

On December 31, 1970, Paul McCartney brought suit to end his partnership with the other three Beatles, making official what had already in fact happened. The four lovable moptops turned countercultural icons had ceased to function as a cohesive unit by the time of *The Beatles* (the White Album, 1968), with *Abbey Road* (1969) pulling them together only as one last defiant act against the dissolution embodied in *Let It Be*. And so "John, Paul, George, and Ringo," for the first time in their adult lives, faced a future as something other than Beatles. These four young men, four Beatles alone but inextricably bound to one another, would spend the next months and years alternately shunning and embracing their storied past. Three ex-Beatles – all but Lennon, who was murdered on December 8, 1980, at the age of forty years – would continue to grapple with their pasts as they entered middle age and beyond. This chapter provides a broad overview of the post-Beatle lives and careers of Lennon, McCartney, Harrison, and Starr, and considers their evolution as individual artists.

As it had been at the time of the Beatles' arrival on US shores in 1964, success in America was the "golden ring" of the entertainment industry in 1970, and was the biggest guarantor of success elsewhere. Hence, though occasionally referring to the British context and sources, the focus here is on the artistic evolution of the four ex-Beatles within the context of their reception by American critics and audiences. This chapter, alone in this book, is *not* about the Beatles. My purpose here is to answer the same question faced by Lennon, McCartney, Harrison, and Starr, not only in 1970, but for the rest of their lives, namely: what does it mean to *not* be a Beatle? This question reverberated in the lives of the solo Beatles. They were stars[1] of the first order, and they – and their audience(s) – had to contend with the band's highly developed image, one bound up in the imaginations of a significant portion of baby-boomers. Accounting for perceptions of the band's artistic supremacy and unrivaled commercial success, and embodying as it did a counterculture / youth culture ideal, the Beatles' image(s) continued to interact with established and emergent societal forces in late twentieth-century America. In the early 1970s, in an environment in which a substantial portion of the audience expected rock music and culture to transcend pleasure into consequence and "meaning," the shimmering fantasia of the Beatles' image cast a long shadow – for none so much as for four ex-Beatles.[2]

A number of forces impacted the careers of the solo Beatles, including both those peculiar to the band and those at work in society. First, the Beatles' unequaled commercial success prompted huge expectations of the solo Beatles, particularly the songwriters, and their solo accomplishments were measured against the commercial achievements of the band. Fans and critics expected successes to be more frequent, and to reach higher heights, than those of run-of-the-mill rock stars. Yet even in the trough, which each at times visited, when critics' barbs were sharpest and record company expectations frustrated, the ex-Beatles continued to release gold-certified albums and singles.[3] Second, in establishing themselves as solo artists, the former Beatles all participated in revision of the Beatles' "story" and deconstruction of their myth, Lennon doing so most famously with revelations of groupies, drug use, and infighting, in the *Lennon Remembers* (1972) interviews with *Rolling Stone*'s Jann Wenner, in late 1970. Part of this process was attribution of the songwriting credits for the Beatles' catalog, particularly – but not exclusively – by Lennon. Ironically, this "clarification" often had the contrary effect of further obscuring the contributions and talents of the individual Beatles to their success, particularly McCartney's production and arranging prowess. There were ramifications for the reception of the former Beatles by various audiences, as can be seen in the relative coolness with which McCartney's superbly crafted but non-committal pop and experimental amalgams were initially received by *Rolling Stone* and other rock publications, compared to the warm reception for more culturally, artistically, and lyrically "committed" works like Harrison's majestic paean to Krishna Consciousness, *All Things Must Pass* (1970), and Lennon's *Plastic Ono Band* (1970) and *Imagine* (1971). Third, the former Beatles – once, communally, catalysts for the transformation of rock and roll into rock, in fact into Art, and focal points for much of the discourse that concerned the youth culture and its relevance – were destined to be considered individually within that framework. Complicating matters, American progressives and conservatives were waging a culture war, which, depending on one's ideological bent, strongly influenced perceptions of rock music and musicians, and of the youth culture. The ex-Beatles, embodying the ideal and ideals of the sixties generation, were inescapably bound up in that battle.

While this chapter offers an account of the careers of the four solo Beatles, the focus is on the first ten years following the breakup, the 1970s, a period during which rock music was still definitive in shaping the youth culture and in which Lennon, McCartney, Harrison, and Starr continued to be viewed as banner-carriers for the youth movement and its values. Additionally, the specter of a Beatles reunion allowed a space for the optimism of the previous decade, a chance for many to re-ignite the ember of idealism that remained from their youths. Lennon's death brought this period to an end, not only as to expectations of the four ex-Beatles, but as to the progressive aspirations of many in that generation.

The decade following the end of the Beatles was the most productive period for the ex-Beatles, certainly within the rubric of rock music. Harrison released six studio albums, and Starr seven, in the 1970s. In the aftermath of Lennon's death, a disenchanted Harrison released only three more studio albums of new compositions before his death in 2001, while Starr released only two albums in the 1980s, 1981's *Stop and Smell the Roses* and *Old Wave* (1983), before a nearly ten-year hiatus from recording of new material (*Time Takes Time* [1992] was followed by sporadic recording and numerous iterations of his nostalgic review, the All-Starr Band [inaugurated in 1989]). McCartney released ten studio albums in the decade following the end of the Beatles, and he retained the work ethic he demonstrated as a Beatle, but, after Lennon's death, his career witnessed a gradual falling off of rock studio albums, and he increasingly pursued other interests, particularly after his classical work, *Liverpool Oratorio*, was released in 1991. Lennon released seven studio albums in the 1970s. One studio album, *Milk and Honey* (1982), and several compilations were released posthumously.

Over the first decade following the end of the band, as rock continued along its path of incorporation by the music industry, a rear guard continued to judge the work of Lennon, McCartney, and Harrison regarding the extent to which it diminished or fortified the perceived values of the youth culture. The solo career of Starr, the most "ordinary" of the Beatles – in the estimation of some, the world's luckiest sideman – was less bound up in the prevailing effort to define rock's function or in the conflict between ascendant conservatism and withering progressivism. Nevertheless, Starr's early solo fortunes rose and fell with his ability to recreate and invoke the bonhomie and communalism that had been so essential to the youth culture's self-perception and to his Beatle persona, and for a time he did indeed "get by" and even flourish with a little help from his friends.

Ringo Starr: "I get by with a little help from my friends"

While he was still a Beatle, Starr's solo efforts were concentrated in acting, and he appeared with varying success in *Candy* (1968) and *The Magic Christian* (1969).[4] But, with the Beatles fragmenting, Starr undertook an ambitious solo recording agenda, releasing two albums in 1970. In fact, with *Sentimental Journey*, he was the first Beatle to record and release a non-experimental studio solo album. A collection of standards from his parents' generation, with arrangements by, among others, George Martin, Quincy Jones, Elmer Bernstein, Maurice Gibb of the Bee Gees, and Paul McCartney, *Sentimental Journey* charted in the USA and UK, despite luke-warm reviews.[5] Its follow-up, *Beaucoups of Blues*, was recorded with some of the best studio musicians in Nashville, including pedal steel guitar player Pete Drake (whom Starr had met on sessions for Harrison's *All Things Must Pass*), who produced and enlisted some of country music's best writers to compose tracks for the album. The collection, which better suited Starr's limited range and vocal quality than did its predecessor, was received more favorably by critics,[6] though performing less well in the charts.

Following the release of his first two albums, Starr became a renaissance man, of sorts, recording and performing at leisure while pursuing interests in other fields, such as film and furniture design.[7] He played on Lennon's *Plastic Ono Band* and Harrison's *All Things Must Pass*. He also joined Harrison for the Concert for Bangladesh benefit. In 1971, Starr recorded the hit single "It Don't Come Easy," a gold record and top five hit in both the US and UK charts. This was followed, in 1972, by the top ten hit, "Back Off Boogaloo." In late 1973, he finally issued another album, the critical and popular hit, *Ringo*.[8] Joining Starr on the album were Randy Newman, Harry Nilsson, members of the Band, Billy Preston, Klaus Voormann, Lennon, Harrison, and McCartney. Lennon penned the album's opener, "I'm the Greatest," and played piano, with Harrison on guitar. Starr's tongue-in-cheek delivery is a perfect foil for the bombast of Lennon's humorous record of life in "the greatest show on earth." Lennon and Harrison's participation on the track fueled speculation that a Beatle reunion might be near (as would any meeting of Beatles, real or imagined, over the next seven years).[9] McCartney and wife Linda wrote the closing track, "Six O'Clock," and contributed elsewhere on the album. Harrison wrote Starr's number one single, "Photograph," as well as "Sunshine Life for Me," and "You and Me (Babe)." "Sunshine Life for Me," recorded with members of the Band and David Bromberg, is perhaps the most lively track on the album, with the backup band and Starr giving the song an authentic country-bluegrass feel. Starr's cover of Johnny Burnett's 1960 recording of "You're Sixteen" was a number one hit in the USA, and "Oh My My" was a top five single. Impressively if loosely produced, the album succeeds because Starr, with his drolly comical delivery, never takes himself too seriously, while those around him both understand his limitations and his appeal and keep him within those bounds. A remarkable album, *Ringo* benefits from the palpable good cheer that went into its creation, of which *Rolling Stone* commented: "In atmosphere *Ringo* is the most successful record by an ex-Beatle."[10]

Goodnight Vienna followed, in late 1974. Critically well received, it reached number eight in the USA, and was certified gold, but climbed no higher than number thirty in the UK charts.[11] Two tracks, covers of the Platters' "Only You (And You Alone)" and Hoyt Axton's "No No Song," were also top ten hits in the USA. *Ringo's Rotogravure*, released in 1976, with contributions from Lennon, McCartney, and Harrison, as well as Eric Clapton and Peter Frampton, garnered only lukewarm reviews and mediocre sales,[12] demonstrating, perhaps, that the formula that had marked his previous two star-laden albums had run its course. Attempts to move away from that formula pushed Starr's limitations to the forefront, as was apparent on the disco-inflected *Ringo the 4th* (1977), an ill-conceived and humorless attempt to find an audience in the burgeoning disco market. That commercial and critical disaster[13] was followed by *Bad Boy* (1978), which *Rolling Stone*, echoing the generally held view, called "ersatz trash."[14] Even a concurrent television special, *Ringo*, failed to resuscitate his stagnating career. In the fall of 1980, Starr, hoping to re-ignite some interest, grasped at his winning formula of the early 1970s, employing some of rock's top names for his next album, tentatively titled *Can't Fight Lighting*. Lennon's murder brought production to a halt.

George Harrison: "Beware of Maya"

Of all the Beatles, Harrison had been the most devoted to the spiritual quest and the most vocal advocate of transcendental meditation and Krishna Consciousness as alternatives to the Judeo-Christian tradition. Whether publicly declaring his devotion, as he did early on, or pursuing his spirituality in a much more private way, as was his later tendency, he sought to break through the fleeting illusion of the physical world, or *maya*, into the transcendent reality of Brahman. "Beware of Maya," he sings on "Beware of Darkness," a track from his first proper studio album following the breakup of the Beatles. It is a sentiment that anchored his artistic and personal life over the next three decades.

Harrison's triple album *All Things Must Pass*, considered by many critics to be one of the three best solo Beatle albums (joining Lennon's *Imagine* and McCartney's *Band on the Run*), was issued on November 30, 1970, just weeks after the debut of *Let It Be*. *The Times*'s Richard Williams reckoned that Harrison was "more than he was being allowed to be" in the Beatles, and, in a review that also evaluated Lennon's *Plastic Ono Band*, found that, of all the solo Beatle albums to date, Harrison's "makes far and away the best listening."[15] The album, featuring a loose, all-star, line-up,[16] was produced by Phil Spector. While the notoriously difficult producer's effort has been criticized, both for his frequent intoxication and the datedness of his vaunted "Wall of Sound" mix,[17] Spector's aesthetic propelled the

soul-inflected "What is Life" and gospel-tinged "My Sweet Lord" to commercial and critical success (*Rolling Stone* called the latter "sensational").[18]
Perhaps even more important to the album's overall sound was the effort
expended on strings and orchestra by Harrison and arranger John Barham,
exemplified on the majestic "Isn't It a Pity," Harrison's supreme warning
about *maya*, "Beware of Darkness," and the album's title track. A spectac-
ular *tour de force*, the album exhibited the influence of Harrison's recent
brushes with soul (producing Doris Troy's self-titled album, in 1970), the
southern blues of Delaney and Bonnie and Friends, and gospel (reflecting
Harrison's recent work producing the Doris Troy set and a Billy Preston
album). It also benefits from his interaction with Bob Dylan and the Band
in the waning days of the Beatles and, of course, his immersion in Hindu
culture. *All Things Must Pass* established with critics Harrison's status as an
artist of stature comparable to that of Lennon and McCartney.[19]

A product of its time, the album took root in a youth culture that had
received international attention for its spirituality. The year of the debut of
All Things Must Pass saw a noticeable increase in media coverage of youth
religiosity, particularly membership in Christ-oriented movements, cults,
and communes. A particularly perplexing issue for the established religions,
which saw their membership continue a postwar decline, it was the focus
of not only the religious press (including *Christianity Today*, *Christian
Century*, and *Commonweal*), but also the mainstream media.[20] It is worth
noting that *All Things Must Pass* spent three weeks in the Billboard album
charts, before being displaced by Andrew Lloyd Webber and Tim Rice's
original cast recording of *Jesus Christ Superstar*,[21] and that the original cast
recording of the stage musical *Godspell*, released in July, 1971, was a top
forty album in the USA. In this environment, the collection of songs, most
grounded in Harrison's spirituality, managed to sit high in the charts in
both the UK and the USA, where it reached number one. The album also
produced "My Sweet Lord," the first solo Beatle single to reach number
one in both the UK and US charts. Though critical of Harrison's tendency
towards earnestness and "taking himself or the subject too seriously," *Rolling
Stone*'s Ben Gerson nevertheless captured a widespread sentiment among
rock critics and fans about Harrison's album and artistry, calling *All Things
Must Pass* an "extravaganza of piety and sacrifice and joy, whose sheer
magnitude and ambition may dub it the War and Peace of rock 'n' roll,"
and applauding Harrison as "perhaps the premier studio musician among
rock band guitarists."[22]

Harrison followed up *All Things Must Pass* with the *Concert for
Bangladesh*, undertaken following a visit by Ravi Shankar, who brought
the plight of flood-ravaged Bangladesh to Harrison's attention. In response,
Harrison released "Bangladesh," the first rock charity single. Days later,

on August 1, 1971, Harrison took the stage with numerous rock luminaries, including Starr, the reclusive Bob Dylan, Eric Clapton, Badfinger, Billy Preston, and Leon Russell, for two performances before 40,000 fans at New York's Madison Square Garden. The Bangladesh benefit pioneered the whole idea of the charity album and single, as well as of the rock concert fundraiser.[23]

In 1973, Harrison released *Living in the Material World* and, from the album, the single "Give Me Love (Give Me Peace on Earth)" (backed with "Miss O'Dell"), which displaced McCartney's "My Love" at the top of the Billboard singles chart. Unlike its predecessor, *Living in the Material World* was an intimate project on which Harrison eschewed the "cast of thousands" approach for a smaller combo. Spector and his "Wall of Sound" were jettisoned in favor of Harrison's far leaner and cleaner production aesthetic, augmented by the sparing use of Barham's string and orchestral arrangements. Harrison's slide-playing is featured throughout, with the swamp-drenched, nocturnal wails of "Sue Me, Sue You Blues," in particular, demonstrating his grasp of the form. The title track is one of Harrison's hardest-rocking recordings, its pulsing bass and driving piano reminiscent of the Beatles' "Old Brown Shoe." "Give Me Love," which opens the album, perfectly encapsulates Harrison's guitar technique and production: economical in notes, it demonstrates virtuosity instead in its augmentation of the melody, rendered in the layering of two or more fluid slide guitar parts painstakingly arranged and impeccably recorded.

For the most part fashioned from new compositions, the album showed that Harrison wasn't dependent on the back catalog of songs that had provided most of the tracks for *All Things Must Pass*. Yet there are hints of qualities that became less attractive to critics and fans in the ensuing years. Tracks like "The Light that has Lighted the World," which carped, "It's funny how people won't accept change," and "Who Can See It," on which Harrison pleads, "I only ask that what I know should not be denied me now . . . my life belongs to me," betrayed sentiments of a man increasingly at odds, not only with an industry narrowly defining success as sales, but also with fans and critics who wanted him to be "Beatle George," or at least to be less fixated on his spirituality. Nevertheless, while receiving variable comment from critics,[24] the album fared well in the charts, reaching number one in the USA and number two in the UK.

In the fall of 1974, in the midst of the deterioration of his relationship with his wife, Pattie Boyd, and battling laryngitis, Harrison hurriedly finished *Dark Horse* to meet the deadline for a tour intended to promote Harrison's newly founded Dark Horse label. In retrospect, Harrison can be faulted for not allowing his voice to strengthen before completing the album and going on tour. The tight deadline also forced him to forsake his normally meticulous recording practices in favor of a more "rough and ready" approach. Songs, rather than being worked out ahead of time, often emerged in the studio. *Dark Horse* was a huge critical debacle – *Rolling Stone*, heretofore one of Harrison's great champions, blasted this "embarrassingly bad record."[25] Similarly, *High Fidelity* commented that the Federal Food and Drug Administration should "bust Harrison for selling a sleeping pill without a prescription, for a downer this definitely is."[26] While Harrison had his defenders,[27] *Rolling Stone*'s relentlessly negative critique was evidence of growing hostility in Harrison's relationship with the rock press. Yet it is difficult to find a justification for the vitriol leveled at the album by *Rolling Stone*. There are a number of strong tracks delivered by musicianship that is first rate. The instrumental opening the album, "Harris on Tour (Express)," is an upbeat rocker that highlights Harrison's slide work and Tom Scott's saxophone. "Maya Love" features Billy Preston's keyboard and a rhythm section driven by Andy Newmark's drumming and Willie Weeks's bass; they allowed Harrison to expand on his earlier experiments with soul and record his most funky and R&B-inflected album to date. Perhaps Harrison's greatest sin, as far as fans and critics were concerned, was that the lyrical content was so relentlessly critical of life as an ex-Beatle. Harrison's solo work had revealed his obsessions, but before this album the focus had been on his spiritual evolution; here, Harrison was, in the view of some, simply wallowing in self-pity. Critics seem also to have lost their senses of humor, with wife Pattie Boyd's and paramour Eric Clapton's backing vocals on "Bye Bye Love" and the over-the-top holiday good cheer of "Ding Dong, Ding Dong" marked for particular scorn. The tour would only contribute to Harrison's deteriorating status with critics.

Harrison took to the road in November, with Billy Preston and Ravi Shankar in tow, thus becoming the first ex-Beatle to stage a major tour of the USA. Reflecting his superstar status, Harrison even visited the White House, as guest of President Gerald Ford's son, Jack. Unfortunately, much to the chagrin of critics and fans, the shows were, in the words of the *New York Time*'s influential critic John Rockwell, "boring and eccentric." At Madison Square Garden, where the tour finished with three dates, Harrison only reluctantly drew from his Beatle past, playing "In My Life" with reworked lyrics (substituting "In my life, I love God more" for "In my life, I love you more"). He also programmed an apathetically received set by Ravi Shankar into the show, and battled a hoarseness that made his singing virtually unintelligible to the audience. Making matters worse, he badgered the audience to buy his albums and concert programs and, perhaps the greatest offense of all, to stop smoking marijuana. Rockwell found that Harrison's backup of Billie Preston on the keyboardist's handful of songs most suited the ex-Beatle – the role of the "'silent Beatle,' humbly taking second billing to those more charismatic than himself."[28] Harrison followed *Dark Horse* with the last album he owed Apple, *Extra Texture*, released in October 1975. Though Harrison's voice was much improved on the collection, which featured autobiographical songs that made fewer direct appeals for the spiritual well-being of its audience, and which was less disparaging of life in the public eye, criticism was only slightly less derisive than that for *Dark Horse*, with *Rolling Stone*'s review judging that "we are faced with the fact that Harrison's records are nothing so much as boring."[29]

His recording career seemingly going into freefall, Harrison started 1976 with a case of hepatitis. Still recovering, he testified in court for three days in the song plagiarism suit brought by Bright Tunes Music over his biggest solo single, "My Sweet Lord" – the court ultimately found that he had unintentionally plagiarized one of the company's properties, the Chiffons' 1963 hit, "He's So Fine." Though quite happy to be freed from his contractual obligations to Apple, the ailing Harrison faced a multi-million dollar lawsuit brought by his current record company, A&M, for "non-delivery of product," which was settled only after Warner Brothers bought Harrison's contract from the company. His first album on his own Dark Horse label, and the first with Warner Brothers, *Thiry-Three & 1/3*, was released in late 1976. Harrison's voice, having healed, was at its strongest in years, and he had a top-notch line-up of musicians, including Billy Preston and Gary Wright on keyboards and Tom Scott on horns, as well as one of the best rhythm sections to appear on a Harrison album – Alvin Taylor on drums, and Willie Weeks on bass. Harrison largely jettisoned spirituality in favor of more traditional, and commercial, ruminations on life and love. The *Village Voice*'s Richard Meltzer was particularly laudatory, noting that the album was Harrison's "best LP since *All Things Must Pass* and on par with, say, [Bob Dylan's] *Blood on the Tracks*." Britain's *Melody Maker* called the collection "a fine album which must regain for [Harrison] the impetus he has lost."[30] The album also fared somewhat better with fans than did the previous two albums; it reached number thirty-five in the UK charts and number eleven in the US Billboard album charts, and spawned two top forty hits on its way to gold certification. Promoting the album, Harrison joined host Paul Simon on *Saturday Night Live*, where he debuted videos for the two singles, "Crackerbox Palace," directed by Monty Python's Eric Idle, and a sendup of the Bright Tunes' "My Sweet Lord" affair, "This Song." He and Simon also played an acoustic set featuring the host's "Homeward Bound" and Harrison's "Here Comes the Sun."

Debuting simultaneously with *Thirty-Three & 1/3* was *The Best of George Harrison*, over half of which, much to Harrison's chagrin (he was powerless to control the content of the EMI/Capitol release), was culled from his Beatles work. Despite his misgivings, and while it failed to chart in the UK, the album did well in the USA with critics[31] and fans, receiving certification as a gold record from the Recording Industry Association of America, as had his previous albums dating back to *All Things Must Pass*. Despite the success, Harrison was increasingly unhappy with the life of the rock star, and throughout 1977 and much of 1978 he pursued other interests and started a new family. Having divorced Pattie Boyd in 1977,[32] Harrison married Olivia Trinidad Arias in September, 1978, a month after the birth of their son, Dhani. Harrison also co-founded Handmade Films, initially to produce comedy troupe Monty Python's *The Life of Brian*. The company specialized in off-beat comedies and became one of the most important producers of independent films.[33] Harrison returned to music in February 1979 with *George Harrison*, which yielded the single, "Blow Away." Co-produced with Russ Titelman, the album was generally well received[34] and continued Harrison's streak of gold albums. Comfortably ensconced in his Friar Park studio, Harrison was enjoying private life at home too much to contemplate a tour and a return to life as a "star," a sentiment present later that year when he published *I Me Mine*, an eccentric collection of lyrics, photographs, and stories, but precious little to quench the thirst of curious Beatles fans. Nevertheless, by late 1980 it was time for another album, and Harrison began work on *Somewhere in England*.

Paul McCartney: "Some people want to fill the world with silly love songs"

Paul McCartney faced a rock press that held him responsible for the demise of the Beatles, and, further, scorned the very things that made him popular with the mainstream audience. With Lennon assuming, and being granted, the role of resident Beatle genius, McCartney's contributions to the band were increasingly viewed as stylistic and commercial by a rock press still arguing for rock's status as an art form carrying forward an anti-establishment worldview. McCartney's first ten years after the end of the Beatles were spent chasing and capturing the heights of commercial and mainstream success, often with unquestionably silly but expertly rendered love songs, while facing the most hostile reception of any ex-Beatle for it from the rock press.

With the demise of the Beatles, McCartney had buried himself in work, writing and producing this first solo album at home, playing all the instruments and providing the vocals (with additional vocals from his wife, Linda). *McCartney* was released in April 1970, just weeks after Starr's *Beaucoups of Blues*, and mere weeks before the release of the Beatles' *Let It Be*, and was accompanied by promotional materials that left little doubt that the Beatles were disbanding, including a questionnaire in which McCartney posed the questions, "Do you miss the other Beatles and George Martin? . . . Do you foresee a time when Lennon-McCartney becomes an active songwriting partnership again?" His answer: "No."[35] The album contained "Maybe I'm Amazed," "That Would Be Something," and "Every Night," the first, a love song for his wife, becoming one of his best-loved and most covered songs, and thereafter a staple on his numerous tours. The album reached the top ten in the USA (number twenty-eight in the UK). Generally well received in the mainstream press, the album was also given a positive review in *Rolling Stone*, though, on editor Jann Wenner's insistence, a positive review was rewritten to take into account McCartney's promotion of *McCartney*: "Why did Paul choose to cover a very beautiful and pleasing record with such tawdry propaganda?"[36]

He followed up his eponymous first effort with the top ten US and UK single "Another Day," backed with "Oh Woman, Oh Why," released in February 1971. Recorded during sessions for an album which would eventually be called *Ram*, the single was a hint of McCartney's musical direction, with "Another Day" introducing a new McCartney vocal sound, comprising his and wife Linda's voices, and the flip-side rocker demonstrating that McCartney had lost little, if any, facility with the rock and roll shout first demonstrated on early Beatles recordings like "Long Tall Sally" and "I'm Down." *Ram* was released in the wake of Lennon's *Plastic Ono Band* and Harrison's *All Things Must Pass*, and expectations were high for McCartney's sophomore project. The album opens with "Too Many People," a catchy, acoustic-based rocker that knocks "too many people preaching practices," which Lennon saw as directed at his and Ono's very public politicking. It was not the only slight perceived by Lennon: the cover collage featured a picture of what appeared to be two beetles coupling, and a shot of McCartney and wife dressed as clowns and ensconced in a bag.[37] (Lennon would have his pound of flesh on *Imagine*.) Controversy aside, the album demonstrates McCartney's pop sensibility with meticulously crafted melodies and arrangements incorporating forms as varied as country, jazz, the blues, hard rock, even the Beach Boys. The latter figure most prominently on "Ram On," with its *Smile* era production, and "Dear Boy," with one of the album's most intricate vocal arrangements. "Smile Away" is one of McCartney's great driving rock and rollers. "Uncle Albert / Admiral Halsey" was the kind of whimsical and ambitious production that had been the Beatles' – and George Martin's – stock in trade, going back at least as far as the effects created for "Yellow Submarine," in 1965. Silly, yet infectious, the track was released as a single in the USA, where it became McCartney's first post-Beatles number one. The album reached number one in the UK charts, and number two in the USA. Yet the album received only fair reviews in the mainstream press, and *Rolling Stone* called it "the nadir in the decomposition of Sixties rock thus far." Further, reviewer Jon Landau hypothesized that, in the Beatles, Lennon "was there to keep McCartney from going off the deep end that leads to an album as emotionally vacuous as *Ram....McCartney* and *Ram* both prove that Paul benefited immensely from collaboration and that he seems to be dying on the vine as a result of his own self-imposed musical isolation."[38]

The apathy, even hostility, with which McCartney's early solo work was received by *Rolling Stone* was part of a process of defining the achievements and legacy of the youth culture that emerged in the 1960s. Prior to the breakup, the music of the Beatles was simply attributed to "Lennon and McCartney," or "the Beatles and George Martin," and so on, vague personifications that did little to explain the specific contributions of any single actor to the creative process. Much of Lennon's interview with *Rolling Stone*'s Jann Wenner, in December 1970, focused on questions of authorship. His attribution of various compositions fostered the creation of nice, neat – and opposed – categories for the two chief Beatles: "Lennon as artist and *avant-gardiste*" and "McCartney as commercial craftsman." Reflecting the values of the counterculture and New Left, writers and editors at *Rolling Stone*, and the readers to which they appealed, often found common cause with John Lennon, while McCartney was often demonized as a commercial hack for his refusal to say anything of consequence.

Lennon's reception by rock critics, as compared to McCartney's, betrays a preference for the written word and, at least in part, a miscalculation of the importance of McCartney's vision to the Beatles' art, particularly that of the post-touring years. McCartney, of all the Beatles, was most drawn to the possibilities of the studio, and his integration of varied past and alternative forms into his rock and pop *oeuvre* demonstrated both the centrality of sound to his art and his prowess as a producer, a dexterity born of patient observation and determination over the years. McCartney's greatest strength may well have been his ability to translate his immediate influences (and those of the other Beatles) for his audience by means of the modern studio. McCartney was the most active of the Beatles in bringing the experimental currents of the times into the work of the band, and the most capable in translating them for the pop milieu. In the mid-1960s, McCartney's preoccupations, fueled by his immersion in London's vibrant artistic environment, and evident on the band's most experimental work, were definitive in rock and roll's evolution into rock, and into art. Equally important were Lennon's lyrics, which, with those of Dylan, were expanding the boundaries of the pop rock *oeuvre*. Yet, speaking primarily of the lyrics of the songs, Lennon's revelations (among many) that masterpieces like "A Day in the Life" and "Strawberry Fields Forever" were primarily his works obscured McCartney's essential contributions, and, so far as much of the activist youth culture was concerned, demonstrated that the Beatles' artistic genius could be attributed largely to Lennon, a product of his wordcraft and artistic vision. Lennon's political radicalism undoubtedly eased acceptance of this assertion among the more "committed" members of the youth culture. In short, for many rock critics, the accessibility of Lennon's commitment to the issues of the time, and to the "higher calling" of "art," embodied most consistently in his lyrics, proved more meaningful than McCartney's commercialism, continuing sonic experimentation, and genre-bending forays.

McCartney continued to draw upon his environment for inspiration as a solo artist, but his situation was completely different from that of the pop art intellectual of 1967, and the domesticity of post-Beatledom was less attractive to a segment of the youth culture audience that continued to expect rock to rebel. In this environment, McCartney's strengths were often discounted by a variably activist rock press, and while he continued to develop as a musician, songwriter, and producer, to be sure, he often did so to little appreciation. In fact, McCartney was held to a much higher standard than contemporaries, such as Jagger and Richards, who were rarely faulted for their catalog's dearth of meaning or message. While the opinions of rock critics gradually came to acknowledge, and occasionally value,[39] McCartney's ease with melodies and his considerable abilities as producer and arranger, there remained an undercurrent of dissatisfaction with a talent perceived as extraordinary but misspent.

Shaken by *Rolling Stone*'s review and lukewarm critical response in the mainstream press, but heartened by *Ram*'s commercial success, McCartney debuted his new band, Wings, in August 1971 (though it did not acquire the name until the following month), with Denny Laine on guitar and Denny Seiwell on drums. *Wild Life*, credited to Wings, was released in November to variable critical response. Attributing the album's banality to "nonchalance" in the face of contractual obligations to a company for which McCartney no longer wished to work (i.e. Apple), *Rolling Stone*'s John Mendelsohn tabbed the album "vacuous, flaccid, impotent, trivial and unaffecting," yet he also found it "nicely . . . executed pop music [that] should be taken or left on that basis alone," an opinion consistent with reaction in the mainstream press.[40] Yet, at a time when even the basic communalism of the youth culture was under fire in the mainstream press,[41] McCartney's talents counted for little among the cultural elites of the youth movement.

McCartney added guitarist Henry McCullough to Wings' line-up, and quickly recorded Wings' first single, "Give Ireland Back to the Irish," written following the Bloody Sunday violence of January 30, 1972.[42] The single was released in late February and promptly deemed "politically controversial" and banned by the BBC. This was not McCartney's only challenge to the system – in the midst of touring, in August, McCartney and his wife were arrested in Sweden for hashish possession, one of numerous similar scrapes with the law.[43] Yet McCartney still failed to gain credibility with the political and cultural left. Certainly hurting any effort he might have expended to ingratiate himself with the youth movement was ABC's broadcast, in April, of the ill-advised[44] bit of schmaltz, *James Paul McCartney*, which was, in the words of the *New York Times*' reviewer, little more than "a series of disconnected routines strung together with commercials for Chevrolet cars." Other critics were similarly dismissive of the effort.[45] McCartney followed in May with Wings' second single, "Mary Had a Little Lamb," a song that had been performed on the special. Written for his daughter Mary, the song is little more than a child's idyll pounded out on the piano. A light, sweet, melody propels the nursery rhyme along to the chorus, "You can hear them singing, la la, la la la," on which McCartney is joined by his wife Linda and daughters Heather and Mary. Rock critics viewed it as vacuous, self-indulgent nonsense.

Despite such critical setbacks, McCartney forged ahead. The Beatle who had most wanted to take the band back on the road, McCartney recognized that reclaiming his stature as a force in the modern music scene required that he reestablish himself before live audiences. A Wings summer tour of Europe in 1972 had allowed the band to grow into a cohesive unit, so much so, in fact, that McCartney felt ready to attempt a tour of the UK the following spring. Not only was Wings getting a reputation as a tight, hard-rocking outfit, but McCartney appeared to be finding his voice again as a writer, and, importantly, the band could now tour in support of the latest album, *Red Rose Speedway*. In the hope of boosting sales above those of *Wild Life*, the album was credited to "Paul McCartney and Wings." Bolstered by the success of the last two singles, "Hi, Hi, Hi" (a hard-rocking song banned by the BBC for "suggestive" lyrics), and, from the album, a new ballad which became a concert favorite and a number one hit in the USA, "My Love," *Red Rose Speedway* continued McCartney's upward climb in the charts; it also marked a changing critical environment for reception of McCartney's work by the rock press. Patti Smith collaborator and guitarist Lenny Kaye, writing in *Rolling Stone*, called the album "the most overall heartening McCartney product given us since the demise of the Beatles."[46] While McCartney's music would continue to be criticized by some commentators as vacuous and facile, Kaye's review appears to mark the point where art of consequence was no longer required of McCartney by rock critics, the opinions of whom were increasingly coming to resemble the generally welcoming reception found in the mainstream press.[47] The album, a blend of country, ballads, and superior arrangement and production, most noticeable on side two's

"Medley," reached number one in the US Billboard chart, and was followed by McCartney's masterful collaboration with George Martin on "Live and Let Die," the theme for the new James Bond film of the same name. With its catchy melody incorporating ska and Hollywood theatrics, most notably the orchestral bombast arranged by Martin, the recording, credited only to Wings, rose to number two on the US singles charts and garnered an Oscar nomination for Best Original Song (though losing to "The Way We Were").

McCartney's breakout came with the release in December 1973 of *Band on the Run*, considered by many critics to be one of the three best solo Beatles albums. Fueled by the success of two singles from the collection – "Jet," a US and UK top ten single released in February 1974, and the title track, a number one hit in the USA, released in June – the album was a worldwide hit and Grammy winner for Best Pop Performance by Duo, Group, or Chorus, and the top-selling album for 1974. *Band on the Run* marks the full flowering and most definitive restatement of McCartney's strengths: an unequaled work ethic and production sense allied with an uncanny ability to find the right sounds with which to render the fruits of his unsurpassed facility with melodies. The title track opens the album, and is reminiscent of Martin's production on side two of *Abbey Road*, as song sections segue seamlessly from one to the next. It is followed by the rolling thunder guitar and synthesizer of "Jet," then the jazz-inflected "Bluebird." Track by track, McCartney demonstrates his mastery of numerous musical forms, much as the Beatles had, particularly from *Rubber Soul* onward. "Mrs. Vanderbilt" highlights McCartney's bouncy and ever-changing bass lines. "Mamunia," in its country feel and deceptively simple arrangement, is reminiscent of his first two solo albums, not to mention "Mother Nature's Song" from *The Beatles*. "No Words" and "Nineteen Hundred and Eighty Five" demonstrate that McCartney had learned a great deal about building song arrangements from George Martin. At last, much as "I Want to Hold Your Hand" had been a single that Capitol could not turn down, *Band on the Run* was a work that critics of all stripes had no choice but to embrace. Reflecting the widespread positive critical reception for the album, the *New York Times* dubbed it "music as natural and fresh as tomorrow," and *Rolling Stone*'s Jon Landau judged the album "(with the possible exception of John Lennon's *Plastic Ono Band*) the finest record yet released by any of the four musicians who were once called the Beatles."[48]

McCartney continued his streak with the next two albums, the critically acclaimed *Venus and Mars*[49] (released May 1975) and *Wings at the Speed of Sound*[50] (released March 1976), both reaching number one in the US and UK album charts. *Speed of Sound* spawned the single "Silly Love Songs," which was McCartney's response to those critical of his music's perceived lack of meaning; it was also his first foray into disco music, and one of

Wings' biggest sellers. McCartney and Wings toured the UK and, at last, the USA, in 1976, with Wings' spring US visit providing the material for McCartney's fifth straight number one US album, the triple disk *Wings Over America*, released in an era in which that form reigned supreme (note, for instance, the success of Peter Frampton's 1976 number one hit, *Frampton Comes Alive*, and Kiss's top ten albums, *Alive!*, released in 1975, and *Alive II*, from 1977). In 1977, Wings released "Mull of Kintyre," a folk-based ode to McCartney's adopted Scottish homeland, where he and his family had lived since the late 1960s. The single, which featured bagpipes, could not have been more different from current trends, most notably the advent of punk, marked by the debuts of the Sex Pistols and the Clash. Nevertheless, "Mull of Kintyre" went to number one in the British charts, and became one of the biggest-selling singles in UK history, displacing the Beatles' "She Loves You" before being displaced by Band Aid's "Do They Know It's Christmas" in 1984.

London Town, released in 1978, received a generally lukewarm reception. After the success of the previous five albums, there was every expectation that McCartney's success would continue, and it did, commercially speaking. But the critical angst over the slickness of his productions and his obvious lack of interest in creating music of "substance" was never far below the surface, and the latest album was found by many to be, in the words of the *New York Times*, "too bland."[51] *Back to the Egg*, released in June, 1979, was the final studio album of Wings. Though reaching the UK and US top ten, and despite its platinum certification for sales (and the inclusion of the Grammy-winning instrumental "Rockestra Theme"), the album reached a new low with the critics.[52] The next album, recorded solely by McCartney, was the minimalist synthesizer-driven *McCartney II*, released in June 1980. Though reaching number three on the US album charts, it fared less well with critics, *Rolling Stone* calling it "an album of aural doodles designed for the amusement of very young children" and "strident electronic junk music." The *New York Times'* John Rockwell allowed that the album had "its moment of charm and even self-revelation," but concluded that it "ultimately seems trivial." He added: "Mr. McCartney seems to need equal collaborators to stiffen the frothier side of his creative spirit. Like John Lennon, for instance. Anybody for a Beatles reunion?"[53] Of course, time was quickly running out for such a gathering.

John Lennon: "I just believe in me"

On December 30, 1969, UK broadcaster ITV televised *Man of the Decade*, which included segments on John Kennedy, Mao Zedong, and John Lennon.

In February, 1970, *Rolling Stone* named John Lennon its "Man of the Year."[54] Lennon had a great deal to prove, particularly with an anti-war left still stewing from Lennon's apparent rejection of it on the Beatles' recording "Revolution." He had begun to address its concerns and seek common cause with his and Yoko Ono's 1969 peace offensive, and was energized by a new freedom denied him as a Beatle. By the release of *Plastic Ono Band* (1970), on which he sang "I don't believe in Beatles . . . I just believe in me," on the track "God," he was speaking his mind and acting upon the issues of his time as an individual, without concern for maintaining the Beatles myth.

The Lennons christened 1970 "Year One AP" (i.e. After Peace). Lennon was pleased with the "bed-in for peace" and "War is Over" events of the past year;[55] in the following months, however, he was less satisfied with symbolic gestures, and took tentative steps toward greater confrontation with the system. A new agenda required a new look, and in late January, Lennon and Ono had their hair shorn, in Lennon's words to "stop being hyped by revolutionary image and long hair,"[56] and donated their locks for auction at a benefit organized by London Black Power leader Michael X.[57] An appearance by the Plastic Ono Band[58] on *Top of the Pops* in mid-February 1970 featured Lennon's new look: dressed in a black turtleneck sweater, hair short and uneven, he played keyboard and sang "Instant Karma," while a similarly coifed and attired Ono sat behind him, her vision obscured by a white blindfold, knitting white yarn. This was a stark picture, one at odds with his Beatles past. For Lennon, ragged and ugly in comparison to the Beatle image, it was a means of breaking even more fully with his pop star past.

Trying to bring some order to their personal lives, Lennon and Ono sought custody (unsuccessfully) of Ono's young daughter, Kyoko. They also underwent four months of primal therapy at Dr. Arthur Janov's Los Angeles Primal Institute clinic, beginning in April 1970. A therapy that attempts to move patients to direct emotional experience of past trauma, thus allowing those repressed feelings to be dealt with openly, Janov's treatment had a profound influence on Lennon and Ono, and much of Lennon's *Plastic Ono Band* album, released in December 1970, was composed while Lennon was in therapy. A masterpiece, this first truly solo project most closely reflected Lennon's vision of art as emerging from pain.[59] In track after track, Lennon bared his soul, in the process skewering every institution that had ever traumatized him, or judged him, or in any sense confined him. This was an album of "Pain," as understood in primal therapy. Songs like "God," "Isolation," "I Found Out," "My Mummy's Dead," "Mother," and perhaps most audibly "Well Well Well" were the direct artistic fruits of Lennon's primal therapy. Not for the timid, the album received mixed reviews,[60] but has since been recognized as one of Lennon's best and most influential albums. Promoting the album, Lennon sat down with *Rolling Stone*'s Jann Wenner for a massive landmark interview. Over the span of two installments, in January and February 1971, readers were transfixed by an account of Lennon's life that, in detailing the band's drug use, groupies, and internal affairs, aggressively sought to shatter the myth of the Beatles, a move welcomed by New Left advocates.[61] The Lennons further aligned themselves with the radicals through various activities and protests in the UK[62] and in the USA, following their relocation to New York later that year.

Lennon's next album, *Imagine*, was released in September 1971, in the USA (October in the UK). The album signaled the return of Lennon to a more commercial sound incorporating a variety of textures that had been absent from the harrowingly single-minded starkness of *Plastic Ono Band*. On the title track, suggested by a line from an Ono poem, Lennon imagines a world in which there are no countries, no greed, no hunger, even no heaven or religion. He imagines "all the people sharing all the world." On numerous tracks, Lennon rejects the establishment and its mechanisms of control. On "I Don't Want to Be a Soldier" he sings: "I don't want to be a soldier, I don't want to die. . . . I don't want to be a lawyer, I don't want to lie . . . I don't want to be a failure, I don't want to cry." On "Gimme Some Truth" Lennon directly challenges the perceived source of so much of the political left's anguish, and declares that he will not be had by "no short-haired, yellow-bellied son of tricky dicky" (i.e. President Nixon). Elsewhere, Lennon, still in confessional mode after *Plastic Ono Band*, continues to reveal his own insecurities, most notably on "Jealous Guy," "Crippled Inside," "It's So Hard," and "How?," which wonders, "How can I go forward when I don't know which way I'm facing?" Lennon declares his love for Ono, who made "everything clear in the world," on "Oh My Love," and the pop-folk hybrid, "Oh, Yoko," featuring Lennon on harmonica, *à la* Dylan. Phil Spector produced the album, though Lennon, like Harrison before him, successfully reined in his tendency toward overproduction. Lennon enlists many of the musicians found on *All Things Must Pass*, with the core band comprising Lennon on vocals, guitar, and piano, Klaus Voormann on bass, and Alan White on drums, augmented with Nicky Hopkins's piano. George Harrison is also in fine form, lending dobro to "Crippled Inside," a delicate guitar part on "Oh My Love," and slide guitar on "I Don't Want to Be a Soldier" and "Gimme Some Truth." His participation on "How Do You Sleep?" – a blistering slide part that is among his best recorded work – only fanned the controversy sparked by the song's lyrics. Irked by perceived slights on McCartney's *Ram*, Lennon lampooned the cover of *Ram*, which shows McCartney restraining a ram by its horns – early pressings of the album included a postcard of Lennon restraining a pig by its ears. But this broadside paled in comparison to "How Do You Sleep?," on which the sounds of an orchestra tuning up – a swipe at McCartney's pretensions to art, here pointedly referring to the opening of *Sgt. Pepper's Lonely Hearts Club Band* – give way to the kind of character assassination associated with Dylan in the mid-1960s, on tracks like "Positively Fourth Street" and "Like a Rolling Stone." While Dylan's targets remain undefined, Lennon spells it out. Humorous, but no less cutting, were lyrics like "The only thing you done was *yesterday*, and since you're gone it's just *another day*," which took a swipe at McCartney's biggest song and one of his latest singles. Lennon sings, "Those freaks was right when they said you was dead," which referred to the "Paul is Dead" hoax of the late 1960s, and "The sound you make is muzak to my ears," which is a particularly pointed comment on the inconsequential nature of McCartney's songs, then the focus of much of the rock press's criticism of his post-Beatles work. Adding insult to injury, Lennon took a swipe at McCartney's relationship with Linda McCartney, singing, "Jump when your momma tell you anything," which might be viewed as somewhat disingenuous given Lennon's very public personal and artistic relationship with Ono. Still, while the Lennon and McCartney tiff made for good press, even Lennon admitted (to a Syracuse University audience, on the day of the album's release), that "How Do You Sleep?" was "an outburst. Things are still the same between us. He was and still is my closest friend, except for Yoko."[63] The album was generally well received by the press[64] and public, reaching number one in the US and UK charts, while the single from the album, "Imagine," was a number three hit in the USA. Yet there was some concern over Lennon's stridency. *Rolling Stone*'s Ben Gerson gave the album a mixed review, which appears prescient given the content of Lennon's next album, *Some Time in New York City*:

> Most insidiously, I fear that John sees himself in the role of truth-teller, and, as such, can justify any kind of self-indulgent brutality in the name of truth ... Personally, I'm interested in John the man, his personal trials and dramas, because he has revealed them to us as John the extraordinary artist. If he does not continue as such, his posturings will soon seem not merely dull but irrelevant. It seems to me that John is facing the most extraordinary challenge of his career, both personally and artistically.[65]

Nevertheless, Lennon's credibility with the New Left was at a new high – even one-time president of the Students for a Democratic Society (SDS), Todd Gitlin, in reacting to Lennon's first two solo albums and the book publication of Lennon's entire *Rolling Stone* interview,[66] applauded Lennon for shedding the myths of the Beatles and the counterculture, and for providing a path for renewal of the badly fragmented and rudderless movement: "Lennon revives the idea of leader as exemplar." Writing in the lay Catholic journal *Commonweal*, Gitlin expressed a desire that Lennon's authenticity and "public struggle to be free" would spark a new "commonality" that might resuscitate political and social activism.[67]

Relocating to New York in September, 1971, the Lennons were befriended by Yippies Jerry Rubin and Abbie Hoffman, and took a sharp turn into radical politics. In November they headlined a benefit for the victims of the Attica prison riot that had taken place the previous month.[68] A month later, Lennon and Ono visited Ann Arbor, Michigan, for a benefit for John Sinclair, leader of the White Panther Party, and manager of the rock band MC5. Sinclair had been sentenced in 1969 to ten years' incarceration after being found guilty of selling two joints to an undercover police officer. Then, in February 1972, Lennon and Ono joined demonstrators outside the New York office of British Overseas Airways Corporation, supporting a boycott of British exports as a protest against the deployment of troops in Northern Ireland. This was followed by a week-long stint as co-hosts of the popular afternoon variety program *The Mike Douglas Show*. The audience was treated to an appearance by Chuck Berry, Lennon's boyhood idol, but the Lennons sparked controversy with guests Jerry Rubin and Black Panther founder (with Huey Newton) Bobby Seale. Lennon was clearly invigorated by the political ferment that engulfed his Greenwich Village neighborhood, and was beginning to piece together an ambitious anti-war agenda. Of particular concern to the Republican administration and party, the Twenty-Sixth Amendment to the US Constitution had been ratified on July 1, 1971, thus granting the vote to eighteen-year-olds, who would now be eligible to vote in the 1972 presidential election, an election that would focus on the Vietnam War. Fearful that Lennon would lead protests at the Republican National Convention and mount a voter registration campaign and tour, and of the forces coalescing into a voting populous that likely would hold Nixon to account for the country's continued presence in Vietnam, Republican Senator Strom Thurmond advised that deportation of Lennon might be the best option. Lennon's misdemeanor drug bust in 1968, for possession of cannabis, was ostensibly the cause for issuance of a deportation order in March 1972, but, as Jon Wiener describes in *Come Together: John Lennon in His Time*, the FBI's campaign of harassment and wire-tapping, under the direction of Nixon administration officials, proved crippling to Lennon's radical activities.[69]

In real fear of being forced to leave their chosen home, and of being unable to pursue the custody of Ono's daughter, Kyoko (eventually granted by the court in March 1972),[70] Lennon dropped his radical agenda, but not before the release of his and Ono's most radical album, *Some Time in New York City*, produced in late 1971 and early 1972 by Phil Spector. Lennon enlisted Elephant's Memory as his backup band for the album. Housed in a sleeve that satirized the front page of the *New York Times*, complete with a doctored photo showing President Nixon and Mao Zedong dancing together, nude, the double-disc album is a relentless assault on chauvinism ("Woman is the Nigger of the World" and Ono's "Sisters, O Sisters"),[71] racism (Lennon and Ono's "Angela"), army affronts in Northern Ireland ("The Luck of the Irish" and "Sunday Bloody Sunday"), US involvement in Vietnam, and the oppressive state ("John Sinclair," "Attica," and Ono's "Born in a Prison"). Disc two was a live recording of the Lennons at New York's Filmore East in June 1971, with Frank Zappa and the Mothers of Invention. Though it is interesting as an historical artifact, the execution is uneven, and, while Lennon is clearly leading the effort, the performances are often dominated by Ono's wailing and Zappa's improvisation, though the versions of "Cold Turkey" and Walter Ward's "Well (Baby Please Don't Go)" show Lennon in top form, aggressive at the mike and bold in his performance. Released in June, 1972, the album was a critical and commercial failure.[72] It is, perhaps, the stridency of Lennon and Ono's messages that was most problematic for the audience. Lennon substituted political commitment and sloganeering for his natural *oeuvre* of lyrics that are at once personal and universal. It was this failure to communicate on the personal level – in stark contrast to *Plastic Ono Band* and *Imagine* – that most disappointed fans and critics. Fans were willing to accompany Lennon as he exorcised his demons, to share in his pain, and to become intimates, because he had been an integral part of their youth and had grown up with them. He had earned the right to confide in them, and his poetics allowed his personal experience to be shared. For some, *Some Time in New York City*, with its harshness and impersonal sloganeering, transgressed this relationship.[73] Crushed by the album's commercial and critical failure, and by the weight of the Nixon administration's efforts to deport him, Lennon's future efforts were less likely to be directed through radical politics.

In September 1973, Lennon and Ono separated, and Lennon was alone for the first time in his adult life. Cracking under the pressure of his separation from Ono and ongoing efforts by the US government to deport him, Lennon spent more than a year drowning his demons and insecurity in alcohol and carousing with friends Harry Nilsson, Ringo Starr, Keith Moon, and Phil Spector. Recorded shortly before his relocation to Los Angeles, the self-produced *Mind Games* was his first solo album without the input of either Spector or Ono. Released in November, it had better sales than its predecessor, but received only lukewarm response from the critics. Nevertheless, *Mind Games* was a top ten album in the USA, and the title track made it into the US top twenty singles. Far more varied and textured than *Some Time in New York City*, Lennon's rockers, "Tight A$" and "Meat City," retain that album's energy without its anger, while tracks like "Aisumasen (I'm Sorry)," "One Day (at a Time)," "Out the Blue," and "You Are Here" mark the return of the fragile artist, here pining for Ono from a deep sense of regret. Lennon's message songs, "Only People" and "Mind Games," are delivered without any of the rancor that blighted much of the message of the previous album. Even "Bring on the Lucie (Freda Peeple)," while taking to task the forces aligned against him, including the Nixon administration, FBI, and INS, and warning that, "your time is up, you better know it," manages to do so in a less aggressive manor, deflating his threat at the beginning of the track with a mock call to arms – "This is it boys. Over the hill!" While the album might not have risen to the level of *Plastic Ono Band* and *Imagine*, for many fans and critics it was a welcome step in the right direction.[74]

Walls and Bridges, issued in October 1974, received fair notices, and was a number one album in the USA, with "Whatever Gets You Thru the Night" topping the singles charts.[75] Perhaps his most Beatle-esque solo album, the collection featured some of Lennon's most intricate arrangements, with "Old Dirt Road," "Nobody Loves You (When You're Down and Out)," and the magnificent "#9 Dream" incorporating strings in textured soundscapes not previously heard on a solo Lennon album. Yet tracks like "Steel and Glass," and, particularly, "I'm Scared," while far more the creatures of studio technique, harken back lyrically to the stark desolation of *Plastic Ono Band*. Lennon also demonstrates that he can still rock, giving one of his best vocal performances on the funky "What You Got." While "Surprise, Surprise (Sweet Bird of Paradox)" revels in the awakening of his romance with May Pang, the assistant Ono had had accompany Lennon during their separation, Ono figures prominently in "Going Down on Love," with its regrets over loss of "something precious and rare," and "Bless You," which hopefully states, "Still we're deep in each other's hearts."

Lennon followed *Walls and Bridges* with *Rock 'n' Roll*, released in February 1975. Though it had been started during the first days of his separation from Ono, excessive drinking by Lennon and producer Phil Spector led to recordings of variable quality. Worse yet, their disorderly conduct led to banishment from the A&M Records studio at which they had been working. Spector then disappeared with the tapes, returning them while Lennon was in the midst of recording *Walls and Bridges*. Lennon revisited the rock and roll project after completion of that album. Growing out of the settlement of a dispute between Lennon and Morris Levy, head of Roulette Records and publisher of Chuck Berry's early catalog, over Lennon's cribbing the line "Here come old flat-top" from Berry's "You Can't Catch Me" for the Beatles' "Come Together," *Rock 'n' Roll* included numerous rock and roll songs from Levy's holdings and others. It was released by Capitol to uneven reviews, though solid sales pushed the album into the US top ten.

In the midst of the booze-fueled holiday, Lennon, surprisingly productive, had released two solo albums and contributed to Starr's *Ringo* and *Goodnight Vienna* albums, as well as to Harry Nilsson's *Pussy Cats*. By late 1974, however, he was ready to return to Ono. Settling a bet struck with Elton John, who had played on "Whatever Gets You Thru the Night," on *Walls and Bridges*, Lennon made good on his promise to play live with John and his band if the track became a US number one, making a surprise appearance at John's November 28 Madison Square Garden concert. He played the single, as well as "Lucy in the Sky with Diamonds," and "I Saw Her Standing There." Ono was in the audience, and a short meeting after the show was followed by Lennon's return to New York and Ono in January 1975. He recorded a version of "Across the Universe" for David Bowie's *Young Americans* album, and co-wrote Bowie's hit from the set, "Fame." He performed live for *A Salute to Sir Lew*, a tribute for British entertainment impresario Sir Lew Grade, which aired on ABC in June.[76] The biggest news of the year, however, was that Ono was pregnant, and on October 9, 1975, Lennon's thirty-fifth birthday, Ono gave birth to a son, Sean. In 1976, his contract with Capitol/EMI lapsed and was not renewed. Lennon was without contractual obligation for the first time in fifteen years. In April, he made a guest appearance, his last for five years, on Starr's *Rotogravure*, supplying Starr with "Cookin' (In the Kitchen of Love)." In July, Lennon's permanent residency application was finally approved, and his fight to stay in the country was over.[77] Freer than he had been since he was a teenager, Lennon settled into fatherhood, domesticity, and house-husbandry.

Over the next five years, Lennon made himself available to the public only sparingly, occasionally appearing in the personality and society pages, as when he and Ono attended Jimmy Carter's Presidential Inauguration Gala in January, 1977, and when they contributed funds for purchasing bullet-proof vests for New York's finest.[78] But this was not sufficient for many within the youth culture. "An Open Letter to John Lennon" appeared in *Rolling Stone* in 1977, imploring Lennon to come out of retirement and respond to the public's curiosity, and give some direction to the failing youth movement.[79] In May 1979, Lennon and Ono took out full-page advertisements in the *New York Times* and London's *Sunday Times*, as well as a Tokyo newspaper. Called "A Love Letter from John and Yoko, To People Who Ask Us What, When and Why," the piece sang the praises of domesticity and "magic," and thanked the public for its good wishes and interest, but gave no indication that Lennon's retirement would end anytime soon.[80]

By mid-1980, Lennon was starting to feel an urge to record again, and, armed with a number of new songs, returned to the studio in August. In late September, Lennon and Ono signed with David Geffen's new independent label, Geffen Records, which released *Double Fantasy* in mid-November.

Lennon and Ono each contributed seven songs to the album, subtitled "A Heart Play." In the wave of nostalgia and grief that followed Lennon's death, the album sent three tracks into the top ten singles charts in the USA, with "(Just Like) Starting Over" reaching number one three weeks after his death, "Woman" rising to number two in March 1981, and "Watching the Wheels" making the top ten in May. Upon its release, however, critical reception of *Double Fantasy*, and its core theme of domestic bliss, was mixed,[81] though the album was greeted by the public as a welcome end to Lennon's seclusion, and a promising rebirth.[82] A reinvigorated peace movement, a Beatle reunion – with Lennon back, anything seemed possible. On the night of December 8, 1980, however, as Lennon and Ono returned home from a recording session, a voice called from the shadows, and in an instant ringing with gunfire, the dream was over.

Lennon's death was met with months of grieving and assessment of his accomplishments and those of the Sixties generation. An editorial in *The Nation* spoke of the loss of an "unacknowledged President who stood for peace."[83] Writing in *The Center Magazine*, one-time president of the SDS Todd Gitlin commented on the mass exhibitions of sorrow and solidarity around the fallen hero: "Could it be that this vast longing for peace . . . this force of, yes, love which had once seemingly come out of nowhere and turned so many lives upside down, could it be in some crazy way that its time, which had once come, could come again?"[84] Yet there was also criticism. Conservatives, flush with Ronald Reagan's election to the Presidency of the United States, crowed over the end of 1960s-era liberalism.[85] Richard Brookhiser, senior editor for the *National Review*, noted: "Lennon and his friends influenced other things besides music, *mostly for the worse*."[86]

The response to Lennon's death encapsulated and highlighted lingering hostility as pundits on the left and right attempted to define the legacy of the 1960s in the USA. Postwar prosperity had ushered in a new class of people educated at the country's colleges and universities. This "progressive" middle class generally opposed the Vietnam War, favored civil rights for black Americans and equal rights for women, and was sympathetic to environmental and consumer causes. The repercussions for American politics were vast, most notably in the alienation from the Democratic Party of many socially conservative (and largely working-class) northeastern Democrats loyal to the Democratic Party since Franklin Roosevelt's New Deal programs of the 1930s. Stressing traditional social and moral values, rejecting the counterculture, and renouncing big government programs, especially those tied to race, conservatives exploited the break in Democratic ranks to court disaffected Democrats.

Ronald Reagan, governor of California from 1967 to 1975, and a fervent opponent of the New Left and counterculture, emerged in 1980 as the Republican nomination for president, and became the overwhelming choice for cultural conservatives, both Republican and Democrat. President Jimmy Carter remained the candidate for progressives. For voters, the lines in the culture war were clearly drawn. Unfortunately for Carter and the Democratic Party, by the mid-1970s the coalition of blacks, women, Jews, organized labor, and environmentalists, which had been a core progressive constituency in the 1960s, was badly fragmented. In the 1980 election, Reagan rolled over Carter in a landslide, ushering in an era of Republican and conservative domination of the executive and judicial branches of government. Thus, in early December 1980, with Reagan's inauguration just over a month away, the Republican ascendancy was at hand, and with it the ruin of 1960s liberalism. With Lennon's passing, the last vestiges of the "movement" fell into a retreat from which it has yet to recover.

"And so dear friends, you'll just have to carry on"

On 1970's "God," Lennon had declared that "the dream is over," bringing to a close the idealism and fantasy of the previous decade. For many fans, however, the chance of a Beatles reunion and reanimation of 1960s era liberalism had postponed this conclusion. For them, his death brought horrific closure to that idealism, and wondering, again quoting "God," how they would "carry on." Lennon's stature was elevated following his death, and his accomplishments and influence amplified, often, perhaps unavoidably, at McCartney's expense. Eventually, in 1981, an exasperated McCartney reacted, confiding to Beatles biographer and friend Hunter Davies (who later, to McCartney's shock, published his comments): "He could be a maneuvering swine, which no one ever realized. Now since the death he's become Martin Luther Lennon. But that wasn't him either. He wasn't some sort of holy saint."[87] For some, however, he had indeed become a kind of secular saint, increasingly beyond reproach, as reaction to publication of Albert Goldman's *The Lives of John Lennon* (1988) indicates. This tawdry exposé of a megalomaniacal, abusive, drug-addled, bulimic recluse was too much for his fans and defenders of the 1960s youth legacy, and led to a public pillorying of its author across a wide swathe of the mainstream media. Most indignant of all, *Rolling Stone* blasted its "mean-spirited scandalousness."[88]

In the wake of Lennon's death, McCartney returned to recording *Tug of War*, with producer George Martin and Beatles engineer Geoff Emerick. "It's a tug of war, what with one thing and another, we were trying to outscore each other, in this tug of war," McCartney sang, and the title track and "Here Today" were taken by many to be his personal address to Lennon. The album also featured a duet with Stevie Wonder, "Ebony and Ivory," which was an international hit on the singles charts. Created under the duress of his friend's murder, and his ambivalent feelings toward him, *Tug of War* is, perhaps, McCartney's most personal album. Critically acclaimed,[89] the album was number one in the US and UK charts.

Disgusted by an industry that dissected and reassembled his work to suit its own interests, and which capitalized on the horror of Lennon's murder, Harrison lost interest in the life of the pop star, and produced only two more albums before taking a five-year hiatus from recording. The first was the revamped *Somewhere in England*, featuring Harrison, Starr, and the McCartneys on "All Those Years Ago," a reworking of a track he originally intended for a new Ringo Starr album, here rewritten to memorialize Lennon and as an indictment of those who "don't act with much honesty" and have "forgotten all about mankind" and God. Pushed by the wave of nostalgia following Lennon's murder, the single quickly went to number two in the US Billboard charts, where it stayed for three weeks in July 1981. Still, the album garnered little attention from the press, with what little there was mixed.[90] The second album was the less than inspired *Gone Troppo*, which ended Harrison's commitment to Warner Brothers and marked the beginning of his retirement from public life until 1985.

With the aid of Harry Nilsson, Ron Wood of the Rolling Stones, Stephen Stills, Harrison, and McCartney, Starr completed *Can't Fight Lighting*, now called *Stop and Smell the Roses* (1981), his best-received album in years. At its best, according to the *New York Times*'s Robert Palmer, the album's pop was "infectious and charming. And since he's Ringo, one doesn't have to plumb it for profundity in order to enjoy it."[91] Nevertheless, disappointing sales prompted RCA to drop Starr in 1982. Though his recording career was flagging, other interests proved more successful. Starr jumpstarted his film career[92] with the slapstick *Caveman*, a minor hit released in 1981. Also that year, Starr married "Bond girl" Barbara Bach, who had appeared in *Caveman*. His success in the film was followed, in 1984, by Starr's first of two seasons as narrator of *Thomas the Tank Engine and Friends*, the popular British children's show later exported to the USA.[93]

Though more uncomfortable than ever with his celebrity status, and generally disenchanted with the industry, Harrison was drawn back to music in 1985, when he appeared with Carl Perkins, Ringo Starr, and Eric Clapton on HBO's *Carl Perkins and Friends* concert. This was the beginning of a particularly productive and happy period in Harrison's life. In November, 1987, Harrison released *Cloud Nine*, which, with a generally positive response from the critics,[94] was his first platinum album since *All Things Must Pass*. Additionally, the first single from the album, "Got My Mind Set on You," was a number one hit in January 1988. Shortly after the success of *Cloud Nine*, Harrison assembled the Traveling Wilburys, including himself, Bob Dylan, Tom Petty, Jeff Lynne and Roy Orbison. The band's first album, *The Traveling Wilburys: Volume One*, released in November 1988, was a triple platinum worldwide hit, reaching number three in the US album charts. This popular and critical success[95] led a year later to the follow-up, *The Traveling Wilburys: Volume Three*, which went platinum. Harrison followed this effort with a thirteen-date tour of Japan in late 1991, some of which made it on to a double disc and documentary in 1992. In the middle of the decade, apart from activities tied to the release of the Beatles' *Anthology*, Harrison was content to withdraw from center stage and act in support of his friends' projects, for example his 1997 collaboration with Ravi Shankar, on *Chants of India*, an album of chants based on Vedic scripture.

In late 1999 Harrison survived a nearly fatal knife attack at the hands of a deranged intruder in his home. Just as Lennon had lost his life to an insane assailant, Harrison, stabbed several times in the chest, very nearly suffered the same fate, and in response withdrew further from public life. Harrison battled cancer throughout the latter part of the 1990s, before finally succumbing to the illness in 2001. In the last year of his life, though gravely ill, Harrison continued to work, opening discussions with his friend, a founder of Cirque du Soleil, Guy Laliberté, about a possible Beatles-inspired production (the successful Cirque du Soleil production, *The Beatles: Love*, premiered in June 2006).[96] Harrison also played on sessions for other musicians,[97] began remastering the Traveling Wilburys' catalog for reissue (the collection was released in 2007), and worked on recordings for *Brainwashed*, an album posthumously completed by Jeff Lynne and Harrison's son, Dhani. Upon Harrison's death, on November 29, 2001, his family released a statement saying he "left this world as he lived in it, conscious of God, fearless of death and at peace, surrounded by family and friends. He often said, 'Everything else can wait, but the search of God cannot wait, and love one another.'"[98]

Brainwashed was released a year after Harrison's death. *New York Times*'s critic and author of *The Beatles* (1995), Allan Kozinn, noted the cohesive thread running through Harrison's solo career, and culminating in this last album: "The new material has a familiar ring. The underlying theme, after all, is one Harrison has explored since *All Things Must Pass* in 1970: that the trappings of success are meaningless compared with the spiritual quest."[99] On this final studio album, as on his first, Harrison warned of *maya*.

Pipes of Peace, released in 1983, was McCartney's last top ten album until 1997's *Flaming Pie*. Pushed by the second of two duets with Michael Jackson, the number one hit, "Say Say Say" (the other, "The Girl is Mine," appeared on Jackson's *Thriller*), the album reached number one in the UK charts, and number four in the USA, though clearly viewed as inferior to *Tug of War*. McCartney also starred in the film *Give My Regards to Broad Street*, for which he also wrote the script. The film, depicting a day in McCartney's life, as he attempts to reclaim master recordings stolen by an unsavory underling, was accompanied by McCartney's soundtrack, which, like the film, included numerous Beatle covers, including "Here, There and Everywhere," "Eleanor Rigby," "Yesterday," and "The Long and Winding Road." Though "No More Lonely Nights" was a top ten hit in the UK and US singles charts, the film and soundtrack debuted in 1984 to a dismal reception.

Press to Play followed, but McCartney's albums of the late 1980s and early 1990s demonstrated his technical prowess more than artistic inspiration, and languished in the charts, revived only by *Flowers in the Dirt* (1989), which peaked at number one in the UK and number 21 in the USA, and included McCartney's collaboration with Elvis Costello, "My Brave Face," which was a hit in the USA and UK. *Flowers in the Dirt* and *Off the Ground* (1993) each spawned successful world tours. While McCartney's pop output for the 1990s centered on live albums,[100] in 1997 he released the critically acclaimed studio album *Flaming Pie*, which the *New York Times* dubbed his "best solo album since his 1982 solo masterpiece *Tug of War*."[101] McCartney continued to exhibit the experimental, even adventurous, proclivities that had marked his work as a Beatle, and he mounted several successful forays into classical music and other forms (which continued into the new century), beginning with 1991's *Paul McCartney's Liverpool Oratorio* (co-written with Carl Davis), which was a number one worldwide hit on the classical charts, as was his second major work of classical music, *Standing Stone*, released in 1997. *Paul McCartney's Working Classical* (1999), featuring classical reworkings of songs from his solo career, also did well on the classical charts. *Liverpool Sound Collage*, released in 2000, was created to accompany an exhibition of the works of Peter Blake (the influential pop artist and designer of the *Sgt. Pepper's Lonely Hearts Club Band* cover), and included, among other things, snippets of Beatles dialog, and the *Liverpool Oratorio*. *Ecce Cor Meum*, released in 2006, did well in the classical charts, and captured the Best Album Award at the UK's Classical BRIT Awards. McCartney also tried his hand at ambient music, recording under the name "The Fireman." In 2005, McCartney released *Twin Freaks*, a double album of remixes by one of England's premier DJs, remixers, and producers, the Freelance Hellraiser.

The loss of Linda McCartney to breast cancer in 1998 sent McCartney into a deep depression, but he emerged from mourning with a collection of rock and roll covers, *Run Devil Run*, released in 1999. Also in 1999, he was inducted into the Rock and Roll Hall of Fame, following in

Lennon's footsteps, whom he inducted in 1994. The retrospective collection *Wingspan: Hits and History* followed in 2001, and was a top ten hit in the USA and UK. *Driving Rain* premiered in November 2001, and included the 9/11-inspired anthem, "Freedom." Generally well received by the critics, the album reached only number twenty-six in the US charts, and fared even worse in the UK, but the tour that followed was a massive worldwide success. McCartney was the first artist to release an album on Starbucks' Hear Music label: *Memory Almost Full*, a top five album in the UK and USA, was promoted heavily on YouTube and Apple Computer's iTunes, and demonstrated McCartney's willingness to approach the audience wherever it might be found.

McCartney, following in the footsteps of Cliff Richard and George Martin, was knighted in 1997, in recognition of his "services to music," but his commercial success undoubtedly played a part in the award. His publishing interests have made him one of the richest men in the world (though he does not own the rights to his own Beatles music). He has continued to play to packed coliseums and stadiums throughout the world. McCartney's advocacy of countercultural values, while often newsworthy, has been measured. Always a proponent of the legalization of marijuana, he reportedly swore off marijuana only after the birth of his daughter with Heather Mills, Beatrice, in 2003. He and wife Linda McCartney supported People for the Ethical Treatment of Animals (PETA), the largest animal rights organization in the world. Additionally, Linda introduced her own line of vegetarian meals, which continued to be sold after her death in 1998. McCartney and Heather Mills (married in 2002) were vocal opponents of the use of landmines and the yearly baby seal hunt in Canada. Their joint activism was short-lived, however, when rancorous divorce proceedings were engaged in 2006.[102]

McCartney has become iconic of the sense of freedom and community that permeated the counterculture. He closed the Live Aid show in 1985 with "Let It Be," and twenty years later he opened the Live 8 concert in London, playing "Sgt. Pepper's Lonely Hearts Club Band" ("It was twenty years ago, today") with U2 singer Bono, and closing the program that night, leading the day's performers and the Hyde Park audience in a rendition of "Hey Jude." In 2003, he and his band played in Moscow; the DVD that followed, *Paul McCartney Live in Red Square*, captured his show and reminiscences by Russians who had developed their own counterculture in the 1960s, and for whom the Beatles had become the supreme model.

Harrison's 1987 "comeback" prompted Starr to contribute drums on *Cloud Nine*'s Beatle-esque "When We Was Fab." Shortly thereafter, having received treatment after years of alcohol abuse, Starr inaugurated his "All-Starr Band," an ever-changing roster of rock notables that has mounted numerous successful tours, the latest taking place in 2006. His recording career was also reinvigorated by collaboration with Mark Hudson, dating back to work Hudson did on *Time Takes Time*, a critical success[103] but commercial failure (prompting Private Music to drop Starr from their label).[104] Nevertheless, Starr and Hudson deepened their professional relationship, and the 1998 album, *Vertical Man*, which received fair reviews[105] but only meager sales, was the start of a collaboration that continued to the end of 2007. Dropped by Mercury, Starr released his next two albums, *Ringo Rama* (2003) and *Choose Love* (2005), on Koch. *Choose Love* was his most critically acclaimed album in years, but failed to chart in the USA and UK. In August 2007, Starr released *Photograph: The Very Best of Ringo Starr*, a compilation of recordings dating back to 1970, and comprising work on Capitol (EMI), Atlantic, Mercury, Boardwalk, Private Music, and Koch. Starr returned to EMI for *Liverpool 8* (released in January 2008), his first with the company since 1975. Starr has retained his attachment to the values of his youth, and is as likely to flash a peace sign today as he was in the heyday of the "flower children."

At the dawn of a new millennium, Starr and McCartney continue to record and perform. Their youth, like that of other baby-boomers, fades into the mists of memory, as do the reasons why they seemed to matter so much. Grown iconic now, like the "Summer of Love," and "Woodstock," the two Beatles carry on. The vision they put forth is less dogmatic and didactic than that of their youth, or of their bandmates, for that matter, and less of a challenge to the powers that be, but, at its heart, it is the same as it always was, since it first sprang forth in a more innocently optimistic time – in Starr's words, "Peace and Love, Peace and Love, Peace and Love." The work of four young men, and that of the two that remain, remains a moving declaration of individual and communal possibilities.

10 Any time at all: the Beatles' free phrase rhythms

WALTER EVERETT

A number of those interested in the music of the Beatles have singled out for discussion its rhythmic inventiveness. Most discussions of the Beatles' rhythmic devices start and end with an appreciation of their remarkably wide-ranging approaches to the metric surface, paying particular attention to asymmetrical meters (those representing measures containing numbers of beats not divisible by two or three, as in the 5/4 meter appearing in "Within You Without You" [*SP*])[1] or the many examples of freely mixed meter (as with the repeated alternation of 4/4 and 3/4 bars in "All You Need is Love" [*MMT*]). Another interesting development in the Beatles' rhythmic invention is their flexibility with strongly accented patterns of syncopation, which arises when normally weak beats or weak parts of beats (such as the second and fourth beats in 4/4 meter, or the second eighth within a quarter-note beat) are accented by strong melodic events (as with a sudden high note), rhythmically unexpected chord changes (normally changing on downbeats but subject to expressive versatility), or obtrusive dynamics (as with the normal rock drumbeat pattern, which loudly accents the snare on beats two and four). Because these and other related effects are manifest for the most part at the beat level (between the barlines), they are all relatively superficial and may be accounted for chiefly in the musical foreground (as opposed to groupings of measures and of phrases, which may be thought to occupy progressively deeper middle-ground and background orientations).[2] But perhaps of even greater significance for the individual character and expressive potential of many of their hundreds of songs is the group's free treatment of phrase rhythm. In this domain, we must recognize a larger-scale manifestation of regular or irregular accent patterns, measured in phrase lengths rather than within measures. These patterns derive from both (1) the manner in which successive downbeats (often made plain by motivic repetition and harmonic changes) relate to one another – some will be stronger than others; and (2) the manner in which multi-measure groupings (often adhering to the scanning of the poetic text) cohere in larger units such as phrases and periodic groupings of phrases. The purpose of this chapter will be to examine the rhythmic nature of the music of the Beatles from a large-scale, hypermetric[3] and phrase-based perspective, making reference to a large number of Beatles

Table 10.1 *The Beatles' canon on compact disc*

(Designation)	Full title	(Recording dates)
(*PPM*)	*Please Please Me*	(1962–3)
(*PM*)	*Past Masters*	(1962–9)
(*WtB*)	*With the Beatles*	(1963)
(*HDN*)	*A Hard Day's Night*	(1964)
(*BfS*)	*Beatles for Sale*	(1964)
(*H!*)	*Help!*	(1965)
(*RS*)	*Rubber Soul*	(1965)
(*Rev*)	*Revolver*	(1966)
(*SP*)	*Sgt. Pepper's Lonely Hearts Club Band*	(1966–7)
(*MMT*)	*Magical Mystery Tour*	(1966–7)
(*YS*)	*Yellow Submarine*	(1967–8)
(WA)	*The Beatles* (the "White Album")	(1968)
(*LIB*)	*Let It Be*	(1969–70)
(*AR*)	*Abbey Road*	(1969)

compositions from throughout their career as recording artists (1962–9). A handful of illustrations will be examined in somewhat closer detail.

The Beatles' phrase rhythms are foursquare often enough to permit the establishment of regular norms (that is, repeated lengths of four bars plus four bars) against which abnormal lengths can be measured. A large number of their songs, however, feature in one section or another various irregularities that will be scrutinized according to the following characteristics, each of which will be defined and exemplified below:

(1) contrasting unit lengths
(2) expanded prototypes
(3) reinterpretations of accent at the hypermetric level
(4) tonicization-related stretching and elision
(5) adjustments required by changes in harmonic rhythm
(6) thoroughly asymmetrical patterns

Because these various approaches to the plasticity of phrase are interwoven with one another in the Beatles' music, they will not necessarily be introduced in turn, but will rather be referred to as they are found to influence our chosen illustrations.

In many cases, irregularities in phrase length are closely tied to the given phrase's formal function within the song as a whole. Because of the presence in each case of a lyric text, some devices have compelling poetic connotations as well. While all three of the composing Beatles (John Lennon, Paul McCartney, and George Harrison) experimented with free phrase rhythms, Lennon was adventurous most often – though the far less prolific Harrison most consistently – in this regard.

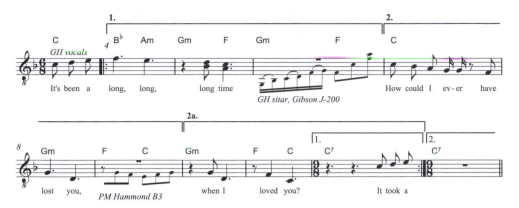

Example 1 "Long Long Long" (verse)

Before we investigate properties of contrasting unit lengths, we should note that metric groupings comprising odd numbers of measures sometimes appear exclusively, without direct comparison to others of the much more "normal" duple-measured lengths. The Beatles often embrace asymmetrical three-bar lengths as their unit of measure, as in "Long Long Long" (WA). The Renaissance-era mensuration system may help us understand the nesting of metric levels in this song: the hypermeasure divided into three bars may be referred to as a "perfection," as opposed to an "imperfection," which would group pairs of measures into hypermeasures. This song's triple division of a hypermeasure into three-bar groups, its normally duple groupings of beats into two-beat measures, and its triple division of a beat into three equal eighths, might be conceived, respectively, as illustrating an example in "perfect modus," "imperfect tempus," and "perfect prolatio." (This metric structure might be notated with beats represented as dotted quarters – perfect prolatio; with two beats per 6/8 measure – imperfect tempus; and with three measures per phrase – perfect modus. In nearly all tonal music, the "imperfect modus" pattern governs most phrase-level ratios that are typically duple in nature, but this was not so much the case in the Renaissance, hence our inspiration to refer to Beatles patterns in somewhat archaic, though unusually appropriate, terms.) The vocal melody and chord patterns for the verse (0:08–0:41)[4] of "Long Long Long," along with a simple analysis of phrase rhythm, are given in Example 1. In this and all following examples, horizontal brackets above the staff demarcate the extent of hypermeasures rather than phrase and subphrase groupings, although there is usually significant overlap between the meter and the phrase articulation. Here, the lyric's reference to an extreme length of time is portrayed through verses divided as three three-bar units (perfections), all in a slow 6/8 meter but for a final, stretched-out bar in 9/8.[5] In each of the three hypermetric units, two bars of vocal melody are appended by a measure-long instrumental tag. Note that the last unit (the hypermeasure labelled "2a" above its bracket [0:30–0:41]) is an extended revision of the melodic-harmonic pattern set forth in the second and third bars of unit 2 (0:23–0:29), and thus an unambiguous representation of a "long, long, long time." A similar example, the song "Wait" (*RS*), had been composed three years earlier by John Lennon, notably on a similar poetic idea, even using the same opening lyric ("it's been a long time . . . "). Here, verses are built as three bars (0:00–0:06) plus three bars (0:06–0:12). Lennon's hypermetric perfection is not unlike the "Ritmo di tre battute" of the Scherzo of Beethoven's Ninth Symphony, and even more like the last movement of Brahms's Opus 25 Piano Quartet. Lennon's uptempo rhythm is more readily comprehensible than that in the ambiguously slow "Long Long Long," but I find Harrison's moody and meditative example more evocative.

Contrasting unit lengths

Often, contrasts are presented between duple and triple units. In McCartney's "You Never Give Me Your Money" (*AR*), square 4 + 4 verses initially in a strict descending-fifth sequence ($I^7 - IV^7 - VII^7 - III - VI^7 - II^7 - V^7 - I$ [0:23–0:46]) are followed by a repeated three-bar double-plagal codetta (1:31–1:39). (I use the term "double plagal" to characterize the descending-fourth progression $\flat VII - IV - I$, which nests one neighboring plagal relationship within another.) The three-bar double-plagal cadence in "You Never Give Me Your Money" (one measure per chord) conveys a timeless quality that exemplifies the lyric's reference to a "magic feeling," hovering gently on Harrison's Leslie-tremolo Telecaster (suddenly switched to the lead pick-up for the slow arpeggiations) as if an aural escape from the standard duple, business-oriented, "money"-preoccupied verse.[6] Contrast in the form of strong internal disagreement is suggested in McCartney's verses of "We Can Work It Out" (*PM*), the first of which (0:00–0:18) begins with the words "Try to see it my way." This is an entire song devoted to the theme of disaccord and hoped-for resolution. Here, eight-bar phrases divide unequally as 3 + 3 + 2. Underlining the thoughts expressed in the lyrics, the hypermetric conflicts pit a stubborn wrong against a declared right. Lennon's ensuing bridge passage ("Life is very short . . . " [0:37–1:03]) paints "fussing and fighting" with the three-against-two metric motive at the beat level, through the use of triplet quarters; the tension is also expressed contrapuntally, with 4–3 suspensions above each V/VI in Lennon's harmonium part (0:44–0:46). As if completing a puzzle, the song's two-bar codetta (2:05–2:13) revisits the triplets on the tonic, which is there ornamented with

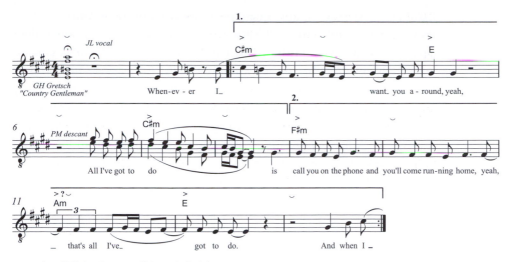

Example 2 "All I've Got to Do" (verse/refrain)

a 4–3 neighboring line reminiscent of the bridge's suspensions. One imagines that the codetta's harmonious resolution of the three-two combination bodes well for the bickering parties portrayed in the poetic text.

Expanded prototypes

Related to the triple-unit perfection is the concept of what I call the "floater," usually a two-bar unit that attaches itself to the front or back end of a hypothetical host four-bar phrase and thus an example of our second type, the expanded prototype. The four-bar phrase will serve as our hypothetical normal length against which all actual phrases are measured, particularly when they are expanded beyond that prototypical length into asymmetrical phrases of, for instance, five or seven bars. The technique of the expanded prototype is heard in the verses of John Lennon's "All I've Got to Do" (*WtB*), the first of which (0:00–0:25) is abstracted in Example 2. Here and henceforth, the beginning of the two-bar floater is marked with an italic "*f*" above the bracket, in this case beginning in measure 7. Note the long anacrusis (the inhalatory upbeat) preceding the double bar that puts the phrase grouping slightly out of phase with the indicated hypermetric divisions. The harmonically ambiguous opening two-bar anacrusis (0:00–0:03) leads to the phrase proper, which seems like it could have been metrically closed after four bars (note the strong/weak accentuation suggested beneath the bracket in measures 3–6). This is followed by the varied repetition of measures 3–4 (0:03–0:07) in measures 7–8 (0:11–0:15), as if a four-bar antecedent (measures 3–6) is to be answered by a parallel four-bar consequent.[7] As it turns out, a contrasting consequent phrase begins only in measure 9, and so the fragment of measures 7–8 is metrically a conclusion of the antecedent phrase, now made up of three two-bar sub-units (and thus analogous to perfections in three-bar units). Grammatically, the passage functions at the same time as a transition to the consequent phrase, which aligns fairly closely with a hypermeasure (measures 9–13 [0:15–0:25]) of an odd five-bar length. This odd length is permitted by a retrospective reinterpretation of measure 11 (where a poignant descending passing tone is introduced with C♮) as weak rather than its initially perceived strong function – thus the notation above measure 11 shows a questioned strong accent replaced by a weak one.

In "All I've Got to Do," we've seen that the floater (measures 7–8) would likely first be perceived as the beginning of an antecedent phrase, as its motivic material is parallel with the opening of the consequent phrase; however, because its idea is abandoned halfway through, the measures are likely reinterpreted as a continuation of the antecedent. Commonly, the correct metric interpretation of the floater, and its motivic and harmonic interdependence with other units, are perceived only upon the completion of the entire passage. This same problem arises along with an emotional outburst in the bridge of John Lennon's "Yes It Is" (*PM*) (the contrasting section that begins with the words "I could be happy..." [1:00–1:18]).[8] The section's third 12/8 bar ("if I could forget her..." [1:08–1:11]) is at first interpreted as the beginning of a consequent phrase, but in retrospect, because of textural, motivic, and poetico-grammatical contrast in the next bar, it floats back to join the antecedent; the original consequent idea has been abandoned and the bridge is left with a phrase rhythm of 3 + 2 bars. In the first vocal phrase of George Harrison's "Something" (*AR*) (0:05–0:26), a two-bar floater (measures 6–7 [0:20–0:26]) impetuously transposes the material of measures 4–5 (0:12–0:19) in harmonic sequence, as if the singer is reaching ever higher to uncover the inscrutable nature of the "something" he tries to describe, resulting in a six-bar opening phrase. In McCartney's "Two of Us" (*LIB*), reduced in Example 3, an unusual half-bar floater (0:23) invades the verse/refrain (0:18–0:49). The irregularity of the floater – especially when followed by two bars (measures 4–5 [0:24–0:28]) sung in a remarkably slowed rhythm – conveys the sense of "riding nowhere, not arriving."

At about the time that McCartney was writing "Two of Us," over the second half of 1968, the same half-bar floater was being used to good effect by Lennon in "Revolution" (*PM* [0:12–0:13] and WA [0:21–0:22]) and by McCartney himself in "Martha My Dear" (WA [0:22]). A list of representative floaters – most often of two bars – appearing throughout the Beatles' career is given in Table 10.2.

Table 10.2 *Representative "floaters" in the Beatles' music*

Lennon's refrain to "Not a Second Time" (*WtB*) [4 + 4 + 2] [0:26–0:45]
McCartney's verses to "Every Little Thing" (*BfS*) [4 + 2, 4 + 2] [0:03–0:14, 0:15–0:26]
McCartney's verses to "Michelle" (*RS*) [2 + 4, 2 + 4] [0:08–0:20, 0:21–0:32]
Lennon's bridge to "We Can Work it Out" (*PM*) [4 + 2, 4 + 2] [0:37–0:50, 0:51–1:03]
Lennon's verse to "A Day in the Life" (*SP*) [4 + 4 + 2] [0:12–0:43]
Lennon's verse to "Revolution" (WA) [2.5 + 4 + 2.5 + 4 + 5.5] [0:16–1:1:02] (cf. *PM*)
McCartney's verse to "Martha My Dear" (WA) [1.25 + 2.5 + 2.5 + 1] [0:19–0:38]
McCartney's bridge to "Two of Us" (*LIB*) [2 + 4] [1:31–1:44]
Lennon's verse to "Because" (*AR*) [4 + 4 + 2] [0:30–1:00]

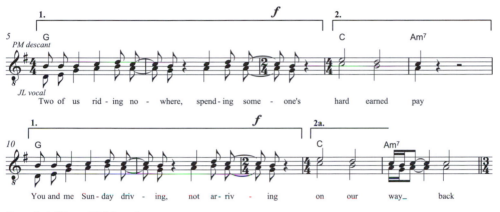

Example 3 "Two of Us" (verse)

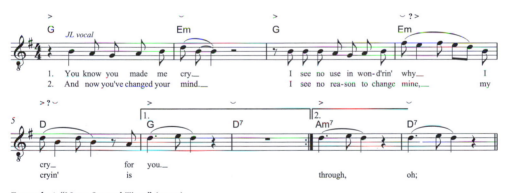

Example 4 "Not a Second Time" (verse)

The floater is an example of how the Beatles expand their basic proto-typical phrases; other devices appear as well. One method combines triple and duple units within the phrase, but elides the connection so that a weak measure will have to be reinterpreted, in hindsight, as strong; this creates seven-bar verses in Lennon's "Not a Second Time" (*WtB* [0:00–0:13]) and McCartney's "Yesterday" (*H!* [0:05–0:22]). The first of these is shown in Example 4. The suggested accent pattern of strong and weak measures is

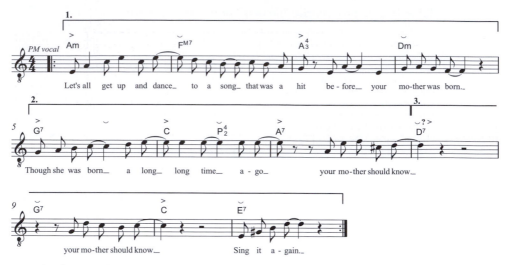

Example 5 "Your Mother Should Know" (verse)

based on harmonic and motivic construction. As the example is heard in real time, the listener must retrospectively reinterpret the hypermetric accent in measures 4 and 5, based on the unequivocal accents heard subsequently in measures 6 and 7. The unusual delayed entrance of the drums in measure 5, however, works against the suggested accent pattern, further complexifying the issue. To my ear, all of this metric confusion portrays exquisitely the emotional uncertainty of the sensitive singer, John Lennon.

Reinterpretations of accent at the hypermetric level

In the verse of McCartney's "Your Mother Should Know" (*MMT*), shown in Example 5, the first hypermeasure (0:04–0:12) is of a simple four bars. In the second unit (measures 5–7 [0:12–0:18]), the vocal phrasing works against the hypermeter, which momentarily ventures into an irregularly doubled harmonic rhythm, confusing the listener who would normally wish to hear its fourth bar as a weak conclusion to the hypermeasure. Instead, the continuing motivic pattern forces a reinterpretation of measure 8 as a strong beginning to the third metric unit (measures 8–11 [0:18–0:26]), thus amputating the second hypermeasure so as to result in a 4 + 3 + 4-bar passage. The metric irregularity coincides with a brief tonicization of the minor key's mediant.

Other expansions are less involved, as in the measured, composed-out fermata that may create an extended anacrusis or cadence. This method of extending the cadence, William Rothstein points out, has been discussed

Example 6 "There's a Place" (verse)

since Kirnberger and Reicha.[9] The extended anacrusis is first heard in John Lennon's "There's a Place" (*PPM*), the first verse of which is shown in Example 6. Here, the first vocal phrase is extended to six bars (measures 4–9 [0:06–0:15]), opening with a two-bar anacrusis (measures 4–5 [0:06–0:08]). The third hypermeasure (measures 14–20 [0:22–0:33]) is expanded further when the same long anacrusis is preceded by a parenthetical repetition ("[and it's my] mind and there's no time"). A similar measured

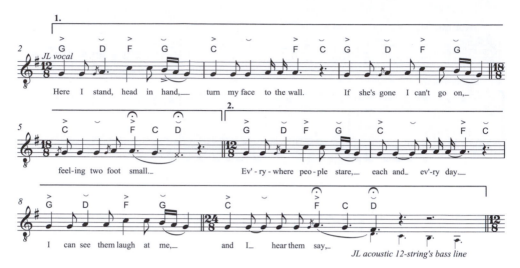

Example 7 "You've Got to Hide Your Love Away" (verse)

fermata (0:10–0:14) opens the chorus of Lennon's textually related "Strawberry Fields Forever" (*MMT*) four years later. The composed-out cadential fermata is heard in the verse of Lennon's "You've Got to Hide Your Love Away" (*H!*), shown in Example 7. In the first phrase (0:02–0:19), I hear the elongation of each of the prototypical third and fourth beats of measure 5, each marked with a fermata, stretched into two beats each. The prototypical fourth beat is expanded even further at the conclusion of the second phrase (0:20–0:38), leading to a passage of twenty-four eighths that functions as a single measure. Other measured cadential fermatas appear in the verses of "The Continuing Story of Bungalow Bill" (WA [0:33–0:37]), "Lucy in the Sky with Diamonds" (*SP* [0:27–0:31]), and – expanded through the orchestral "glissando" – "A Day in the Life" (*SP* [1:33–2:16]), all, significantly, Lennon compositions.

Tonicization-related stretching and elision

Phrase rhythm must adapt to harmonic and formal requirements in several songs. In both Lennon's "Yes It Is" (*PM* [2:20–2:40]) and McCartney's "I Will" (WA [1:07–1:33]), and in their jointly composed "I Want to Hold Your Hand" (*PM* [2:08–2:23]), phrases are expanded in the codas to permit final Mozartean deceptive harmonic developments.[10] Extra bars are required for tonicizations in "Lucy in the Sky with Diamonds." In Lennon's "You're Going to Lose That Girl" (*H!*), a two-bar floater (0:52–0:55) permits a rhythmically fluid transition from I to ♭III for the bridge, but an abrupt retransition to the verse through a tritone-substitute for V (1:06–1:08) cuts

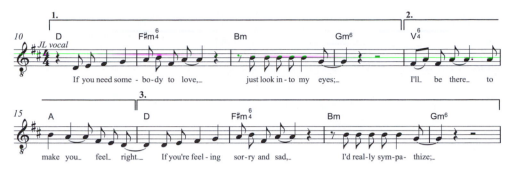

Example 8 "Any Time at All" (verse)

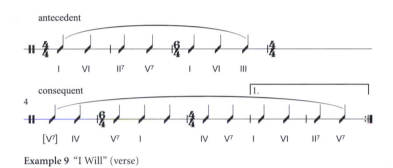

Example 9 "I Will" (verse)

the bridge's second phrase one bar short. The harmonic surprise takes the breath out of the phrase, cutting the last metric unit to three bars.

Enjambments (measures that enjoy simultaneously beginning and ending functions) and elisions (functioning but absent measures) appear often.[11] Both techniques work together in the verse of Lennon's "Any Time at All" (*HDN*), reduced in Example 8. Here, a harmonically static four-bar subphrase (0:15–0:21) is followed by a harmonically active consequent (0:21–0:24) that misses its third and fourth bars, displaced by the metrically enjambed opening of the second period with unit three (0:24–0:31). The second antecedent subphrase (marked as unit 3) is answered by a normal four-bar consequent (0:31–0:38). Lennon repeats the same fluid enjambment in "Julia" (0:14) four years later. Hurried phrases result from elisions in the same composer's "Cry Baby Cry" (*WA* [2:08]); the elision here of measures within phrases represents a large-scale version of the Beatles' penchant for eliding beats within measures of mixed meter. In Lennon's "It Won't Be Long" (*WtB*), as in "Any Time at All," the regulation of time itself is the song's subject. Here, a prototypical fourth bar is elided because an impatient Lennon apparently decides that the third bar (0:19–0:20) has already served this function; he rarely likes to tread water.

As shown in Example 9, the opening phrase of McCartney's "I Will" (*WA*) comes to an abrupt halt when the roadblock of a non-functional mediant harmony (0:08), with attendant ambiguity of hypermetric accent,

Example 10 Voice-leading analysis of "I Should Have Known Better"

appears in an extended measure 3 (two bars of 4/4 conclude with a single bar of 6/4). Because the phrase dangles on the weak III chord, there is a strong sense of elision. The consequent phrase has two different lengths, both longer than the antecedent, depending upon whether it returns to another verse (with one bar of 4/4, one of 6/4, and three bars of 4/4 [0:09–0:21]) or moves on, through the second ending (totaling one bar of 4/4, one of 6/4, and another single bar of 4/4 [0:30–0:40]), to the bridge. Other examples of enjambments or elisions can be found in the retransitions of both McCartney's "She's Leaving Home" (*SP*), where the only bar containing a tonally and hypermetrically expected V (following 1:17) is entirely removed and thus exists only hypothetically, and Lennon's "Sexy Sadie" (WA), the bridge of which returns abruptly to its verse via an elision (1:10). Also see the verse (0:21) of "Being for the Benefit of Mr. Kite!" (*SP*) and the chorus (0:07) of "The Continuing Story of Bungalow Bill" (WA), both songs by Lennon.

In Lennon's "I Should Have Known Better" (*HDN*), the Beatles join an aborted second verse and a bridge with the "linkage" technique, which Oswald Jonas defined as "a new phrase [taking] its initial idea [from] the end of the immediately preceding one."[12] The second verse has a length of 6 + 2 (0:25–0:40) as opposed to the initial verse's length of 6 + 4 (0:07–0:25). This complex example warrants closer inspection. The voice-leading sketch given in Example 10, which for convenience reduces the entire song to its basic tonal structure, elucidates the interrelated parts of the melodic design. The growth of the sixth scale degree, **E**, from neighboring motion through passing motion at **A** and through roothood to tonicized status at **C** is the tonal focus in these sections, which are joined by an enlarged motivic overlap, the "linkage," that has a profound effect upon phrase rhythm. The second verse (**B**) is cut short to eight bars because of the unexpected appearance of V^7/VI in support of the melodic leading tone F sharp at measure 22 (0:38). This initiates a transition to the lyrical and expansive E-minor melody of the bridge (**C**). (The applied chord is amplified in importance by the entrance in measure 22 of Harrison's electric twelve-string guitar, which chimes with the bridge's changes as if accompanying a measured recitative.) The melodic drop to an inner-voice b^1 at measure 23 (a pitch class highlighted later in the bridge with a dramatic register shift to b^2) only briefly interrupts the rise to the eighth scale degree, g^2, that would have marked the conclusion of the *second* verse had it continued as did the *first*. In the graph, this rise at letters **A** and **B** from the ornamented initial tone d^2 through passing sixth and seventh scale degrees to the eighth is marked with a slur and the italic lower-case a.[13] From the end of the second verse, the rise is completed at measure 24 (0:42), effecting a motivic overlap of the verse, transition, and bridge that expresses the singer's great determination to communicate ("can't you see, when I tell you . . . and when I ask you . . ."). With the boost to scale degree 8 from the inner realm of b^1, Lennon reaches a new depth of understanding not heard in the previously blithe neighboring and passing treatment of the sixth scale degree, portrayed in a new setting of the tonic scale degree with VI of the tonicized VI. It is as if this area, the submediant, is where Lennon was headed all along, but even he could not have known so; the tonal evolution of the sixth scale degree can thus be heard as a portrayal of the deep hindsight that inspires the song. So my sense is that some level of phrase continues beyond the metric and harmonic closure at the double bar following measure 22.

The Beatles achieve their most original phrase rhythm effects in Lennon's "Sexy Sadie" (WA) and "Because" (*AR*). In each, the strong and weak accentual characteristics of phrases within verses are reinterpreted in codas by virtue of appearances there of new superimposed melodic parts. "Because," the last verse and coda of which are given in full score in Example 11, will illustrate. Preceding verses had each ended with an unusual half cadence in instruments only, halting on a fully diminished seventh chord (0:58–1:00). The function of this chord is clarified as VII of IV only after the second verse, by the beginning of the bridge (1:30). In the analogous place following the verse that begins in measure 35 (1:42), shown in Example 11, the diminished-seventh harmony (falling in measure 44 [2:09–2:11]) carries on as it had instrumentally. That is, the instruments behave as if the half cadence has been reached in bar 44, and restart in measure 45 (2:12)

Example 11 "Because" (last verse and coda)

Example 11 (*cont.*)

with a complete verse structure, beginning with the Moog's statement of the C-sharp minor arpeggio.[14] The singers' newly added wordless parts, however, are dreamily out of phase with the instrumental backing: whereas the instruments believe they are beginning anew in bar 45, the singers had gotten a head start and actually cadence authentically at this point; whereas the instruments attempt a half cadence as before in measure 48 (2:21–2:23), the singers continue, insisting that the phrase cadence deceptively in bar 49 (2:24). Thus the song's first two verses group phrases into 4 + 4 + 2 (0:30–1:00) and 4 + 4 + 2 (1:00–1:30) bars, but the third and final verses rearrange the accentuation so as to group them as 4 + 4 + 4 + 4 + 4 (1:42–2:44). The phrase grouping and hypermeter are far more acutely out of phase than in examples provided by Lerdahl and Jackendoff and by Rothstein.[15] The same effect had been achieved a year earlier in "Sexy Sadie," where scant new vocal phrases in the coda (2:13–3:12) work against the instrumental hypermeter; the sly, lasciviously slithery harmonic ambiguities of "Sadie" enable the metric playfulness.

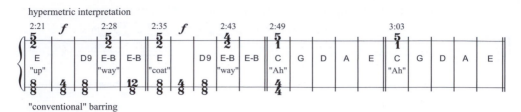

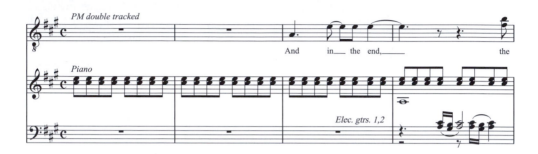

Example 12 "A Day in the Life" (bridge)

Example 13 "The End" (concluding couplet)

Adjustments required by changes in harmonic rhythm

But perhaps most interesting are the free phrase rhythms that result from the Beatles' play with tempo. In some cases, such as in "I Want to Hold Your Hand" (0:22) and "Your Mother Should Know" (0:18), a doubled harmonic rhythm doubles the density so that phrase lengths may be halved.[16] A more majestic such relationship empowers McCartney's bridge of "A Day in the Life" (*SP* [2:16–3:17]). This passage opens with the piano-led rhythm section pounding out frenetic eighths, grouped conventionally as shown in the lower single-line staff of Example 12; the first word of each phrase, timings, and all chord changes are given for the reader's reference. Four phrases appear, each of the first three comprising a total of 2.5 bars of 8/8 (barred either 8/8 + 4/8 + 8/8 or 8/8 + 12/8). The fourth phrase, in contrast, is shortened to a more regular two bars of 8/8. With this new regularity as its only preparation, the tempo slows (at 2:49) to exactly one half of its value, as regularly recurring 4/4 bars lead to the end of the bridge in a dreamy retransition in falling fourths (C − G − D . . .). But these regular bars are grouped into asymmetrical hypermeasures, five 4/4 measures in each of the last two phrases (indicated in the upper staff as two hyperbars of 5/1). In retrospect, it can be determined that the first three phrases of the bridge, asymmetrical on the surface with their changing meter, can also be heard in hypermetric groupings of five. But because of the faster tempo in relation to the retransition, these earlier phrases occupy hypermeasures of 5/2. So it seems that despite the fact that the rhythmic and melodic-harmonic materials of the 5/2 and the 5/1 sections are unrelated, McCartney develops his phrase rhythms in a motivic way, emphasizing five-bar units.

Finally, the Beatles create their own examples of metric modulation in both Lennon's "Lucy in the Sky" (0:48) and McCartney's "The End" (*AR* [1:40]), both of which coincide with tonal modulations.[17] In the latter, excerpted in Example 13, subtle shifts in both phrase rhythm and tonal relations reflect the construction of Paul McCartney's equation of "the love you take" and "the love you make," uncovering the key to the ideas in the second half of *Abbey Road* with a seven-bar phrase whose prototype's duration is altered not with a halving of tempo or a composed-out fermata, but with a composed-out ritard.

I hope that, in this limited space, this chapter has been able to suggest something of the astounding variety of large-scale rhythmic effects in Beatles songs. The constant flexibility of these composers in juggling irregular hypermetric lengths (occasionally the result of large-scale perfections but much more often the product of expansions of hypothetical prototypes) and structural changes in tempo and harmonic rhythm, and their manifold demands that the listener reinterpret phrase-level accent patterns to align with changing tonal, formal, and instrumentational relationships, all make this music constantly fresh and dynamic. Combined with the Beatles' poetic interests in the portrayal of emotional conflicts, contrasts, parenthetical embellishments, or changing perspectives of time itself, all phrase-rhythm techniques work together with the multi-leveled meanings of their lyrics to create one of several dimensions in which this group produced some of the most compellingly expressive music of its era.

PART THREE

History and influence

11 The Beatles as zeitgeist

SHEILA WHITELEY

The sixties and cultural politics

In July 2006, I was invited to take part in a day of national and regional press interviews. The topic was "The 60s: The Beatles Decade," a five-part series by UKTV History which explored the influence of music on the 1960s. The series was accompanied by a survey which compared the experiences of those growing up in the sixties, seventies, and eighties, and revealed that over a third (34 percent of the 3,000 adults interviewed) conceded that at one time or another they have embroidered their past in order to gain the respect of their family and friends. A quarter of these claimed that they were flexible with the truth in order to appear "cool" to their children. Yet only 15 percent of those growing up in the seventies, and a mere 5 percent of those growing up in the eighties, admitted to lying about their past.

In particular, those growing up in the sixties were most likely to ex-aggerate their "beat generation" credentials – with a quarter claiming that they were a part of or had associations with the hippy movement, when in reality a mere 6 percent could really lay claim to this being true. One in five admitted lying about the drugs they had taken. Twenty-two percent of those questioned admitted that they had used the line, "I was too stoned to remember the sixties," whereas in reality a mere 8 percent had tried cannabis and only 1 percent had tried acid.

Claiming to have attended rock festivals and to have seen popular bands such as the Beatles live was also a popular telltale for the sixties generation, with 9 percent claiming to have been at famous concerts when in reality they actually saw the footage on TV. Eleven percent of the sixties respondents also claimed that they knew people who had attended a "love-in," with 9 percent claiming they had been invited to one. In fact these were fabrications, with just 4 percent knowing someone who had, and 1 percent actually invited to attend a love-in. Claims to have met famous people from the sixties decade were also revealed to be lies – 12 percent of those questioned had "made up" an encounter with someone famous to impress their friends, the most popular fabrication being an encounter with Paul McCartney.

For the seventies children of the revolution, the overwhelming reasons for lying about their past experiences were ill-advised fashion decisions, a desire to be associated with famous people, and a misguided love of

Table 11.1 *Top lies told by people who grew up in the sixties,
seventies, or eighties*

	Percentage
1960s	
Was a hippy	27
Experimented with soft drugs	20
Meeting someone famous from the Beat Generation	12
Knowing someone who took part in a love-in	11
Seeing the Beatles live	9
1970s	
Regularly in the disco	33
Wore platform shoes	17
Hated prog rock	11
Meeting someone famous	11
Avoided orange or brown interior furnishings	9
1980s	
Didn't watch Charles and Diana's wedding on TV	35
Didn't wear shoulder pads	29
Didn't vote Tory	15
Owned a computer	11
Attended Live Aid	2

Survey, information and write-up from Lesley Land, Taylor Herring Public Relations, London

indulgent prog rock! It seems the eighties were worth keeping quiet about, with many of generation X now ashamed of their political stance (the dreaded Margaret Thatcher), their shoulder pads, and their "uncool" fixation with the royal family. (See Table 11.1.)

I will return to some of these points later, but I would add that it is very common for people to look back on their younger, rock and roll days through rose-tinted glasses. In reality, however, the experience of growing up in the sixties, for most people, would be more conservative than they would like to make out: more akin to Cliff Richard than to Keith Richards. Even so, what most colors our feelings about an era is the cultural politics, and here, there is no doubt that it is the music that gives it the real edge. As all the programs in UKTV History's series stated:

> There was a change across the decade from a Conservative Government led by Harold Macmillan to a Labour Government led by Harold Wilson. By the end of the decade censorship was over, the pill freed up sex, music and drama became part of life; there was a growing consumer society and increasingly this meant taking holidays abroad. The Beatles were at the heart of this transformation, the symbol of a decade: four lads from Liverpool who took on the establishment and won!

The last sentence is telling. On the one hand, it reveals the particular slant of the programs; on the other, it suggests that the Beatles were fully engaged in cultural politics; that their music can be interpreted as responding to the political and ideological shifts that took place over the sixties while at the same time, instigating change.

It is also significant that the sixties are encapsulated by the phrase "the Beatles decade" – and not, say, "the Rolling Stones decade." While this could be attributed to the longevity of the band – 1960, John, Paul, and George playing the Jacaranda as the Silver Beetles;[1] 1969, in public still united, in private splitting up, with McCartney finally leaving the band on April 10, 1970 – it is suggested that their songs are unique in mirroring the changing face of the decade: from the buoyant optimism of the early years, through to the overarching feeling in the years 1969–70 that the party was well and truly over. For those of us of a comparable age, the Beatles seemed to mirror our own growing up: as teenagers no longer tethered by postwar austerity, we had a certain amount of disposable income,[2] and, with a new emphasis on attitude – attributable in part to the 1950s advent of rock and roll, coffee bars, the jukebox, and such role models as Elvis Presley and Buddy Holly – the paralyzing grayness that had characterized British society during the postwar period was replaced, almost overnight, by Carnaby Street color, youth culture, and the Beatles. As Philip Norman observes, "the hormonal balance of the body was irrevocably upset by the dramatisation of teenage life";[3] we were different, no longer mini-versions of our parents, but rather teenagers with a particular identity of our own, an identity fueled by the potency of beat.

Clearly, it would be an exaggeration to suggest that the Beatles were the principal catalysts of change, albeit that the series of programs appeared on a dedicated history channel. Britain in the fifties and sixties was a society in transition, and the emerging teenage culture was, in part, a response to this situation. Not least, the increased spending power among teenagers reflected both an overall rise in the standard of living and a trend toward personal consumption – fashion, records, and record-players, cinema and other entertainment, including coffee bar culture. Significant, in this context, are the specifics of consumption, not least lifestyle and leisure. Hence while 1950s American artists such as Elvis Presley, Buddy Holly, and Chuck Berry are undoubtedly important in highlighting teenage life, the Beatles provided a new and specific focus on both national and regional identity which resonated with the particular experiences of their young fans. Suddenly, Liverpool was hip and England was where it was happening.

It is interesting, at this early stage of my discussion, to posit the question of whether the Beatles' three stages of composition – from beat to self-conscious artistry via the super-pop of *Rubber Soul* (1965) and the "mélange of style and substance" of *Revolver* (1966)[4] – were simply fortuitous or whether they provided a particular insight into the shifting sociocultural politics of the time. In the early 1960s, for example, Presley was in the army,

Motown and Stax records were beginning to make an impact, the twist became the new hit dance, and local bands, stimulated both by the DIY culture of skiffle (popularized by Lonnie Donegan)[5] and the examples of such home-grown pop stars as Cliff Richard and Tommy Steele, sprang up in major cities across the UK. In 1961 there were more than 400 bands in Liverpool alone, with the Beatles' lunchtime gig at the Cavern introducing a growing fan base to cover versions of Chuck Berry, Little Richard, and Carl Perkins.

The Beatles first came to national attention with their debut single, "Love Me Do," and their subsequent appearance on British television's *Thank Your Lucky Stars* on February 13, 1963. This appearance allowed the band to debut their new single, "Please Please Me," before 6 million viewers, and marked a pivotal moment in their career. Successive hits, including "From Me to You" and "She Loves You" – especially the song's catchy chorus, "Yeah, yeah, yeah" – ensured that they became household names as their catchphrase was echoed in newspaper headlines and television alike. By 1964, after an appearance on the *Ed Sullivan Show*, their popularity in the United States overshadowed their preeminence in Great Britain. By April, they held an unprecedented top five spots on the *Billboard* Hot 100, and in Canada they boasted nine records in the Top Ten. They quickly spearheaded a new direction in popular music, one that extended peripherally into fashion and the arts and, more specifically, ousted the solo singer in favor of an irrepressible flow of Merseybeat talent that focused on group dynamics.

The relationship between fashion, the arts, and popular music was pivotal to 1960s popular culture. Art colleges "were providing a free and easy world for clever but wayward boys and girls,"[6] not simply as an alternative to university, but rather as a place to explore ideas, spawning such charismatic and influential artists as Mary Quant, John Lennon, and Pete Townshend. By the mid-sixties, London became the epicentre of the "swinging scene," the focus for European fashion, art, design, music, and theatre. It was "the place to be seen," with Allen Ginsberg, Julie Christie, Twiggy, Mick Jagger, Michael Caine, and David Bailey, to name but a few, frequenting the most glamorous restaurants and nightclubs. Its atmosphere captured by Peter Whitehead in his documentary *Tonite Let's All Make Love in London* (1967) and in the American weekly magazine *Time*, which, in 1966, dedicated an entire issue to "the Swinging City," London was eulogized as the epitome of modern urban culture. Even shopping became a fashion in itself as boutiques proliferated; Mary Quant in New Bond Street, Granny Takes a Trip just off King's Road, Biba in High Street, Kensington, and Bazaar on King's Road, with UK magazines such as *Queen*, *Honey*, and *Petticoat* promoting the new fashions to their young readers.

It was also a period of celebrity culture, with films such as Antonioni's *Blow Up* (1966), inspired by fashion photographer David Bailey's career, and Nicolas Roeg's film *Performance* (1969), starring Mick Jagger, providing a particular insight into both the glamor and the decadence of the period.[7] Meanwhile, writers such as Arnold Wesker, John Braine, Alan Ayckbourn, Harold Pinter, and John Osborne were hailed as the "angry young men" of the theatre, while Michael Caine, as "Alfie," celebrated the dubious glamor of working class roots. It was, however, British music that promoted the London "look" to the world, and arguably the catalyst was the Beatles; but to what extent did their music really challenge the status quo?

Modernity, meritocracy, and change

Perhaps one of the most notable changes over the period was the challenge to embedded class deference, at the time a defining characteristic of British social relations.[8] The end of the class war – promised by the postwar British Labour party on the premise of reformed capitalism, and appropriated by a reformed Conservative government under the slogan "capitalism for the people" – seemed initially unlikely. Their defeat at the Orpington by-election (1962) was, however, a strong indication that the Conservatives were out of touch, and in the subsequent "night of the long knives" Harold Macmillan expelled one third of his cabinet. Humiliating defeats in foreign policy – not least the rejection of the UK's application to join the Common Market (1963) – an increasing subordination to US interests, political scandal – the Profumo affair, and Kim Philby's defection to the Soviet Union (1963) – were all grist to the Labour Party's mill, and Harold Wilson's masterly speech highlighting the fragility of British Intelligence arguably precipitated Macmillan's resignation. In retrospect, his replacement, Sir Alec Douglas-Home – a Scottish landowner – served as a timely reminder that the upper classes could no longer expect to be in charge, or indeed respected, simply because of their hereditary status. Rather, public opinion indicated that the country needed a new aristocracy, a new image. This was provided by Harold Wilson, a former grammar school boy with a fundamental grasp on the new media age. The 1964 general election was the first to be televised, and Labour was returned with a majority of four. Their focus on modernity, technology, and change proved a popular strategy, and two years later Labour were once again returned, this time with a majority of ninety-six.

While the change in political profile seemed to indicate a more contemporary, "with-it" leadership, there is little doubt that Labour initially benefited from the corrosive portrayal of Macmillan and Douglas-Home in

Private Eye, and the popularity of Ned Sherrin's Friday night radio satire, *That Was the Week That Was*. In essence, these were characterized by a sense of pungent irreverence for the establishment, and the Beatles were quick to follow suit. Invited to perform at the televised Royal Command Performance in November 1963, John Lennon prefaced "Twist and Shout" with "Would the people in the cheaper seats clap your hands, and the rest of you, if you'll just rattle your jewellery!" His famous wit also punctured the formalities of the 1964 Royal Variety Show. When they were presented with the Variety Club Silver Heart Award by Harold Wilson, Lennon's "Thanks for the purple heart – sorry, silver heart!" and Ringo's "Good old Mr. Wilson should have one!" were further indications that the age of blind deference was coming to an end. Nevertheless, the award of Member of the Order of the British Empire to the Beatles in 1965 was considered by many inappropriate, with some existing MBEs returning their medals. Lennon's response, that the award was "for exports," can be interpreted both as an astute recognition of the Beatles' real value to the country, and as a refusal to acquiesce in the "somewhat patronizing endorsement" of their artistic merit. Either way, it was the first step into today's world where celebrities are rewarded for their services to Queen and country, and an indication that the separation between high culture and popular culture was on the wane. Less forgivable, not least by the US Bible belt, was Lennon's 1966 oft-quoted comments on Jesus Christ to rock journalist and friend Maureen Cleave:

> Christianity will go. It will vanish and shrink . . . We're more popular than Jesus now; I don't know which will go first – rock 'n' roll or Christianity. Jesus was all right, but his disciples were thick and ordinary. It's them twisting it that ruins it for me.

As William Northcutt observes, "Christ's disciples in the southern United States answered en masse. Record burnings and protests, death threats and bomb scares dogged the Beatles through the South."[9] Pungent irreverence had, it seemed, little place in the Southern States of America, where equality was still "a dream" and where civil rights were compromised by continuing racial discrimination.

While it could be argued that the UK was also experiencing problems in race relations, not least those involving Commonwealth immigrants, who were encountering widespread discrimination in housing and employment,[10] the country, as a whole, was gradually moving toward a less class-driven society. The death of Churchill, in particular, seemed to symbolize the drift towards greater equality. He had been active in politics since the Edwardian era, and, although controversial, had proved an inspirational leader during the war years. In retrospect, his state funeral, on January 30, 1965, heralded the end of an era. Deference toward the aristocracy was being replaced by Harold Wilson's emphasis on a meritocracy based on technology and modernity. Epitomized by the Post Office Tower, high-rise flats, wonder plastics, nylon, and the Mini, Britain's trendy profile was nevertheless compromised by economic crisis. The Labour party had inherited huge debts – including a massive war loan from the United States – and the period of growth promised by Wilson proved untenable. By the end of the sixties, a wage freeze, cuts in public expenditure, union disputes, a seamen's strike, and a move to more coercive and punitive measures in the sphere of industrial relations led increasingly toward a harsh "control culture." This, in turn, was accompanied by a series of measures directed against the rising tide of permissiveness characterized partly by an emerging drug culture and so-called increase in sexual promiscuity.[11]

Sex, love, relationships, and social reforms

In the early 1960s, the consequences of sex before marriage were considered a serious matter. There were still shotgun weddings; John Lennon married Cynthia Powell, whom he had been dating since 1958, because she was pregnant.[12] Ninety-six percent of adults over forty-five were married; at many universities and colleges, immediate expulsion followed being caught in a room occupied by the opposite sex – by the end of the decade this was modified to allow visits between the hours of 3:00 and 4:00 p.m.[13] Even so, the sixties did see changes in sexual attitudes, largely brought about by the media attention given to Dr. Spock (how to bring up your baby),[14] the Pill (no more unwanted pregnancies), and the Kinsey Reports[15] (discussing previously taboo subjects, including masturbation and the female orgasm). Parliament also confronted outmoded laws with the Homosexual Reform Act (1967), the abolition of capital punishment (1965),[16] and the Abortion Act (1967).[17] There was also support for the more general concerns about freedom of expression that underpinned such previously censored texts as D. H. Lawrence's *Lady Chatterley's Lover*, Henry Miller's *Tropic of Cancer* and *Tropic of Capricorn*, and William S. Burroughs' *The Naked Lunch* and *Dead Fingers Talk*, which attracted adverse criticism from such contemporary writers as Dame Edith Sitwell. Violence as spectacle also had a particular resonance in the 1960s, not least in Antonin Artaud's Theatre of Cruelty. Glenda Jackson (now a British Labour Member of Parliament) appeared as Christine Keeler, "stripped, bathed and ritually clothed as a convict to the recitation of the words of the Keeler court case."[18] She was also featured as a wildly erotic Charlotte Corday in *The Persecution and Assassination of Marat as Performed by the Inmates of Charenton under the Direction of the Marquis de Sade*. Even so, the extent to which this so-called loosening up of sexual attitudes affected the majority of the population is debatable. Despite an upswing in premarital sexual behavior, the traditional pathway for the majority of women remained either marriage or being "left on the shelf."

As I discussed in "Love, Love, Love: Representations of Gender and Sexuality in Selected Songs by the Beatles" (2006), early Beatles songs are characterized by their ebullient and catchy qualities; while there is a certain shift in emphasis from the imperative of "Love Me Do" to the discursive of "She Loves You," their songs, like their moptop image at the time, maintain a certain naivety that renders them unthreatening. They construct an imaginary ideal whereby the teenager is invited to mentally negotiate the experience of being young and in love. The underlying, omnipresent beat adds to the experience – it is music to dance to, to flirt to. Not least, the songs deflect the teenage girl's experience of sexuality on to the terrain of romance, so providing a way of negotiating that experience through a series of male and female roles. As Angela McRobbie observes, "If female adolescence is defined as a period of independence from parental restraints, it is also a period of high risk in which the girl might go off the rails . . . As such, the romantic code is like a transmission belt which carries the girl over the limbo of adolescence, [and] delivers her safely from the family of origin to the family of destiny."[19] Given the upswing in premarital sexual behaviour across the 1960s, maybe one should add that this is an ideal situation, albeit one that reflects the emphasis of the Beatles' early love ballads.

But what of the women who don't marry? Lennon and McCartney also provided a particular take on the loneliness that characterized so many women's experience at the time. Paradoxically, it is a track on which the group made no instrumental contribution. Rather, it is tethered by an austere string arrangement by George Martin, and has an acute sense of observation which resonates with both pathos and social realism, invoking both a nostalgic and monochromatic portrait of loneliness. This is enhanced by the matter-of-factness of the lyrics, where descriptions of the mundane ("darning his socks in the night when there's nobody there") fill the two-bar phrases, culminating in a sense of resignation as the final syllable is held over the next bar and followed by a pragmatic evaluation of personal worth (the "nobody came" of Eleanor Rigby's funeral; the "what does he care" of the equally lonely priest).

The mood of austerity and restraint is particularly evident in George Martin's string writing, where a heavy use of repetition – similar to the chromaticism and unresolved dissonances in Bernard Hermann's music for *Psycho* – creates suspense and underpins the references to death: "Father McKenzie, wiping the dirt from his hands as he walks from the grave." Forty years on, the inclusion of a classical infrastructure within a popular song is less than revolutionary. At the time, it gave "Eleanor Rigby" a freshness of approach in terms of musical arrangement which was also appropriate to the mood of the lyrics, which, in turn, resonated with the experience of countless women who had neither family, friendship, nor support from that bastion of respectability, the established church. And this, surely, is why this is a political, cultural, and socially conscious song.

In particular, the refusal of the Catholic Church to reform its attitude to birth control seemed little less than hypocrisy, given the increasing numbers of the poor in the so-called developing countries of the Third World and South America. In the UK and the Republic of Ireland, illegitimacy was still treated with a moral superiority that resulted in countless women being imprisoned in welfare nursing homes not too different from those of the Victorian poor houses of the nineteenth century. Birth control, backstreet abortions, and unnecessary death were thus essential items on the feminist agenda,[20] and while the liberalism of the sixties had borne legislative fruit in the spheres of legalized abortion and "no blame" divorce, for many people such reforms either came too late or were considered less weighty than the dictates of the church. Eleanor Rigby's drab and joyless destiny, it appears, was simply to be buried, along with her name – a sad indictment on a church which is arguably the richest and most powerful in the Christian world.

The Beatles were not unique in drawing attention to the problems surrounding religion, marriage, and personal relationships. As Theodor Roszak wrote in 1971, rock generally provided a means whereby young people could explore the politics of consciousness, "love, loneliness, depersonalization, the search for the truth of the person."[21] To some extent this is reflected in the Beatles' songs – not least those concerned with relationships. As they tellingly wrote, "Try to see it my way" ("We Can Work it Out," 1965), a plea arguably at odds with the ebullience associated with their earlier songs, and perhaps more in tune with older fans who had themselves experienced failing relationships and whose expectations of lasting love were somewhat jaded. Not least, the institution of marriage itself was under scrutiny by the state, and legislative reform under Roy Jenkins[22] (Labour Home Secretary from 1965 to 1967) was directed at a relaxation in divorce laws. His "no blame" divorce reflected his view that the right sort of legal framework would provide for greater self-determination in social life and relationships, and this, in turn, stimulated discussion about the constitution of the family itself, with many considering the nuclear family model oppressive, and other models, such as a committed partnership, or a commune, a viable alternative.

As Polly Toynbee observes, this was a period of unparalleled social legislation and social activism.

Peter Hain was campaigning brilliantly against apartheid, Tessa Jowell worked for the new campaign Mind, Paul Boateng worked in an idealistic new law centre, Nick Raynsford was emergency officer for homeless action group Shac, Frank Field ran the Child Poverty Action Group and Patricia Hewitt and Harriet Harman ran the National Council for Civil Liberties. Most of that Labour generation came to politics via the myriad new campaigns that sprang up from a passionate social engagement of those days. Not since the Victorians was there such an explosion of new voluntary organisations – Help the Aged, Age Concern, Sane, Action Aid, Shelter, Crisis, Centrepoint, Community Service Volunteers, pre-school playgroups and toy libraries filling voids in state provision.[23]

Social reforms were, however, costly, and Britain's economic situation was worsening. The USA remained committed to winning the war in Vietnam through massive B-52 bombing campaigns, and Robert McNamara and Lyndon B. Johnson were putting pressure on the UK to send troops to Vietnam. Wilson's refusal resulted in the USA withdrawing support for sterling, and Britain's economic situation worsened. Wages were frozen and the Labour government began to fall apart.

The end of an era: war, political protest, and cultural conflicts

By 1968 the war in Vietnam was in its seventh year,[24] and television coverage had brought the atrocities into the family living room. Protests escalated, with student demonstrations across American campuses, horrifying self-immolations,[25] and breaking news of a massacre in My Lai (March 16, 1968). The anti-war movement swept across Europe with uprisings in Paris, Rome, Berlin, and Czechoslovakia. In the UK the Grosvenor Square demonstration turned into a riot after an eighteen-year-old girl became trapped underneath a police horse.

It would be misleading to suggest that the Beatles were directly involved in political protest against the war in Vietnam. Unlike Mick Jagger, who was at the Grosvenor Square demonstrations and whose song "Street Fighting Man" resonated with his personal experiences on the day, the Beatles were more aligned with the philosophy of love that characterized hippy philosophy. Their 1968 song "Revolution" spelled it out: "We all want to change the world / But when you talk about destruction / Don't you know that you can count me out." Their solution, "change your head . . . free your mind," and the importance of love as empowering change ("All You Need is Love," 1967), relates to drug culture,[26] to the metaphysical,[27] and to "flower power," a slogan used by hippies in the late sixties and early seventies as a symbol of their non-violence ideology, rooted in their opposition to the Vietnam War. Therefore, it is not too surprising that their 1967 album, *Sgt. Pepper's Lonely Hearts Club Band,* was less a political protest and more, in Allen Ginsberg's words, "an exclamation of joy, a discovery of joy and what it was to be alive . . . It was actually a cheerful look around the world: the first time, I would say, on a mass scale."[28] Despite the murder of Che Guevara, the race riots in Detroit, and the gathering discontent at universities in both the USA and the UK, *Sgt. Pepper* seemed at the time to exemplify a mood of "getting better." "Holes" were being "fixed," love would still be there at sixty-four, and the Band promised to "turn you on."

"For anyone who was young at the time," writes Steve Turner, "the music automatically evokes the sight of beads and kaftans, the sound of tinkling bells and the aroma of marijuana masked by joss sticks."[29] Peter Blake's pop art design for the record sleeve became instantly collectable, and even the pseudo-military figure of Sgt. Pepper himself seemed little more than a send-up of the infamous Kitchener recruitment poster from the 1914–18 war. It was Edwardian chic, drawing on the current craze for military uniforms, quickly echoed in Biba's Carnaby Street fashions, and copied by fans worldwide. "The kids tried to identify with their heroes' music," writes Greil Marcus. "They wanted costumes, Salvation Army band coats, bells, beads, painted faces and all the other absurd paraphernalia."[30] Even so, despite its mood of optimistic escapism – appropriate to 1967's Summer of Love – there was confrontation in the apocalyptic vision of the final song, "A Day in the Life."

Opening with softly strummed acoustic guitar chords, the verse describes a suicide with a conciseness comparable to that displayed in "Eleanor Rigby": "I read the news today, oh boy." Built on a series of tense, reflective passages, followed by soaring releases, the dispassionate account of events is reinforced by the simplicity of narration, both verbally and through the music. There is no extraneous detail, and the pentatonic melody follows the natural inflection of the words. The lack of modulation also works to make the imagery more powerful as it evokes the monotonous repetition of newscasting and the reading of horrendous events which are passively consumed and then forgotten. Conformity ("A crowd of people stood and stared") conjures up images of the amorphous mass, the mindless credulity of "them." Materialism is confronted by the headlines "about a lucky man who made the grade," the response "Well I just had to laugh" linking the song to George Harrison's metaphysical "Within You Without You," "the people who gain the world and lose their soul."[31]

The "out there" is then rejected, with the refrain "I'd love to turn you on" precipitating an electronic crescendo, a musical metaphor for a drug-induced "rush," as the audience is moved on to a differently coded though thematically connected idea. The music has a nervous dissonance as the percussive drumbeat melts into a panting chug, but again there is a move toward psychedelic flight and release, "Found my way upstairs and had a smoke / Somebody spoke and I went into a dream." The dream, however, is more an evocation of a nightmare, and the final "I'd love to turn you on" leads directly into a cacophony of noise, suggesting both anarchy and chaos.

As the final song on the album, "A Day in the Life" takes on board "the lonely people," and, with wit, tenderness, and a cutting-edge musical arrangement by George Martin, calls into question the meaning of contemporary society. To ignore the vision is to invoke the consequence, and the final instrumental crescendo paints a scenario of devastation that is balanced only by Lennon's invitation to psychedelic experience, "I'd love to turn you on." The connection between hallucinogenics and visionary religion thus falls into place; they are complementary pathways in the search for an alternative reality to the atrocities of war. As Timothy Leary observed at the time, the album "gave voice to a feeling that the old ways were out . . . it came along at the right time that summer."[32] Exactly one month after its release, the famous editorial by William Rees-Mogg, "Who Breaks a Butterfly on a Wheel," appeared in *The Times*, defending the position of the Rolling Stones, who had been imprisoned after admitting to taking drugs. Some three weeks later, the same paper published an advertisement advocating the legalization of marijuana, to which the Beatles were signatories.

It is, perhaps, extraordinary that the Beatles should follow *Sgt. Pepper* with a double album that reflects on their five-year musical history. It was musically clever, but for many the so-called "White Album" (*The Beatles*, November 1968) suggested that the group was disintegrating, that this was both an ironic take on their earlier successes and a testimony to Lennon and McCartney's individual talents, with little to suggest either literary or musical unity. Unlike in their earlier collaborations, the majority of songs on the album were sung by the author: John Lennon, "I'm So Tired," "Happiness is a Warm Gun," "Sexy Sadie," "Dear Prudence," "Julia," "Glass Onion," "Revolution 1," and "The Continuing Story of Bungalow Bill"; Paul McCartney, "I Will," "Mother Nature's Son," "Helter Skelter," "Honey Pie," "Martha My Dear," "Rocky Raccoon," and the opening track, "Back in the USSR," which satirizes the absurdities of the Cold War by situating nostalgia within Soviet Georgia. Even so, the fact that the album failed to demonstrate any particular theme or conceptual reference point compromised their role as "spokesmen for their generation," not least with student activists. The year 1968 was a period of violence, with the assassination of Martin Luther King and Senator Robert F. Kennedy foregrounding the problems of racial conflict and continuing mass protest against the war in Vietnam. The fact that "Revolution" was released only three days after the student uprising in Paris (May 6), and that their response to murder and conflict was little more than an ironic 'Marseillaise' within a framework of "Love, Love, Love," seemed to many a total disregard of serious political issues. This, it seems, was left to John and Yoko, whose much publicized quest for peace in Vietnam is narrated in "The Ballad of John and Yoko" (May 1969) and "Give Peace a Chance" (1969).

Meanwhile, the *Torry Canyon*, the world's first supertanker, had broken up on the coast of Cornwall; a gas explosion in Tower Hamlets, London, had brought down a block of high-rise flats; dockers, Post Office workers and civil servants were on strike, and Commonwealth immigrants were being made the scapegoats for the country's problems. It seemed to many that the party was over. The association of LSD with Satanism, which had resulted in the murder of Sharon Tate and six others by the Manson family (August 9, 1969), and the violence at the Rolling Stones concert at Altamont (December 6, 1969), provided a grim reminder that the freedoms promised by the sixties cultural revolution were little more than a stoned dream. LSD was made illegal under the Dangerous Drugs Act, pirate radio was suppressed, the Youth International Party was formed, and the Pentagon was exorcised.

By 1969 the Beatles were splitting up, and despite the release of *Abbey Road* (1969), their final group album, and the subsequent release of *Hey Jude* and *Let It Be* (1970), there was an increasing involvement with their individual careers, with five solo albums released that year. Paul had married Linda Eastman, Ringo was a father, and John had divorced Cynthia and married Yoko Ono.[33] Apple,[34] which had been set up in 1968 to support new bands and make films, was losing money, and the rows over who owned what arguably contributed to the breakup. Paul left on April 10, 1970, and on June 19 the Conservative Party was returned to power. While I do not wish to imply a simplistic cause and effect, for many the two events seemed to herald the end of an era.

Time, place, and cultural change

This raises the question of the extent to which the Beatles can be considered an intrinsic part of the decade's sociocultural zeitgeist. With regard to popular music, there is no doubt that their songs became the foremost expression of the poetry of everyday life. Written in the vernacular, they revealed a world of colorful images, with McCartney constructing stories and characters and Lennon writing first-person testimonies, including his exploration of the metaphysical through hallucinogenics. Their albums opened up new avenues within popular music: pastiches of goodtime twenties songs, simple rock and roll, folk songs, tongue-in-cheek parodies, country and western ballads, hints of Elizabethan romanticism, surrealism, comedy, wit, and sentimentality. Yet, as much as the Beatles offered a mood of contemporeity – not least in their engagement with Carnaby Street culture, psychedelia, and hippy philosophy – they also provided insights into their past. In "Polythene Pam" Lennon recalls his Liverpool club days, "Lovely Rita" eulogizes a "meter maid," while "Penny Lane" and "Strawberry Fields Forever" are lasting reminders of the Liverpool of their youth. It is, however, their stubborn northern-ness, their Liverpool humor, and their disregard and contempt for the pomposity of class-based social relations that situate them most accurately in the zeitgeist of the sixties. As Mick Jagger observed at the time, "The Stones might speak to one's personal condition in a way that the Beatles did not, but the Beatles were universal."[35] They may not have offered solutions to the problems of a society which revolved around materialism, repressive affluence, and individual conformity, but they nevertheless provided insights, celebrating what was, for their countless fans worldwide, a cheerful alternative.

12 Beatles news: product line extensions and the rock canon

GARY BURNS

The record-collector magazine *Goldmine* has a department now called "All Things Elvis" but formerly called "Elvis News." I once mentioned to a friend, much more a Presley enthusiast than I, that I did not see how there could be such a magazine column or much "news" about Elvis, who had already been dead many years. My friend looked at me as if I were crazy – how could I be so unaware of the perpetual flow of reissues, newly discovered recordings, books written by Presley's acquaintances, accomplishments by or tabloid stories about daughter Lisa Marie Presley, and developments involving Graceland or Elvis's estate?

Viewed this way, most of the actual, journalistic "news" (loosely defined) is about Elvis's aftermath – either his survivors or the latest product line extensions growing from his 1950–70s career. Another type of "news" is the abundant research (again, loosely defined) that continues to be produced by writers ranging from scholars to amateur memoirists to fanzine publishers.

There is, obviously and justifiably, substantial and ongoing interest in Elvis. The "news" about him is actually the discursive and commercial afterlife of celebrity.[1] Elvis is no longer here, but "news" about him still arises, often in the form of pseudo-events and public relations.

A similar phenomenon is observable with respect to bands that no longer exist but whose members are still alive. Cream, the Who, the Police, Van der Graaf Generator, the Stooges, and many others have recently re-formed, creating new music to write about. Surviving members of bands that do not re-form generate new solo albums or other projects, not to mention almost inevitable speculation and interview questions about possible future reunions.

Aside from Elvis Presley, the most prominent musical act that generates "news," despite being defunct, is the Beatles. For years following their dissolution there was immense interest in the activities of the individual Beatles and in the possibility of a reunion. Even after John Lennon died in 1980, there was hope of John's son Julian Lennon substituting for his father in some future reunion.[2] A reunion of sorts finally happened in 1995, with the surviving "Threetles" adding accompaniment to two

John Lennon demo tapes ("Free as a Bird" and "Real Love"). The recordings were released under the Beatles' name in conjunction with the *Anthology* project (a video documentary, three double-CD packages, and eventually a book). A music video was produced and released for each of the "new" songs.[3] All of this activity garnered much press attention and spurred sales of new and old Beatles product.

In the last few years there has been, not surprisingly, quite a bit of Beatles "news." Much of this is reported on such websites as www.whatgoeson.com, www.thebeatles.com, www.georgeharrison.com, www.johnlennon.com, www.paulmccartney.com, and www.ringostarr.com. The band itself had a "new" album in 2006, *Love*, consisting of mashups and remixes by the Beatles' producer, George Martin, and his son Giles. The album was a spinoff project connected with a Cirque du Soleil stage production, also called *Love*, built around Beatles recordings. The second installment of reissues of the Beatles' original US albums on Capitol appeared in 2006. In 2007 Apple Records settled a long dispute with Apple, Inc., the computer company, over use of the word "Apple" as a trademark. Speculation was rampant that the Beatles' catalog of recordings would soon be made available for downloading, possibly through Apple, Inc.'s iTunes service. The individual Beatles have also been in the "news." Paul McCartney's acrimonious divorce from Heather Mills was tabloid fodder. He performed at *Live 8* in 2005 and released two new albums in 2006 and another in 2007. Ringo Starr released a new album in 2005. George Harrison's album *Living in the Material World* was reissued in 2006. And a John Lennon movie, *The U.S. vs. John Lennon*, appeared at about the same time that the "final" FBI files on John Lennon were released to historian Jon Wiener following "twenty-three years of litigation."[4] Between April 2006 and April 2007 each Beatle was the subject of a cover story in *Goldmine*.

As Ian Inglis states: "While it may appear trite to repeat it, the Beatles have indeed changed the world, and our perceptions of it, in a way that only a handful of popular entertainers – Chaplin, Monroe, Presley, Dylan – have been able to do."[5] The Beatles have been "in the news" internationally since about 1963, and are still "in the news" in the same manner as Elvis Presley and also in ways that Elvis never achieved. Truly, the Beatles are a cultural touchstone, alive in both "dream and history," as Devin McKinney put it in the subtitle of his own obsessive, sprawling book on the subject.

While it may seem preposterous to treat the Beatles' commercial success separately from their status as sociocultural icons, that is what I am going to do in this analysis of the Beatles as public figures. It is clear that the Beatles, aided by savvy business allies, were quite deliberate in their effort to become the world's biggest and greatest rock band. At the same time, they could not possibly have known how fruitful their striving would be or what their stardom would ultimately mean for themselves or for the world. Thus it is possible to observe the Beatles and their agents as producers, constantly honing their craft, seeking publicity, hawking product; and, somewhat alternatively, as objects of admiration, imitation, critique, study, and parasitism.

The commercial and artistic afterlife of the Beatles is mostly a function of deliberate, skillful marketing of various product line extensions derived from the Beatles brand. Much of this activity has been traditional music industry practice, but some has been innovative and trendsetting.

The marketing of a b(r)and

The Beatles brand originally referred to the group as a working band, then quickly to the classic songs and sound recordings that today constitute the Beatles' "canon." From their earliest days as recording artists the Beatles also promoted their brand by engaging in radio and television appearances, both as musicians and as celebrities in a broader sense. John Lennon and Paul McCartney wrote songs for other recording artists, including songs that were not also recorded by the Beatles. Songs written and recorded by the Beatles were widely covered by other recording artists, contributing to the image of the Beatles as virtuoso writer-performers and earning a bonanza of songwriting and publishing royalties.

The American licensing and release of the Beatles' original UK recordings took an unusual path that continues to have commercial ramifications. Capitol, the US affiliate of the Beatles' UK label, EMI/Parlophone, declined to release some of the earliest Beatles recordings, which resulted in one of the first US Beatles albums being released by the independent label Vee-Jay. Capitol later reissued most of this material on an album called *The Early Beatles*. Meanwhile, as Beatlemania erupted in 1964, some pre-EMI recordings of the Beatles surfaced. On these tracks, the Beatles appear mostly as a backup band for singer Tony Sheridan, but the numerous reissues of this material have all stressed the Beatles' authorship more than that of the more audible Sheridan.

These complications diluted EMI's control of the Beatles brand, and even today the Tony Sheridan recordings – admittedly a minor part of the Beatles product line – are owned by Universal rather than EMI. In addition, the US versions of Beatles albums, with a few exceptions, differed greatly from their UK counterparts. The reason for this was that US customers were used to about twelve songs per LP, whereas in the UK about fourteen songs per album was the norm. The UK market was also accustomed to EP (extended play) releases – 7-inch discs featuring, usually, two songs per side. In the US market EPs were not a customary format.

As a result, and as an example, the UK album *With the Beatles*, containing fourteen tracks, was issued in the United States as *Meet the Beatles*, with twelve tracks. *Meet the Beatles* included three songs not found on *With the Beatles* and excluded five songs from the latter album, all of which showed up in the United States on *The Beatles' Second Album* (an album that was not issued in the UK). The Beatles were so prolific as recording artists in the middle and late 1960s that some of their albums in the US market consisted almost entirely of displaced tracks from previous UK albums and EPs, singles not included on UK albums, and movie soundtrack music not included on UK albums (i.e. orchestral [non-Beatles] music recorded for the Beatles films *Help!* and *Yellow Submarine*). Beatles purists then and now have generally objected to the US Beatles albums because of their lack of faithfulness to the UK originals, because of their low value to the customer on a tracks per dollar basis, and because they appeared to be rather thoughtlessly packaged. The Beatles themselves were irked by the treatment their albums received from Capitol. Legend has it that the infamous, withdrawn "butcher" cover art of the USA-only *Yesterday . . . and Today* album was intended by the Beatles as a protest against what they saw as the butchering of their albums by Capitol.

The US versions of the Beatles' albums have seen a curious resurrection on compact disc. Originally, the definitive UK versions of the albums were the only CDs released, and, what's more, the earliest albums were issued on CD in mono only, because it was thought they did not sound good in their primitive and sometimes artificial stereo versions. These aesthetic justifications notwithstanding, a reissue program for the US Capitol albums began in 2004, with each album presented in both mono and stereo. Thus the original problems of Capitol's avarice and poor execution have become a latter-day opportunity for further product line extension – an occasion both for additional avarice and to address genuine demand by completist and nostalgic fans.

Similarly, the Beatles famously resisted "greatest hits" repackagings of their works and generally did not appear on label samplers or other compilation albums, partly because, in today's parlance, such actions would dilute the Beatles brand. After the band's demise, such repackaging became common. It continued in 2000 with *1*, a compilation of Beatles number-one chart hits. A package like this can serve to introduce the band to a new generation of fans and as a handy career-spanning summary even for fans who already own some or all of the original albums.[6]

The Beatles' forays into television and radio have already been mentioned as means by which the Beatles brand was propagated across media.

The main commercial purpose of these appearances was to promote record sales. Other cross-media ventures, while still serving to promote Beatles records, also generated new product for immediate sale. John Lennon published two books (*In His Own Write* and *A Spaniard in the Works*) that became bestsellers and received critical acclaim.[7] Other books by and about the Beatles have followed by the dozen. Those that do not generate money directly for the Beatles do so indirectly by keeping the brand visible. The 2000 book *The Beatles Anthology* is remarkable for many reasons, but especially as a major new literary and pictorial product emanating from a long-defunct collective.

The Beatles also spread their brand to film in *A Hard Day's Night* (1964), *Help!* (1965), *Magical Mystery Tour* (a 1967 telefilm), *Yellow Submarine* (1968), and *Let It Be* (1970). It was hardly a new idea for recording stars to appear in films, but the Beatles were exemplary practitioners of this type of crossover. In particular, *A Hard Day's Night* and *Yellow Submarine* were groundbreaking works, notwithstanding the Beatles' tenuous connection with the latter film.[8] John Lennon and Ringo Starr also had minor careers as film actors (Lennon: *How I Won the War* [1967]; Starr: *Candy* [1968], *The Magic Christian* [1969], and occasional later work). Paul McCartney (*The Family Way* [1966]) and George Harrison (*Wonderwall* [1968]) dabbled in film music. Harrison's *Wonderwall Music* soundtrack album was the first solo album by a Beatle, and, along with Lennon's duo albums with Yoko Ono, paved the way for the Beatles' solo careers.

The breakup of the Beatles into four solo acts is an event that looms with mythic importance in the history of rock music and, indeed, in the history of the equally mythic 1960s. From about 1964 to 1970 the Beatles and the entity called the "counterculture" seemed to be "together." Shortly after that came disco, corporate rock, the "me" decade, the "culture of narcissism," and "psychobabble."[9] The fragmentation of the Beatles seemed to correspond, at least in some ways, with individualistic trends in American society. McCartney became domesticated, Lennon participated in primal scream therapy, and Harrison became more religious. These are caricatures, of course, but the fact is that the Beatles brand persisted, and its strength enabled each Beatle to have a successful solo career, albeit without any individual developing a "product line" as distinguished as that of the band. Despite the band's unfortunate dissolution, it must also be said that the breakup was a commercial success, producing numerous hit singles and albums, perhaps in greater number than a united band would have achieved. For completist fans it became, and remains, necessary to keep up with four careers instead of one.

In addition to the well-established means of product line extension discussed above, the Beatles have been pioneers and early adopters of other innovative commercial techniques. Most importantly, the Beatles created Apple, originally conceived as a sort of countercultural conglomerate with operations not only in music but also in fashion, electronics, and film.[10] All branches other than the music division quickly fell by the wayside, but the Apple record label still exists and has belatedly and perhaps surprisingly become an effective vehicle for the ongoing commercial exploitation of Beatles product. (Frank Sinatra had established Reprise Records in 1960, but Apple was the first instance of a rock band starting a record label of any significance. The model set by the Beatles with Apple was quickly copied by other rock bands seeking some measure of independence from the much-despised major record labels. Rock band boutique labels established over the next several years included the Moody Blues' Threshold label, Jefferson Airplane's Grunt, and the eponymous Rolling Stones label.) Apple went about its business rather chaotically but released numerous hits by the Beatles as a band and as individuals. Further, recording artists including Mary Hopkin, Badfinger, James Taylor, and Billy Preston had hits on the Apple label.

More recently Apple and the surviving Beatles have tinkered with existing recordings in various ways to produce new Beatles product. As already mentioned, the "newest" Beatles album, *Love*, is an authorized mashup, possibly inspired by Danger Mouse's unauthorized 2004 mashup *The Grey Album*, which combined the Beatles' 1968 White Album (officially titled *The Beatles*) with Jay-Z's 2003 release *The Black Album*.

Another "new" product, *Let It Be . . . Naked*, released in 2003, is a remixed and reordered version of the 1970 album *Let It Be*. Phil Spector's production, which either ruined or saved the original album, depending on one's opinion, is removed in the 2003 revision.

The *Anthology* CDs included other examples of altered tracks in addition to numerous archival, unreleased recordings. As mentioned, the long-anticipated, albeit virtual, reunion realized in "Free as a Bird" and "Real Love" was a highlight of the *Anthology* project. A third reunion track, "Now and Then" (also known as "Miss You"), remains unfinished and unreleased, but may eventually be completed by McCartney and Starr.[11] If such a prospect seems both desperate and tantalizing, it is a sign that the Beatles remain the apotheosis of both commercial popularity and canonical textuality in rock music.

The Beatles in the rock pantheon

In fact, and as a preface to my discussion of the Beatles as canonical figures, it is worth emphasizing that popularity and eminence are reciprocal, at least in rock music and at least sometimes. One reason the Beatles became so popular is that people thought they were good. And one reason people think the Beatles are good is because they were so popular. To be both "popular" and "good" is, at least potentially, to be "important."

Prior to the late 1960s it probably was not widely believed that rock or most other popular music was "important." Now few people would dispute that it is. There is a Rock and Roll Hall of Fame and Museum, an International Association for the Study of Popular Music, a journal called *Popular Music* published by no less a cultural arbiter than Cambridge University Press, and an Institute of Popular Music at the University of Liverpool, in the Beatles' home town. These institutions are only a few of the hundreds of organizations and publications devoted to the reverent but critical – and, most importantly, serious – study of popular music. This enterprise owes its existence, in no small measure, to the Beatles.

We may identify three types of canon pertinent to the study of rock music – sociological, literary, and musicological. The Beatles are canonical figures in all three of these domains. By "canon" I mean a group of founders or revered persons or master practitioners (such as the Beatles); or a group of texts thought to be masterpieces or "standard" works or representative specimens (such as the Beatles' songs); or a group of texts that constitute an artist's finished, published, official corpus of work in some format (such as the Beatles' EMI and Apple albums and the songs therein).

Rock's sociological canon

The Beatles are foundational members in what I am calling the sociological canon of rock music. They were crucial in establishing the importance of rock as a social phenomenon. After the Beatles, rock, whatever its artistic merit, could no longer be viewed as a trivial force in Western culture. Despite their long apprenticeship, which later came to light in biographies, in most people's awareness the Beatles seemed to burst upon the scene as something fresh, unprecedented, and overwhelming. This was Beatlemania, and its manifestation in the United States in early 1964 was quickly and lastingly taken to be not merely the latest musical fad but a response to the assassination of President John F. Kennedy.[12]

Following Beatlemania, the Beatles continued to prove they were not only hit-makers but news-makers. John Lennon's 'more popular than Jesus' comment caused a religious backlash in the United States. Upon the death of their manager, Brian Epstein, the Beatles' presence at a retreat in Bangor, Wales, with Maharishi Mahesh Yogi, became widely known and drew attention to the band's flirtation with Eastern religion. Indian music, drugs, and an overarching psychedelicism became a fad over the next few years, spurred partly by the Beatles' 1967 album *Sgt. Pepper's Lonely Hearts Club*

Band and by imagery such as the psychedelic photo portrait of John Lennon on the cover of the January 9, 1968, issue of *Look* magazine.

A perception of the Beatles as anti-establishment avatars grew from their dress and hairstyles, from the aforementioned trappings of psychedelia, from their formation of Apple (notwithstanding Apple's status as a capitalist undertaking), and from their song lyrics. Lennon was the only Beatle to become seriously political, and mostly that happened after he left the Beatles.[13] Still, the political implications of songs like "Nowhere Man," "Taxman," "Piggies," "Revolution," and the Plastic Ono Band's "Give Peace a Chance" were hard to overlook and generally added momentum to the leftward movement of youth culture at the time, as did Lennon's, Starr's, and especially Harrison's pioneering ventures into benefit rock in the early 1970s.

The rumored death of Paul McCartney in 1969 and John Lennon's actual death in 1980 provided definitive proof, if any were still needed, that the Beatles were more than musicians. The McCartney farce is a case study in the sociology of rumor, but is more illuminating in its baroque elaboration as a conspiratorial, utopian, but apocalyptic myth.[14] Lennon's murder, on the other hand, was a shattering reality that touched the world as few events had since the very assassination of JFK that Beatlemania had purportedly assuaged.[15] This is an extraordinary fact.

If we want to discern why Lennon's death was such a shock we should perhaps make some comparisons. Elvis Presley's death only three years earlier in 1977 did not stop the world the way Lennon's death did. One could argue that the difference is explained by the fact that Lennon was murdered. But Marvin Gaye, who died in 1984, was also shot dead, and by his own father. Arguably, then, Gaye was less famous, a lesser star, than Lennon. Then again, George Harrison's death in 2001 was not violent, although he had been stabbed by an intruder at his house in 1999. Harrison was fifty-eight when he died – Lennon was forty. None of this satisfactorily explains why the death of John Lennon was a defining moment of the late twentieth century. The breakup of the Beatles had been, to borrow a cliché, the end of an era. But the breakup could always be undone, thereby extending or reviving the "era" that had seemed to have passed. When Lennon died, that truly was the end of the Beatles and of the hope that they could ever be resurrected, and of the innocent, comforting, naïve belief that the world at large could, somehow, be "together" in the 1960s sense of the term.

Rock's literary canon

If Lennon is the most important of the Beatles in a sociological sense, he was also the most accomplished wordsmith in the band, and it is mainly because of him that the Beatles belong in what I am calling the literary canon of rock music. The towering figure in any such canon must be Bob Dylan, but if the Beatles rank below Dylan as rock poets, it is not far below, and their skill as musicians easily makes them (i.e. Lennon and McCartney) better overall songwriters than Dylan.

But that is not a very significant distinction. Both Dylan and the Beatles (along with others) made people notice that rock songs were well written and meaningful. Prior to this, popular music had been largely ignored or treated as sub-art or as a social problem by critics. Adorno didn't like the music in the 1940s. Hayakawa didn't like the words in the 1950s.

In the 1960s, scholars and other serious observers finally started to write favorably about popular music, and by then they had something indisputably good to write about (although there had always been literary and musical quality, often unnoticed, in pop). It helped that John Lennon was a book author and that the books were clever and substantial and praised by critics. As I will explain below, the Beatles' songs and records have by now been repeatedly and microscopically analyzed, with close attention to both words and music. It nonetheless bears emphasizing that the Beatles' words have sometimes been the subject of analyses that downplay or ignore the musical aspects of the Beatles' art. James Sauceda's book *The Literary Lennon* treats Lennon as an author, as distinct from a songwriter, and says practically nothing about the Beatles' songs.[16] David Pichaske, one of the foremost literary analysts of song lyrics, includes the lyrics to the entire *Sgt. Pepper* album, plus numerous other songs by the Beatles and others, in his poetry textbook and anthology *Beowulf to Beatles*.[17] Pichaske devotes a chapter to the Beatles in his critical and analytical tome *The Poetry of Rock*.[18] The Beatles' song lyrics have been published many times, with and without accompanying sheet music.[19] Paul McCartney has published a book of poetry and lyrics (*Blackbird Singing*)[20] and a children's book.[21] Harrison published a rather skimpy autobiography-cum-lyric-anthology. The Beatles' lyrics as a body of work are subjected to statistical content analysis in a study by West and Martindale[22] that concludes that the Beatles evolved as creative songwriters over the course of their career as a band.

Rock's musical canon

However, the Beatles' exalted position in the popular music pantheon derives only partly from the words they wrote. Well-crafted song lyrics made English professors take note, which was a crucial event in the ultimate legitimation of what tardily became known as popular music studies. But even before the celebration of the Beatles as songwriters it was clear that they were phenomenal performers and recording artists, which placed them, almost from the beginning of Beatlemania, in what I am calling rock's musical canon.

The British Invasion of the mid-1960s, led by the Beatles, brought dozens of UK recording artists to concert venues and radio and TV airwaves in the United States. During this period British acts had hundreds of hit recordings in the USA and around the world. The Beatles were first among equals in this musical movement. Then they adapted to changing conditions (as some of their compatriots did not) and proved their durability as leaders in the emerging rock culture.

It is hard for those too young to have been teenagers in the 1960s to believe, but the Dave Clark Five and Herman's Hermits were, at that time, almost as big as the Beatles. If there had been a rock canon at the time, the DC5 and Herman would have been in it. Critical opinion nowadays would place them in a second tier behind the Beatles and about a half dozen other British Invasion bands that are more respectfully remembered than are Clark and Herman. In this more elite, probably canonical, group are the Rolling Stones, the Kinks, the Who, the Animals, the Yardbirds, and Pink Floyd.

This group of bands and the Beatles, along with others including (canonical) "response" bands such as the Byrds and the post-Invasion Beach Boys, established conventions of artistic practice and understanding that defined "rock" for many years. These conventions still have great influence, despite erosion over the years, and still affect some of our judgments about quality. I will expound briefly on five of these conventions.

First, in "rock" it became important for performers to write their own songs – Kill Brill, we might say. The Beatles excelled at this; Herman's Hermits did not.

Second, "rock" is an art, whereas it had been unnecessary or difficult to think of popular music in this way prior to the mid-sixties. The art school background of many British rock musicians, documented by Frith and Horne,[23] undoubtedly contributed to an art-based ideology, as did critical acclaim for the Beatles' use of such devices as the Aeolian cadence, discussed below.

Third, "rock" posited the LP album as an art form, whereas the primary unit of recorded popular music had, heretofore, been the individual song of about three minutes' duration. The landmark album for purposes of this discussion is the Beatles' *Sgt. Pepper*, notwithstanding the fact that their earlier albums *Rubber Soul* and especially *Revolver* are today sometimes regarded as better than *Sgt. Pepper*.

There is also dispute about whether *Sgt. Pepper* was the first "concept album," although it was in any case *one of* the first. It was the album to live up to after its debut in 1967. It was one of the first albums to include printed lyrics, a gatefold cover, and elaborate packaging. It was one of the first albums to be built around a theme, such as it was, and around a dramatic pretense (the Beatles in costume and in character as another band). *Sgt. Pepper* included no hit singles. It was one of the first albums in which the end of one song overlapped with the beginning of the next, conveying the impression of a larger work.

Fourth, "rock" musicians played their own instruments, although, fifth, "rock" music also expanded the palette of musical instruments, musical styles, and studio production techniques acceptable in combination with status quo practices inherited from the early 1960s music industry. Thus it was important that the Beatles were good musicians and singers, whereas it was a problem for the Monkees, initially, that they did not play their own instruments (more precisely, it was a problem that this fact became widely known). The use of session musicians was a bad thing if they substituted for the credited band, a good thing if they supplemented and were in some way directed by the credited band and used to advance the art form.

We see in these conventions an emerging romantic, auteurist ideology of originality, expression, transcendent genius, and authenticity. This ideology played out in teen magazines, which quickly mutated, parallel to the music itself, into more ambitious and ostensibly more high-minded journalistic outlets such as *Rolling Stone*, *Crawdaddy*, and *Fusion* (which had begun as *New England Teen Scene*). The writing in these magazines ranged from teen or celebrity gossip to rigorous analysis.

The Beatles were one of the first rock bands susceptible to this level of analysis, and were thus instrumental, at least indirectly, in the founding of popular music studies. Even before the teen magazines became more serious, the Beatles had been praised in *The Times* – in 1963! – for, among other things, using an "Aeolian cadence" in their rather insubstantial song "Not a Second Time."[24] An Aeolian cadence is a chord change, at the end of a song, from vi to I. A better example than "Not a Second Time" is "Help!" – but "Help!" was not released until 1965.[25] The remarkable thing is not that the Beatles were using Aeolian cadences (without knowing the name for them) but that a music critic for *The Times* was noticing it in 1963.[26]

The comment about the Aeolian cadence has, ever since, been used as a joke and as an example of overanalysis, the academicization of something the Beatles did instinctively or spontaneously or with knowledge drawn from real-world apprenticeship and experimentation and creativity. Still, the Beatles' mastery – instinctive or otherwise – of the rules of mainstream tune-writing was so striking that it allowed and practically demanded acknowledgment by critics and, indeed, by scholars.

Just as English professors have analyzed Beatles lyrics as poetry, music professors have written exhaustively about the musical qualities of the

Beatles' songs and records. The Beatles' entire catalog (i.e. canon) of record-ings has been transcribed and published in musical scores.[27] Starting as early as 1973 with a book by Wilfrid Mellers,[28] there have been numer-ous, extended analyses of the Beatles' musical *oeuvre*, often on a song-by-song basis, sometimes including analysis of lyrics along with the music, and sometimes highly technical in their use of music theory. Treatments in this vein, besides that of Mellers, include those of O'Grady,[29] Riley,[30] Dowlding (a journalistic, song-by-song discussion with little musical or lyri-cal analysis),[31] MacDonald,[32] Hertsgaard,[33] Pollack,[34] and Walter Everett's monumental two-book set.[35] In addition, several Beatles albums have entire books devoted to them.[36] My point is not that the Beatles deserve this level of scholarly, quasi-scholarly, journalistic, and fan attention – they probably do, but in any case the publications indicate that the Beatles enjoy a canoni-cal status that is unprecedented for popular musicians. Even for the Beatles' contemporaries of elevated stature, such as Bob Dylan, the Rolling Stones, and the Beach Boys, the books are not as numerous, as serious, or as good. The Dave Clark Five are not even on this "chart."

The Beatles and Popular Music Studies

As I have suggested, the Beatles were an important spur to academic activ-ities that resulted eventually in a somewhat formalized field of popular music studies. For decades prior to the 1960s, there had been scholarly studies of popular music (in the broad sense) published in journals such as *American Quarterly*, *Et Cetera*, *Ethnomusicology*, the *American Journal of Sociology*, and the *Journal of American Folklore*. One of the first academic studies of *rock* music was an article about Beatlemania published in 1966.[37] Another Beatlemania study[38] and an analysis of Beatles lyrics[39] followed in 1969. Larry Smith's PhD dissertation about the Beatles, which may be the first dissertation about rock music, appeared in 1970.[40] The *Journal of Popular Culture*, early in its history, published a colloquy from 1969 to 1971 about the Beatles and the "serious" study of popular music.[41] Shortly thereafter, in 1971, the journal *Popular Music and Society* began, partly as a sort of academic product line extension of the *Journal of Popular Cul-ture*. Throughout its history *Popular Music and Society* (which I now edit) has published numerous articles about the Beatles, including several for a special issue on the band in 1998 and a recent *tour de force* analysis by Barbara Bradby[42] suggesting, among other things, that the odd use of pro-nouns in "She Loves You" positioned the singing Beatles as go-betweens or "vehicles of female discourse,"[43] representing a "breakthrough for girls."[44] Even though I am drastically truncating and oversimplifying the argument developed in Bradby's article, it should be clear that Bradby has a novel and compelling explanation for at least part of the power and popularity of the Beatles.

I close with this example because I believe it represents the best in recent studies of the Beatles and provides the academic community with a model for ongoing scholarship. It opened my ears to new ways of understanding the Beatles' music – ways that had not occurred to me in forty years of reasonably careful listening, thinking, and writing. To me, Bradby's article was news – good news. It is a safe bet that there will continue to be Beatles news for many years to come, much of it commercially motivated, some driven by fan obsession and admiration, some seeking to understand and explain this most singular band, their canonical music, and the mania that has still not quite stopped swirling around them.

13 "An abstraction, like Christmas": the Beatles for sale and for keeps

JOHN KIMSEY

When, in a generation or so, a radio-active, cigar-smoking child, picnicking on Saturn, asks you what the Beatle affair was all about – Did you actually *know* them? – don't try to explain all about the long hair and the screams! Just play the child a few tracks from this album and he'll probably understand what it was all about. The kids of AD 2000 will draw from the music much the same sense of well being and warmth as we do today.   DEREK TAYLOR[1]

Beatles press officer Derek Taylor got some things wrong in his 1964 liner notes for *Beatles for Sale.* Certainly he was off with the Saturn bit, and the claim with which he closed – *Beatles for Sale* "is the best album yet" – missed the mark by 180 degrees, at least if you accept the critical consensus that sees the band's fourth LP as a cover-filled rush job, the exhausted gasp that pretty much had to follow the ecstatic peak of *A Hard Day's Night.*

But Taylor was on to something about AD 2000. On November 13 of that year, Apple Corps released *1,* a CD collecting twenty-seven chart-topping Beatles singles which, in its first week, sold 3.6 million copies, a sales pace that held up for weeks, such that *1* became the year's biggest-selling album and the top seller "in 30 countries."[2] In the same month, ABC television broadcast a two-hour documentary, *Beatles Revolution,* which featured luminaries such as Salman Rushdie, J. K. Rowling, Al Green, and President Bill Clinton attesting not just to the Beatles' tunefulness but to their transformative impact on world culture. The month before had seen the Rock and Roll Hall of Fame and Museum unveil a huge exhibit entitled *Lennon: His Life and Work,* an installation designed to showcase its late subject as both multimedia artist and world-historical individual. Late fall was also rollout time for the print edition of the *Beatles Anthology,* the last phase of a documentary project which first went public (in televisual and audio form) in November 1995. And oh yes, in December, *A Hard Day's Night,* the band's cheeky, innovative film debut, was re-released in select US theaters. When, at the end of 2005, the show business bible *Variety* marked its hundredth anniversary by publishing a list of the 100 entertainment "Icons of the Century," the Beatles took another trophy. The top ten included Louis Armstrong, Marilyn Monroe, Mickey Mouse, and Elvis Presley, but *Variety* ranked the Beatles toppermost of the poppermost.[3]

It was the turn of the century of course, and the millennium to boot, and hence a season for lists, retrospectives, and nostalgia-mongering. Striking, though, was the Beatles' prominence in both sales charts and less quantifiable registers of meaning. According to the editors of *In My Life*, a late nineties collection of writing inspired by the Beatles, "Their music circumscribes a small but important evolutionary history of the changing politics, spirituality and mores of the second half of the twentieth century," so that a book about "encounters with the Beatles" is also "a book about each one of us."[4]

Whether we define "popular" in terms of units purchased or people's experience – by the numbers or by the zeitgeist – the Beatles seem to have it covered, and this has long been one of their tricks, this ability to bridge domains. Thus, in the sixties they managed both to dominate show business and make music seen as having "the highest artistic quality."[5] If, as many analysts have suggested, the twentieth century marks the moment when the boundaries delimiting high from mass culture were once and for all dissolved, then it seems apt to regard the Beatles as epochal.

But it has not always seemed so. The band's progress from sixties stardom to millennial symbol was not inevitable. As early as 1976, rock critic Greil Marcus saw himself having to defend the Beatles from a "consensus" that dismissed them as "imitative, lightweights, yea-sayers, softies, ordinary musicians, vaguely unhip, unimaginative lyrically, and, above all, 'clever' – that is, merely clever. You know, the Beatles just wanted to hold your hand, while the Stones wanted to pillage your town, etc."[6] And following punk, the Beatles' stock fell further: "As the Seventies advanced, the apolitical Beatles came to seem irrelevant," writes Ian MacDonald, "and by the Eighties they were regarded by the pop press as museum pieces. Only when a psychedelic revival occurred in pop culture during the late Eighties did the Beatles' records start to make emotional sense to their young descendants."[7]

Coincident with this revival was the reintroduction, in 1987, of the Beatles catalog through the then young medium of the compact disc, a move timed to mark the twenty-year anniversary of *Sgt. Pepper's Lonely Hearts Club Band* – the LP widely regarded as the Beatles' magnum opus, the apotheosis of psychedelia, and/or the most influential rock album of all time.

In the same year, EMI commissioned Beatles researcher Mark Lewisohn to write *The Complete Beatles Recording Sessions* (published in 1988), a compendious diary chronicling the group's studio history. Based on pioneering work by EMI engineer John Barrett, the book mapped the mass of mixes, submixes, mastertakes and outtakes housed in the Abbey Road vaults – hundreds of hours' worth of Beatles material, never before archived coherently. Abbey Road's Ken Townsend described Lewisohn's book as "the first and only one to tell the story of [the group's] recording career" and "the definitive reference work for Beatles' fans everywhere."[8] Lewisohn's book in turn nourished several others. For example, Ian MacDonald's *Revolution in the Head: The Beatles' Records and the Sixties*, published in 1994, drew on Lewisohn's raw session data and added rich, critically astute song-by-song commentary to produce a book that made the Beatles come alive for many readers too young to have witnessed things first-hand. In the post-punk interval, a scholarly discourse on the Beatles as *recording* artists – as masters of what Evan Eisenberg terms "phonography," the art of using the studio not simply to store but to construct musical compositions – began to emerge and, alongside it, a more friendly critical climate.[9]

In 1992, rumors began to appear in the press suggesting that yet unheard Beatles songs were secreted away in the Abbey Road vaults. Then, in a January 1994 *New Yorker* article begun as a profile of Lewisohn, journalist Mark Hertsgaard confirmed that the Beatles were planning to issue unreleased material culled from the archives. Moreover, this project would see the three surviving Beatles coming together to work on new material. Hertsgaard had been invited by EMI to listen to some of the closely held archive tapes, something he portrayed as a great privilege.[10] His follow-up book, *A Day in the Life* (1995), attempted to make the case to a broad, non-technical audience that the Beatles were, above all, exemplary modern artists.

This foreshadowed the carefully executed, massively promoted *Beatles Anthology* project of the mid-nineties. While some complained that the *Anthology* was mostly hype, others, such as musicologist Walter Everett, saw great value in it: "While the *Anthology* . . . closes a very long chapter in Beatles history, it also inspires a very strong sense that the Beatles are beginning anew."[11] The *Anthology* racked up tremendous sales numbers, with many purchases being made by young consumers. It came out during the heyday of Britpop, a new movement that looked for inspiration to the sixties British Invasion. As a lavish retrospective on the band synonymous with sixties cultural change, *Anthology* helped position the Beatles for the millennium sweepstakes.

None of this had to happen, of course. It's not as if with the *Anthology* Apple finally perfected mass-mediated mind control. The 2006 *Love* album received press coverage almost as breathless as that for the *Anthology* without making a comparable impact. But in exerting control over "the repertoire of products available for cultural consumption," Apple and EMI helped prepare the way for the *Anthology*'s enthusiastic reception.[12] In the words of Simon Frith, while consumers can make "creative" meanings for the products of the culture industries, both "what is available to us" and "what we can do" depend in part on "decisions made in production, made by musicians, entrepreneurs and corporate bureaucrats, made according to governments' and lawyers' rulings, in response to technological opportunities."[13] This chapter will consider such factors while tracing attempts, by Apple Corps and EMI, individual Beatles and their representatives, to invoke, inscribe, or re-frame the band's historical legacy – a legacy that is at once cultural and economic. It will concentrate on the period from the late eighties to 2007.

The Beatles on CD

In 1987, Beatles music was made available for the first time in the compact disc format. With George Martin overseeing the remastering process, EMI/Parlophone released twelve Beatles albums on CD: *Please Please Me*; *With the Beatles*; *A Hard Day's Night*; *Beatles for Sale*; *Help!*; *Rubber Soul*; *Revolver*; *Sgt. Pepper's Lonely Hearts Club Band*; *Magical Mystery Tour*; *The Beatles* (a.k.a. the White Album); *Abbey Road*; and *Let It Be*.[14] This sequence mirrored the Beatles' LPs as they had been originally released in the UK.[15] In addition, the 1988 follow-up CDs, *Past Masters Volumes 1* and *2*, collected tens of single releases – e.g., "We Can Work It Out"/"Day Tripper" – which had not been included on UK albums.[16]

As is well known, Beatles LPs released in the US during the 1960s were, up through *Revolver*, configured quite differently from their UK counterparts. This was due to Capitol Records' policy of stretching the product for the American market. At Parlophone in the UK, it was standard practice to include fourteen songs on a Beatles LP. Moreover, "UK chart protocol" militated against including single releases on albums.[17] In the USA, pop/rock customs were different. A typical LP – e.g., *Beach Boys Today!*, or the Byrds' *Fifth Dimension* – featured ten to twelve songs and often included recently released singles as part of the package. Knowing what the market would bear, Capitol simply lopped a few songs off each UK Beatles album, creating a surplus which could then be exploited. By tossing a half dozen such surplus tracks together with, say, two recent singles, Capitol could come up with ten "extra" Beatles tracks, enough to generate a "new" album. Though it was the band's sixth album on Parlophone, *Rubber Soul* was its eighth on Capitol. Moreover, if one takes into account the two US-only LPs that appeared on labels other than Capitol – *Introducing the Beatles* (Vee Jay, 1963) and *A Hard Day's Night* (United Artists, 1964) – then *Rubber Soul* counts as the band's tenth LP in the American market.

So, in December 1965, UK consumers were offered a *Rubber Soul* containing fourteen tracks, the first of which was "Drive My Car." Meanwhile, US consumers were offered an LP of the same name containing only twelve tracks, with "Drive My Car" not among them. Instead, the US *Rubber Soul* kicked off with "I've Just Seen a Face," a song from the UK version of *Help!* (an LP that, in its US version, filled out nearly half its length with orchestral passages from the film soundtrack). Additional songs (such as "Nowhere Man," "If I Needed Someone," and "What Goes On") which were integral to *Rubber Soul* as the Beatles assembled it were not included on the US release.

The sort of slicing and dicing which Capitol engaged in was perhaps excusable early on, when the Beatles seemed like a singles-based hit-making machine and British beat just another youth craze. But by *Rubber Soul,* the Beatles had begun to see themselves less as teen market tunesmiths and more as artists with a musical vision, and were crafting LPs accordingly. In this light, Capitol's blithe reconfiguration of opuses like *Rubber Soul* and *Revolver* – and its creation of chimeras like *Yesterday & Today* (an album, non-existent in the UK, which the American audience was led to think came between *Rubber Soul* and *Revolver*) – seems at best heavy-handed, and at worst brazenly dismissive of the authors' intentions. Of course, in 1965, the very notion that pop singers might be *auteurs* with notable intentions was new. Along with Bob Dylan, the mid-sixties Beatles would be key to pop's transformation into something people took seriously.

Generations of Americans had grown up listening to the Capitol LPs and hence to arguably impoverished versions of masterworks like *Revolver* or landmarks like *Please Please Me*.[18] The 1987 CD releases meant to correct this distorted image by returning to the UK selections and sequences. From 1987 to 2003, the only officially available Beatles CDs were the Parlophone editions. Thus, a new generation of Beatles listeners was to be raised on what one might call the band's proper albums and intentions.

And yet this itself produced a new demand from Beatles fans who, back in the sixties, had come of age with the Capitol releases.[19] In a few years, bootleggers were creating their own CD versions of the Capitol albums as well as rarities such as the mono mix of *Sgt. Pepper*.[20] Not having access to master tapes, bootleggers such as "Dr. Ebbets" of the Dr. Ebbets Sound System relied on pristine vinyl LPs of the type produced in limited edition by Mobile Fidelity Sound Lab in the early eighties.[21] Such bootleggers transferred the vinyl LPs to CD using higher sampling rates than those available to Martin and company in the mid-eighties. Some listeners think these bootlegs sound better than the 1987 CD remasters, which are held to have a harsh, "tinny" quality thought to be typical of digital audio of the mid-eighties period.[22]

As if in response to this trend, in 2004 Capitol released the first of several projected CD boxed sets presenting the Capitol LPs in both mono and stereo formats along with the original artwork and lavish additional packaging. The Capitol CDs also faithfully reproduced other features peculiar to the

Capitol Records releases: for instance, Capitol in the sixties was in the habit of adding extravagant doses of reverb to Beatles mixes, with the thought that this would make them "jump" more when aired on car radios. This no doubt irked the Beatles and their production team, who, by *Rubber Soul*, were using minimal amounts of reverb in their recordings.[23]

Nonetheless, even in a narrative that privileges the Beatles' artistry over Capitol's commercialism, the Capitol releases can be said to play an important role. Consider again the Capitol version of *Rubber Soul*: lacking four songs that appeared on its UK counterpart, it can seem a travesty. And yet this is the LP – the American *Rubber Soul* – that shook Brian Wilson, such that he was inspired to embark on *Pet Sounds*, a record which sustained moods, textures, and lyrical themes across an album's length and which strongly influenced *Sgt. Pepper*:

> I was sitting around a table with friends, smoking a joint, when we heard *Rubber Soul* for the very first time; and I'm smoking and getting high and the album blew my mind because it was a whole album with good stuff! It flipped me out so much I said, I'm going to try that, where the whole album becomes a gas.[24]

Starting with the bluegrass-flavored, acoustic twelve-string-driven "I've Just Seen a Face," segueing into the Celtic modalism of "Norwegian Wood," strolling on through "Michelle," "Girl," "I'm Looking Through You," and "In My Life," the Capitol *Rubber Soul* seems dominated by woody instrumental textures and gentle, laidback rhythms. Start the same LP with the faux-Memphis funk of "Drive My Car," add the glistening, metallic sheen of "Nowhere Man" and "If I Needed Someone," and a very different spell is cast. Listening to the Capitol *Rubber Soul*, many Americans assumed that the Fabs had gone folk – in post-MTV parlance, unplugged – for an entire LP. This was a fortuitous consequence of Capitol's fiddling with Parlophone products. To the extent that it inspired *Pet Sounds*, though, the accident might be deemed a happy one.

Live at the BBC

In 1989, Apple Corps won a longstanding legal dispute with EMI concerning underpaid royalties. In addition to a multi-million pound settlement, Apple chief Neil Aspinall secured veto power over any future Beatles releases from EMI.[25] This cleared the way for Apple to roll out a sequence of carefully researched retrospectives featuring previously unreleased material. Though the *Anthology* is the best-known of these, prior to the *Anthology* came *The Beatles Live at the BBC*, released in 1994. This double-CD set assembled nearly seventy tracks by the band, all recorded at BBC studios for radio broadcasts during 1962–5, many of them live to tape. The collection included Lennon-McCartney hits and funny interview bits, but the great majority of numbers were cover tunes. Indeed, *Live at the BBC* provides a picture window on to what the Beatles must have been like as a working club band. They rip through fifties era numbers with rollicking ease and show themselves to have been even closer students of artists such as Chuck Berry, Arthur Alexander, Carl Perkins, and the Everly Brothers than their early LPs would suggest. And, as showcased here, the Beatles appear to have been particular devotees of obscure rockabilly B sides by groups like the Johnny Burnette Trio and the Jodimars. Indeed, if one wished to argue, as some have, that the early Beatles were at heart a rockabilly band, one could point to *Live at the BBC* as Exhibit A. A report on the band's radio audition, written by the BBC producer in charge at the time, seems to concur. Producer Peter Pilbeam described the early Beatles as "an unusual group. Not as 'Rocky' as most, more country and western with a tendency to play music."[26] *Live at the BBC* provides an extended look at this "unusual group" and the music it favored in its formative years.

The *Anthology*

In 1995, the *Beatles Anthology* debuted. A sweeping chronicle of the band's career produced in house by Apple, the *Anthology* took the form of a ten-hour, eight-part documentary film, three double-CD sets featuring previously unreleased material, and a stylishly appointed, 368-page coffee-table book which reproduced selected images and most of the dialog from the film. The sheer maximalism of the project might suggest delusions of grandeur, but the *Anthology* was enthusiastically received and "made the Beatles an enormous media property again."[27] The first of the CD sets was issued in 1995 and contained music recorded as early as 1958 and as late as 1964; the *Anthology 2* and *3* sets, covering the band's middle and late periods respectively, were released a few months apart in 1996. All featured track-by-track annotations by Lewisohn.

Anthology 1 also included a new Beatles song recorded in the 1990s, an intended coup that brought to mind clichés about the magic of technology. The process began in 1994 at the ceremony inducting John Lennon, solo artist, into the Rock and Roll Hall of Fame.[28] At the ceremony, where McCartney did the honors for his old partner, Ono gave McCartney some cassette tapes containing demos Lennon had made at home in the late 1970s.[29] Collaborating with producer Jeff Lynne and engineer Geoff Emerick, the three surviving Beatles – nicknamed the Threetles – proceeded to add voices and instruments, hooks and countermelodies to Lennon's rough, lo-fi voice/piano renditions of "Free as a Bird" and "Real Love." Thus adorned, the two songs became the opening tracks, respectively, of the CD sets *Anthology 1* and *2*, and were also released as CD singles.[30] A third demo was slated for the same treatment and same slot on *Anthology 3*, but after completing work on the second song, Harrison declined to participate further and work on the third demo ceased.[31]

Of course, expectations for such a record were huge and, as a Beatles effort, "Free as a Bird" was judged decidedly sub-par by close critics such as MacDonald and Tim Riley. Riley mistakenly attacked McCartney for the song's hackneyed middle eight (composed, except for a few words, by Lennon), while MacDonald found the only high point to be the key change setting up Harrison's soaring, horn-like slide guitar solo.[32] Other astute listeners were clearly moved by a virtual Beatles reunion: at a King Crimson concert ten days after the song's release, rock avantist Adrian Belew stunned the crowd by dialing up a piano patch on his guitar synthesizer and giving a pitch-perfect solo rendition of "Free as a Bird." It was a hail-to-the-chief gesture, the flip side to Jimi Hendrix whipping out the *Sgt. Pepper* theme at the Saville Theatre just three days after that album's release on June 1, 1967.[33]

The bulk of all three *Anthology* CD compilations consists of previously unreleased demos, outtakes, and live recordings of songs from the Beatles repertoire that are, as songs, mostly familiar. Notable exceptions include "If You've Got Trouble" and "That Means a Lot," Lennon-McCartney compositions recorded during the *Help!* sessions but absent from the album or film. Yet even with known songs, alternative renditions of the type collected here can be revelatory: Harrison's pensive, acoustic-guitar-and-voice demo for "While My Guitar Gently Weeps" from *Anthology 3* contrasts strikingly with the thudding rock number found on the White Album. Illuminating too is take 1 of "Tomorrow Never Knows," included on *Anthology 2*. This landmark Beatles creation appears here shorn of its most distinctive features – the tambura, the syncopated drum figure, the harmonic shift to the mixolydian VII, the backwards guitar solo, and, above all, the otherworldly tape loops that stir the song's "seething dazzle."[34] Titled "Mark I" at this nascent moment, the song bears paltry resemblance to "the thrilling orgy of sound" which closes *Revolver*.[35] In particular, the *Anthology* outtake allows one to appreciate the power of McCartney's contribution to this visionary Lennon song, for it was he who cooked up the tape loop idea, as well as the loops themselves – the *coup de grâce* so notable by its absence here.[36]

The video *Anthology* debuted in November 1995 when a three-part, six-hour version was broadcast by ITV in the UK and ABC TV in the USA. The film became available for retail purchase in the fall of 1996. In its DVD boxed set incarnation the *Anthology* is divided into eight parts, and clocks in at over ten hours, with an additional eighty-one minutes of special features.[37] Directed by Geoff Wonfor and produced by Apple chief Neil Aspinall and Chips Chipperfield, the documentary draws on a store of footage, much of it collected during the sixties by Aspinall, who at the time served as the Beatles' road manager. Aspinall was gathering material for a retrospective eventually given the working title *The Long and Winding Road*. With the breakup of the band and the many years of ensuing infighting, the project was put aside, even as Aspinall went on to become *de facto* CEO of Apple.[38] When, in 1989, the aforementioned lawsuit with EMI was settled, the moment seemed right for a return to the project. Known for his skill at mediating between all concerned even when the various Beatle camps were feuding, Aspinall convinced McCartney, Starr, Ono, and even a reluctant Harrison to come aboard.[39] To add to the store of material already collected, new interviews were done with the three surviving Beatles in both one-on-one and group settings. Lennon's voice was included by way of the many audio and video interviews he had given during the period 1963–80. These were then woven together to create a narrative that, starting with recollections of childhood, closely tracks the group through formation, struggle, mania, and megastardom to its official dissolution in 1970. In place of a single voiceover narrator, the *Anthology* presents the voices of the four Beatles in a polyphonic tapestry. The *Anthology* is thus described as the Beatles' story "in their own words."[40]

This is both a strength and a weakness of the project. It is, for instance, most intriguing to hear the Beatles themselves discuss, say, meeting Elvis Presley, or being roughed up by the Marcos government of the Philippines, or whether Magic Alex may have had a hand in the uproar at Rishikesh in 1968. At the same time, it can be frustrating, for the Beatles' are nearly the only voices one hears on such topics. The other prominent interviewees are Aspinall, Derek Taylor, and George Martin, all members of the band's inner circle. As MacDonald notes, once Ono declined to take part as an interviewee, then "other wives and lovers were ruled out," and this, combined with the fact that the project was controlled from top to bottom by Apple, gives the *Anthology* a "Party Line tinge."[41]

Another drawback to this approach is that the Beatles, quite understandably, have difficulty making the case for their own artistic greatness. Autobiographers usually do, as one doesn't want to boast, and anyway, one may have written a masterpiece like, say, "Eleanor Rigby" and still have little of interest to say about the fact or artifact. Commentary and analysis is not the artist's job; it does, however, seem necessary to any attempt at a definitive portrait. In the *Anthology*, the Beatles' greatness is taken for granted; nowhere is it explained, explored, or considered in any critical depth. In this sense, though it offers much to the Beatles fan, the film preaches to the choir. It's doubtful whether a young person not already familiar with the band and its enormous impact would, on viewing *Anthology*, comprehend what all the fuss has been about.

Contrast this approach to that taken by the 1987 Granada Television special *It Was Twenty Years Ago Today*, produced to mark the twentieth anniversary of the release of *Sgt. Pepper*. This documentary – assembled, like the *Anthology*, in close consultation with Derek Taylor – featured fresh interviews with the surviving Beatles, but also talking heads as diverse as Allen Ginsberg, Roger McGuinn, Barry Miles, Abbie Hoffman, Wilfred Mellers, William Mann, William Rees-Mogg, Paul Kantner, and Michelle Phillips. It argues for the album's greatness, but does so by placing it in a broad cultural and historical context while offering a range of viewpoints, including the odd dissenting voice:

> INTERVIEWER: Is love all you need? . . .
>
> ABBIE HOFFMAN: *No*. (Smiles.) It's nice to have. (Laughs.) It's *nice*, as is peace. But it is not, and this is basically the flaw in Beatle politics: *Justice* is all you need.[42]

By comparison, the *Anthology* film seems guarded, centripetal. There is a telling moment near the end when Harrison remarks, concerning Beatlemania, "You know [the fans] gave their money and . . . their screams, but the Beatles kind of gave their nervous systems, which is a much more difficult thing to give."[43] It is as if the Beatles, having expended so much, now mean to take something back. That something is, of course, their own story, and their strategy for reclaiming it in the *Anthology* involves not only banishing outsiders, but also revealing certain things while concealing others. (There is, for instance, virtually no mention of the orgiastic escapades the group got up to during their concert tours.) The gaps, though, are overshadowed by the great size of the edifice – all that film, tape, talk, and music. Harrison's wry remark evokes spectacle and sacrifice, something on the order, say, of a bullfight. Juxtaposed in the film with Starr's and McCartney's affirmations of love – love among "four guys" and "love" and "peace" as the band's "spirit" – it hints at something messianic.[44] But then every autobiography is a piece of mythology, constructing an identity for its author/subject while pretending to reveal the already-there. Approached with this in mind and supplemented with critical and contextualizing material, the *Anthology* becomes a vital resource on Beatles music and culture.

Revisionisms

In November 2002, McCartney released *Back in the US*, a live double album documenting his recent North American concert tour.[45] Lennon-McCartney songs accounted for nineteen of the album's thirty-five tracks, and in the listings for these, McCartney reversed the authors' credit so that his own name came first. The songs in question were indeed McCartney compositions, whether in whole (e.g., "Hey Jude") or in large part (e.g., "We Can Work It Out"), but the move sparked cries of foul from some Beatles fans and from Yoko Ono. Her spokesman, Elliot Mintz, called McCartney's action "a misguided act of Beatle revisionism" and "an attempt to rewrite history." Meanwhile McCartney rep, Geoff Baker, attributed the move to McCartney's concern about his "place in history."[46]

In the previous twenty-four months, McCartney had released a new solo album, supported it with a record-setting world tour, and headlined the Queen's Jubilee, the Superbowl, and the post-9/11 Concert for New York. He had also published a book of poetry, exhibited a collection of his abstract paintings, and overseen the release of both a Wings anthology and the experimental opus *Liverpool Sound Collage*. In spring 2001, he also gave several high-profile interviews in which he sounded a persistent theme: "With the computer generation coming in and data being stored . . . there probably is a scenario in the future where someone will think that 'Hey Jude,' 'Let It Be,' 'The Long and Winding Road' . . . were written by the guy who came first."[47] Envisioning a time when data banks might abbreviate Beatles songwriting credits to something on the order of, say, "jlennon&," McCartney feared he was headed for history's delete file.

To many, such talk seemed inappropriate if not absurd. In one interview, CNN's Larry King remarked, "There's no one who doesn't know you," as if to reassure this most famous, wealthy, and talented of celebrities that everything was OK.[48] Yet as early as 1981 McCartney had voiced concern that, in the wake of Lennon's murder, a "cult" had emerged – one which deified Lennon, often at his own expense.[49] Of course, since his murder, Lennon's image, legend, and aura have grown so that they cast a long shadow, not just over McCartney, but over contemporary culture. Anthony Elliott has argued that "since his tragic death in 1980 at the age of 40 . . . Lennon has become an object of mourning, of fantasy, of intense feelings of hope and dread" – a "transcendent hero" who "haunts our culture."[50]

What appears to haunt McCartney is the impossibility of meeting and competing with such a figure on a level playing field.

> KING: Do you ever think he gets more credit than you?
> McCARTNEY: No, I – what's happened since he died is that . . .
> KING: There's a martyrdom.
> McCARTNEY: You can't blame people. You know, there's a lot of sympathy. It was such a shocking way to go that you want to try and give him everything. But the trouble is that there is . . . revisionism, where certain people were saying, "Well . . . the only thing Paul ever did was book the studio."[51]

In *Paul McCartney: Many Years From Now*, a biography written in close collaboration with its subject, Barry Miles argues that public perception of the Lennon-McCartney collaboration has been skewed by Lennon and Ono's one-sided account, which has been ubiquitous in the media. During the 1970s, he claims, "John and Yoko did as many as ten interviews a day," whereas Paul remained quiet, a situation *Many Years From Now* means to correct with detailed reflections from McCartney, particularly regarding the artistic practices and processes that informed Beatles music-making.[52]

For a sense of what Miles is talking about, consider the following passage by Jann Wenner, editor and publisher of *Rolling Stone*. Wenner hitched his magazine's wagon to the Lennon-Ono star in 1971 with the publication of the book-length interview, *Lennon Remembers*. In his Introduction to the new edition (2000), Wenner writes: "The publication of these interviews was the first time that any of the Beatles, let alone the man who had founded the group and was their leader, stepped outside that protected, beloved fairy tale and told the truth" about "the sugar-coated mythology of the Beatles and Paul McCartney's characterization of the breakup."[53] Some of the tropes deployed here have become crude common sense about Lennon and the Beatles. According to Wenner, Lennon is the founder, leader, and truth-teller, while the Beatles, and McCartney in particular, are sugar-plum fairies. Note too that the structuring opposition – courage and risk-taking on one side, sentimentality and scheming on the other – is heavily gender-coded. This reproduces rock orthodoxy's masculinist agenda, where those things read off as "feminine" are disdained as mere "pop."[54]

According to Miles, then, a certain kind of "Beatles revisionism" is long overdue. It's a delicate business, though, for since his death Lennon has been canonized as "St. John," and so "any attempt at . . . objective assessment of his role in the Beatles" risks looking like bad form.[55] *Many Years From Now* cuts against popular images of McCartney as "cute Beatle" or sappy balladeer, portraying its subject as a quintessential sixties bohemian who embraced the artistic *avant garde* well before his partner. This characterization works to bolster McCartney's rock credentials in that the figure of the "edgy innovator" fits with rock codes of authenticity in a way that, say, "effervescent tunesmith" does not.[56] Indeed, the stock narrative that pits Lennon the uncompromising rocker against McCartney the calculating showman is a version of rock's never-ending story, the conflict between being real and selling out. According to George Martin, that story reduces both parties to caricature and arguably says more about the workings of rock ideology than it does about the Lennon-McCartney partnership.[57]

Drawing on Miles among many other sources, Ian MacDonald's updated *Revolution in the Head* portrays McCartney as the "*de facto* musical director" of the band from *Revolver* onward.[58] In his recent memoir, *Here, There and*

Everywhere: My Life Recording the Beatles, Geoff Emerick, the band's chief engineer during that second half of its career, concurs:

> It might have been [Lennon's] band in the beginning, and he might have
> assumed the leadership role in their press conferences and public
> appearances, but throughout all the years I would work with them, it always
> seemed to me that Paul McCartney, the soft-spoken bass player, was the real
> leader of the group, and that nothing got done unless he approved of it.[59]

Summer of Love, George Martin's account of the making of *Sgt. Pepper*, paints a similar picture. In the face of what Emerick calls "conventional wisdom" about the Beatles,[60] such accounts amount to an emerging counternarrative.

Let It Be . . . Naked

Released in 2003, the *Let It Be . . . Naked* CD presented a remixed version of the Beatles' *Let It Be* LP from 1970. Liner notes characterized *Let It Be . . . Naked* as a restoration project in tune with the original agenda of *Let It Be*, which began as a back-to-basics effort in January 1969. At first titled *Get Back*, the 1969 project aspired to show the Beatles "as nature intended," without frills or production flourishes, but in a few weeks' time the whole thing unraveled.[61] Over a year later, Lennon, Harrison, and Allen Klein brought producer Phil Spector in to assemble the tapes into a soundtrack album for the forthcoming *Let It Be* film. Lennon was pleased with Spector's work, but McCartney was appalled, particularly at Spector's addition of orchestra and choir to his sparsely arranged ballads "Let It Be" and "The Long and Winding Road," moves on which the composer was not consulted.[62] By contrast, *Let It Be . . . Naked*, produced by Paul Hicks, Gary Massey, and Allan Rouse, received McCartney's enthusiastic support. Indeed, the CD amounted to something he had long sought – an edition of the album from which all traces of Spector had been scrubbed. Though Spector-less versions of *Let It Be* had circulated for years among bootleggers, *Let It Be . . . Naked* purported to have better sound quality than the bootlegs and something else besides. Digital technology had been used to clean up the old tracks, a twenty-first-century intervention that, according to the liner notes, removed a layer of unwanted interference. The authentic music could now stand revealed: "It's just the bare tapes," said McCartney, "just the bare truth."[63]

Talk of bare truth aside, though, *Let It Be . . . Naked* had a case to make; namely, that the popular reading of the 1970 album and film – as documenting the group's hateful, hurtful collapse – is wrong. In his liner notes, Kevin Howlett attributes this impression to director Michael Lindsay-Hogg's having cut the film to emphasize moments of conflict. In fact, says Howlett, a fuller picture of the project shows it had plenty of "happy moments."[64] As if to underscore the point, *Let It Be...Naked* includes a bonus "Fly on the Wall" disc containing excerpts, most less than thirty seconds long, in which the band can be heard talking, singing, and having a jolly good time. This audio montage may presage a new edition of the film, cut to a similar template.

Museum politics[65]

Meanwhile, Lennon's star hovers far above the fray. This is partly due to his status as "transcendent hero" and partly to Ono's tireless promotion of her late husband as a champion of peace.

In November 2006, she took out a full-page ad in the *New York Times* calling for December 8th, the anniversary of Lennon's killing, to become an annual occasion for "healing ourselves" and the world.[66] In late April 2007, Amnesty International announced the forthcoming release of a "historic double CD," *Instant Karma: The Amnesty International Campaign to Save Darfur*. The Warner Brothers album features over twenty Lennon songs performed by rock and pop stars ranging from U2 to Christina Aguilera. At Ono's behest, all proceeds go to Amnesty's campaign to "focus attention and mobilize activism around the urgent catastrophe in Darfur and other human rights crises."[67] Earlier in the same month, the BBC announced that one of Lennon's former possessions, the upright piano on which he composed "Imagine," would be carried to Memphis, Tennessee, to the site of the National Civil Rights Museum on the anniversary of Martin Luther King's assassination. There it would be photographed, for the piano, which is owned by pop star George Michael, is set "to tour global sites of past violence to promote peace." A "documentary film and photo album" would come out of the tour, with proceeds marked for "charity."[68]

These news items attest to the particular quality of Lennon's enduring presence. He once suggested that, with songs such as "Give Peace A Chance," he meant to be an advertising man – a jingle-writer – but one who sold peace instead of detergent powder.[69] In the sign economy of the twenty-first century, it is not just anthems like "Imagine" that function as mythic signifiers of "change";[70] Lennon's iconic aura is such that an object once touched by him can be treated as if imbued with mana, like a piece of the true cross. Lennon the man died in 1980, but John Lennon the symbol continues to inspire idealism, promote causes, and generate revenue – in other words, to do cultural work.

Ono is a close overseer of her late husband's estate and the chief custodian of his memory. By funding selected projects and controlling access to his *oeuvre*, she helps shape the Lennon image and keep it in the public eye. Thus, a recent BBC documentary project was canceled, reportedly because Ono was displeased with its depiction of Lennon.[71] On the other hand, *The U.S. vs. John Lennon*, a 2006 documentary detailing the couple's anti-war activism, received her full support. The makers of this independent film acknowledge they could not have succeeded in their work without the support Ono provided, which included access to Lennon's solo catalog.[72] The film portrays Lennon and Ono as exemplary advocates who, in the late sixties, made a bold commitment – to put the weight of their celebrity behind the crusade to stop the Vietnam War, something they did at great risk to their own safety and well-being. It does not, however, highlight Lennon's later repudiation of his New Left involvements, even though in one of his last interviews he described "Power to the People" – a song trumpeted in the film – as having been "written in the state of being asleep and wanting to be loved by Tariq Ali and his ilk."[73] Indeed, in the same interview, he said: "I dabbled in so-called politics in the late Sixties and Seventies . . . out of guilt . . . for being rich" and "against my instincts."[74] The film-makers hope to shed light on Orwellian outrages like the FBI's COINTELPRO operation and to inspire contemporary anti-war activists with Lennon and Ono's example. A film more attuned to the mercurial, even contradictory, shifts of Lennon's political views has yet to be made.

Given Ono's art world background, it is perhaps not surprising that she has nurtured numerous galleries, installations, and museums undertaking to honor the Lennon corpus. The exhibit *Lennon: His Life and Work*, which was unveiled at the Rock and Roll Hall of Fame and Museum in fall 2000, is a case in point. This massive, exquisitely appointed exhibit was timed to coincide with what would have been Lennon's sixtieth birthday. It also fitted neatly with the millennial year, framing Lennon as an epochal figure, an embodiment of the late twentieth-century zeitgeist.[75]

Featuring an array of striking artifacts as well as audio, video, and interactive components, the exhibit culminated in what Marsha Ewing called a "Song Sanctuary" – a "hushed" space on the Hall's top floor where the lyrics to more than twenty Lennon compositions were mounted on the wall.[76] The curatorial commentary accompanying these told a story cut from the classic rock template. Curator James Henke placed Lennon's early Beatles writing (and, by implication, the Beatles themselves) under the sign of artifice and alienation, noting that with potboilers like "Run For Your Life" Lennon had been churning out product and not expressing his inner self.[77] He framed "In My Life" as the turning point at which Lennon found his own voice and vocation, a quest for authenticity that eventually mandated he leave the Beatles.[78]

In the Introduction to the exhibit catalog, Henke calls Lennon "the leader of the biggest rock group ever," while going on to claim that

> his influence extended well beyond rock and roll. He excelled as a poet, a writer, a filmmaker and an artist. He was a political activist. He had a huge social conscience, and an enormous wit. Though it may sound like a cliché, he was, truly, a spokesperson for a generation. And perhaps more important than anything else, he was a seeker of the truth, a person whose life reflected the values and beliefs that he spoke of.[79]

To portray Lennon as the epitome of truth, Henke follows rock ideological practice and constructs an inauthentic Other to serve as counterfoil. "Conventional wisdom" comes in handy here, as McCartney gets stuck with the role.[80]

Thus, while the catalog entry paints "In My Life" as Lennon's breakthrough to truly personal, inner-directed songwriting, it concludes on a competitive note: "The British music magazine *Mojo* . . . recently ranked 'In My Life' the 'Greatest Song of All Time,'" beating out three other songs including "the McCartney composition, 'Here, There and Everywhere.'"[81] Implicitly pitting the partners against each other, the entry also assumes that "In My Life" is solely Lennon's invention, a dubious assumption at best. By contrast, McCartney claims to have set the entire lyric to music, while Lennon himself said that Paul "helped with the middle eight musically."[82] Pointing to musicological features, McCartney says: "The melody structure's very me."[83] On this point MacDonald agrees, noting that the tune's wide interval skips reflect McCartney's "vertical" approach to melody as opposed to Lennon's "horizontal" one.[84] Acknowledging this difference in characteristic styles, Everett[85] points out that the pair nevertheless worked together so long and intimately that "each seems to have internalized . . . the style of the other."[86] Given this, Everett concludes that the question is ultimately undecidable.[87]

Whatever the answer, such information seems pertinent to any discussion of "In My Life" as a "work." It can be said to point up not just a disagreement between the two partners, but also the profound complexity of their collaboration. However, the exhibit leaves the impression that there is no debate about attribution and no reason to consider the duo's unique collaborative dynamic.

It does, however, treat as profound Lennon's collaboration with Ono, highlighting, through a range of installations and displays, their performance art, activism, love affair, and family life. This is unsurprising, in that Lennon himself frequently affirmed their partnership as having no equal. But it must be said that the exhibit reflects Ono's particular version of things, something it does not advertise prominently. At the very back of the 176-page catalog, following the lyric and photo credits, one reads: "All artifacts collection of Yoko Ono Lennon." This perhaps accounts for the fact that out of seventy-two artifacts listed in the catalog, only eighteen refer to the Beatles.[88]

Calling "the establishment of collections a form of symbolic conquest," Eileen Hooper-Greenhill argues that museum displays work to "produce visual narratives that are apparently harmonious, unified and complete." This tendency, combined with the fact that such displays are typically "presented with anonymous authority," has a naturalizing effect.[89] The constructed quality of the narrative is elided, and parochial viewpoints begin to look like plain truth. Timothy Luke argues for reading exhibitions partly in terms of what they omit or leave out, since displays "are part of an ongoing struggle by individuals and groups to establish what is real, to organize collective interests and to gain command over what is regarded as having authority."[90] *Lennon: His Life and Work* allows Ono to present a version of the Lennon story with which it is difficult to argue; part of the difficulty, though, lies in the fact that the story is visually materialized but not verbally explicit.

The Lennon exhibit remained at the Rock Hall for two years. Meanwhile, Ono has shepherded similar projects, including the establishment, in 2000, of a Lennon museum at the Saitama arena in Tokyo,[91] and the 2005 exhibit *John Lennon: Unfinished Music*, put on by the Cité de la Musique in Paris. A 240-page volume, published to accompany the Cité exhibit, presents fifteen essays from a variety of journalists, art critics, and academics, all of whom build on the notion that Lennon was "un artist '*complet*'" – a *total* artist whose endeavors as a writer, designer, and "*plasticien*" crossed boundaries in liberating ways and deserve to be considered on the same plane as his music.[92] Art historian Emma Lavigne, curator of the Cité exhibit, begins her essay "*John Lennon: Unfinished Music*, une exposition inachevée," with a quote from a 1970 encounter between Lennon and Marshall McLuhan. Lennon complains that the Beatles have become "a museum, an institution," by which he means an oppressive, ossified structure, something that we have to "obliterate . . . or change."[93] She goes on to say that *Unfinished Music* does not intend to "museumize" Lennon.[94] Nonetheless, the man who once said, "*Avant garde* is French for bullshit," appears poised to become an art world hero in a way that, say, McCartney, Harrison, and Starr do not.[95]

Love

Projects like Amnesty International's *Instant Karma*, which yoke rock music and media to humanitarian relief efforts, descend from the Concert for Bangladesh, the star-studded benefit organized by George Harrison in 1971 to raise awareness about, and money for, famine relief in south Asia. Concurrent with the 1973 release of his solo album *Living in the Material World*, Harrison announced the founding of the Material World Charitable Foundation, an organization which has gone on to provide support to organizations such as Médecins Sans Frontières and "hundreds of individuals . . . with . . . special needs."[96] In November 2002, family and friends organized the Concert for George, a memorial staged at the Royal Albert Hall on the first anniversary of Harrison's death. Proceeds from the concert and the related CD and DVD went to the Foundation. The concert featured a bevy of rock artists, almost all close friends of the deceased, performing Harrison songs with an all-star band led by Eric Clapton. Starr and McCartney gave moving tributes, and Monty Python, whose films Harrison had funded, fended off false piety by baring some famous behinds. The concert also featured, at its outset, an hour's worth of Indian music, the high point of which was a composition, "Arpan," written by Ravi Shankar especially for the occasion. Calling for both Indian and European instruments as well as performance styles, the piece was rendered by a virtuosic ensemble led by Shankar's daughter Anoushka. It was a poignant salute to a man who had used his celebrity to push "open the door that . . . had separated the music of much of the world from the West."[97]

In his last years, Harrison laid the groundwork for an innovative and controversial Beatles collaboration. The *Love* project began in talks between Harrison and Guy Laliberté, founder of Cirque du Soleil, the wildly inventive circus troupe known for blending high-wire derring-do with high Romantic fantasy. In 2000, Harrison attended a party thrown by Laliberté following the Montreal Grand Prix, and they began to discuss the possibility of a Cirque show set to Beatles music.[98] The fit seemed apt: both the Beatles and Cirque could be said to have taken a street art form – rock and roll in one case, circus acrobatics in another – and turned it into something giddily sublime.[99] Harrison and his wife, Olivia, secured McCartney's support by squiring him to the Cirque spectacle *O*, from which McCartney emerged duly impressed. With Starr and Ono also giving the nod, Apple and its lawyers began a long negotiation with Cirque concerning what would become "the first authorized theatrical show" ever set to Beatles music.[100] By the end of June 2006, *Beatles: Love* was up and running at the Mirage Hotel on the Las Vegas strip "in a purpose-built theatre erected at the cost of $120 million."[101]

Taking particular inspiration from the band's psychedelic period, the show offers in place of, say, bewigged Beatles imitators, a phantasmagoric joyride with controls set for "sensory overload."[102] To this end, the audience is bathed in "360-degree" electronic sound sent through more than 6,000 speakers, some looming from the rafters, some so tiny they tuck into the headrest of one's seat.[103]

Then there is the soundtrack itself, also "purpose-built" to exact spec-ifications. The main architect is Giles Martin, son of Sir George and a successful producer/engineer in his own right. George Martin oversaw his son's work and is credited as producer, but he left the audio heavy lifting to Giles. The resulting soundscape promises to present Beatles music "as never before," while adding nothing new to sounds the Beatles actually recorded.[104] It does so by remixing, recombining, and recontextualizing such sounds, interventions made feasible by twenty-first-century digital audio technology. In the words of the elder Martin: "The brief on this show was that I should use all previous recordings in any way I wanted. It gave us *carte blanche* to muck about."[105]

To start, Giles ventured into the vaults and reviewed every scrap of Beatles material found there. In addition to mixes of songs (final or otherwise), he also examined the multi-track tapes from which such mixes had been generated. In the process, he discovered that basic maintenance was long overdue, as the original tapes had never been properly backed up, that is, copied in high fidelity against the possibility of deterioration or loss. His first step then was to make safeties of all the tracks, and he did so by transferring them from the analog to the digital domain.[106]

With the sounds thus separated and stored as computer data, it became possible not just to remix Beatles tracks, but to apply to them the full panoply of production tricks offered by digital mixing programs like Pro Tools.[107] One could slash and sample and generate mashups – uprooting, say, Ringo's lead vocal from "Octopus's Garden" and replanting it among the lush, cinematic strings of "Good Night." No matter that the former song was recorded in the key of E and the latter in G; the string track can be pitch-shifted to E without changing its tempo, something impossible in the analog domain, where pitch is a function of tape speed. Before pursuing such radical options, though, the Martins paused to get approval from McCartney, Starr, Olivia Harrison, and Ono. Giles created a demo, the highlight of which was the superimposition of vocals and melody instruments from "Within You, Without You" on the rhythm track of "Tomorrow Never Knows." McCartney was particularly enthused at the Martins taking things so "far out," and with that they proceeded accordingly.[108]

The *Love* soundtrack was released in November 2006 in both CD and DVD-audio form, the latter featuring 5.1 surround sound and an additional three minutes of material beyond the CD's 78 minutes.[109] As a single-disc attempt to encompass the range of the band's work, *Love* recalls the *1* compilation. But where *1* drew its selections from the top of the pop charts and hovered, one might say, near the surface of Beatles music, *Love* plumbs mysterious depths. Thus, while *1* omitted "Strawberry Fields Forever" on the ground that it did not quite top the charts, *Love* makes this extraordinary song a centerpiece. True, *Love*'s version of "Strawberry Fields" is a creature of the remix process, assembled from disparate takes, some previously unheard; but one could argue that this is in keeping with the spirit of the original, which was itself "partly cut into shape physically, like electronic music" and which never fully satisfied Lennon.[110] Numerous reviewers of the *Love* album recounted skepticism turning to delight, with many noting the vibrant sound quality of the recordings. Such writers also paid homage to Starr, whose one-of-a-kind drum style comes mightily to the fore in the remixes.[111] Geoff Emerick, though, decried the project as a presumptuous meddling with masterpieces.[112]

Unauthorized digital meddling with Beatles music has created a stir in recent years. DJ Danger Mouse's *Grey Album* (2004) mashed up instrumental segments of the White Album with vocals from Jay-Z's *Black Album*, while the Beachles' *Sgt. Pet Sounds' Lonely Hearts Club Band* (2006) jammed chunks of *Sgt. Pepper* together with vocal and instrumental tracks retrieved from the Beach Boys' *Pet Sounds* box. In both cases, EMI responded with cease and desist orders, but the *Grey Album* became a *cause célèbre* on the internet, where postmodern music fans organized to facilitate its mass free distribution.[113] Some young listeners no doubt got an Oedipal jolt from seeing the godlike Beatles thus brought down to earth. Thirtysomething Giles Martin was, one might say, the right man to provide a riposte while keeping things well within the family. In discussing the Martins' painstaking approach, Giles insisted: "We're concerned about the Beatles' legacy."[114] *Love* can be seen, then, as an officially approved, major-label-backed mashup, an effort to contain the profligate dissemination of Beatles music in the digital domain. And, like the *Anthology* film, the *Love* soundtrack seems to say that the Beatles make world enough; no need to go mixing with outsiders.

Making and taking

Reportedly miffed at Capitol's lackluster promotion of both the *Love* soundtrack and his own 2005 release *Chaos and Creation in the Back Yard*, McCartney announced in March 2007 that he was leaving EMI/Capitol, the label he had been associated with for most of his career. His upcoming album, *Memory Almost Full*, would be released on Hear Music, a new, upstart label created by the international coffee shop chain Starbucks in partnership with Concord Music.[115] Media reports noted that older, established rock artists have difficulty getting new releases played on the radio, such that their core audience often remain in the dark about such things. Claiming "It's a new world," McCartney expressed hope that with Starbucks bistros in more than twenty countries playing his music, he would be able to reach listeners, old and young, more directly.[116] In addition to being released on CD, *Memory Almost Full* was made available for online downloading, a move that foreshadowed the announcement, in May, that EMI would soon release McCartney's full post-Beatles catalog "across all digital platforms."[117] In June, EMI announced that Starr's solo back catalog was set for online release as well.

For weeks, rumors had swirled that summer 2007 would see the Beatles catalog itself made available for legal downloading. In its customary fashion, Apple Corps had resisted the downloading trend, making Beatles music conspicuous by its absence from the online realm. Apple Corps' reservations reportedly concerned the sound quality of mp3s, the prospect that sales of mp3s might hurt sales of CDs, and the fact that online music consumers typically purchase individual songs as opposed to full-length albums, the format thought to feature the Beatles at their best.[118] Several 2006 stories on the *Love* project mentioned that the entire Beatles catalog had of late been digitally remastered, welcome news for those purists who complain that the 1987 CD remasters sound sketchy – inferior to the original LPs and outdated in the light of more recent advances in digital technology.[119] In addition, in February and March 2007, Apple Corps settled two long-standing lawsuits seen as roadblocks to any online venture. The first determined that Apple Corps could not prevent Apple Inc., makers of the Mac and the iPod, from using the Apple logo in music-related endeavors, a resolution that some thought would free the two corporations to collaborate on, say, a pre-loaded Beatles iPod, if not an exclusive deal with Apple Inc.'s iTunes Music Store.[120] The second suit, claiming that EMI had grossly underpaid royalties during the period 1994–9, was settled in Apple Corps' favor, with the Beatles receiving a "multi-million pound" payout from EMI.[121]

Analysts speculated that a Beatles downloading craze might bring EMI out of the financial doldrums in which it, like other music industry giants, had been stuck for some time.[122] But in April it was announced that EMI and Apple Inc. had struck a deal, one which included scores of EMI artists, but not the Beatles.[123] McCartney indicated that details of an online Beatles launch were "virtually settled," but provided no target.[124]

April's biggest Beatles news concerned the departure, after decades of service, of Neil Aspinall as Apple Corps CEO. Some reports indicated that the move had long been in the works, and that, with the settlement of the two lawsuits, the moment was right for the sixty-five-year-old to bow out gracefully.[125] However, other accounts sounded a note of alarm, suggesting that differences between Aspinall and the Apple Corps board had become irreconcilable. In these, Aspinall was depicted as the calm, cool hand who had steered the Beatles back to superstar status with ambitious, tasteful projects like the *Anthology* – someone who, having been present at the creation, was deeply averse to moves that might be seen as crassly commercial. Hinted at was a shameless scheme to "flood the market" with Beatles merchandise, a scheme which Aspinall supposedly could not stomach.[126]

Flood the market? Some would argue that the damage had already been done with Aspinall-led undertakings like *Anthology*, *1*, and *Love*. Others might say that if there's profit to be made from "I Am the Walrus" ring-tones, then a CEO, particularly one from the entertainment business, can be fairly expected to chase it. Aspinall's replacement as chief of Apple Corps is the fifty-one-year-old Jeff Jones, a respected music industry executive who has devoted his career to repackaging and relaunching superstar back catalogs.[127] As a Vice President at Sony/BMG, Jones oversaw the media giant's Legacy division, which has won plaudits for carefully organized, well-annotated reissues such as the expanded 2005 edition of Miles Davis's *'Round About Midnight*. Still, news stories taking Aspinall's part emphasized Jones's involvement in seemingly endless repackagings of the Elvis Presley catalog. Apparently, right-thinking people don't want the Beatles going the way of the Reese's Peanut Butter Cup "King" pack.[128] In public statements, Jones has affirmed the notion that forthcoming Apple projects should strive to balance commercial opportunity with "Beatle credibility."[129] Moving the Beatles catalog online is said to be at the top of his priority list.[130]

Band and brand

In January 2007, the Official UK Charts Company announced a change in how it tallies the chart position of singles. Henceforth, online downloads would be counted alongside purchases of physical units, an approach taken by *Billboard* in the US nearly two years earlier. More significantly for the Beatles, downloads of "golden oldies" would be counted as well.[131] British bookmakers were soon taking bets on which Beatles track would go to number one once the catalog officially comes online. Some even foresaw an all-Beatles Top Ten in the offing, while others derided this as wishful thinking.[132]

Thirty-seven years after their breakup, and at a moment when the landscape of the music business appears to be shifting seismically, the Beatles are still a focus of hope and concern: perhaps the pop charts will once again be dominated by "quality" music; perhaps a Beatles downloading craze will save an ailing record industry; perhaps an online Beatles launch will confirm that the digital medium has at last truly arrived. Then again, such events might also signal the death of the long-playing album, the format that the Beatles, among others, made synonymous with serious rock.

Such scenarios speak to the Beatles' unique status within rock culture. According to Keir Keightley, rock ideology is founded on a "paradox."[133] Though "rock has involved millions of people buying a mass-marketed, standardized commodity . . . available virtually everywhere, these purchases have produced intense feelings of freedom, rebellion, marginality, opposi-tionality, uniqueness and authenticity."[134] Unlike, say, folk or jazz, which have fostered such feelings while remaining distant from the commercial mainstream, rock wants it both ways: On one hand, it reproduces the cri-tique of mass culture that sees forces of mass production, consumption, and communication as threats to the autonomy and integrity of the individual. On the other, it re-frames that critique, claiming that one can consume the products of mass culture without compromising one's integrity, provided one searches out those mass culture artifacts or experiences that are authen-tic and shuns those that are alienated. Of course, qualities like authenticity and alienation do not inhere in artifacts. They are rhetorical constructions whose meanings are loaded and ambiguous; so much so that "negotiating the relationship between the 'mass' and the 'art' in 'mass art' has been the distinguishing ideological project of rock culture since the 1960s."[135]

This is a project to which the Beatles have been central. They are protag-onists of a rock historical narrative that turns on the question: Is it possible to sell out (be immensely popular) without selling out (compromising one's integrity)? For many, the Beatles prove that this ideological project is not an impossible dream.

Treating the Beatles as a prestige brand, in the manner indicated by Aspinall and Jones, may simply be savvy marketing – a canny nod to con-sumers who cherish this conception of the Beatles and rock music. Or it may be that such executives are themselves true believers who aspire to balance the "bad" kind of selling out with the "good." Fears over flooding the market bespeak what John Storey calls the "elitist and reactionary" idea that "more (quantity) always means less (quality)," a position he associates with critics of popular culture.[136] Keightley argues that rock is a form of popular culture built on elitism and moralism – on "processes of exclusion" having to do with taste, and a conception of taste that blends aesthetic considerations about beauty with ethical ones about complicity with the system.[137]

Thus far, the Beatles, perhaps more than any comparable figures, have been able to serve both masters. They continue to epitomize the rock ideal of the band – music as "organic" expression, as something made by a "self-sufficient . . . self-contained" gang of talented, uppity autodidacts.[138] They also define the music industry model of a brand – music as signature commodity, as merchandising empire, as golden goose.[139] For the moment at least, band and brand abide. Will this continue to be the case? Though one cannot predict the path of Beatles reception, a few trends seem worthy of note.

If the Britpop movement of the mid-nineties is an indication, then Beatles music retains the power not just to impress – or oppress – young musicians, but to inspire them directly. Britpop aligned grunge with encroaching Americanization, purporting to enlist sixties British icons like the Beatles and the Kinks in a campaign of homegrown resistance. Whatever this pop war's substance, a new generation of hipsters and hypesters found current uses for decades-old British rock.[140] More recently, the mashup trend, as exemplified by Danger Mouse and the Beachles, suggests that digital musicians regard the Beatles' records as rich pop "compost," despite EMI's attempts to police such poaching.[141] Composer James Russell Smith has argued that the Beatles' do-it-yourself approach helped demystify artistic "creation" for a generation of music enthusiasts. Writing their own songs, playing their own instruments, taking lead roles in arranging the music and producing the records, the Beatles disrupted the division of labor that had structured popular music-making for a half century and suggested to sixties era amateurs "that maybe, just maybe we too could strike a spark from the once forbidden fires of genius."[142] Smith has expressed concern that, to later generations, the Beatles' human-scale achievements may seem as distant and magical as those of Romantic titans, but developments such as these suggest the music persists as part of a useable past.[143] According to MacDonald, such engagement "can only be fruitful for young pop musicians," for "together and individually, the Beatles amount to a veritable academy of pop cultural values and talents."[144]

In this regard, it should be noted that, starting in the 1980s, popular music and the Beatles in particular began to be taken up by the traditional academy. As volumes like this one attest, major educational institutions now see the Beatles as a *bona fide* topic of scholarly inquiry. Beatles studies – what one might call Fabology – is a growing field that engages historians, cultural theorists, sociologists, and musicologists. It would appear that the Beatles' place in the history books, if not the pop charts, is assured.

Moreover, the Beatles are now at home in the nursery: generations of parents have introduced their children to the music in what has become a secular ritual, something that's not the case with, say, the music of the Rolling Stones.[145] In the words of Ritchie Unterberger, "waves and waves of kids continue to discover and get enthusiastic about [the Beatles] year after year, decade after decade."[146] In fact, this phenomenon is so widespread it has become the butt of jokes, as in the 1998 film *Sliding Doors*, where one character quips, "Everybody's born knowing the Beatles lyrics instinctively.

They're passed into the fetus subconsciously along with the amniotic stuff. In fact, they should be called 'The Fetals.'"[147] On this view, one might shrug at the Beatles flooding the market, as they appear to have flooded everything else.

Unterberger continues: "There's a timelessness about the joy, curiosity, and ceaseless, almost self-actualizing hunger they had to constantly change that's immediately tangible, almost overpowering, in their music."[148] Seen simultaneously as agents of change and vessel of family values, the Beatles make an appealing myth for modern liberalism – which, like rock, wants to have it both ways.[149] In such light, another statement from Derek Taylor comes to mind, this one made years after he retired from Apple. In Hertsgaard's *A Day in the Life*, Taylor is quoted as saying the Beatles are "an abstraction, like Christmas."[150] According to him, they stood for "hope, optimism, wit, lack of pretension, [the idea] that anyone can do it, provided they have the will to do it. They just seemed unstoppable."[151] One could add that over the years, the Beatles have, like Christmas, performed a cultural as well as an economic function – serving at once as symbol of high idealism and engine of mass consumption. Indeed, at Christmas time in the modern West, humane sentiments cohabit with hyper-commerce, as if compassion and capital had no quarrel. And when the old songs come on, it's hard not to be carried along.

Notes

1 Six boys, six Beatles: the formative years

1 Antonio Gramsci, *Selections from the Prison Notebooks*, ed. and trans. Quintin Hoare and Geoffrey Nowell Smith (London: Lawrence & Wishart, 1971), 324.

2 Billy Shepherd, *The True Story of the Beatles* (London: Beat Publications, 1964); Hunter Davies, *The Beatles* (New York: McGraw Hill, 1968; rev. edns., New York: Norton, 1985, 1996); Barry Miles, *Paul McCartney: Many Years From Now* (London: Secker & Warburg; New York: Holt, 1997); and The Beatles, *The Beatles Anthology* (London: Cassell; San Francisco: Chronicle, 2000).

3 Albert Goldman, *The Lives of John Lennon* (New York: William Morrow, 1988); Ray Connolly, *John Lennon 1940–1980: A Biography* (London: Fontana, 1981); and Henry W. Sullivan, *The Beatles with Lacan: Rock 'n' Roll as Requiem for the Modern Age* (New York: Peter Lang, 1995).

4 Epstein, *A Cellarful of Noise*; Cynthia Lennon, *A Twist of Lennon* (London: Star Books, 1978); Sutcliffe and Thompson, *Stuart Sutcliffe*.

5 Three examples of biographical confusion can be adduced here. The earliest "official" biography, by Billy Shepherd, published in 1964, mistakenly dated the meeting of Lennon and McCartney at Woolton Fete as July 1955, when Paul was only thirteen, instead of 1957. This error was repeated as late as 1981 by an eminent American critic in the authoritative *Rolling Stone* history of rock (Greil Marcus, "The Beatles," in Jim Miller [ed.], *The* Rolling Stone *Illustrated History of Rock and Roll* [London: Picador, 1981], 177–89). Second, the occupational status of Lennon's uncle George Smith is given by most authors as the owner of a small dairy business; but Pauline Sutcliffe claims, without supporting evidence, that he was simply an employee and that John had exaggerated his uncle's importance and his own social status (Pauline Sutcliffe and Douglas Thompson, *Stuart Sutcliffe: The Beatles' Shadow and His Lonely Hearts Club* [London: Sidgwick & Jackson, 2001], 34). Meanwhile, Bob Spitz says that at some stage Uncle George left the dairy business to become a bookmaker, quoting Lennon's cousin Stanley Parkes from an unpublished interview made in 1985 for Goldman's book (*The Beatles* [New York: Little, Brown, 2005], 2). Perhaps betraying some incredulity at this revelation, Spitz adds that "no one was sure how George squared such activities with upright Mimi." Thirdly, until 2000, it was widely accepted that the first Brian Epstein had heard of the Beatles was when "Raymond Jones," a regular customer of Epstein's NEMS music store, placed an order for a copy of the German single "My Bonnie." This was attested by Epstein himself in his memoir (*A Cellarful of Noise* [London: Souvenir Press, 1964], 43), and by his assistant Alastair Taylor (with Martin Roberts, *Yesterday: The Beatles Remembered* [London: Sidgwick & Jackson, 1988], 6). No subsequent biographer was able to trace Jones, but this did not shake their faith in the story. Only the *Mersey Beat* editor Bill Harry, in a 1997 interview with Bob Spitz (which was not published until nine years later), was skeptical of the role of "Jones" in bringing the existence of the band to Epstein's attention, since this supposed event occurred several months after Harry had supplied Epstein with copies of *Mersey Beat* in which the Beatles were heavily featured (*The Beatles*, 265–6). Meanwhile, in 2000, Alastair Taylor admitted in the late Debbie Geller's television documentary and book about Epstein that he had invented "Raymond Jones" because, while a number of individuals had enquired after the disc, he needed to show that an order had been placed so as to persuade Epstein to buy a box of discs from Polydor in Germany (Debbie Geller and Anthony Wall (eds.), *The Brian Epstein Story* [London: Faber & Faber, 2000], 35). Nevertheless, as late as 2003, Philip Norman, in the "revised and updated" edition of his *Shout! The True Story of the Beatles* ([London: Sidgwick & Jackson, 2003], 126), once again repeated the story that Jones was "an 18-year-old Huyton boy" and even that Epstein remembered him as a fan of Carl Perkins. Norman's book may have been updated, but clearly not revised, at least on this point!

6 Sutcliffe and Thompson, *Stuart Sutcliffe*, 74.

7 Ray Coleman, *Brian Epstein* (Harmondsworth: Penguin, 1990), 507.

8 Barry Miles, *The Beatles: A Diary – An Intimate Day by Day History* (New York: Barnes & Noble, 2004), 4.

9 Peter Hennessey, *Having It So Good: Britain in the Fifties* (London: Allen Lane, 2006), 9.

10 Ibid., 19.

11 The Beatles, *The Beatles Anthology*, 38.

12 Miles, *The Beatles: A Diary*, 55.

13 Ibid.

14 John Lennon was won over to the producer George Martin when he realized that Martin had produced albums by the group and by Peter Sellers, who starred in the Goon Show with Spike Milligan and Harry Secombe. Another link was Dick Lester, the director of the two Beatles films. Lester had directed the Goons' short *The Running, Jumping and Standing Still Film*.

15 Peter Townshend, *The Family Life of Old People* (London: Routledge & Kegan Paul, 1957), 108.

16 Peter Brown, with Steven Gaines, *The Love You Make: An Insider's Story of the Beatles* (London: Macmillan, 1983), 29.

17 Sutcliffe and Thompson, *Stuart Sutcliffe*, 18.

18 Townshend, *The Family Life of Old People*, 108.

19 Sutcliffe and Thompson, *Stuart Sutcliffe*, 47.

20 Miles, *The Beatles: A Diary*, 20.

21 *The Beatles Anthology*, 36.

22 The Beatles, *The Beatles Anthology* (London: Cassell; San Francisco: Chronicle, 2000), 36.

23 Tony Judt, *Postwar: A History of Europe since 1945* (London: Heinemann, 2005), 395.

24 Dominic Sandbrook, *Never Had It So Good: A History of Britain from Suez to the Beatles* (London: Abacus, 2000), 206.

25 Ian MacDonald, *Revolution in the Head: The Beatles' Records and the Sixties* (London: Fourth Estate, 1994), 65.

26 Ibid., 457.

27 Miles, *The Beatles: A Diary*, xi.

28 Sullivan, *The Beatles with Lacan*, 86.

29 Ibid., 86.

30 Ibid., 61.

31 Hennessey, *Having It So Good*, 69–70.

32 Ibid., 74.

33 Ibid., 75–6.

34 Miles, *The Beatles: A Diary*, 40–3.

35 Originating in the East End of London, the Teddy boys (or Teds) were a much reviled youth group. They were linked to rock and roll and the cinema "riots" that occurred during showings of *Rock Around the Clock*. Some Teddy boys were prominent in the attacks on Caribbean immigrants in the Notting Hill "riots" of 1958 in London. For non-metropolitan teenagers such as Lennon and Harrison, it was possible to detach the look of the Teds from their subculture or lifestyle.

36 Alan Clayson and Pauline Sutcliffe, *Backbeat: Stuart Sutcliffe – The Lost Beatle*, (London: Pan, 1994), 17.

37 Simon Frith and Howard Horne, *Art Into Pop* (London: Methuen, 1987).

38 Miles, *The Beatles: A Diary*, 50.

39 Phil Bowen, *A Gallery To Play To: The Story of the Mersey Poets* (Exeter: Stride Publications, 1999).

40 Royston Ellis, *Rave* (Northwood: Scorpion Press, 1960).

41 Miles, *The Beatles: A Diary*, 53.

42 Coleman, *Brian Epstein*, 172.

43 John Lennon, *School Days*, which he wrote during his time at grammar school (no record of publication).

44 Michael Wood, "John Lennon's Schooldays," in Elizabeth Thomson and David Gutman (eds.), *The Lennon Companion: Twenty-Five Years of Comment* (London: Macmillan, 1987, 146 (originally published in *New Society*, June 27, 1968).

45 Miles, *The Beatles: A Diary*, 23.

46 On the character and history of skiffle see Brian Bird, *Skiffle: The Story of Folk-Song with a Jazz Beat* (London: Robert Hale, 1958); Chas McDevitt, *Skiffle: The Definitive Inside Story* (London: Robson, 1997); and Michael Brocken, "Was It Really Like That?: *Rock Island Line* and the Instabilities of Causational Popular Music Histories," *Popular Music History* 1/2 (2006), 147–66.

47 Roland Barthes, "Musica practica," in Roland Barthes, *Image–Music–Text*, trans. Stephen Heath (London: Fontana; New York: Noonday Press, 1977), 149.

48 Alan J. Porter, *Before They Were Beatles: The Early Years 1956–60* (Bloomington, IN: Xlibris, 2003), 18.

49 Quoted in Richard Mabey, *The Pop Process* (London: Hutchinson Educational, 1965), 48.

50 The Beatles, *The Beatles Anthology*, 36–7.

51 Porter, *Before They Were Beatles*, 152.

52 Eve Kosofsky Sedgwick, *Between Men: English Literature and Male Homosexual Desire* (New York: Columbia University Press, 1985), 89.

53 Cynthia Lennon, *A Twist of Lennon*, 134.

54 Bob Spitz, *The Beatles: The Biography*, 2nd edn. (New York: Little, Brown, 2007), 37. Brian Bird's 1958 book *Skiffle* made a parallel point. He wrote that for young men, singing was a "sissy extra" in school and "whereas in the past a young man sang only in his bath" – as private as Lennon and Shotton's sylvan seclusion – "now he does so openly on every occasion when he foregathers with his friends" (56–7). Thanks to Simon Frith for this reference.

55 Porter, *Before They Were Beatles*, 33.

56 Miles, *The Beatles: A Diary*, 30.

57 Julia Baird, with Geoffrey Guiliano, *John Lennon: My Brother* (New York: Henry Holt, 1988), 30 (emphasis added).

58 Miles, *The Beatles: A Diary*, 24.

59 The addition of new words had a very practical dimension: songs were often learned from radio broadcasts and it was impossible to memorize or even note down all the lyrics at one listening. This necessity – to create new words to fill in gaps – was undoubtedly a spur to the composition of wholly new songs. Alan Porter mentions another example from the early days of the group: a Burl Ives record of "Worried Man Blues" was so scratched that some lyrics were indecipherable, so John improvised replacements (Porter, *Before They Were Beatles*, 37).

60 Coleman, *Brian Epstein*, 169.

61 Miles, *The Beatles: A Diary*, 36–7; Coleman, *Brian Epstein*, 182.

62 Miles, *The Beatles: A Diary*, 51.

63 Ibid., 52–3.

64 Barbara Bradby, "She Told Me What to Say: The Beatles and Girl-Group Discourse," *Popular Music and Society* 28/3 (2005), 359–90.

65 Quoted in the Beatles, *The Beatles Anthology*, 49.

66 Ibid.

67 Lutgard Mutsaers, "Indorock: An Early Eurorock Style," in *Popular Music* 9/3 (1990), 307–20.

68 In 1961, Stuart Sutcliffe decided to leave the group and remain in Hamburg with his new girlfriend, Astrid Kirchherr, and to study art there with Eduardo Paolozzi. He died in Hamburg in April 1962.

69 George Martin, quoted in Kenneth Womack, *Long and Winding Roads: The Evolving Artistry of the Beatles* (New York: Continuum, 2007), 51.

70 MacDonald, *Revolution in the Head*, 93.

71 These include Clayson and Sutcliffe, *Backbeat*; MacDonald, *Revolution in the Head*; Spitz, *The Beatles*; Jeff Russell, *The Beatles Album File and Complete Discography*, rev. edn. (London: Blandford, 1989); and Bill Harry, *The Book of Beatle Lists* (Poole: Javelin, 1985).

72 Listed in Kevin Howlett, *The Beatles at the Beeb 1962–65: The Story of Their Radio Career* (London: BBC Publications, 1982).

2 The Beatles as recording artists

1 Gareth Pawlowski, *How They Became the Beatles* (New York: Dutton, 1989), 36.

2 The Beatles Ultimate Experience website, First Radio Interview, October 28, 1962, at www.beatlesinterviews.org/db1962.1028.beatles.html (accessed May 18, 2009).

3 Hunter Davies, *The Beatles* (New York: McGraw Hill, 1968), 107.

4 Quoted in David Simons, *Studio Stories* (San Francisco: Backbeat Books, 2004), 18.

5 All quotations from the author's telephone interview with Van Dyke Parks, March 2007.

6 From www.nonesuch.com/artists/brian-wilson.

7 Brian Wilson interviewed by Andy Battaglia, August 30, 2005 at www.avclub.com/content/node/40133/2 (accessed May 18, 2009).

8 Author's telephone interview with Van Dyke Parks, March 2007.

9 Jim Irvin, "The *MOJO* Interview: George Martin," *MOJO* 160 (March 2007), 37.

10 Paul McCartney, quoted on the Beatles Ultimate Experience website: www.beatlesinterviews.org/dba01please.html (accessed May 28, 2009).

11 Geoff Emerick, and Howard Massey, *Here, There, and Everywhere: My Life Recording the Music of the Beatles* (New York: Gotham, 2006), 44.

12 George Harrison, interviewed with the other Beatles by Larry Kane in Chicago, August 20, 1965; at the Beatles Ultimate Experience website: www.beatlesinterviews.org/db1965.0820.beatles.html (accessed May 28, 2009).

13 Ibid.

14 Emerick and Massey, *Here, There, and Everywhere*, 70–1.

15 Ibid., 70.

16 Mark Lewisohn, *The Complete Beatles Recording Sessions*, 36.

17 Ibid., 38.

18 Emerick and Massey, *Here, There, and Everywhere*, 81.

19 Ringo Starr, interviewed on the US radio program *Inner-view* in two parts, 1976; at the Beatles Ultimate Experience website: www.beatlesinterviews.org/db1976.00rs.beatles.html (accessed May 18, 2009).

20 Keith Badman, *The Beatles: Off the Record* (New York: Omnibus, 2000), 210–11.

21 As reported on http://www.rarebeatles.com/photopg7/nonusa/php7466.htm.

22 Author's interview with Van Dyke Parks, March 2007, continued by email.

23 Ringo Starr, interviewed on *Inner-view*.

24 George Harrison, interviewed by *Crawdaddy* magazine, February 1977.

25 Lewisohn, *The Complete Beatles Recording Sessions*, 63.

26 Paul McCartney, interviewed by Alan Smith on June 16, 1966, and published in the *New Musical Express*, June 24, 1966; at the Beatles

Ultimate Experience website:
www.beatlesinterviews.org/db1966.0616.
beatles.html (accessed May 18, 2009).
27 Lewisohn, *The Complete Beatles Recording
Sessions*, 64.
28 Ibid., 67–9.
29 Ibid., 70.
30 Badman, *The Beatles*, 206.
31 Geoffrey Giuliano, *The Lost Beatles
Interviews* (New York: Plume Books, 1994),
236.
32 Emerick and Massey, *Here, There, and
Everywhere*, 120–3.
33 Ibid., 84.
34 Badman, *The Beatles*, 208.
35 Emerick and Massey, *Here, There, and
Everywhere*, 116.
36 Ibid.
37 Badman, *The Beatles*, 209.
38 Ibid., 208.
39 John Lennon, interview in *New Musical
Express*, March 11, 1966; at the Beatles Ultimate
Experience website:
www.beatlesinterviews.org/db1966.0311.
beatles.html.
40 Paul McCartney, interviewed by Alan Smith.
41 Badman, *The Beatles*, 256.
42 Emerick and Massey, *Here, There, and
Everywhere*, 190.
43 Badman, *The Beatles*, 263.
44 Emerick and Massey, *Here, There, and
Everywhere*, 135.
45 Ibid., 139.
46 Ibid., 141.
47 John Lennon, quoted in *Playboy*, "*Playboy*
Interview with John Lennon," 1980, as
reproduced at www.john-lennon.com/
playboyinterviewwithjohnlen-
nonandyokoono.htm.
48 Badman, *The Beatles*, 265.
49 Lewisohn, *The Complete Beatles Recording
Sessions*, 91.
50 Badman, *The Beatles*, 257.
51 Jeff Russell, *The Beatles Complete
Discography* (New York: Universe Publishing,
2006), 97.
52 Badman, *The Beatles*, 269.
53 John Harris, "Sgt. Pepper, the Day the World
Turned Day-Glo," *MOJO* 160 (March 2007),
72.
54 Emerick and Massey, *Here, There, and
Everywhere*, 88.
55 Lewisohn, *The Complete Beatles Recording
Sessions*, 204.
56 Ibid., 95.
57 Harris, "Sgt. Pepper," 76.
58 Emerick and Massey, *Here, There, and
Everywhere*, 189.

59 John Lennon, "John Lennon and Yoko Ono:
Candid Conversation."
60 Ibid.
61 Lewisohn, *The Complete Beatles Recording
Sessions*, 99.
62 Ibid.
63 Badman, *The Beatles*, 288.
64 Lewisohn, *The Complete Beatles Recording
Sessions*, 96.
65 Ibid.
66 Emerick and Massey, *Here, There, and
Everywhere*, 188.
67 Badman, *The Beatles*, 289.
68 John Lennon, interviewed by Norrie
Drummond on May 19, 1967, published in the
New Musical Express, May 27, 1967; at the
Beatles Ultimate Experience website:
http://www.beatlesinterviews.org/db1967.0519.
beatles.html.
69 John Lennon, quoted in *Playboy*, "*Playboy*
Interview with John Lennon," 1980, at
http://www.john-lennon.com/
playboyinterviewwithjohnlennonandyokoono.
htm (accessed May 29, 2009).
70 Badman, *The Beatles*, 389.
71 Ringo Starr, interviewed on *Inner-view*.
72 Walter Everett, *The Beatles as Musicians:
Revolver Through the Anthology* (New York:
Oxford University Press, 1999), 175.
73 Lewisohn, *The Complete Beatles Recording
Sessions*, 138.
74 Badman, *The Beatles*, 387.
75 Ibid., 397.
76 Ringo Starr, interviewed on *Inner-view*.
77 Badman, *The Beatles*, 344.
78 Ibid., 381.
79 Emerick and Massey, *Here, There, and
Everywhere*, 260–1.
80 Badman, *The Beatles*, 381.
81 Ibid.
82 Kenneth Womack, *Long and Winding Roads:
The Evolving Artistry of the Beatles* (New York:
Continuum, 2007), 1.
83 Russell, *The Beatles Complete Discography*,
153.
84 Lewisohn, *The Complete Beatles Recording
Sessions*, 168–9.
85 Emerick and Massey, *Here, There, and
Everywhere*, 277.
86 Ibid., 280.
87 Womack, *Long and Winding Roads*, 293.
88 Russell, *The Beatles Complete Discography*,
142.
89 Ibid.
90 Lewisohn, *The Complete Beatles Recording
Sessions*, 191.
91 Emerick and Massey, *Here, There, and
Everywhere*, 322.

3 Rock and roll music

1 Paul McCartney, quoted in The Beatles, *The Beatles Anthology* (London: Cassell; San Francisco: Chronicle, 2000), 23.

2 John Lennon, quoted in ibid., 67.

3 Quoted in Mark Lewisohn, *The Complete Beatles Recording Sessions: The Official Story of the Abbey Road Years* (London: Hamlyn, 1988), 16.

4 Quoted in ibid., 24.

5 Ibid.

4 "Try thinking more": *Rubber Soul* and the Beatles' transformation of pop

1 Mary Gaitskill, *Veronica* (New York: Vintage, 2005), 28–9.

2 The darker flipside of this latter type, the "beautiful but suddenly dead teenager" genre represented in songs such as "Endless Sleep" (death is foiled in this one), "Patches," "Teen Angel," "Last Kiss," and "Leader of the Pack" largely affirms a romanticized notion of adolescent love rather than prompting any soul-searching. Notable among other parodists of the "death rock" genre, Jimmy Cross alludes to Beatlemania in setting up the tragedy: "I remember we were cruising home from the Beatles concert. I'd had such a wonderful evening, sitting there watching my baby screaming, and tearing her hair out, and carrying on. She was so full of life." Baby dies in a car crash on the way home, of course, but months later Cross's narrator digs up her corpse.

3 Paul McCartney claimed that the title riffed on an "old blues guy's" disparaging comment about Mick Jagger's "plastic soul." Quoted in The Beatles, *The Beatles Anthology* (London: Cassell; San Francisco: Chronicle, 2000), 193.

4 "Love Me Do," the Beatles' first single, appeared on October 5, 1962, while the *Rubber Soul* sessions commenced on October 12, 1965. See William J. Dowlding, *Beatlesongs* (New York: Fireside, 1989), 29, 112.

5 Greg Clydesdale disputes this, arguing that "the Beatles' early compositions showed no sign of their later genius": "Creativity and Competition: The Beatles," *Creativity Research Journal* 18 (2006), 129–39, 132.

6 Kari McDonald and Sarah Hudson Kaufman cite the *Rubber Soul* sessions as integral to the more sophisticated aesthetic: "In earlier recording sessions, the Beatles followed strict studio guidelines, defining where, when, and how they were to record. Beginning with *Rubber Soul*, the Beatles began to break these rules by extending their hours in the studio. By *Revolver*, this was common practice": "'Tomorrow Never Knows': The Contributions of George Martin and His Production Team to the Beatles' New Sound," in Russell Reising (ed.), *"Every Sound There Is": The Beatles'* Revolver *and the Transformation of Rock and Roll* (Aldershot: Ashgate, 2002), 151.

7 See Mark Lewisohn, *The Complete Beatles Chronicle* (London: Hamlyn, 2000), 136–79.

8 Lewisohn remarks, however (ibid., 181), that the band's frustration with their live audience's inability to listen quietly prompted them to give up trying to replicate their earlier inspired performances at the Cavern Club and drove Lennon to shout (inaudible) obscenities at the crowds. Such vexation no doubt contributed to the Beatles' embracing of the studio, a secure space where they could control the quality of their music (indeed, where they could hear their music!) and reward careful listeners with richly brocaded sounds and thoughtful lyrics.

9 Quoted in The Beatles, *The Beatles Anthology*, 193.

10 Quoted in ibid., 197.

11 Indeed, many of the Beatles' fans were disappointed, despite the band's more measured approach to change.

12 One need not cite the riots provoked by the radical musical innovations of Stravinsky, Schoenberg, Berg, and others to understand the shock and frustration of audiences over abrupt experimentalism. In one notorious example, the Beatles' contemporary Bob Dylan faced the wrath of his traditional folk audience when he merged pop technology ("going electric") with his folk aesthetic. In Dylan's case, the experiment resulted in a wider audience, but countless examples of the reverse exist. Some notable ones include Rick Nelson (use of honky-tonk aesthetic), Elvis Costello (experimentation with multiple non-pop/rock genres), and the Violent Femmes (inclusion of "Christian" lyrics). Too much adherence to one's "brand," however, can lead to charges of being formulaic, stale, etc.

13 Theodor Adorno, "On the Contemporary Relationship of Philosophy and Music," in Richard Leppert (ed.), *Essays on Music* (Berkeley: University of California Press, 2002), 135.

14 Theodor Adorno, "Why Is the New Art so Hard to Understand?," in Richard Leppert (ed.), *Essays on Music* (Berkeley: University of California Press, 2002), 128, 131.

15 Theodor Adorno, "On Popular Music," in Richard Leppert (ed.), *Essays on Music* (Berkeley: University of California Press, 2002), 453. Adorno further notes that in typical pop music, "recognition" becomes an end in itself, thus stifling the spontaneity necessary for

advanced art. In *Rubber Soul*, the Beatles move between the two modes.

16 Lewisohn, *The Complete Beatles Chronicle*, 202.

17 Walter Everett, *The Beatles as Musicians: The Quarry Men Through* Rubber Soul (New York: Oxford University Press, 2001), 315. Everett adds that the quirky intro results "from an apparent overdub of McCartney's bottleneck-slide guitar over the bass/drum track."

18 Tim Riley, *Tell Me Why: The Beatles – Album by Album, Song by Song, the Sixties and After* (Cambridge, MA: Da Capo, 2002), 157.

19 Indeed, when the song carries the sexual metaphor to its conclusion, he, not she, will be the driver, and her body, potentially the site of her autonomy, becomes reinscribed as a car, an object.

20 Quoted in Barry Miles, *Paul McCartney: Many Years From Now* (London: Secker & Warburg; New York: Holt, 1997), 270.

21 The Beatles, of course, have a history of toying with their interviewers and duping them with bogus responses.

22 Riley, *Tell Me Why*, 158. Riley correctly identifies as innovative the song's strategy of "inference rather than . . . description." This methodology comes closer to Adorno's conception of the "tension" required by serious music. See Adorno, "On Popular Music," 440.

23 Walter Everett, quoted in The Beatles, *The Beatles Anthology*, 193.

24 Everett, *The Beatles as Musicians*, 333.

25 Interestingly, Dowling reports that Lennon exclusively penned "No Reply," while McCartney was solely responsible for "You Won't See Me." See Dowlding, *Beatlesongs*, 82, 116.

26 Kenneth Womack, *Long and Winding Roads: The Evolving Artistry of the Beatles* (New York: Continuum, 2007), 118.

27 Michael Fraenkel, *"Passing of Body" in Death Is Not Enough: Essays in Active Negation* (London: C. W. Daniel, 1939), 24.

28 John Lennon, quoted in The Beatles, *The Beatles Anthology*, 193.

29 Devin McKinney, *Magic Circles: The Beatles in Dream and History* (Cambridge, MA: Harvard University Press, 2003), 100; Theodor Adorno, "The Aging of the New Music," in Richard Leppert (ed.), *Essays on Music* (Berkeley: University of California Press, 2002), 181.

30 Adorno, "Why Is the New Art so Hard to Understand?," 130.

31 Riley, *Tell Me Why*, 163.

32 Everett, *The Beatles as Musicians*, 329.

33 Womack, *Long and Winding Roads*, 120.

34 Riley, *Tell Me Why*, 165. Riley aptly notes that "none of them mean the same thing below the surface."

35 McKinney, *Magic Circles*, 115.

36 Womack, *Long and Winding Roads*, 124. Womack reminds readers that the song was written for *Help!*, which no doubt helps explain its relative lack of sophistication.

37 Sheila Whiteley, "Love, Love, Love: Representations of Gender and Sexuality in Selected Songs by the Beatles," in Kenneth Womack and Todd F. Davis (eds.), *Reading the Beatles: Cultural Studies, Literary Criticism, and the Fab Four* (Albany: State University of New York Press), 65.

38 John Lennon, quoted in The Beatles, *The Beatles Anthology*, 197. Lennon further adds that he disliked "Run for Your Life."

39 Everett provides a possible rationale with his observation that "Run for Your Life" and "Drive My Car" function as "effective bookends [being] the only two straightforward hard-rocking blues-oriented numbers": *The Beatles as Musicians*, 312.

40 Adorno, "On Popular Music," 439. Adorno contrasts this with "serious" music, which relies on a "concrete totality" in which details are never "an enforcement of a musical scheme." Adorno suggests that the pop listener focuses on differences in the details and avoids contemplation of the whole. In *Rubber Soul*, the Beatles had not yet abandoned the pop musical scheme as dramatically as they were to do in albums such as *Revolver* and *Abbey Road*.

5 Magical mystery tours, and other trips: yellow submarines, newspaper taxis, and the Beatles' psychedelic years

1 Stanislav Grof, MD, *LSD Psychotherapy: Exploring the Frontiers of the Hidden Mind* (Alameda, CA: Hunter House, 1980), 25.

2 See Steve Turner, *The Gospel According to the Beatles* (London: Westminster John Knox Press, 2006), for a full discussion of the evening.

3 Bob Spitz, *The Beatles: The Biography* (New York: Little, Brown, 2005), 564–6.

4 Dr. Max "Feelgood" Jacobson, a personal "Dr. Robert" for Timothy Leary, Andy Warhol, and others, also served as John F. Kennedy's personal physician during his presidency, and often administered "vitamin" injections that left JFK flushed and excited (Martin A. Lee and Bruce Shlain, *Acid Dreams: The Complete Social History of LSD: The CIA, the Sixties, and Beyond* [New York: Grove Press, 1985], 102).

5 Steve Turner, *A Hard Day's Write: The Stories Behind Every Beatles Song* (New York:

HarperCollins, 1999; London: Carlton, 2000), 111.

6 Timothy Leary, Ralph Metzner, and Richard Alpert, *The Psychedelic Experience: A Manual Based on "The Tibetan Book of the Dead"* (New Hyde Park, NY: University Books, 1964), 14.

7 For our more detailed analysis of the psychedelic dimension of *Sgt. Pepper's Lonely Hearts Club Band*, see Russell Reising and Jim LeBlanc, "The Whatchamucallit in the Garden: *Sgt. Pepper* and Fables of Interference," in Olivier Julien (ed.), *Sgt. Pepper and the Beatles: It Was Forty Years Ago* (Aldershot: Ashgate, 2009). For two excellent cultural histories of psychedelia, from which we have both learned, see Lee and Shlain, *Acid Dreams*.

8 Timothy Leary, *Flashbacks: An Autobiography – A Personal and Cultural History of an Era* (New York: Putnam, 1983), 261.

9 Timothy Leary, *High Priest* (Berkeley: Ronin, 1995), 4, 6, 7. Leary also changes "Albert Hall" to "Alpert Hall," a reference to his colleague, Richard Alpert (later Baba Ram Das), in the following: "Now he knows how many moles it takes to fill the Alpert Hall."

10 Cited in Jay Stevens, *Storming Heaven: LSD and the American Dream* (New York: Atlantic Monthly Press, 1987), 57.

11 Albert Hofmann, *LSD: My Problem Child* (Los Angeles: Tarcher, 1983), 15.

12 Leigh Henderson, "About LSD," in *LSD: Still with Us after All These Years* (New York: Lexington Books, 1994), 45–6.

13 Jim DeRogatis, *Kaleidoscope Eyes: Psychedelic Rock from the '60s to the '90s* (Secaucus, NJ: Carol Publishing Group, 1996), 10.

14 Sheila Whiteley, *The Space between the Notes: Rock and the Counter-Culture* (London: Routledge, 1992), 4.

15 Geoff Emerick, with Howard Massey, *Here, There, and Everywhere: My Life Recording the Music of the Beatles* (New York: Gotham, 2006), 167.

16 Russell Reising, "Introduction: 'Of the Beginning,'" in Russell Reising (ed.), *"Every Sound There Is": The Beatles'* Revolver *and the Transformation of Rock and Roll* (Aldershot: Ashgate, 2003), 7.

17 Tim Riley, *Tell Me Why: A Beatles Commentary* (New York: Knopf, 1988), 176.

18 Spitz, *The Beatles*, 596–7, 600.

19 Mark Lewisohn, *The Complete Beatles Chronicle* (London: Hamlyn, 2000), 216.

20 For more on Starr's work on "Tomorrow Never Knows," and on *Revolver* in general, see Steven Baur, "Ringo Round Revolver: Rhythm, Timbre, and Tempo in Rock Drumming," in Reising (ed.), *"Every Sound There Is,"* 171–82.

21 Emerick, *Here, There, and Everywhere*, 8–10.

22 Barry Miles, *Paul McCartney: Many Years from Now* (New York: Henry Holt, 1997), 291–2.

23 See, for instance, Stuart Madow and Jeff Sobul, *The Colour of Your Dreams: The Beatles' Psychedelic Music* (Pittsburgh: Dorrance Publishing, 1992), 4; and Riley, *Tell Me Why*, 178.

24 Walter Everett, *The Beatles as Musicians:* Revolver *through the* Anthology (New York: Oxford University Press, 1999), 44.

25 Ibid., 49.

26 Lewisohn, *The Complete Beatles Chronicle*, 220.

27 For more on the Beatles' frequent use of the subtonic (♭VII) chord during this period, see Ger Tillikens, "A Flood of Flat-Sevenths," in Reising (ed.), *"Every Sound There Is,"* 121–36.

28 Miles, *Paul McCartney*, 286–7.

29 Everett, *The Beatles as Musicians*, 66.

30 Ibid., 66.

31 The Beatles, *The Beatles Anthology*, vol. 3 of the televised series, directed by Geoff Wonfor (Apple, 1996).

32 While scholars like Everett maintain that *Sgt. Pepper*, along with the single that preceded it in the winter of 1967, "capture the Beatles at their peak of creativity, and the introspective psychedelia in the words and sounds of these records would revolutionize popular music even more thoroughly than the Beatles did in 1964," others, like Tim Riley, feel that "*Sgt. Pepper* is the Beatles' most notorious record for the wrong reasons – a flawed masterpiece that can only echo the strength of *Revolver*" (Everett, *The Beatles as Musicians*, 87; Riley, *Tell Me Why*, 203). For a thorough summary of critical responses to *Revolver* since the 1960s, see Reising, "Introduction: 'Of the Beginning,'" 2–9.

33 Lewisohn, *The Complete Beatles Chronicle*, 235.

34 The Beatles, *The Beatles Anthology*, vol. 6, directed by Geoff Wonfor (Apple, 1996).

35 Everett, *The Beatles as Musicians*, 84.

36 Miles, *Paul McCartney*, 303–6, 349–50.

37 George Harrison, *I Me Mine* (San Francisco: Chronicle Books, 2002), 106.

38 Everett, *The Beatles as Musicians*, 132; Lewisohn, *The Complete Beatles Chronicle*, 253.

39 Everett, *The Beatles as Musicians*, 138, 143.

40 Ibid., 141.

41 David Sheff, "John Lennon and Yoko Ono: Candid Conversation," *Playboy*, January 1981, 112.

42 Grof, *LSD Psychotherapy*, 29.

43 R. D. Laing, *The Politics of Experience* (New York: Ballantine, 1967), 190.

44 Leary, *High Priest*, 234. Leary summarized the impact of his first LSD experience in representative terms: "It was the classic visionary voyage and I came back a changed man. You are never the same after you've had that one flash glimpse down the cellular time tunnel. You are never the same after you've had the veil drawn" (34).

45 Sidney Cohen, *The Beyond Within: The LSD Story* (New York: Atheneum, 1966), 177.

46 Everett, *The Beatles as Musicians*, 104.

47 Alan Bisbort and Parke Puterbaugh, *Rhino's Psychedelic Trip* (San Francisco: Miller Freeman, 2000), 74.

48 Stevens, *Storming Heaven*, 57.

49 The first words spoken (by John Lennon) in the 1967 television movie *Magical Mystery Tour*. "Mystery tours" were popular, low-budget getaways in Britain during the period, involving day trips on buses to surprise locations.

50 Cam Cloud, *The Little Book of Acid* (Berkeley: Ronin, 1999), 11.

51 Cohen, *The Beyond Within*, 108.

52 Madow and Sobul, *The Colour of Your Dreams*, 62, 68.

53 Emerick, *Here, There, and Everywhere*, 214–16.

54 See Marsha Alexander, *The Sexual Paradise of LSD* (North Hollywood: Brandon House, 1967); and Warren Young and Joseph Hixson, *LSD on Campus* (New York: Dell, 1966). See also R. N. Ellson, *Sex Happy Hippy* (San Diego: Corinth, 1968).

55 G. Gordon Liddy, *Will: The Autobiography of G. Gordon Liddy* (New York: St. Martin's, 1996), 148.

56 Lee and Shlain, *Acid Dreams*, 117. As the authors note, Liddy's later "arsenal of dirty tricks included LSD and other hallucinogens to neutralize political enemies of the Nixon administration."

57 Miles, *Paul McCartney*, 190. Lennon's comment is cited in G. Barry Golson, *The Playboy Interviews with John Lennon and Yoko Ono: The Final Testament* (New York: Berkeley, 1981), 191.

58 Ian MacDonald, *Revolution in the Head: The Beatles' Records and the Sixties* (New York: Henry Holt, 1994), 258.

59 Emphasis added.

60 Stevens, *Storming Heaven*, 206.

61 Malden Grange Bishop, *The Discovery of Love: A Psychedelic Experience with LSD-25* (New York: Dodd, Mead & Co., 1963), 134.

62 Ibid., 139.

6 Revolution

1 These included John Lennon's acting role in *How I Won the War* (Dick Lester, 1967), Paul McCartney's music for *The Family Way* (Roy Boulting, 1966), George Harrison's film score for *Wonderwall* (Joe Massot, 1968) and Ringo Starr's acting role in *Candy* (Christian Marquand, 1968).

2 Christopher Booker, *The Neophiliacs: The Revolution in English Life in the Fifties and Sixties* (London: Collins, 1969), 311–13.

3 Mark Hertsgaard, *A Day in the Life: The Music and Artistry of the Beatles* (New York: Delacorte, 1995), 228.

4 Ian MacDonald, *Revolution In The Head: The Beatles' Records and the Sixties* (London: Fourth Estate, 1994), 187–8.

5 T. J. O'Grady, *The Beatles: A Musical Evolution* (Boston: Twayne, 1983), 148.

6 David Sheff, *The Playboy Interviews with John Lennon and Yoko Ono*, ed. G. Barry Golson (New York: Playboy Press, 1981), 172.

7 Bob Neaverson, *The Beatles Movies* (London: Cassell, 1997), 92.

8 Bruno Edera, *Full Length Animated Feature Films* (London: Focal Press, 1977), 87.

9 Derek Taylor, sleeve notes, The Beatles, *Yellow Submarine* (Apple PMC 7070, 1969).

10 Barry Miles, *Paul McCartney: Many Years from Now* (London: Secker & Warburg, 1997), 449.

11 George Harrison, *I Me Mine* (London: W. H. Allen, 1982), 118.

12 Sheff, *The Playboy Interviews*, 162–3.

13 Wilfrid Mellers, *Twilight of the Gods: The Beatles in Retrospect* (London: Faber & Faber, 1973), 138.

14 Miles, *Paul McCartney*, 465.

15 Walter Everett, *The Beatles As Musicians: Revolver through the Anthology* (New York: Oxford University Press, 1999), 195.

16 Sheff, *The Playboy Interviews*, 158.

17 See, for example, the comments of Apple director Denis O'Dell, in Denis O'Dell and Bob Neaverson, *At The Apple's Core: The Beatles from the Inside* (London: Peter Owen, 2002), 101–2; and of *Rolling Stone* editor and founder Jann Wenner, in Nicholas Schaffner, *The Beatles Forever* (New York: McGraw Hill, 1977), 113.

18 The Beatles, *The Beatles Anthology* (London: Cassell, 2000), 305.

19 See, for example, Lennon's angry response to Epstein's comments during the recording of "Till There Was You," in Ray Coleman, *Brian Epstein* (Harmondsworth: Penguin, 1990), 175.

20 Mark Lewisohn, *The Complete Beatles Recording Sessions: The Official Story of the Abbey Road Years* (London: Hamlyn, 1988), 141.

21 Geoffrey Giuliano, *Two of Us: John Lennon and Paul McCartney Behind the Myth* (New York: Penguin, 1999), 128.

22 Jann Wenner, *Lennon Remembers: The Rolling Stone Interviews* (Harmondsworth: Penguin, 1971), 51.

23 David Quantick, *Revolution: The Making of the Beatles' White Album* (London: Unanimous, 2002), 13.

24 O'Dell and Neaverson, *At the Apple's Core*, 133–4.

25 Hertsgaard, *A Day in the Life*, 254.

26 Chris Salewicz, *McCartney: The Biography* (London: Queen Anne Press, 1986), 202.

27 Malcolm Doney, *Lennon and McCartney* (New York: Hippocrene, 1981), 89.

28 Philip Norman, *Shout! The True Story of the Beatles* (London: Hamish Hamilton, 1981), 340.

29 Ed Whitley, "The Postmodern White Album," in Ian Inglis (ed.), *The Beatles, Popular Music and Society: A Thousand Voices* (New York: St. Martin's, 2000); Jan Wenner, *Lennon Remembers* (London: Macmillan, 2000), 105–25.

30 Allan Kozinn, *The Beatles* (London: Phaidon, 1995), 180.

31 O'Grady, *The Beatles*, 150.

32 Whitley, "The Postmodern White Album," 122–3.

33 Schaffner, *The Beatles Forever*, 111.

34 Quantick, *Revolution*, 141.

35 Mellers, *Twilight of the Gods*, 131–2.

36 Double albums released in the preceding two years included Bob Dylan, *Blonde on Blonde* (May 1966); Frank Zappa and the Mothers of Invention, *Freak Out* (July 1966); Donovan, *A Gift from a Flower to a Garden* (April 1968); and Cream, *Wheels of Fire* (June 1968).

37 Giuliano, *Two of Us*, 132.

7 On their way home: the Beatles in 1969 and 1970

1 Walter Everett, *The Beatles as Musicians: Revolver through the* Anthology (New York: Oxford University Press, 1999), 244–5.

2 Ibid., 144.

3 The last session, that is, until the three surviving Beatles regrouped to finish John's demos "Free as a Bird" in 1994 and "Real Love" in 1995.

4 This version contradicts the common assumption voiced by Mark Lewisohn (*Day by Day: A Chronology 1962–1989* [New York: Harmony, 1990], 114), Ian MacDonald (*Revolution in the Head: The Beatles' Records and the Sixties* [London: Fourth Estate, 1994], 264), and Steve Matteo (*33 1/3: Let It Be* [New York: Continuum, 2004], 48) that George left because of chronic mistreatment at Paul's hands.

Granted, Paul had been riding George hard, but the rehearsal tapes reveal that "George had finally had enough of John's unwillingness (or inability) to engage in rational communication. His resentment was heightened by Yoko's habitual and presumptuous tendency to speak in John's place which, if accepted, would give her a voice in the future of the group equal to or overshadowing his own" (Doug Sulpy and Ray Schweighhardt, *Get Back: The Unauthorized Chronicle of the Beatles' "Let It Be" Disaster* [New York: St. Martin's, 1997], 169).

5 Sulpy and Schweighhardt, *Get Back*, 177.

6 Philip Norman, *Shout! The Beatles in Their Generation* (New York: MJF, 1981), 383.

7 Paul recalls: "It was like when he told Cynthia he was getting a divorce. He was quite buoyed up by it" (The Beatles, *The Beatles Anthology*, 347).

8 Nicholas Schaffner gives the date as April 9 (*The Beatles Forever* [Harrisburg, PA: Cameron House, 1977], 131), adding that the insert was placed inside "British copies of the album, but deleted by Klein . . . from the American ones" (135). According to McCartney, however, only the press received the insert-added albums: Barry Miles, *Paul McCartney: Many Years From Now* (New York: Henry Holt, 1997), 574; see also Barry Miles, *The Beatles: A Diary – An Intimate Day by Day History* (New York: Barnes & Noble, 2004), 316; and Mark Lewisohn, *The Complete Beatles Chronicle* (New York: Harmony, 1992, 2000), 341.

9 The two key studies are, respectively, William K. Wimsatt, Jr., and Monroe C. Beardsley, "The Intentional Fallacy," in Vincent B. Leitch (ed.), *The Norton Anthology of Theory and Criticism* (New York: Norton, 2001), 1374–87; and Roland Barthes, "The Death of the Author," in Roland Barthes, *Image–Music–Text*, trans. Stephen Heath (New York: Noonday Press, 1977), 142–8. "The evaluation of the work of art remains public; the work is measured against something outside the author," write the former (1381). "A text is not a line of words releasing a single 'theological' meaning (the 'message' of the Author-God) but a multi-dimensional space in which a variety of writings, none of them original, blend and clash," writes Barthes (146).

10 The concept of "timeless" art, although making a post-2000 comeback, is a tenet of modern and romantic notions of art – in short, of humanism. In this vein, Kennneth Womack argues that "the Beatles espouse a sense of hope and the promise of humanity and sameness in the face of an increasingly inexplicable present" (298); they urge "us to embrace the restorative powers of love, friendship, and a universalizing belief in a redeemable past" (*Long and Winding*

Roads: The Evolving Artistry of the Beatles [New York: Continuum, 2007], 306).

11 This is not to say that postmodern approaches have no place in the analysis of Beatles music in 1969 and 1970; however, it is to say that reliable readings begin with knowledge of the history of these so-called swan-songs. On the topic of closure alone, *Let It Be* and *Abbey Road* confound the conventional idea of ending, thus bringing into question postmodernism's much-debated concept of origins in works of art.

12 As late as his last interviews in 1980, Lennon denied any paranoia. He insisted that Paul sabotaged his (John's) songs by cultivating "this atmosphere of looseness and casualness and experimentation . . . I begin to think, well maybe I'm paranoid. But it's not paranoid; it's absolute truth" (David Sheff, *The Playboy Interviews with John Lennon and Yoko Ono*, ed. G. Barry Golson [New York: Playboy Press, 1981], 162). Ian MacDonald accuses Lennon of being the real saboteur: "McCartney left no technical blemish on any Beatles tracks, whoever wrote them. By comparison, Lennon's crude bass playing on "The Long and Winding Road" . . . amounts to sabotage when presented as finished work" (*Revolution in the Head*, 272). In 1969, John, not Paul, was the one usually unfocused, out of tune, tuned out, or late to sessions.

13 John Lennon, quoted in Bob Spitz, *The Beatles: The Biography* (New York: Little, Brown, 2005), 803.

14 This division of labor occurred in February, all Beatles consenting to it.

15 Variously recorded in the main sources, John's outburst was, "I'm sick of being fucked about by men in suits sitting on their fat arses in the city."

16 Mark Lewisohn, *The Beatles Recording Sessions* (New York: Harmony, 1988), 172–6.

17 Miles, *Paul McCartney*, 548.

18 In their study of the Apple saga, Peter McCabe and Robert Schonfeld accuse Paul of hypocrisy: "For somebody who claims to have been so repulsed by Allen Klein, Paul McCartney was nevertheless quite prepared to reap a lot of benefits of Klein's hard work . . . When things went well and Klein secured good deals, Paul promptly placed his signature on the dotted line. When he felt things were not going his way, or were not to his liking, he ran to the open arms of the Eastmans, who were only too delighted to have the opportunity to denounce Allen Klein as a terrible person" (Peter McCabe and Robert D. Schonfeld, *Apple to the Core: The Unmaking of the Beatles* [New York: Pocket Books, 1972], 175–6).

19 Paul had a right to be angry. John had already released three non-Beatle albums (*Unfinished Music, No. 2: Life with the Lions*, *Wedding Album*, *Plastic Ono Band Live Peace in Toronto*) and two singles ("Give Peace a Chance," "Cold Turkey") – all 1969 – and one single ("Instant Karma") in 1970; George had released one solo album (*Electronic Sound*) in 1969, and Ringo had released one solo album in 1970 (*Sentimental Journey*).

20 Psychedelic/baroque pop trailed the Beatles like bad karma into 1969 in the form of the *Yellow Submarine* soundtrack (UK release January 17, 1969), which included indulgences like "Only a Northern Song" and "It's All Too Much."

21 Lewisohn, *The Complete Beatles Chronicle*, 306, 309.

22 Wenner, *Lennon Remembers*, 118.

23 Tim Riley, *Tell Me Why: A Beatles Commentary* (New York: Knopf, 1988), 292.

24 Matteo, *33 1/3*, 49–55.

25 Ibid., 127.

26 These official versions were "recorded at Savile Row on 28 January and remixed on 7 April" (Lewisohn, *The Beatles Recording Sessions*, 172).

27 Sex and religion were sufficiently taboo subjects in 1969 that an audacious use of them – "Christ, you know it ain't easy . . . They're going to crucify me"; "We're only trying to get us some piece/peace" – got John's "ballad" banned on the BBC and many American radio stations.

28 George Martin, quoted in The Beatles, *The Beatles Anthology*, 337.

29 Perhaps a bit melodramatically, Bob Spitz describes Lennon on two typical days in the first half of 1969: "With his painfully thin frame, gaunt face, stringy unkempt hair, and bloodshot eyes, John looked demonic, like a zombie had claimed his tormented soul" (*The Beatles*, 813); he "jabbered incessantly in a thickening Liverpool brogue, but incoherently, like a lunatic, and his appearance reflected it; he looked gaunt, sickly, from the heroin he ingested, his hair long, unkempt, and stringy" (834).

30 MacDonald, *Revolution in the Head*, 292.

31 Spitz, *The Beatles*, 338.

32 *Abbey Road*, Ringo told Max Weinberg, "was tom-tom madness. I had gotten this new kit made of wood, and calfskins, and the toms had so much depth. I went nuts on the toms" (ibid., 185).

33 Paul's contribution (piano and bass) to the tune's "swampiness" is discussed in Miles, *Paul McCartney*, 553.

34 Linda Martin and Kerry Segrave, *Anti-Rock: The Opposition to Rock 'n' Roll* (New York: Da Capo, 1993), 47.

35 Geoff Emerick remembers that John "flatly refused to participate at all in the making of 'Maxwell's Silver Hammer,' which he derisively dismissed" (Geoff Emerick and Howard Massey, *Here, There, and Everywhere: My Life Recording the Music of the Beatles* [New York: Gotham, 2006], 280–1). "Rococo craftsmanship on a Gothic but hollow shell," Walter Everett calls the tune, a judgment shared by the other three Beatles "marking their exits" (*The Beatles as Musicians:* Revolver *Through the* Anthology, 253, 251).

36 More conflicting reports: While MacDonald says the tune "appealed strongly to all four of them" (*Revolution in the Head*, 275), Emerick, who was there, says Paul "was very unhappy, not only with the song itself, but with the idea that the music . . . was being obliterated with noise . . . [He] seemed too beaten down to argue the point with a gleeful Lennon, who seemed to be taking an almost perverse pleasure at his bandmate's obvious discomfort" (*Here, There, and Everywhere*, 300).

37 Sheff, *The Playboy Interviews*, 171.

38 Everett, *The Beatles as Musicians:* Revolver *Through the* Anthology, 259.

39 Emerick, *Here, There, and Everywhere*, 293–4.

40 Ibid., 289.

41 Ibid., 295.

42 Paul recast "Cold Turkey" to brilliant effect as "Let Me Roll It" on 1973's *Band on the Run.*

43 Wenner, *Lennon Remembers*, 120.

44 John Lennon, quoted in Peter Doggett, *Let It Be / Abbey Road* (New York: Schirmer, 1998), 123.

45 By Everett's reckoning. Sulpy and Schweighhardt (*Get Back*, 276) time the track at 8:23.

46 Where millions hear majesty in "Let It Be," Ian MacDonald hears "complacent uplift rather than revelation" (*Revolution in the Head*, 270).

47 Dickinson wrote (*c.* 1862): "Renunciation – is a piercing Virtue – / The letting go / A Presence – for an Expectation" (Poem 745, in Thomas H. Johnson (ed.), *Final Harvest: Emily Dickinson's Poems* [Boston, MA: Little, Brown, 1961]).

48 *Let It Be . . . Naked*'s bonus disc of studio chatter is a paltry twenty-two minutes culled from thousands.

9 The solo years

1 See Richard Dyer's landmark study of the Hollywood movie star apparatus, *Stars* (1980; London: British Film Institute, 1998), which offers detailed commentary on critical and theoretical approaches to the study of star images. A star's image is an evolving composite of traits emanating from a wide range of media texts including promotion (that is, materials created specifically to advance the star) and publicity (or what the media learn about a star – though this is sometimes "planted" by the star in service of their publicity), as well as work product (here, the music, films, books, etc., of the former Beatles), and commentary about a star's work and life (63). See also Christine Gledhill's introduction to her edited volume, *Stardom: Industry of Desire* (London: Routledge, 1991), in which she defines the star as "an intertextual construct produced across a range of media and cultural practices" (xiv–xv).

2 For a detailed account of the Beatles' evolving image and its context in the 1960s, see Michael Frontani, *The Beatles: Image and the Media* (Jackson: University Press of Mississippi, 2007).

3 The Record Industry Association of America (RIAA) began certifying gold albums (500,000 units sold) in 1958, and platinum albums (1 million units sold) in 1976. From 1958 to 1988, the RIAA required sales of 1 million units to certify a single as gold, and 2 million for platinum certification. In 1989, these requirements for singles were lowered to 500,000 and 1 million units sold for gold and platinum certification, respectively.

4 See Renata Adler, "Screen: "Candy," Compromises Galore," review of *Candy* (Cinerama Releasing Corporation movie), *New York Times*, December 18, 1968, 54: "The movie . . . manages to compromise . . . almost anyone who had anything to do with it." *Candy* was followed by a better-received starring role in director Joseph McGrath's *The Magic Christian* (1969), co-starring Peter Sellers. The *New York Times*'s Roger Greenspun called Starr's performance "fine," in a film that was "funny," and full of "lovely victories" ('Screen: Satirical 'Magic Christian,'" *New York Times*, February 12, 1970, 29).

5 See William C. Woods, "Ringo Goes it Solo, Pleasantly Enough," review of the sound recording *Sentimental Journey* (Apple LP), *Washington Post*, May 17, 1970, 142: "pleasant enough . . . [but] nothing is revealed in this collection . . . except that Ringo can't sing, which we knew already, and that he doesn't know it, which we didn't know." Lennon felt "embarrassed" about the album (see Jann Wenner, *Lennon Remembers: The* Rolling Stone *Interviews* (London: Verso, 1971).

6 See Don Heckman, "Recordings: Making a Star of Starr," review of the sound recording *Beaucoups of Blues* (Apple LP), *New York Times*, November 22, 1970, 133: "What is remarkable is . . . that he does it so well."

7 In addition to a documentary he made about British glam rocker T Rex, *Born to Boogie* (1972), Starr appeared in a number of films of variable quality, including Frank Zappa's surrealist depiction of life on the road with the Mothers of Invention, *200 Motels* (1971), Ferdinando Baldi's spaghetti western *Blindman* (1971), the critical and commercial failure *Son of Dracula* (directed by Freddie Francis, 1974), and Ken Russell's *Lisztomania* (1975). Noteworthy more for their directorial excess than the contributions of their actors, these films did little to further Starr's acting career.

8 The *New York Times*'s Loraine Alterman called Ringo an "instant knockout" and "sensational album" ("Ringo Dishes Up," *New York Times*, November 25, 1973, 188).

9 Most notable were those surrounding promoter Bill Sargent's 1976 offer of $50 million for one performance, and those circulating at the time of the Concerts for Kampuchea in 1979, though reunion rumors were a permanent fixture of the 1970s, often fanned by the four principals.

10 See Ben Gerson, "Records: Ringo," review of the sound recording *Ringo* (Apple LP), by Ringo Starr, *Rolling Stone*, December 20, 1973, 73. Gerson expanded on his point: "It is not polemical and abrasive like Lennon's, harsh and self-pitying like Harrison's, or precious and flimsy like McCartney's, but balanced, airy and amiable."

11 *Rolling Stone*'s reviewer called it a "pleasant collection . . . in the winning tradition of Ringo's breakthrough album, *Ringo*" (Tom Nolan, "Good Night Vienna," April 24, 1975, 62).

12 See Larry Rohter, "No Reason to Cry," *Washington Post*, November 3, 1976, D14: "*Rotogravure* is a routine album." Even a positive review in *Melody Maker*, which called it "such a nice jolly record," could not help the album on to the British charts. See "Jolly Nice, Ringo," October 23, 1976, 27.

13 See Chris Welch, "Albums: Ringo Starr: *Ringo the 4th*," *Melody Maker*, February 11, 1978, 20: "There comes a point where a man singing flat and stripped of all legend and nostalgia becomes just a man singing flat." See also, Stephen Holden's review ("Ringo the 4th," *Rolling Stone*, November 17, 1977, 94), in which he judges the album to be "little more than the seedy extravagance of an exiled aristocrat whose legend resounds ever more faintly."

14 See Tom Carson, "Bad Boy," *Rolling Stone*, July 12, 1978, 52. Indicating a growing disaffection with the ex-Beatles, Carson continues, "but a record like Wings' London Town is trash with pretensions, which is worse."

15 See Richard Williams, "Solo Beatles," review of the sound recording *All Things Must Pass* (Apple LP), by George Harrison, *The Times Saturday Review*, January 23, 1971, 17.

16 Among musicians playing on *All Things Must Pass* were Ringo Starr, Alan White (drums), Klaus Voormann (bass), Gary Brooker, Gary Wright, and Billy Preston (keyboards), Pete Drake (pedal steel guitar), members of Badfinger (acoustic guitars) and, late of Delaney and Bonnie and Friends, and now evolving into Derek and the Dominoes, Eric Clapton (guitar), Carl Radle (bass), Jim Gordon (drums), and Bobbie Whitlock (organ and piano), as well as Dave Mason (guitar), and Jim Price and Bobby Keys (trumpet and saxophone, respectively).

17 According to Simon Leng, in his detailed 2006 study of Harrison's solo work, *While My Guitar Gently Weeps* (New York: Hal Leonard, 2006), even Harrison considered some of the album "overcooked" (85). In the booklet accompanying his 2001 remaster of the album, Harrison acknowledged Spector's help in getting the record made, and, in a flash of his understated sense of humor, noted: "In his company I came to realize the true value of the Hare Krishna Mantra."

18 See Jon Landau, "Singles: 'My Sweet Lord'/'Isn't It A Pity," *Rolling Stone*, December 24, 1970, 56. "My Sweet Lord" was number one in the US singles chart, and, backed with "What Is Life," number one in the UK.

19 See Tom Zito's "Within Him, Without Them: The Consciousness of George Harrison" (*Washington Post*, January 3, 1971, F1–F2). Zito judged that the album "would add much speculation to the still unanswered question" – "Who was really the genius behind the Beatles?" *Time* magazine found the album an "expressive, classily executed personal statement . . . one of the outstanding rock albums in years" (William Bender, "Let George Do It," November 30, 1970, 57). The *New York Times*'s Don Heckman wrote: "If anyone had any doubts that George Harrison was a major talent, they can relax . . . This is a release that shouldn't be missed" ("Pop: Two and a Half Beatles," December 20, 1970, 104).

20 See, for example, "Fellow Traveling with Jesus" (*Time*, September 6, 1971, 54–5), which described the Way and the Process, two movements enjoying some popularity among the young. The "Jesus Craze" was the focus of a *Life* feature, also from 1971 (December 31, 1971,

38–9). Additionally, *Look* published a lengthy feature on the growth in popularity of revivals among American youth (Brian Vachon, "The Jesus Movement is Upon Us," February 9, 1971, 5–21).

21 Interestingly, late in 1969, there were press rumors that Lennon would play Christ in the Tim Rice / Andrew Lloyd Webber musical *Jesus Christ Superstar*, to be performed at St. Paul's Cathedral. Apparently he was interested, but it was decided that "a relative unknown should have the starring role," for "someone like Lennon would imprint his own personality to such an extent that people would read the star's character into the character of the part" (See "John and Yoko's Christmas Gifts," *Rolling Stone*, January 21, 1970, 6).

22 See Ben Gerson, "Records: All Things Must Pass" (*Rolling Stone*, January 7, 1971, 46). The *New Yorker*'s Ellen Willis was impressed by the album's "beautiful sound" and an Indian influence that had been "integrated quietly" ("Rock, Etc.: George and John," review of *All Things Must Pass* [Apple LP], by George Harrison, and *John Lennon/Plastic Ono Band* [Apple LP], by John Lennon, *New Yorker*, February 27, 1971, 95–7).

23 The single, the concert, and the resulting *Concert for Bangladesh* album and film, were forerunners of Bob Geldof and Midge Ure's efforts for Ethiopian hunger relief, including the Band Aid project and the single "Do They Know It's Christmas" (1984), and the Live Aid concert (1985) and resulting film and recordings, as well as Michael Jackson and Lionel Ritchie's charity single for East African famine relief, "We Are the World" (1985), Farm Aid (held annually since 1985), Live 8 (2005), and the Live Earth (2007) concerts, films, and recordings. McCartney also followed Harrison's lead, organizing, with UN Secretary-General Kurt Waldheim, the Concerts for the People of Kampuchea, to benefit the victims of Pol Pot's regime in Cambodia, in December 1979.

24 See Stephen Holden, "Records: Living in the Material World," *Rolling Stone*, July 19, 1973, 54: "A seductive record . . . the album stands alone as an article of faith, miraculous in its radiance." Less impressed, the *New York Times*'s Ian Dove called it an "informally produced . . . mélange . . . Introspection . . . abounds here, but it sounds like notes in passing" ("Records: Harrison's Turn," June 6, 1973, 37). See also David Sterritt, "Latest from ex-Beatles McCartney, Harrison," *Christian Science Monitor*, June 29, 1973, 12: "The music never jells solidly enough to support the lyrics' mystical didacticism." *Melody Maker* judged:

"there isn't a bad cut, but at the same time there aren't as many obvious stand-outs as there were on [*All Things Must Pass*]" (Michael Watts, "Living in the Material World," June 9, 1973, 3).

25 See Jim Miller, "Dark Horse: Transcendental Mediocrity," *Rolling Stone*, February 13, 1975, 76. Miller painted a bleak picture: "Stripped of the Beatles' company . . . Harrison's weaknesses as a musician have gradually surfaced." Specifically, "his voice has always been dogged by a limited range and poor intonation, just as his guitar playing, adequate for fills within precise arrangements, has always been rudimentary and even graceless in an affecting sort of way . . . How long will his fans continue to tolerate such mediocrity? . . . George Harrison has never been a great artist, as he himself must know . . . the question becomes whether he will ever again be a competent entertainer."

26 See "Dark Horse," *High Fidelity*, April 1975, 101.

27 The ever-welcoming *Melody Maker*, though approaching the album "with some trepidation, fearing a lot of whining sitar, thudding tablas and groaning out-of-tune voices," happily found that "the Sacred Cowboy has produced a good one" ("Harrison: Eastern Promise," December 21, 1974, 36).

28 See John Rockwell, "Music: George Harrison," *New York Times*, December 21, 1974, 19. See also Larry Rohter, "For Harrison, Some Things Must Pass," *Washington Post*, December 14, 1974, C1, which notes the Washington DC audience's bewilderment at Harrison's musical arrangements and the paucity of Beatles tunes. The *New Yorker* was similarly unimpressed ("At the Garden," January 13, 1975, 30).

29 See Dave Marsh, "Extra Texture," review of *Extra Texture (Read All About It)*, by George Harrison, *Rolling Stone*, November 20, 1975, 75.

30 For positive comment, see Richard Meltzer, "George Harrison Surrenders the Goodies," *Village Voice*, December 20, 1976, 89; see also "Harrison regains his Rubber Soul," *Melody Maker*, November 27, 1976, 23. The *New York Times*'s influential critic John Rockwell, however, found that the album, exhibiting "a certain plodding monotony," "just isn't very interesting" ("Pop Life," *New York Times*, December 24, 1976, 44). *High Fidelity* painted much of the album as "semi-listenable dreck – some of it pallid, some of it self-righteous and stupid" ("George Harrison: Thirty-Three & 1/3," March 1977, 140).

31 The *New York Times*'s John Rockwell found the Beatle era music "delightful," while finding that the solo material retained a "flowing appeal"("Pop Life," *New York Times*, December

24, 1976, 44). The *Washington Post*'s Larry Rohter called the album "an absolute delight" ("Dear Santa: All I Want for Christmas Is No. 11578," *Washington Post*, December 19, 1976, 147).

32 Though not ending until 1977, the marriage had been rife with turmoil for years. Boyd, who had long been the object of Eric Clapton's desire (voiced in his recording "Layla"), married the guitarist in 1979 (divorced 1988).

33 Films include *Time Bandits* (1981), Neil Jordan's *Mona Lisa* (1986), the disastrous *Shanghai Surprise* (1986, starring newlyweds Madonna and Sean Penn), and director Bruce Robinson's critically acclaimed *Withnail and I* (1987) and *How to Get Ahead in Advertising* (1989).

34 See Robert S. Spitz, "George Harrison on the Move," *Washington Post*, March 4, 1979, A1. Later the writer of the respected and mammoth *The Beatles: A Biography* (2005), Spitz praised the album's "sense of structure," which had been absent from the previous four "dreadful mistakes." Here, Harrison "once again proves a first-rate composer." The *Christian Science Monitor* reviewer found the album "not so cloying," but judged that it "suffer[ed] from a blissfully droning and boring sameness" (Sara Terry, *George Harrison*, *Christian Science Monitor*, March 22, 1979, 22). *Rolling Stone*'s Stephen Holden noted that co-producer Russ Titleman and Harrison had presented arrangements that were "the most concise and springy to be found on any Harrison record" ("George Harrison," *Rolling Stone*, April 19, 1979, 90). *High Fidelity* opined that the album seemed to demonstrate that Harrison was "ageing more gracefully than expected" ("George Harrison," May 1979, 125).

35 See Nicholas Schaffner, *The Beatles Forever* (New York: McGraw-Hill, 1978), 135; John Blaney, *Lennon and McCartney: Together Alone* (London: Jawbone Press, 2007), 31–2.

36 See Langdon Winner, "Records: McCartney" (*Rolling Stone*, May 14, 1970, 50). Regarding Wenner's alteration of Winner's review, see Robert Draper, *Rolling Stone Magazine: The Uncensored History* (New York: Doubleday, 1990), 99. The mainstream press was less bothered by the album's promotion. The *Christian Science Monitor*'s David Sterritt applauded McCartney's effort: "Here one realizes again what a crucial factor to the Beatles' success was his talent as both songwriter and singer . . . It's [*McCartney*'s] simple and slight, and it's all deliberately delightful," and judged: "With Paul, unquestionably, lies the future path for Beatle fans" ("Discs: Hello, Paul – Bye-bye

Beatles," June 29, 1970, 8). Similarly, *Time*'s review, though judging it inferior to his Beatles classics, called the album a "tour de force" that "in mood and style . . . marks the same kind of return to simple pleasures . . . that characterizes Bob Dylan's recent work . . . Overall, the new album is good McCartney – clever, varied, full of humor" ("Music: Hello, Goodbye, Hello," April 20, 1970, 57). *Newsweek*'s Hubert Saal opined: "What's extra special about the record is the incredible richness of melody, the tastefulness and wit of the lyrics and the expressive range of McCartney's voice," and, of the album's fourteen songs, "There's not a loser in the bunch" ("The Beatles Minus One," April 20, 1970, 95).

37 Lennon took the photo to be a dig at his and Ono's "bagism" of the 1969 peace campaign, during which he and Ono appeared at press conferences and other public events completely covered by a bag, hence, they maintained, freeing their message of peace of the stereotypes and bigotry that would otherwise attend their appearances.

38 See Jon Landau, "'Ram,'" *Rolling Stone*, July 8, 1971, 42. *Melody Maker* called the album, which failed to "match up" to Harrison's and Lennon's albums (*All Things Must Pass* and *Plastic Ono Band*, respectively), a "good album, by anybody's standards," but, "you expect too much from a man like Paul McCartney. It must be hell living up to a name" (Chris Charlesworth, "Mutton dressed as Ram?," *Melody Maker*, May 27, 1971, 11). The *Christian Science Monitor*'s David Sterritt criticized McCartney's use of "second-hand Beatlisms . . . But this is an eclectic package . . . All in all, it looks like another Beatle has done it again" ("On the Disc Scene: 'Ram,'" *Christian Science Monitor*, July 7, 1971, 4).

39 Robert Palmer, reviewing *Tug of War* (1981), grasped an essential fact about McCartney's compositions: "One can't lambaste Mr. McCartney too strenuously for writing sentimental, home-and-hearth lyrics; that's the kind of person he is. And one of the big changes the Beatles made . . . was their insistence that artists write their own kind of songs, about their own realities" ("Paul McCartney's Latest is Exquisite but Flawed," *New York Times*, April 25, 1982, Section 2, pp. 1, 19).

40 See John Mendelsohn, "'Wild Life,'" review of *Wild Life* (Apple LP), by Wings, *Rolling Stone*, January 20, 1972, 48; and David Sterritt, "Discs: Hello, Paul – Bye-bye Beatles," review of *McCartney* (Apple LP), by Paul McCartney, *Christian Science Monitor*, June 29, 1970, 8.

41 See, for example, Craig McGregor's "Rock's 'We Are One' Myth" (*New York Times*, May 9, 1971, D15). In the aftermath of Altamont, which blighted the countercultural ideal of community under an alcohol and drug-fueled explosion of thuggery and violence, McGregor questioned the most idyllic and cherished claim of the counterculture, "We are all one."

42 British troops fired on civil rights protesters in Derry, Northern Ireland, killing fourteen, including six minors.

43 McCartney's interaction with the law included a 1980 arrest for cannabis possession while entering Japan for a Wings tour.

44 Sir Lew Grade convinced McCartney to make the special, produced by the same team responsible for Elvis Presley's "comeback special" on NBC, in 1968. Grade, who controlled half the publishing royalties for McCartney's songs, questioned the co-writing credits that Linda McCartney was getting on a number of songs on *Ram*. He agreed to stop pressing the issue if McCartney would do the special.

45 Among the "routines" were McCartney giving an acoustic performance of a medley including "Blackbird," "Bluebird," "Michelle," and "Heart of the Country," while his wife snapped photographs; Wings performing "Mary Had a Little Lamb" in a pastoral setting; and a Busby Berkeley-inspired dance number featuring McCartney singing "Gotta Sing, Gotta Dance" and hoofing it with dancers attired in half woman / half man regalia. See John J. O'Connor's "TV: McCartney and His Group on ABC Tonight" (*New York Times*, April 16, 1973, 75), in which he judged that the performances by McCartney and Wings made the special "definitely worth watching." Yet the *Washington Post*'s Tom Zito, ("Hamming and Homage," April 17, 1973, B6) bemoaned the emphasis placed on Linda McCartney, leading him to "speculate what heights McCartney, and also John Lennon, might be able to reach were they not respectively Paul and Linda and John and Yoko . . . Mrs. McCartney's previous careers . . . certainly don't qualify her to perform in public." *The Times*'s reviewer Alan Coren jibed that it "was not the sort of programme you make a come-back with. It was the sort of programme you make a come-back after" ("James Paul McCartney," May 11, 1973, 11).

46 See Lenny Kaye, "Red Rose Speedway," *Rolling Stone*, July 5, 1973, 68.

47 The *Christian Science Monitor* noted a "sometimes facile, sometimes vulgar hipness . . . but nothing quite disturbs the quiet listenability of Paul's cheery work" (Sterritt, "Latest From ex-Beatles McCartney, Harrison,"

12). The *New York Times*'s Ian Dove noted that McCartney, "the romantic, the seeker after melody," had fared less well with the critics than Lennon's introspection and Harrison's blossoming talent – approaches "more fashionable to trendy critical ears" – but judged the new LP McCartney's best to date ("Records by McCartney," May 2, 1973, 37).

48 See Loraine Alterman, "Pop: Paul's Grooves Will Grab You," *New York Times*, December 2, 1973, 208. See also Jon Landau, "Band on the Run" (Apple LP), *Rolling Stone*, January 31, 1974, 48, 50. The *Washington Post*'s Tom Zito called it "largely enjoyable, insubstantial fluff ensconced in some of the best rock melodies currently being written" ("The Beatles: Looking Back," P8). *High Fidelity* called *Band on the Run* McCartney's "best since *Ram*," and noted: "Not everyone need be a poet . . . and the music's lack of lyrical import diminishes the product not at all" ("Paul McCartney: Band on the Run," April 1974, 124).

49 The *Washington Post*'s Tom Zito called *Venus and Mars* the "first true post-Beatles Beatles album," mixing "clever, provocative lyrics, hummable melodies, unusual tonalities, classical timbres and a refined audio approach . . . in brief, just the sort of things we'd expect of a new Beatles record" ("Hey, Venus, Could That Be a New Beatles Album?," July 6, 1975: 71). *Melody Maker* concluded that "this new collection of songs will eventually sink into the collective rock consciousness and become widely appreciated as another triumph for Wings and their song writing bass player" ("Wings: Shooting Stars!," May 31, 1975, 22).

50 *Rolling Stone*'s Stephen Holden found *At the Speed of Sound* to lack the "effervescence" of its predecessor, but nevertheless applauded McCartney's ability to "play the studio like an instrument," so evident on this 'spectacularly well arranged and recorded' effort. More proof that McCartney had gained some level of acceptance with the once hostile *Rolling Stone* critics, the review of "Silly Love Songs" found it an "acceptably didactic" and "clever retort" to his critics. Nevertheless, Holden registered concern over McCartney's studio dexterity hampering his songwriting, for "the best McCartney songs will most certainly outlast all the studios in which they were recorded" ("On the Wings of Silly Love Songs," May 20, 1976, 67, 69).

51 See Mark Kernis, "McCartney and Wings Just Won't Fly," *Washington Post*, April 16, 1978, A1. Kernis griped about "music so light that it may disappear altogether." *Rolling Stone*'s Janet Maslin found the album "so lighthearted" that

the "feeling of familial strength and affection is virtually the only thing that binds it to earth" (June 15, 1978, 89, 91–2). *High Fidelity*, however, applauded the album as a distinct improvement over the "melodic milk" of *At the Speed of Sound*, and welcomed the deeper complexity of the lyrics which indicated a "more complete artist" (Toby Goldstein, "London Town: So What's Wrong with Silly Love Songs?," July 1978, 120).

52   *Rolling Stone* quipped that "McCartney's gross indulgence is matched only by his shameless indolence, and *Back to the Egg* represents the public disintegration of a consistently disappointing talent" (Timothy White, "Back to the Egg," August 23, 1979, 56). The *Washington Post* was somewhat more charitable, finding that, from "a purely pop standpoint," the album was "difficult to fault," but that McCartney was sounding "more like a McCartney imitator" (Harry Sumrall, "Paul McCartney's Scrambled 'Egg,'" July 22, 1979, A1). The *New York Times*'s John Rockwell found the album "curiously indifferent and casual" ("The Pop Life," June 29, 1979, C24).

53   See Stephen Holden, "McCartney II," *Rolling Stone*, July 24, 1980, 54. See also Rockwell, "The Pop Life," C14. The *Washington Post*'s Richard Harrington ("McCartney and Sinatra: The Past Is Still Best," June 15, 1980, A1) found the album a "miserable mistake."

54   See Jann Wenner, "Man of the Year: John Lennon," *Rolling Stone*, February 7, 1970, 24–5.

55   See Wenner, *Lennon Remembers*, 41.

56   Ibid., 75.

57   The proceeds financed a black-culture center in London.

58   The Plastic Ono Band was Lennon and Ono's ever-changing band – in effect, whoever they were playing with at the time. Among those playing in the band were Eric Clapton, Yes drummer Alan White, bassist Klaus Voormann, Harrison, and Starr. In September 1969, Lennon, Ono, Clapton, Voorman, and White played the Toronto Rock and Roll Revival. Their performance was released as *Live Peace in Toronto, 1969*, in December of that year, and rose to number ten in the US album charts.

59   Lennon described the role of the artist in the 1971 *Rolling Stone* interview: "If I could be a fuckin' fisherman, I would! . . . It's no fun being an artist . . . I resent performing for fuckin' idiots who won't know – who don't know – anything. 'Cause they can't feel – I'm the one that's feeling, 'cause I'm the one expressing what they are trying to. They live vicariously through me and other artists . . . But the pain . . .

ignorance is bliss or something" (Wenner, *Lennon Remembers*, 106).

60   The *Christian Science Monitor*'s David Sterritt commented on the "excruciatingly powerful" solo effort: "The overall tone of the record is so open and self-revelatory that it seems as impolite for the listener to quarrel with them as it is for Lennon to inflict them on his audience" ("Plastic Ono Band," 4). The *New York Times*'s Don Heckman, however, was less impressed, calling the album a "group of empty selections," and continuing: "Curiously, the album resembles Paul McCartney's recent solo outing [i.e. *McCartney*] in its dogged emphasis upon musical self-centeredness. Clearly, these are two artists who lost something important when their intimate working partnership deteriorated" ("Pop: Two and a Half Beatles," 104). *The Times Saturday Review*'s Richard Williams called the album "almost unbearably stark. It is not an album I can put on for pleasure" ("Solo Beatles," January 23, 1971, 17). The *New Yorker*'s Ellen Willis in her generally positive review of the album, called the music "artfully simple," with lyrics that are "mostly spare, sometimes biting, sometimes self-indulgent" ("George and John," February 27, 1971, 97).

61   New Left radical and one-time president of the Students for a Democratic Society (SDS) Todd Gitlin, in reacting to Lennon's first two solo albums and the publication of *Lennon Remembers*, applauded Lennon for shedding the myths of the Beatles and the counterculture, and for providing a path for a badly fragmented and rudderless movement: "Lennon revives the idea of leader as exemplar." He expressed a desire that Lennon's authenticity and "public struggle to be free" might spark a new "commonality" that could resuscitate political and social activism ("John Lennon Speaking . . . .," *Commonweal*, September 22, 1972, 500–3).

62   Among causes picked up by Lennon and Ono was the plight of members of a Scottish shipbuilders union threatened with losing their jobs due to the withdrawal of subsidies from the British government. They also protested against the presence of British troops in Northern Ireland, backed efforts to have the case of convicted A6 murderer James Hanratty reexamined (Hanratty was the last man executed in Great Britain, in 1965), and supported the editors of *Oz*, an underground paper that was on trial for obscenity.

63   See Tom Zito, "Peace, Love, Art, and Yoko," *Washington Post*, October 9, 1971, C1.

64   *Melody Maker*'s Roy Hollingsworth gushed: "It's the best album of the year and for me it's

the best album he's done, with anything or with anyone at any time" ("Pop Albums: Imagine," October 9, 1971, 21). The *Christian Science Monitor*'s David Sterritt called the album "solid and likeable" ("Will the Real Beatle Please Sing Out?," January 28, 1972, 13). The *Washington Post*'s Tom Zito called it an "ambitious and almost fully realized effort. Far and away better than his first solo album" ("Christmas Records," November 28, 1971, 128).

65 See "Records: 'Imagine,'" review of the sound recording Imagine (Apple LP), by John Lennon, *Rolling Stone*, October 28, 1971, 48.

66 Wenner, *Lennon Remembers*.

67 See Gitlin, "John Lennon Speaking . . . ."

68 Inmates had seized prison guards, leading to a four-day standoff that culminated with New York governor Nelson Rockefeller ordering an assault by New York state troopers, leaving twenty-eight prisoners and nine hostages dead.

69 See Jon Wiener, *Come Together: John Lennon in His Time* (1984; Chicago: Illinois University Press, 1991). Wiener's brilliant study of Lennon's political evolution, with his *Gimme Some Truth: The John Lennon FBI Files* (Berkeley: University of California Press, 1999), paints a harrowing picture of a paranoid Nixon administration run amok in the maintenance of its power.

70 A contentious custody battle with Ono's former husband, Tony Cox, continued for years and ended with Cox defying the court's granting of custody to the Lennons and disappearing with Kyoko in 1977. Kyoko reestablished contact with her mother in the early 1990s.

71 According to the *New York Times*, the single "Woman is the Nigger of the World"/"Sisters, O Sisters") received a citation from the New York chapter of the National Organization of Women (NOW), for its "strong profeminist statement" (Laurie Johnston, "Women's Group to Observe," August 25, 1972, 40).

72 "What can one say when confronted with incipient artistic suicide?" wondered *Rolling Stone*'s Stephen Holden, over this "shallow and derivative" and condescending album: "Their [Lennon and Ono's] strategy seems to be to try to radicalize what they must envisage as an ignorant stupid mass of working-class teenagers and ghetto dwellers by 'getting down to their level'" ("Records: *Some Time in New York City*," July 20, 1972, 48). Even Britain's *Melody Maker*, loath to criticize the work of the solo Beatles, commented, "I'm afraid people are right when they criticize him for sitting comfortably at home in New York and writing about something on which he's in no way qualified to pontificate." Particularly troubling were Lennon's – and

McCartney's – "Irish" songs: "How sad that the only thing in years on which he and Paul have agreed should have drawn from both their very worst work. Neither "The Luck of the Irish" nor [McCartney's] "Give Ireland Back to the Irish" can do anything but increase the bigotry of the already ignorant" ("Albums: *Some Time in New York City*," 25). Yet, in an earlier review appearing in the magazine, Roy Hollingsworth called it "the full fist of revolt . . . It is certainly the most valid, most relevant snarl at The Powers That Be that there ever has been" ("The People's Album," Roy Hollingsworth, "Albums: *Some Time in New York City*," review of *Some Time in New York City* [Apple LP], by John Lennon and Yoko Ono, with the Plastic Ono Band, *Melody Maker*, June 10, 1972, 9).

73 Reviewing Lennon's previous album, *Imagine*, *High Fidelity*'s critic identified Lennon's unique perspective and appeal: "Lennon . . . demands that his audience not only judge his music but judge him as well. Pop albums rarely make such intriguing demands on the listener; for that alone John Lennon passes muster with me" (Henry Edwards, "The Provocative Lennon–Ono Marriage," January 1972, 77).

74 The *New York Times*'s Loraine Alterman judged the album "a fascinating piece of work" ("Ringo Dishes Up," November 25, 1973, 188). The *Washington Post*'s Tom Zito noted that the album was full of "raunchy rock 'n' roll as well as bouncy, soaring, string-infused songs, but it's Lennon's heavy lyrics about politics and life that really matter." The review was mildly critical of Lennon's paeans to Ono: "Lennon's lyrics . . . sometimes get so personal that they bore the listener" ("The Beatles: Looking Back Ten Years," February 17, 1974, P8). Calling the album "an attractive rock-oriented collection," *High Fidelity*'s Henry Edwards wrote: "I think John Lennon best serves his talents when he dispenses with the heavy-handed propaganda that has marred his recent recorded excursions. *Mind Games* offers promise for the future" ("Mind Games," March 1974, 109). *Rolling Stone*'s Jon Landau, while critical of Lennon's "worst writing yet," nevertheless marked the album as an improvement over *Some Time in New York City*. *Mind Games* revealed "another major artist of the Sixties [i.e. Dylan is also singled out] lost in the changing musical environment of the Seventies, helplessly trying to impose his own gargantuan ego upon an audience that has already absorbed his insights and is now waiting hopefully for him to chart a new course" ("Mind Games," January 3, 1974, 61).

75 *Rolling Stone*'s Ben Gerson applauded the album's "relative clear-headedness" ("Walls and Bridges," November 21, 1974, 76).

76 Lennon and his band played "Imagine," "Slippin' and Slidin'," and "Stand By Me." Lennon, whose relationship with Sir Lew Grade had suffered since Grade's purchase of Lennon and McCartney's publishing rights from Dick James in 1969, had decided to follow McCartney's lead and make peace with Grade. Grade's ATV had distributed McCartney's *James Paul McCartney* special.

77 In October 1975, the New York State Supreme Court reversed the deportation order, chastised the INS for its "selective prosecution" of the Lennons, and ordered that his application for residency be reconsidered.

78 See Laurence Shames's lengthy account of trying to track down the reclusive Lennon, "John Lennon, Where Are You?," *Esquire*, November 1980, 32.

79 See Dave Marsh's "An Open Letter to John Lennon" (*Rolling Stone*, November 3, 1977, 50). Marsh's piece perfectly captures the unique leadership role filled by rock stars in the 1960s, and retained by some part of the audience in the 1970s: "Always before, you've been there, if not defining the issues and causes for us, at least putting them in some kind of context or blowing any smug and silly convictions apart. I am not of the opinion that you are the only person in the world who can do that – for me, doing it is the essence of what being a rock star (rather than an entertainer or whatever) is all about. But you always did it best."

80 See John Lennon and Yoko Ono, "A Love Letter from John and Yoko, To People Who Ask Us What, When and Why," *New York Times*, May 27, 1979, E20.

81 *Melody Maker*'s Ian Pye blasted the album as a "godawful yawn [that] reeks of an indulgent sterility" ("Double Fantasy," November 22, 1980, 26). The *Washington Post*'s Richard Harrington labeled it "commercial, easy-listening pablum . . . What's obvious from "Double Fantasy" is that Lennon and Ono are no longer avant-gardists, but derriere guards" ("Pap From John and Yoko," November 26, 1980, A1). But Lennon and Ono had defenders, including the influential Robert Palmer and Robert Christgau. Palmer, reviewing the single "(Just Like) Starting Over," backed with Ono's "Kiss Kiss Kiss," in the *New York Times*, noted that Lennon's track, though "sentimental and somewhat obvious," confirmed his stature as a consummate pop tunesmith ("The Pop Life: '[Just Like] Starting Over,'" October 24, 1980, C15). Christgau, in a review appearing in the

Village Voice a month after Lennon's murder, called *Double Fantasy*, with "its rich, precise sound, command of readymades from New Orleans r&b to James Brown funk, from magical mystery dynamics to detonating synthesizers," one of "the two albums released in 1980 (Poly Styrene's dreamlike *Transluscence* is the other) to put the anonymous usages of studio rock to striking artistic purpose" ("Symbolic Comrades," January 14, 1981, 32). *High Fidelity*'s Mitchell Cohen grieved the loss of Lennon and the transformation of the album by his murder from a welcome "step" to "a stop" ("John Lennon's Last," February 1981, 92). And *Rolling Stone*'s Stephen Holden, in a review perhaps softened in the wake of his slaying, noted of Lennon that he seemed "calm, confident, and content . . . He doesn't appear driven to deliver a major statement – so naturally he does" ("Lennon's Music: A Range of Genius," January 22, 1981, 70).

82 In the wake of Lennon's death, *Double Fantasy* was awarded the 1981 Grammy for Album of the Year.

83 "Lennon Has a Legacy," *Nation*, December 20, 1980, 657.

84 Todd Gitlin, "The Lennon Legacy," *The Center Magazine*, May/June 1981, 4.

85 See Terry Eastland, "In Defense of Religious America," *Commentary*, June 1981, 45; also Dorothy Rabinowitz, "John Lennon's Mourners," *Commentary*, February 1981, 58–61.

86 See Richard Brookhiser, "John Lennon, RIP," *National Review*, December 31, 1980, 1555. He continued: "It is hard to think of a zany idea zipping through the ether which the Beatles, as cultural lightning rods, did not conduct – psychedelia, Maharishi Mahesh Fakir, all we are saying is give peace a chance."

87 See Chet Flippo, *Yesterday: The Unauthorized Autobiography of Paul McCartney* (New York: Doubleday, 1989), 373–4.

88 See David Wild, "'The Lives of John Lennon,'" *Rolling Stone*, October 6, 1988, 21. Irish rock band U2's lead singer, Bono, went after the author on 1988's *Rattle and Hum* album, where, on the obviously Lennon-inspired "God Part II," he sings of Goldman: "Instant karma's gonna get him, if I don't get him first."

89 The *Village Voice*'s Davitt Sigerson commented: "After a decade of drivel, it has taken McCartney only six tunes' worth of *Tug of War*'s meaty entertainment to get us ready for some more of the old charm. Readier, indeed, than at any time since *Abbey Road*" ("Paul Carries That Weight," May 11, 1982, 64). The *New York Times*'s Robert Palmer called the

album an "exquisitely crafted though lyrically flawed new album . . . his most ambitious piece of work in a number of years . . . as finely crafted as his work with the Beatles. It's too bad Mr. Lennon isn't around to goad him into making a masterpiece" ("Paul McCartney's Latest is Exquisite but Flawed," *New York Times*, April 25, 1982, Section 2, pp. 1, 19). *Stereo Review*'s Mark Peel was less convinced, stating: "McCartney has been coasting on inoffensive product for so long that when he tries to turn up the energy this time out, not a lot happens" ("McCartney and Friends," June 1982, 76).

90 Critics, both those applauding and those criticizing the album, agreed that Harrison largely ignored contemporary music currents. *Melody Maker*'s Ray Coleman said of Harrison: "Remaining true to himself and his convictions, he's produced an album redolent of a more optimistic, positive period in our history, musical and otherwise" ("George Harrison: Somewhere in England," June 6, 1981, 27). The *New York Times*'s Robert Palmer applauded "All Those Years Ago" for being "plainspoken and musically effective." Yet he also criticized Harrison, who "has said most of what he says here before, and in more effective songs." Further, the "studio players and rock veterans who back him sound utterly anonymous and interchangeable; Mr. Harrison's crying guitar is the album's only distinctive instrumental voice, and there isn't nearly enough of it" ("Two Icons of Rock Music," May 31, 1981, D23). *Rolling Stone*'s critic concluded a generally negative review of the album with this characterization of Harrison: "The most paradoxical of the ex-Beatles, George Harrison is an enigmatic mixture of exquisite craftsmanship and heavy-handed hack work, touching sincerity and plain disingenuousness. As it stands, *Somewhere in England* is neither here nor there" (August 6, 1981, 44).

91 See Robert Palmer, "The Pop Life: Did Ringo Starr Alone Escape Trap of Beatles?," *New York Times*, November 11, 1981, C26. See also Nicholas Schaffner, "Stop and Smell the Roses," *Rolling Stone*, February 4, 1982, 55, in which the album is judged "altogether innocuous and intermittently engaging."

92 In addition to a documentary he made about British glam rocker T Rex, *Born to Boogie* (1972), he appeared in a number of films of variable quality, including Frank Zappa's surrealist depiction of life on the road with the Mothers of Invention, *200 Motels* (1971), Ferdinando Baldi's spaghetti western, *Blindman* (1971), the critical and commercial failure *Son of Dracula* (1974), and Ken Russell's *Lisztomania*

(1975). Noteworthy more for their directorial excess than for the contributions of their actors, these films did little to further Starr's acting career.

93 Starr also played "Mr. Conductor" on the American spinoff *Shining Time Station*, which debuted at the end of the decade.

94 See Stephen Holden, "Pop View: Rock Grows Up, Gracefully and Otherwise," *New York Times*, November 8, 1987, H29. Holden found *Cloud Nine* to be a "pleasingly tuneful album" which "explicitly evokes the Beatles' more romantic psychedelic music of the late 1960s." Holden found that the arrangements "may even be an improvement over those on Mr. Harrison's 1970 post-Beatle blockbuster, *All Things Must Pass*." The *Christian Science Monitor* was similarly impressed by "an amiable collection of songs . . . [several of which] happily recall the Beatles" (Amy Duncan, "Soundtakes: George Harrison, *Cloud Nine*," November 18, 1987, 21). *Rolling Stone*'s David Wild called the album an "expertly crafted, endlessly infectious record" – Harrison's best since *All Things Must Pass*. The album was "an especially heartwarming return to form because it suggests Harrison has come to terms with his own Beatledom . . . *Cloud Nine* is a totally fab record that lives up to the legacy of all those years ago" ("'Cloud Nine,'" December 3, 1987, 80).

95 The *New York Times*'s John Rockwell judged that *Traveling Wilburys: Volume One*, "in its buoyant good spirits, clever songwriting and impassioned singing and playing," is "as good-spirited an album as you're likely to hear this year" ("Old Timers Out for a Spin Cut a Couple of Disks," November 13, 1988, H27). The *Washington Post*'s Mike Joyce called the album "hard to resist" ("Records: Traveling Wilburys Vol. 1," November 16, 1988, D7).

96 After three years of negotiations between the surviving Beatles, the Beatle widows, Apple Corps Ltd., Cirque du Soleil, and the MGM Mirage, and after two years of production, *The Beatles: Love* premiered in June 2006, and continues to play in the theater constructed for it.

97 Harrison's guest appearances included work on Jeff Lynne's 2001 Electric Light Orchestra album *Zoom*, as well as a new composition, "Horse to the Water," which appeared on Jools Holland's *Small World, Big Band* (2001), and had been the focus of Harrison's last recording session, barely two months before his death.

98 See Adam Bernstein, "George Harrison Dies, 58, Pushed Fab Four in New Directions," *Washington Post*, December 1, 2001, A01.

99 See Allan Kozinn, "Music of a Beatle Who Never Stopped," *New York Times*, November 17, 2002, A27. Kozinn called the music "vintage Harrison" – "Harrison's trademark slide guitar shines through everywhere ... This is not a guitarist who retired to the garden."

100 Live collections include *Unplugged* (1991), *Paul is Live* (1993), and *Tripping the Live Fantastic*.

101 See Stephen Holden, "Songs of Innocence and Experience for the Pop Fan of a Certain Age," *New York Times*, November 28, 1997, E1, 33.

102 The divorce was settled in July 2007, with Mills reportedly receiving a settlement of £70 million.

103 Reviewing Starr's follow-up, *Vertical Man*, the *New York Times*'s Alann Kozinn, in discussing Starr's decade-long effort at "rekindling a career," noted that *Time Takes Time* "should have done the trick: it was bright, energetic and pleasantly Beatlesque, but it disappeared without hitting the charts" ("Ringo Outdistances His Past, Finally," June 21, 1998, AR28).

104 Starr recognized that his recording career had hit hard times, telling the *New York Times*: "From *Goodnight Vienna* on, the records were going downhill ... It wasn't the producers' or the musicians' fault, but mine. I was just turning up, really. I wasn't involved" (Alann Kozinn, "Ringo Starr, a 60's [*sic*] Relic? Not if He Can Help It," May 31, 1992, H24).

105 The *New York Times*'s Alan Kozinn called *Vertical Man*, with its roster of guests (including Harrison and McCartney, Joe Walsh, Tom Petty, Steve Cropper, Brian Wilson, Steven Tyler, Ozzy Osbourne, and Alanis Morisette), "a tightly crafted, appealingly upbeat album ... clearly meant as entertainment rather than innovation" ("Ringo Outdistances His Past, Finally," June 21, 1998, AR28).

10 Any time at all: the Beatles' free phrase rhythms

1 This essay is based on presentations made in 1996 to Music Theory Midwest in Kalamazoo and to the Society of Music Theory in Baton Rouge. Each song title mentioned in the text is followed by an abbreviation in parentheses indicating the compact disc on which the reader may locate the song. Table 10.1 provides identifying features of these albums.

2 These concepts have been well rehearsed, but, with regard to related topics, I wonder why interest has not been recorded in the freely ametrical introductions to "Drive My Car" and "Here, There and Everywhere," or in the

similarly ametrical speech-based rhythms in "Happiness is a Warm Gun," done in a manner similar to those in "Across the Universe," of which Lennon himself has said, "Such an extraordinary meter and I can never repeat it!" G. Barry Golson (ed.), *John Lennon and Yoko Ono: The Final Testament* (New York: Berkley Books, 1981), 202.

3 Hypermeter, a term coined by Edward T. Cone in *Musical Form and Musical Performance* (New York: Norton, 1968), in which book it is a central issue, refers to the combinations of measures, the downbeats of which have alternately strong and weak accents, so that a metric pattern, often repeated in a regular way such as four bars plus four bars, exists at levels greater than that within the bar. Cone's hypermeter is a refinement of a method of rhythmic analysis, relating patterns of rhythmic modes to the accents of prosody, developed by Grosvenor W. Cooper and Leonard B. Meyer in *The Rhythmic Structure of Music* (Chicago: University of Chicago Press, 1956).

4 Numbers in parentheses refer to the corresponding timings programmed into the compact discs.

5 It should be made clear that because the Beatles did not notate their music in any way, all determinations as to time signatures in any discussion or transcription of the Beatles' music are based solely upon a listener's interpretation of accent and tempo. So whereas the Beatles often played "shuffle" rhythms that divided beats into three parts, they would have been unaware that they were playing in 6/8, 9/8, or 12/8 meters. And any discussion below as to meters such as 18/8 or 24/8 simply reflects compound measures that are extended by one or more (two, or four, in these two examples) dotted quarter-beats. Not only did the Beatles not read music, but they only rarely resorted to the notation of even the chord changes; they normally played and sang all of their own parts "by memory," teaching parts to each other via "head arrangements." They often had trouble recalling the correct lyrics, and so sometimes recorded their vocals while reading from their lyrics.

6 In many 1969 recordings with the Beatles, Harrison routes his amplified guitar signal through a Leslie cabinet, characterized by its rotating horns, originally intended for a Hammond organ. The rotating speaker produces a Doppler-shifted vibrato along with a strong tremolo in dynamics, giving the sustaining guitar tones an atmospheric, whirring quality. The Telecaster is a solid-body Fender guitar known for its metallic tone,

chiefly through its wide use through the 1960s in country music. A guitar's lead pickup is closest to the bridge, thus having the best location to amplify the string's upper partials, for a biting tone that cuts through the texture better than the "rhythm pickup," closer to the middle of the string for more emphasis on the fundamental and warmer lower partials.

7 While other arrangements are common, phrases usually group themselves into pairs, so that an initial phrase, the antecedent, poses a problem (as by ending with a half cadence) that is solved by an "answering" phrase, the consequent (which always closes with a more conclusive authentic cadence). Such an arrangement, even if the group contains more than a single antecedent or consequent phrase, is referred to as a period, a standard tonal form for hundreds of years before it was adopted by the Beatles.

8 In usage (chiefly British) pertaining to classical music, the term "bridge" usually refers to a transition. In popular music, it connotes instead a section that contrasts with the verses and chorus. It frequently begins with a tonicized subdominant and often leads to a tonicized dominant, ending with a dissonant, retransitional dominant seventh to prepare the return of the following verse. And the term "verse" is not synonymous with its use in relation to the introductory section of a Tin Pan Alley number. Instead, the verse of a rock song is the passage that is repeated numerous times in between choruses, with different stanzas of lyrics for at least its first two appearances.

9 William Rothstein, *Phrase Rhythm in Tonal Music* (New York: Schirmer, 1989), 80–1.

10 Mozart's frequent dependence upon such a conclusory extension is the topic of Janet Schmalfeldt, "Cadential Processes: The Evaded Cadence and the 'One More Time' Technique," *Journal of Musicological Research* 12 (1992), 1–52.

11 The term "elision" is often used either to indicate (1) the simultaneous ending of one phrase with the beginning of another, or (2) the absence of some material that is either present only hypothetically, or was present in a previously heard version and is later abbreviated. For the sake of clarity, the term "enjambment" will be taken from the study of prosody to indicate here only the first of these two meanings, and "elision" will refer only to the second.

12 Oswald Jonas, *Introduction to the Theory of Heinrich Schenker*, trans. and ed. John Rothgeb (1934; New York: Longman, 1982), 7–9. Jonas's German term is "*Knupftechnik.*"

13 This and following sentences are based upon the Schenkerian method, which clarifies the relationship between surface and structural levels of harmony and counterpoint. According to this theory, a single melody (in our case the lead vocal line sung by John Lennon) is a composite of several structural voices governed by stepwise motion: (1) a controlling upper voice, which at its deepest level represents a stepwise descent from the primary tone (the initiating fifth scale degree, Sol) to the first scale degree (Do), a descent that is ornamented by neighbors and other material of lesser structural value, and (2) inner voices that may be initiated by members of the upper voice but then descend below it, and may even, through registral transfer, place "inner-voice" material up above the lay of the "upper" voice. Thus, a single melodic part is a polyphonic web, arpeggiating among several underlying voices. The upper and inner voices are all supported by the bass voice, which carries most of a passage's harmonic information. I have written elsewhere about the expressive relationships between upper and inner voices in the vocal music of Mozart, Schubert, the Beatles, Billy Joel, and Paul Simon. While developed for music from the common practice period, Schenkerian analysis is quite applicable to a great deal of rock and other popular musics, particularly examples, such as "I Should Have Known Better," that reside completely or mostly within the major-minor system. The system is chosen here, at the risk of its being new to many readers, because of the great musicality it reveals in terms of metric, phrasal, registral, and expressive relationships.

14 The Moog is a module-based analog electronic instrument controlled by a keyboard through which voltages are given particular waveshapes, and are filtered and amplified, according to "patches" that lead one circuit to control another at the performer's discretion. Most popular among the English progressive rock bands of the 1970s, the Beatles – at George Harrison's instigation – were among the pioneers of the Moog in *Abbey Road*.

15 For Fred Lerdahl and Ray Jackendoff, a melodic anacrusis, thus beginning a phrase before the (hypermetric) downbeat, has the grouping out of phase with the (hyper)metrical structure. (Such is the device discussed above in regard to the extended example in "There's a Place" but also evident on the surface of many other references, beginning with Example 1.) See their *A Generative Theory of Tonal Music* (Cambridge, MA: MIT Press, 1983), 33–4. Rothstein discusses this phenomenon in *Phrase Rhythm in Tonal Music*, 21–2.

16 In rock music, harmonic rhythm usually determines where the barlines fall, as metric patterns are always based on chords changing on downbeats (this pattern, once established, is often contradicted later), and because chords tend to change once per measure. For example, "I Want to Hold Your Hand" opens with a verse of two four-bar phrases, chords changing for each of the eight bars. This verse is followed by a four-bar phrase of eight chords, changing twice per measure, thus doubling the harmonic rhythm.

17 Metric modulation is a term coined by Elliott Carter for a type of transition perhaps invented by Alban Berg but favored in his own compositions. The effect is based on durations remaining constant while their context as beat divisions changes. For example, the eighth notes that in one passage may divide the beat into two parts may serve as the pivotal connecting tissue to another passage where the same eighths, moving at the same tempo, may be reinterpreted as triplet eighths because beats now contain three, not two, of these values. Thus, the beat-marked tempo is altered significantly (sometimes through a 2:3 or 3:2 ratio, but often through much more complex subdivisions) while submetrical units (such as beat-dividing eighths) remain constant.

11 The Beatles as zeitgeist

1 John Lennon's original skiffle group, the Quarrymen, was joined by Paul McCartney in 1956 and George Harrison in 1958. The group's name subsequently changed to Moondogs and eventually the Silver Beetles (in emulation of Buddy Holly and the Crickets). Ringo Starr finally joined the Beatles in 1962, replacing drummer Pete Best.

2 As Mark Abraham estimated in his early study, *The Teenage Consumer* (London: London Press Exchange, 1959) (since supported by further studies), there was a growth in the real earnings of unmarried teenagers of 50 percent as compared with 1938. This was double the rate for adult earnings in the same period. Most significant was the proportion of uncommitted or "discretionary" spending money available – calculated to be about £900 million.

3 UKTV History, *The 60s: The Beatles Decade*, program 1.

4 Russell Reising, *"Every Sound There Is": The Beatles' Revolver and the Transformation of Rock and Roll* (Aldershot: Ashgate, 2002), p. 6.

5 John Lennon's band, the Quarrymen, being one such example.

6 UKTV History, *The 60s: The Beatles Decade*, program 1.

7 Donatella Maraschin, "The Swinging 60s," in *London: Summer Living* (London: Morris Visitor Publications, June–July 2006), 29–32.

8 For culturalist Marxist historian Edward Thompson, class remained a product of nineteenth-century modernity. As Andy Wood observes: "One of the achievements of the middle-class student revolt of the era [the 1960s] was the establishment of social history as a key contender in academic historical writing" (Andy Wood, *The Politics of Social Conflict: The Peak Country, 1520–1770* [Cambridge: Cambridge University Press, 1999], 10). See, for example, Edward Thompson, *The Making of the English Working Class* (1963; New York: Penguin, 1975).

9 William M. Northcutt, "The Spectacle of Alienation: Death, Loss, and the Crowd in *Sgt. Pepper's Lonely Hearts Club Band*," in Kenneth Womack and Todd F. Davis (eds.), *Reading the Beatles: Cultural Studies, Literary Criticism, and the Fab Four* (Albany: State University of New York Press, 2006), 130.

10 Problems surrounding racial discrimination continued throughout the 1960s. The passing of the Race Relations Act (1968) had been opposed by Enoch Powell, Conservative MP for Wolverhampton South West; and his "Rivers of Blood" speech (April 20, 1968) set out his premise that unless immigrants were repatriated, the streets of Britain would come to be "foaming with much blood," like the River Tiber (an allusion to Virgil's *Aeneid*).

11 In the minds of most social historians, the sexual revolution was primarily the product of the 1960s. While acknowledging the earlier rise of Alfred Kinsey, Hugh Hefner, and an increasingly defiant youth culture, most scholars portray these pre-sixties developments as precursors of the rapid liberalization of sexual behavior that was soon to follow. This is to say, while most scholars identify a general loosening of sexual attitudes during the forties and fifties, they do not detect a significant upswing in premarital sexual behavior until the 1960s. See Alan Petigny, "Illegitimacy, Postwar Psychology, and the Reperiodization of the Sexual Revolution," *Journal of Social History* 38/1 (2004), p.1.

12 John Lennon married Cynthia Powell on August 23, 1962. He later said he married Cynthia because she was pregnant with his child (Julian) and he felt it was the right thing to do.

13 UKTV History, *The 60s: The Beatles Decade*, program 5.

14 Benjamin McLane Spock (1903–98), an American pediatrician, published *The Common Sense Book of Baby and Child Care* in 1946. His approach to childcare influenced several

generations of parents to be more flexible and affectionate toward their children, and to treat them as individuals, rather than focusing on discipline.

15 The Kinsey Reports are two books on human sexual behavior, *Sexual Behavior in the Human Male* (1948) and *Sexual Behavior in the Human Female* (1953), by Dr. Alfred C. Kinsey, Wardell B. Pomeroy, and others. Kinsey was a zoologist at Indiana University and the founder of the Institute for Sex Research. The findings challenged conventional beliefs about sexuality and discussed subjects that had previously been taboo, including masturbation, the female orgasm, homosexuality, and sadomasochism.

16 In 1965 the Labour MP Sydney Silverman, who had committed himself to the cause of abolition for more than twenty years, proposed a Private Member's Bill on abolition which was passed on a free vote in the House of Commons by 200 votes to 98. (A free vote, traditional for issues of conscience such as abortion and capital punishment, is one in which the party whips do not issue directions to MPs.) It was subsequently adopted by the House of Lords by 204 to 104 against.

17 The Abortion Act (1967) regulates abortion by registered practitioners and provides free medical aid through the National Health Service. It was introduced by David Steel as a Private Member's Bill backed by the government, and after a heated debate and a free vote passed on October 27, 1967. It came into effect on April 27, 1968.

18 A. S. Byatt, *Babel Tower* (London: Vintage, 1997), 168.

19 Angela McRobbie, "*Jackie* Magazine: Romantic Individualism and the Teenage Girl," in Angela McRobbie, *Feminism and Youth Culture* (London: Macmillan, 1991), 135–88 (first published as "*Jackie*: An Ideology of Adolescent Femininity," Stencilled Occasional Paper 53, Women's Series [Birmingham: Centre for Contemporary Cultural Studies, 1978]).

20 Betty Friedan's 1963 book *The Feminine Mystique* challenged the view that women can find satisfaction in the exclusively traditional role of wife and mother; radical feminists identified patriarchy – as a system characterized by power, dominance, hierarchy, and competition – as both universal and oppressive, while the emerging women's movement of the late 1960s identified sisterhood as a cohesive revolutionary force for developing self-identity. *Spare Rib*, *Women's Voice*, *Women's Report*, and the *Red Flag* provided communication networks.

21 Theodor Roszak, *The Making of a Counter Culture: Reflections on the Technocratic Society and its Youthful Opposition* (New York: Faber & Faber, 1971).

22 Roy Jenkins was also responsible for the abolition of theater censorship. As Home Secretary he had given government support to David Steel's Private Member's Bill for the legalization of abortion, and Leo Abse's Bill for the decriminalization of homosexuality.

23 Polly Toynbee in the *Guardian*, July 21, 2004, at www.guardian.co.uk/politics/2004/jul/21/labour.politicalcolumnists (accessed May 28, 2009).

24 The US involvement in Vietnam goes back to the 1950s, but President J. F. Kennedy's 1961 dispatch of 400 Special Operations Forces-trained (Green Beret) soldiers to teach the South Vietnamese how to fight what was called counter-insurgency war against Communist guerrillas in South Vietnam provides one starting date. When Kennedy was assassinated in November 1963, there were more than 16,000 US military advisers in South Vietnam, and more than 100 Americans had been killed. Kennedy's successor, Lyndon B. Johnson, committed the United States most fully to the war. In August 1964, he secured from Congress a functional (not actual) declaration of war: the Tonkin Gulf Resolution. Then, in February and March 1965, Johnson authorized the sustained bombing, by US aircraft, of targets north of the 17th Parallel, and on March 8 he dispatched 3,500 Marines to South Vietnam. Legal declaration or no, the United States was now at war (John Whiteclay (ed.), *The Oxford Companion to American Military History* [Oxford: Oxford University Press, 1999]).

25 These included Alice Herz, an eighty-two-year-old survivor of Nazi terror, who set herself on fire in Detroit shortly after President Johnson announced major troop increases and the bombing of North Vietnam (March 15, 1965); Quaker Norman Morrison, setting himself on fire and dying outside Secretary of Defense Robert McNamara's Pentagon office (November 2, 1965); and Catholic worker Roger Laporte, self-immolating opposite the United Nations Building.

26 Their 1966 album *Revolver* is now interpreted as transforming the vocabulary of popular music, with "Tomorrow Never Knows" topping the list of British psychedelia (Jon Savage, "100 Greatest Psychedelic Classics," *MOJO* 43 [June 1997], 61), attempting to "recreate what tripping actually sounds like" (Russell Reising, *"Every Sound There Is": The Beatles' Revolver and the Transformation of Rock and Roll* [Aldershot: Ashgate, 2002], 235).

27 In 1966–7 the Beatles retreated into Hinduism and Transcendental Meditation, adopting the Maharishi Mahesh Yogi as spiritual guide; and they all admitted that they had taken drugs – including LSD. George Harrison remained a Hindu throughout his life, donating a manor house in Watford, UK, to the Krishna movement.

28 Allen Ginsberg in *It Was Twenty Years Ago Today*, directed by John Sheppard for Granada Television, UK, 1987.

29 Steve Turner, *A Hard Day's Write: The Stories Behind Every Beatles Song* (New York: HarperCollins, 1999; London: Carlton, 2000), 144.

30 Peter McCabe and Robert D. Schonfeld, *Apple to the Core: The Unmaking of the Beatles* (New York: Pocket Books, 1972), 86–7.

31 By 1967, after 300 tours worldwide, the Beatles withdrew from public performances and engaged totally with studio production.

32 Timothy Leary, cited in Charlie Gillett, *The Sound of the City* (London: Souvenir Press, 1970), 353.

33 Their seven-bedroom house in Weybridge had cost John Lennon £20,000, but was on the market in 2006 for £5.95 million. John and Yoko recorded their album *Two Virgins* there in May 1968. It was released in November that year.

34 Apple Records was launched in 1968 with Ron Kass as Managing Director, Peter Asher as the company A&R (artists and repertoire) person, and Tony Bramwell in charge of promoting the products. Apple advertisements and posters announced the venture and asked for tapes to review, but very few artists were signed as a result. Most who were signed owed their success to personal preferences of the directors. The first artist signed to this label was James Taylor. Badfinger was a true success story for Apple Records. Mary Hopkin, James Taylor, and Billy Preston had their moments in the sun. Of course, the Beatles and their solo Apple Records faired well, but Apple Records received only two non-Beatles gold record awards (Mary Hopkin, "Those Were the Days," and Badfinger, "Come and Get It"). Apple Records lasted from August 1968 through May 1976.

35 Carey Schofield, *Jagger* (London: Methuen, 1983), 130.

12 Beatles news: product line extensions and the rock canon

1 There are several books on this subject, including Gail Brewer-Giorgio, *Is Elvis Alive?* (New York: Tudor, 1988; Greil Marcus, *Dead Elvis: A Chronicle of a Cultural Obsession* (New York: Doubleday, 1991); George Plasketes,

Images of Elvis Presley in American Culture, 1977–1997: The Mystery Terrain (New York: Haworth Press, 1997); G. L. Reece, *Elvis Religion: The Cult of the King* (London and New York: Tauris, 2006); and G. B. Rodman, *Elvis After Elvis: The Posthumous Career of a Living Legend* (London and New York: Routledge, 1996).

2 This proposal was mentioned by Paul McCartney on camera in *The Beatles Anthology* TV special in 1995.

3 See Gary Burns, "Refab Four: Beatles for Sale in the Age of Music Video," in Ian Inglis (ed.), *The Beatles, Popular Music and Society: A Thousand Voices* (Basingstoke: Macmillan, 2000), 176–88.

4 Jon Wiener, "The Last Lennon File," *The Nation*, January 8–15, 2007, 4; see also his *Gimme Some Truth: The John Lennon FBI Files* (Berkeley: University of California Press, 1999).

5 Ian Inglis, *The Beatles, Popular Music, and Society*, "Introduction," xv.

6 An amusing and very grumpy critique of Beatles reissues and pseudo-reunions appears in J. Lewis, "'Over My Dead Body!,'" *Uncut* (May 2007), 75.

7 See also Lennon's posthumously published *Skywriting by Word of Mouth and Other Writings, Including The Ballad of John and Yoko* (New York: Harper & Row, 1986).

8 *Yellow Submarine* is an animated film in which the Beatles are represented visually as cartoon figures. On the soundtrack we hear actual Beatles records, but during dialog segments the Beatles' lines are spoken by voice actors rather than by the Beatles themselves. This idiosyncratic approach was borrowed from the 1964–7 TV cartoon series *The Beatles*, which was innovative in its own right but not an artistic achievement in the same league as *Yellow Submarine*. See Mitchell Axelrod, *BeatleToons: The Real Story Behind the Cartoon Beatles* (Pickens, SC: Wynn Publishing, 1999); "The Beatles," *Television Chronicles* 3 (1995), 8–15; P. Gorman, "Badly Drawn Boys," *MOJO* (July 2000), 20–1; Robert R. Hieronimus, *Inside the Yellow Submarine: The Making of the Beatles' Animated Classic*, editing and compilation assistance by Laura Cortner (Iola, WI: Krause Publications, 2002).

9 See Gary Burns, "The Myth of the Beatles," *South Atlantic Quarterly* 86 (1987), 169–80; T. Wolfe, "The 'Me' Decade and the Third Great Awakening," *New York*, August 23, 1976, 26–40; Christopher Lasch, *The Culture of Narcissism: American Life in an Age of Diminishing Expectations* (New York: Norton, 1978); R. D. Rosen, *Psychobabble: Fast Talk and Quick Cure in the Era of Feeling* (New York: Atheneum, 1977);

and Theodor Roszak, *The Making of a Counter Culture: Reflections on the Technocratic Society and its Youthful Opposition* (Garden City, NY: Doubleday, 1969).

10 See Stefan Granados, *Those Were the Days: An Unofficial History of the Beatles Apple Organization 1967–2002* (London: Cherry Red Books, 2000).

11 "Method in Their Fabness," *MOJO*, May 2007, 14.

12 See Inglis, *The Beatles, Popular Music, and Society*.

13 See Jon Wiener, *Come Together: John Lennon in His Time* (New York: Random House, 1984).

14 See Donald Alport Bird, Stephen C. Holder, and Diane Sears, "Walrus Is Greek for Corpse: Rumor and the Death of Paul McCartney," *Journal of Popular Culture* 10 (1976), 110–21; Burns, "The Myth of the Beatles"; R. Gary Patterson, *"The Walrus Was Paul": The Great Beatle Death Clues of 1969* (Oak Ridge, TN: Excursion Productions and Publications, 1994); A. J. Reeve, *Turn Me On, Dead Man: The Complete Story of the Paul McCartney Death Hoax* (Ann Arbor, MI: Popular Culture Ink, 1994); and Barbara Suczek, "The Curious Case of the 'Death' of Paul McCartney," *Urban Life and Culture* 1 (1972), 61–76.

15 See Vic Garbarini, Brian Cullman, and Barbara Graustark, *Strawberry Fields Forever: John Lennon Remembered* (New York: Bantam Books, 1980); Fenton Bresler, *The Murder of John Lennon* (London: Sidgwick & Jackson, 1989); Fred Fogo, *"I Read the News Today": The Social Drama of John Lennon's Death* (Lanham, MD: Rowman & Littlefield, 1994); and Anthony Elliott, *The Mourning of John Lennon* (Berkeley: University of California Press, 1999); see also Jack Jones, *Let Me Take You Down: Inside the Mind of Mark David Chapman, the Man Who Killed John Lennon* (New York: Villard Books, 1992).

16 James Sauceda, *The Literary Lennon: A Comedy of Letters – The First Study of All the Major and Minor Writings of John Lennon* (Ann Arbor, MI: Pierian Press, 1983). See also M. E. Roos, "The Walrus and the Deacon: John Lennon's Debt to Lewis Carroll," *Journal of Popular Culture* 18.1 (1984), 19–29, for a primarily literary analysis.

17 David R. Pichaske (ed.), *Beowulf to Beatles: Approaches to Poetry* (New York: Free Press, 1972).

18 David R. Pichaske, *The Poetry of Rock: The Golden Years* (Peoria, IL: Ellis Press, 1981).

19 An example is Alan Aldridge (ed.), *The Beatles Illustrated Lyrics* (London: Macdonald, 1969).

20 Paul McCartney, *Blackbird Singing: Poems and Lyrics 1965–1999*, ed. A. Mitchell (New York: Norton, 2001).

21 Paul McCartney, Geoff Dunbar, and Philip Ardagh, *High in the Clouds* (New York: Dutton Children's Books, 2005). McCartney has also published a book (*Paintings* [Boston: Little, Brown, 2000]) that consists mainly of photographic reproductions of his paintings. This is not, strictly speaking, a literary venture, but is perhaps relevant because it is a book.

22 Alan West and Colin Martindale, "Creative Trends in the Content of Beatles Lyrics," *Popular Music and Society* 20/4 (1996), 103–25.

23 Simon Frith and Howard Horne, *Art Into Pop* (London and New York: Methuen, 1987).

24 "What Songs the Beatles Sang . . . ," *The Times*, December 27, 1963, Arts section, 4 (uncredited article "From Our Music Critic," who was William Mann).

25 Other examples include "All My Loving" and "It's Only Love."

26 As Walter Everett points out, Arthur Alexander's song "Anna (Go to Him)," which the Beatles had recorded, was a "likely model" for "Not a Second Time" (*The Beatles as Musicians: The Quarry Men Through* Rubber Soul [New York: Oxford University Press, 2001], 192). And to *The Times* critic's comparison of "Not a Second Time" with Mahler's *Das Lied von der Erde*, Everett responds: "Good grief! It's 'Mama Said' or 'When My Little Girl Is Smiling,' not Mahler" (ibid., 392).

27 *The Beatles Complete Scores* (Milwaukee: Hal Leonard Corporation, 1989).

28 Wilfrid Mellers, *Twilight of the Gods: The Beatles in Retrospect* (London: Faber & Faber, 1973).

29 T. J. O'Grady, *The Beatles: A Musical Evolution* (Boston: Twayne, 1983).

30 Tim Riley, *Tell Me Why: A Beatles Commentary* (New York: Knopf, 1988; Vintage, 1989), revised as *Tell Me Why: The Beatles – Album by Album, Song by Song, the Sixties and After* (Cambridge, MA: Da Capo, 2002).

31 William J. Dowlding, *Beatlesongs* (New York: Fireside, 1989).

32 Ian MacDonald, *Revolution in the Head: The Beatles' Records and the Sixties* (London: Fourth Estate; New York: Henry Holt, 1994).

33 Mark Hertsgaard, *A Day in the Life: The Music and Artistry of the Beatles* (New York: Delacorte, 1995).

34 Alan W. Pollack, "Notes on . . . " series of online analyses of Beatles songs, the "Official" rec.music.beatles home page (1989–2001), at www.recmusicbeatles.com.

35 Everett, *The Beatles as Musicians: The Quarry Men Through* Rubber Soul, and *The Beatles as Musicians:* Revolver *Through the Anthology* (New York: Oxford University Press, 1999). See also Todd Compton's article in the *Journal of Popular Culture*, a painstaking attempt to determine which Beatle made what authorial contribution to every Beatles song. And see Kenneth Womack and Todd F. Davis's collection, *Reading the Beatles: Cultural Studies, Literary Criticism, and the Fab Four* (Albany: State University of New York Press, 2006), for excellent analyses of the Beatles as canonical figures in each of the three realms under consideration in the present study – sociological, lyrical, and musical.

36 *Revolver:* Russell Reising, *"Every Sound There Is": The Beatles'* Revolver *and the Transformation of Rock and Roll* (Aldershot: Ashgate, 2002); *Sgt. Pepper:* George Martin, with William Pearson, *Summer of Love: The Making of* Sgt. Pepper (London: Macmillan, 1994); Allan F. Moore, *The Beatles:* Sgt. Pepper's Lonely Hearts Club Band (Cambridge: Cambridge University Press, 1997); *The Beatles* (the White Album): David Quantick, *Revolution: The Making of the Beatles' White Album* (London: Unanimous; Chicago: A Cappella, 2002); Peter Doggett, *Let It Be / Abbey Road* (New York: Schirmer; London: Prentice Hall International, 1998); and Steve Matteo, *Let It Be* (New York and London: Continuum, 2004).

37 A. J. W. Taylor, "Beatlemania – A Study in Adolescent Enthusiasm," *British Journal of Social and Clinical Psychology* 5 (1966), 81–8.

38 Evan Davis, "Psychological Characteristics of Beatle Mania," *Journal of the History of Ideas* 30 (1969), 273–80.

39 L. P. R. Santiago, "The Lyrical Expression of Adolescent Conflict in the Beatles' Songs," *Adolescence* 4 (1969), 199–210.

40 Larry R. Smith, "The Beatles as Act: A Study of Control in a Musical Group," PhD thesis, University of Illinois at Urbana-Champaign (1970).

41 Geoffrey Marshall, "Taking the Beatles Seriously: Problems of Text," *Journal of Popular Culture* 3 (1969), 28–34; N. V. Rosenberg, "Taking Popular Culture Seriously: The Beatles," *Journal of Popular Culture* 4 (1970), 53–6; G. W. Lyon, Jr., "More on Beatles Textual Problems," *Journal of Popular Culture* 4 (1970), 549–52; R. A. Peterson, "Taking Popular Music Too Seriously," *Journal of Popular Culture* 4 (1971), 590–4; see also Henry Pleasants, "Taking the Beatles Seriously," *Stereo Review* (November 1967), 52–4.

42 Bradby, "She Told Me What to Say."

43 Ibid., 359.

44 Ibid., 371.

13 "An abstraction, like Christmas": the Beatles for sale and for keeps

I would like to thank the following individuals: research assistant Steve Gibons, who did translations from French; George Healey, Linda Healey, and Jim Kimsey, who helped in gathering materials; and Reg Gant, Maureen Hennessey, and Carol Kimsey, who got me to the show on time.

1 Derek Taylor, liner notes, *Beatles for Sale* CD, 1987 (original 1964).

2 "Year 2000 Annual Review," online posting, www.cyber-beatles.com/year2000.htm (accessed May 21, 2009).

3 "Beatles named 'icons of the century,'" BBC News website, October 16, 2005, at http://news.bbc.co.uk/go/pr/fr/-/2/hi/entertainment/4344910.stm (accessed April 28, 2007).

4 Robert Cording, Shelli Jankowski-Smith, and E. J. Miller Laino (eds.), *In My Life: Encounters with the Beatles* (New York: Fromm International, 1998), "Introduction," n.p.

5 Mark Hertsgaard, *A Day in the Life: The Music and Artistry of the Beatles* (New York: Delta, 1995), 318.

6 Greil Marcus, "The Beatles," in Jim Miller (ed.), *The* Rolling Stone *Illustrated History of Rock and Roll*, rev. and updated edn. (New York: Random House, 1980; London: Picador, 1981), 184.

7 Ian MacDonald, *Revolution in the Head: The Beatles' Records and the Sixties*, fully updated edn. (London: Pimlico, 1998), 328.

8 Ken Townsend, "Preface" to Mark Lewisohn, *The Complete Beatles Recording Sessions: The Official Story of the Abbey Road Years* (London: Hamlyn, 1988), 4. Regarding "definitive" accounts of the Beatles' recording history and practices, Lewisohn's book has now been supplanted by Kevin Ryan and Brian Keyhew, *Recording the Beatles: The Studio Equipment and Techniques Used to Create Their Classic Albums* (Houston: Curvebender, 2006).

9 Evan Eisenberg, "Phonography," in *The Recording Angel: The Experience of Music from Aristotle to Zappa* (New York: Penguin, 1987), 158–9.

10 Hertsgaard, *A Day in the Life*, 324.

11 Walter Everett, *The Beatles as Musicians:* Revolver *through the* Anthology (New York: Oxford University Press, 1999), 295.

12 John Storey, "The Politics of the Popular," in *An Introductory Guide to Cultural Theory and*

Popular Culture (Athens, GA: University of Georgia Press, 1993), 199.

13 Simon Frith, "Introduction: Everything Counts," in his *Music for Pleasure: Essays in the Sociology of Pop* (New York: Routledge, 1988), 6.

14 While he remastered all the Parlophone LPs during the mid-eighties, Martin went a step further with both *Help!* and *Rubber Soul*. Citing dissatisfaction with the original mixes, he actually remixed these two 1965 LPs. See Ryan and Keyhew, *Recording the Beatles,* 402.

15 An exception was made in the case of *Magical Mystery Tour*, a record that originally appeared as a six-song EP on Parlophone in the UK. The CD version of *Magical Mystery Tour* mirrored the 1967 Capitol/US release, which added singles such as "Penny Lane" and "Strawberry Fields Forever" to the Parlophone EP lineup to form an eleven-song LP. Also, it should be noted that, during the same mid-eighties period, the soundtrack of *Yellow Submarine* was remastered and released on CD along with the twelve "official" albums.

16 During the period 1973–82, several LP compilations of Beatles music were released: the double albums *The Beatles 1962–1966* and *The Beatles 1967–1970* (a.k.a. the "red" and "blue" albums) both appeared on Apple in 1973, while in ensuing years Capitol released *Rock and Roll Music* (1976), *Love Songs* (1977), *Rarities* (1980), *Reel Music* (1982), and *20 Greatest Hits* (1982). In addition, Capitol released a live album, *The Beatles at the Hollywood Bowl*, in 1977. Of all these, only *The Beatles 1962–1966* and *The Beatles 1967–1970* have been officially released on CD, and they appeared in 1993.

17 MacDonald, *Revolution in the Head*, 201. According to this UK custom, "anything issued as a single could not be included in an LP released in the same year" (201). The Beatles observed this rule strictly except in the case of their first Parlophone LP, *Please Please Me*, which included four songs previously released as singles.

18 The Capitol version of *Revolver* provides a striking illustration. It contains three fewer tracks than its Parlophone counterpart, all of them Lennon songs, a serious misrepresentation of Lennon's contribution to the album many consider the Beatles' finest.

19 Mark Brown, "Beatles fans kept waiting on remasters," March 18, 2006, *Rocky Mountain News*, at www.rockymountainnews.com/drmn/spotlight_columnists/article/0,2777,DRMN_23962_4475849,00.html (accessed March 20, 2006).

20 The mono mix of *Sgt. Pepper* has never been officially released in CD form even though Martin, Emerick, and the Beatles all agree that the mono (as opposed to stereo) mix is the one into which the team put its greatest effort.

21 These audiophile vinyl editions of the Beatles' LPs, made by Mobile Fidelity Sound Lab from original masters, have been out of print for many years.

22 Brown, "Beatles fans kept waiting"; see also Alex Petridis, "The Beatles, Love," *Guardian*, November 17, 2006, at http://arts.guardian.co.uk/film-andmusic/story/0,,1949254,00.html (accessed November 17, 2006).

23 Ryan and Keyhew, *Recording the Beatles*, 407.

24 Quoted in Geoffrey Guiliano, *Two of Us: John Lennon and Paul McCartney Behind the Myth* (New York: Penguin, 1999), 64. See also Philip Lambert, *Inside the Music of Brian Wilson* (New York: Continuum, 2007), 224.

25 MacDonald, *Revolution in the Head*, 331. See also Allan Kozinn, "A high-wire feat for Beatles music," *International Herald Tribune*, June 23, 2006, at www.iht.com/-articles/2006/06/23/news/beatles.php (accessed June 24, 2006).

26 Quoted in Kevin Howlett, "The Beatles' Radio Sessions 1962–65," in CD booklet, *The Beatles Live at the BBC* (Apple, 1994), 7.

27 MacDonald, *Revolution in the Head*, 335.

28 The Beatles had been inducted as a band at the Rock Hall's inaugural ceremony in 1988; McCartney and Harrison waited, respectively, until 1999 and 2004 to be inducted as solo artists.

29 MacDonald, *Revolution in the Head*, 330.

30 The CD single releases were called maxi-singles and configured like EPs of old: the first led off with "Free as a Bird" and followed it with three tracks of outtakes from the period covered by *Anthology 1*. The second led with "Real Love" and followed it with three tracks of outtakes from the period covered by *Anthology 2.*

31 This third song is sometimes referred to by the title "Now and Then." Scattered news items during 2006–7 reported that McCartney and Starr had returned to working on "Now and Then" with a plan to incorporate "archive tracks" featuring Harrison. See, for example, "Unheard Beatles 'last great song' set for release," Webindia.com, April 30, 2007, at http://news.webindia123.com (accessed May 1, 2007).

32 Tim Riley, *Tell Me Why: The Beatles – Album by Album, Song by Song, the Sixties and After* (Cambridge, MA: Da Capo, 2002), 406; MacDonald, *Revolution in the Head*, 332.

33 King Crimson in concert, Rosemont Theatre, Rosemont, Illinois, November 29, 1995.

34 MacDonald, *Revolution in the Head*, 170.

35 Mark Lewisohn, liner notes, *The Beatles Anthology Volume 2*, CD (Apple Corps Ltd. / EMI Ltd., 1996), 19.

36 Barry Miles, *Paul McCartney: Many Years From Now* (New York: Henry Holt, 1997), 291–2; Geoff Emerick and Howard Massey, *Here, There, and Everywhere: My Life Recording the Beatles* (New York: Gotham Books, 2006), 111–12. McCartney oversaw the selection of music for the *Anthology*.

37 The DVD boxed set appeared in 2003. The *Anthology* film had previously been available in VHS and laser disc formats.

38 As an Apple executive, Aspinall always eschewed formal titles.

39 MacDonald, *Revolution in the Head*, 331.

40 Todd Leopold, "Ladies and gentlemen, the Beatles! – in their own words," CNN, October 5, 2000, at http://archives.cnn.com/2000/books/news/10/05/beatles.anthology (accessed May 15, 2007).

41 MacDonald, *Revolution in the Head*, 334.

42 *It Was Twenty Years Ago Today*, film, directed by John Sheppard (Granada Television, UK, 1987).

43 *The Beatles Anthology*, DVD boxed set (Apple, 2003), "Episode 8: Abbey Road."

44 Ibid.

45 Much of the discussion in this section draws on John Kimsey, "Spinning the Historical Record: Lennon, McCartney, and Museum Politics," in Ken Womack and Todd F. Davis (eds.), *Reading the Beatles: Cultural Studies, Literary Criticism and the Fab Four* (Albany: State University of New York Press, 2006), 197–213.

46 "Paul McCartney defends songwriting credit switch," *AP Wire*, December 18, 2002, at www.salon.com/wire/2002/12/18/mccartney (accessed December 19, 2002).

47 Terry Gross, interview with Paul McCartney, *Fresh Air*, National Public Radio, WHYY, Philadelphia, April 30, 2001.

48 Larry King, "Paul McCartney Discusses 'Blackbird Singing,'" interview, *Larry King Live*, CNN, New York, June 12, 2001.

49 Hunter Davies, *The Beatles*, 2nd rev. edn. (New York: Norton, 1996), 368.

50 Anthony Elliott, *The Mourning of John Lennon* (Berkeley: University of California Press, 1999), 1, 4.

51 King, "Paul McCartney Discusses 'Blackbird Singing.'"

52 Miles, *Paul McCartney*, x.

53 Jann Wenner, *Lennon Remembers: The Rolling Stone Interviews* (1971; New York: Verso, 2000), x.

54 Keir Keightley, "Reconsidering Rock," in Simon Frith, Will Straw, and John Street (eds.), *The Cambridge Companion to Pop and Rock* (Cambridge and New York: Cambridge University Press, 2001), 109–42, 117.

55 Miles, *Many Years From Now*, x.

56 Keightley, "Reconsidering Rock," 136.

57 George Martin, with William Pearson, *Summer of Love: The Making of Sgt. Pepper* (London: Pan Books, 1995), 137–8.

58 MacDonald, *Revolution in the Head*, 153.

59 Emerick and Massey, *Here, There, and Everywhere*, 43.

60 Ibid., 98.

61 *The Beatles Anthology* (San Francisco: Chronicle Books, 2000), 319.

62 Ibid., 323.

63 Quoted in Kevin Howlett, liner notes, *Let It Be . . . Naked*, CD booklet (Apple Corps Ltd. / EMI Records Ltd., 2003), n.p.

64 Ibid.

65 The term "museum politics" comes from the writing of political scientist Timothy Luke. See his *Museum Politics: Power Plays at the Exhibition* (Minneapolis: University of Minneapolis Press, 2002).

66 Quoted in "John Lennon's widow calls for healing," *USA Today*, November 26, 2006, at www.usatoday.com/life/people/2006–11-26-ono_x.htm (accessed November 28, 2006).

67 "Artists unite in donating tracks to 'Instant Karma: The Amnesty International Campaign to Save Darfur,' to be released by Warner Bros. Records June 12," *Market Wire News*, April 30, 2007, at www.marketwire.com/mw/release (accessed May 6, 2007).

68 "Lennon's piano to make peace tour," BBC News website, April 3, 2007, at http://news.bbc.co.uk/2/hi/entertainment/6521055.stm (accessed May 26, 2007).

69 David Sheff, *All We Are Saying: The Last Major Interview with John Lennon and Yoko Ono*, ed. G. Barry Golson (New York: St. Martins, 2000), 216; see also *John and Yoko's Year of Peace*, film, directed by Paul McGrath (Canadian Broadcasting Corporation, 2000).

70 Ono, quoted in "Artists unite in donating tracks to 'Instant Karma.'"

71 "Controversial Lennon film is axed," Metro.co.uk, February 21, 2007, at www.metro.co.uk/fame/article.html?in_article_id=38284-&in_page_id=7&in_a_source (accessed February 22, 2007).

72 John Scheinfeld, "In Bed with Yoko Ono," *Guardian Unlimited* Arts Blog, December 7, 2007, http://blogs.guardian.co.uk/film/2006/12/

in_bed_with_yoko_ono.html (accessed December 7, 2006).

73 Sheff, *All We Are Saying*, 216.

74 Ibid., 96.

75 Kimsey, "Spinning the Historical Record," 202. My discussion throughout this section draws closely on this 2006 essay. For a more detailed discussion of the Lennon exhibit, the reader is referred to that piece.

76 Marsha Ewing, "John Lennon: his life and work – shaking up the house that rock built," *Instant Karma*, October 21, 2000, at www.instantkarma.com/jolrockhallstory1.html (accessed November 3, 2002); quoted in Kimsey, "Spinning the Historical Record," 203.

77 James Henk (ed.), *Lennon: His Life and Work* (Cleveland, OH: Rock and Roll Hall of Fame and Museum, 2000), 101.

78 Ibid., 98.

79 Ibid., 9.

80 Kimsey, "Spinning the Historical Record," 209.

81 Henke (ed.), *Lennon: His Life and Work*, 98.

82 Sheff, *All We Are Saying*, 178.

83 Quoted in Miles, *Many Years From Now*, 277. It should be noted that McCartney has no history of prevaricating about such matters.

84 MacDonald, *Revolution in the Head*, 151.

85 Everett, *The Beatles as Musicians:* Revolver *through the* Anthology, 319.

86 Kimsey, "Spinning the Historical Record," 208.

87 Everett, *The Beatles as Musicians:* Revolver *through the* Anthology, 320.

88 Kimsey, "Spinning the Historical Record," 206.

89 Eileen Hooper-Greenhill, *Museums and the Interpretation of Visual Culture* (New York: Routledge, 2000), 151; quoted in Kimsey, "Spinning the Historical Record," 206.

90 Luke, *Museum Politics*, xxiv; quoted in Kimsey, "Spinning the Historical Record," 205.

91 Diana Plater, "Yes, Yoko Ono approves," news.com.au, n.d., at www.news.com.au/travel/story/0,23483,21491474–27983,00.html (accessed April 3, 2007).

92 Laurent Bayle, "Preface" to *John Lennon: Unfinished Music, Musée de la Musique, 20 Octobre 2005–25 Juin 2006* (Paris: Cité de la Musique, 2005), 7. All translations from French in this chapter were done by my research assistant Steve Gibons.

93 Quoted in Emma Lavigne, "John Lennon: Unfinished Music, Une Exposition Inachevée," *John Lennon: Unfinished Music, Musée de la Musique, 20 Octobre 2005–25 Juin 2006* (Paris: Cité de la Musique, 2005), 9–12, 9.

94 Ibid., 9.

95 "Avant-garde is . . . ": quoted in Sean O'Hagan, "Macca beyond," *Observer*, September 18, 2005, at http://observer.guardian.co.uk/omm/story/0,1569834,00.html (accessed May 28, 2007).

96 "Material World Foundation," George Harrison.com, n.d., at www.georgeharrison.com/mwf (accessed April 16, 2007). Over the years, McCartney and Starr have also been strong on charitable work, Starr as founder of the Lotus Foundation, McCartney as supporter of the Adopt a Minefield campaign and People for the Ethical Treatment of Animals, among other groups.

97 Philip Glass, "George Harrison, World-Music Catalyst and Great-Souled Man: Open to the Influence of Unfamiliar Cultures," *New York Times*, December 9, 2001, Section 2, 33.

98 "It's big-top Beatles, by George," June 30, 2006, *Sydney Morning Herald*, www.smh.com.au/news/arts/its-bigtop-beatles-by-george/2006/06/29/1151174333873.html (accessed May 21, 2009).

99 Guy Laliberté, dedicatory remarks, *The Beatles Love / Cirque du Soleil* program, 2006, n.p.

100 "It's big-top Beatles, by George."

101 Tom Doyle, "Love Story: George and Giles Martin Remixing the Beatles," *Sound on Sound* 22/5 (March 2007), 152–7, 157.

102 Olivia Harrison, quoted in Ann Powers, "Fab foray by Cirque du Soleil," *Los Angeles Times* Calendarlive.com, June 30, 2006, at www.calendarlive.com (accessed June 30, 2006).

103 Doyle, "Love Story," 157.

104 Jasper Rees, "The Beatles as never before," *Daily Telegraph*, October 25, 2006, at www.telegraph.co.uk (accessed October 26, 2006). The one exception is "While My Guitar Gently Weeps," where George Martin, working at the request of Olivia Harrison, composed a string part to accompany her husband's acoustic demo, the same one featured on *Anthology 3*.

105 Quoted in Doyle, "Love Story," 153.

106 Ibid., 154.

107 Ibid.

108 Ibid., 153; "far out": see Dan Cairns, "The next big thing will be Beatlemania," *Times Online*, June 4, 2006, at http://entertainment.timesonline.co.uk/tol/arts_and_entertainment/articles670037.ece (accessed June 4, 2006).

109 The *Yellow Submarine Songtrack*, released in 1999, was the first Beatles release to feature 5.1 surround sound mixes.

110 Pete Townshend, "I Know That It's a Dream," *MOJO* Special Edition: John Lennon (Winter 2000), 146.

111 Cairns, "The next big thing"; see also Pete Paphides, "Beatles and mash with the fifth Fab," *Times Online*, November 17, 2006, at http://entertainment.times-online.co.uk (accessed November 18, 2006). See also Petridis, "The Beatles: Love."

112 Mark Caro, "Yesterday . . . and Today – Why We Still Love it When the Beatles Turn Us On," *Chicago Tribune*, February 11, 2007, Arts and Entertainment, 1.

113 "Grey Tuesday: Free the Grey Album," *Grey Tuesday*, February 24, 2004, at www.greytuesday.org (accessed April 14, 2007).

114 Quoted in Chris Goodman, "Beatles take bigger bite out of Apple," *Daily Express*, April 22, 2007, at www.express.co.uk/posts/view/5048 (accessed April 22 and 25, 2007).

115 "McCartney Inks Deal with Starbucks," Songwriters Guild, n.d., at www.songwritersguild.com/mccartney.html (accessed April 2, 2007).

116 Quoted in Jeff Leeds, "Plunge in CD sales shakes up big labels," *New York Times*, May 28, 2007, at www.nytimes.com/2007/05/28/arts/music/-28musi.html?ei=5090&en=89793f4128e3ba8e&ex=1338004800 (accessed May 29, 2007).

117 Quoted in "McCartney's back catalogue heading online: EMI," CBC Arts, May 15, 2007, at www.cbc.ca.arts/music/story/2007/05/15/mccartney-emi-online.html (accessed May 15, 2007).

118 Caro, "Yesterday . . . and Today"; see also Mark Savage, "Will the Beatles go digital at last?," BBC News website, February 7, 2007, at http://newsvote.bbc.co.uk (accessed February 9, 2007).

119 Brown, "Beatles fans kept waiting on remasters"; see also Petridis, "The Beatles: Love."

120 Goodman, "Beatles take bigger bite"; see also Terry Lawson, "Beatles iPod could signal end of the CD," *Philadelphia Daily News*, March 1, 2007, at www.philly.com/mld/dailynews/living/16807441.htm (accessed March 1, 2007).

121 Christopher Hope, "Beatles join the iPod revolution," *Daily Telegraph*, April 12, 2007, at www.telegraph.co.uk/news/main.jhtml?xml=/news/2007/04/12/nbeatles12.xml (accessed April 12, 2007).

122 Goodman, "Beatles take bigger bite."

123 Evan Hansen and Michael Calore, "Apple still can't buy Beatles' love," *Wired*, April 3, 2007, at www.wired.com/entertainment/music/news/2007/04/emibeatles_0403 (accessed May 29, 2007).

124 Quoted in Brian Garrity, "Exclusive: McCartney Goes Digital, Beatles 'Virtually Settled,'" *Billboard*, May 10, 2007, at www.billboard.com/bbcom/news/article-display.jsp?vnu_content_id=1003583922 (accessed May 11, 2007).

125 On March 24, 2008, less than a year after stepping down from his position as head of Apple, Neil Aspinall died of lung cancer. He was sixty-six. See Richard Williams, "Obituary: Neil Aspinall," *Guardian*, April 25, 2008, www.guardian.co.uk/music/2008/mar/25/uk.obituaries (accessed April 26, 2008).

126 Quoted in Fiona Cummins, "Mad Apple: Exclusive – Fifth Beatle quits in row with 'money-crazy' board," *Daily Mirror*, April 11, 2007, at www.mirror.co.uk/news/topstories/tm_headline=madapple&method=full&objectid=18886813&siteid=89520-name_page.html (accessed April 12, 2007); see also Goodman, "Beatles take bigger bite."

127 Dean Goodman, "'Fifth Beatle' Aspinall quits top job," *Reuters*, April 10, 2007, at www.reuters.com/article/industryNews/idUSN1041291820070411 (accessed April 10 and 11, 2007).

128 The packaging for this candy product features Presley's image.

129 Goodman, "Beatles take bigger bite."

130 Aidan Malley, "Beatles unlikely to turn up on iTunes until 2008," *Apple Insider*, June 1, 2007, at www.appleinsider.com/articles/07/06/01/beatles_unlikely_to_turn_up_on_itunes_until_2008.html (accessed June 2007, 1).

131 "New Chart Rules," Official UK Charts Co. website, December 30, 2006, at www.theofficialcharts.com/rules_press-release.php (accessed January 7, 2007).

132 Savage, "Will the Beatles."

133 Keightley, "Reconsidering Rock," 125.

134 Ibid., 109.

135 Ibid., 109.

136 Storey, "The Politics of the Popular," 197.

137 Keightley, "Reconsidering Rock," 109, 133.

138 Ibid., 134.

139 Greg Kot, "Toppermost of the Poppermost," in June Skinner Sawyers (ed.), *Read the Beatles* (New York: Penguin, 2006), 324. See also John Robinson, "Chewing on the Apple Corps," *Guardian Unlimited*, September 16, 2006, http://arts.guardian.co.uk/features/-story/0,1873555,0.html (accessed September 22, 2006).

140 John Dower, writer/director, *Live Forever*, film (Passion Pictures, 2003).

141 "If you think of culture as a great big garden, it has to have its compost as well": Brian Eno, quoted in Michael Jarrett, "Authenticity," in his *Sound Tracks: A Musical ABC*, 3 vols. (Philadelphia: Temple University Press, 1998), I, 193.

142 Ed Smith, "Following the Genius with Four Heads; or, Why I Became a Composer," in Cording, Jankowski-Smith, and Miller Laino (eds.), *In My Life*, 239.

143 Ibid., 243.

144 MacDonald, *Revolution in the Head*, 335.

145 Thanks to Ellis Clark for this comparison.

146 Quoted in *Inkwell*: Artists and Authors Topic 285: Ritchie Unterberger, "The unreleased Beatles: music and film," October 29, 2006, www.well.com/conf/inkwell.vue/topics/285/Ritchie-Unterberger-The-Unrelease-.html (accessed November 1, 2006).

147 *Sliding Doors*, film, directed by Peter Howitt (Intermedia Films, 1998).

148 Quoted in *Inkwell*.

149 See Frith, "Everything Counts," 2: "Far from being counter-cultural, rock articulated the reconciliation of rebelliousness and capital."

150 Quoted in Hertsgaard, *A Day in the Life*, 191.

151 Ibid.

Beatles discography, 1962–1970

UK Singles releases

"My Bonnie"/"The Saints"; January 5, 1962, Polydor NH 66–833 (as Tony Sheridan and the Beatles)

"Love Me Do"/"P.S. I Love You"; October 5, 1962, Parlophone R 4949

"Please Please Me"/"Ask Me Why"; January 11, 1963, Parlophone R 4983

"From Me to You"/"Thank You Girl"; April 11, 1963, Parlophone R 5015

"She Loves You"/"I'll Get You"; August 23, 1963, Parlophone R 5055

"I Want to Hold Your Hand"/"This Boy"; November 29, 1963, Parlophone R 5084

"Can't Buy Me Love"/"You Can't Do That"; March 20, 1964, Parlophone R 5114

"A Hard Day's Night"/"Things We Said Today"; July 10, 1964, Parlophone R 5160

"I Feel Fine"/"She's a Woman"; November 27, 1964, Parlophone R 5200

"Ticket to Ride"/"Yes It Is"; April 9, 1965, Parlophone R 5265

"Help!"/"I'm Down"; July 23, 1965, Parlophone R 5305

"We Can Work It Out"/"Day Tripper"; December 3, 1965, Parlophone R 5389

"Paperback Writer"/"Rain"; June 10, 1966; Parlophone R 5452

"Eleanor Rigby"/"Yellow Submarine"; August 5, 1966, Parlophone R 5493

"Strawberry Fields Forever"/"Penny Lane"; February 17, 1967, Parlophone R 5570

"All You Need Is Love"/"Baby, You're a Rich Man"; July 7, 1967, Parlophone R 5620

"Hello Goodbye"/"I Am the Walrus"; November 24, 1967, Parlophone R 5655

"Lady Madonna"/"The Inner Light"; March 15, 1968, Parlophone R 5675

"Hey Jude"/"Revolution"; August 30, 1968, Apple [Parlophone] R 5722

"Get Back"/"Don't Let Me Down"; April 11, 1969, Apple [Parlophone] R 5777 (as the Beatles with Billy Preston)

"The Ballad of John and Yoko"/"Old Brown Shoe"; May 30, 1969, Apple [Parlophone] R 5786

"Something"/"Come Together"; October 31, 1969, Apple [Parlophone] R 5814

"Let It Be"/"You Know My Name (Look Up the Number)"; March 6, 1970, Apple [Parlophone] R 5833

UK EP releases

Twist and Shout, July 12, 1963, Parlophone GEP 8882 (mono)
   A: "Twist and Shout"; "A Taste of Honey." B: "Do You Want to Know a Secret"; "There's a Place."

The Beatles' Hits, September 6, 1963, Parlophone GEP 8880 (mono)
   A: "From Me to You"; "Thank You Girl." B: "Please Please Me"; "Love Me Do."

The Beatles (No. 1), November 1, 1963, Parlophone GEP 8883 (mono)
   A: "I Saw Her Standing There"; "Misery." B: "Anna (Go to Him)"; "Chains."

All My Loving, February 7, 1964, Parlophone GEP 8891 (mono)
   A: "All My Loving"; "Ask Me Why." B: "Money (That's What I Want)"; "P.S. I Love You."

Long Tall Sally, June 19, 1964, Parlophone GEP 8913 (mono)

> A: "Long Tall Sally"; "I Call Your Name." B: "Slow Down"; "Matchbox."

Extracts from the film *A Hard Day's Night*, November 6, 1964, Parlophone GEP 8920 (mono)

> A: "I Should Have Known Better"; "If I Fell." B: "Tell Me Why"; "And I Love Her."

Extracts from the album *A Hard Day's Night*, November 6, 1964, Parlophone GEP 8924 (mono)

> A: "Any Time at All"; "I'll Cry Instead." B: "Things We Said Today"; "When I Get Home."

Beatles for Sale, April 6, 1965, Parlophone GEP 8931 (mono)

> A: "No Reply"; "I'm a Loser." B: "Rock and Roll Music"; "Eight Days a Week."

Beatles for Sale (No. 2), June 4, 1965, Parlophone GEP 8938 (mono)

> A: "I'll Follow the Sun"; "Baby's in Black." B: "Words of Love"; "I Don't Want to Spoil the Party."

The Beatles' Million Sellers, December 6, 1965, Parlophone GEP 8946 (mono)

> A: "She Loves You"; "I Want to Hold Your Hand." B: "Can't Buy Me Love"; "I Feel Fine."

Yesterday, March 4, 1966, Parlophone GEP 8948 (mono)

> A: "Yesterday"; "Act Naturally." B: "You Like Me Too Much"; "It's Only Love."

Nowhere Man, July 8, 1966, Parlophone GEP 8952 (mono)

> A: "Nowhere Man"; "Drive My Car." B: "Michelle"; "You Won't See Me."

Magical Mystery Tour, December 8, 1967, Parlophone MMT-1 (mono) / SMMT-1 (stereo)

> A: "Magical Mystery Tour"; "Your Mother Should Know." B: "I Am the Walrus." C: "The Fool on the Hill"; "Flying." D: "Blue Jay Way."

UK Album releases

Please Please Me, March 22, 1963, Parlophone PMC 1202 (mono) / PCS 3042 (stereo)

> Side 1: "I Saw Her Standing There"; "Misery"; "Anna (Go to Him)"; "Chains"; "Boys"; "Ask Me Why"; "Please Please Me." Side 2: "Love Me Do"; "P.S. I Love You"; "Baby It's You"; "Do You Want to Know a Secret"; "A Taste of Honey"; "There's a Place"; "Twist and Shout."

With the Beatles, November 22, 1963, Parlophone PMC 1206 (mono) / PCS 3045 (stereo)

> Side 1: "It Won't Be Long"; "All I've Got to Do"; "All My Loving"; "Don't Bother Me"; "Little Child"; "Till There Was You"; "Please Mister Postman." Side 2: "Roll over Beethoven"; "Hold Me Tight"; "You Really Got a Hold on Me"; "I Wanna Be Your Man"; "Devil in Her Heart"; "Not a Second Time"; "Money (That's What I Want)."

A Hard Day's Night, July 10, 1964, Parlophone PMC 1230 (mono) / PCS 3058 (stereo)

> Side 1: "A Hard Day's Night"; "I Should Have Known Better"; "If I Fell"; "I'm Happy Just to Dance with You"; "And I Love Her"; "Tell Me Why"; "Can't Buy Me Love." Side 2: "Any Time at All"; "I'll Cry Instead"; "Things We Said Today"; "When I Get Home"; "You Can't Do That"; "I'll Be Back."

Beatles for Sale, December 4, 1964, Parlophone PMC 1240 (mono) / PCS 3062 (stereo)

Side 1: "No Reply"; "I'm a Loser"; "Baby's in Black"; "Rock and Roll Music"; "I'll Follow the Sun"; "Mr. Moonlight"; "Kansas City"/"Hey! Hey! Hey! Hey!" Side 2: "Eight Days a Week"; "Words of Love"; "Honey Don't"; "Every Little Thing"; "I Don't Want to Spoil the Party"; "What You're Doing"; "Everybody's Trying to Be My Baby."

Help!, August 6, 1965, Parlophone PMC 1255 (mono) / PCS 3071 (stereo)

Side 1: "Help!"; "The Night Before"; "You've Got to Hide Your Love Away"; "I Need You"; "Another Girl"; "You're Going to Lose That Girl"; "Ticket to Ride." Side 2: "Act Naturally"; "It's Only Love"; "You Like Me Too Much"; "Tell Me What You See"; "I've Just Seen a Face"; "Yesterday"; "Dizzy Miss Lizzy."

Rubber Soul, December 3, 1965, Parlophone PMC 1267 (mono) / PCS 3075 (stereo)

Side 1: "Drive My Car"; "Norwegian Wood (This Bird Has Flown)"; "You Won't See Me"; "Nowhere Man"; "Think for Yourself"; "The Word"; "Michelle." Side 2: "What Goes On"; "Girl"; "I'm Looking through You"; "In My Life"; "Wait"; "If I Needed Someone"; "Run for Your Life."

Revolver, August 5, 1966, Parlophone PMC 7009 (mono) / PCS 7009 (stereo)

Side 1: "Taxman"; "Eleanor Rigby"; "I'm Only Sleeping"; "Love You To"; "Here, There, and Everywhere"; "Yellow Submarine"; "She Said She Said." Side 2: "Good Day Sunshine"; "And Your Bird Can Sing"; "For No One"; "Doctor Robert"; "I Want to Tell You"; "Got to Get You into My Life"; "Tomorrow Never Knows."

A Collection of Beatles Oldies, December 9, 1966, Parlophone PMC 7016 (mono) / PCS 7016 (stereo)

Side 1: "She Loves You"; "From Me to You"; "We Can Work It Out"; "Help!"; "Michelle"; "Yesterday"; "I Feel Fine"; "Yellow Submarine." Side 2: "Can't Buy Me Love"; "Bad Boy"; "Day Tripper"; "A Hard Day's Night"; "Ticket to Ride"; "Paperback Writer"; "Eleanor Rigby"; "I Want to Hold Your Hand."

Sgt. Pepper's Lonely Hearts Club Band, June 1, 1967, Parlophone PMC 7027 (mono) / PCS 7027 (stereo)

Side 1: "Sgt. Pepper's Lonely Hearts Club Band"/"With a Little Help from My Friends"; "Lucy in the Sky with Diamonds"; "Getting Better"; "Fixing a Hole"; "She's Leaving Home"; "Being for the Benefit of Mr. Kite!" Side 2: "Within You Without You"; "When I'm Sixty-Four"; "Lovely Rita"; "Good Morning, Good Morning"; "Sgt. Pepper's Lonely Hearts Club Band (Reprise)"; "A Day in the Life"; "Sgt. Pepper's Inner Groove" [unlisted].

The Beatles [the "White Album"], November 22, 1968, Apple [Parlophone] PMC 7067–7068 (mono) / PCS 7067–7068 (stereo)

Side 1: "Back in the USSR"; "Dear Prudence"; "Glass Onion"; "Ob-La-Di, Ob-La-Da"; "Wild Honey Pie"; "The Continuing Story of Bungalow Bill"; "While My Guitar Gently Weeps"; "Happiness Is a Warm Gun." Side 2: "Martha My Dear"; "I'm So Tired"; "Blackbird"; "Piggies"; "Rocky Raccoon"; "Don't Pass Me By"; "Why Don't We Do It in the Road"; "I Will"; "Julia." Side 3:

"Birthday"; "Yer Blues"; "Mother Nature's Son"; "Everybody's Got Something to Hide Except Me and My Monkey"; "Sexy Sadie"; "Helter Skelter"; "Long Long Long," Side 4: "Revolution 1"; "Honey Pie"; "Savoy Truffle"; "Cry Baby Cry"; "Can You Take Me Back" [unlisted]; "Revolution 9"; "Good Night."

Yellow Submarine, January 17, 1969, Apple [Parlophone] PMC 7070 (mono) / PCS 7070 (stereo)

Side 1: "Yellow Submarine"; "Only a Northern Song"; "All Together Now"; "Hey Bulldog"; "It's All Too Much"; "All You Need Is Love." Side 2: "Pepperland" (instrumental); "Sea of Time"/"Sea of Holes" (instrumental); "Sea of Monsters" (instrumental); "March of the Meanies" (instrumental); "Pepperland Laid Waste" (instrumental); "Yellow Submarine in Pepperland" (instrumental).

Abbey Road, September 26, 1969, Apple [Parlophone] PCS 7088 (stereo)

Side 1: "Come Together"; "Something"; "Maxwell's Silver Hammer"; "Oh! Darling"; "Octopus's Garden"; "I Want You (She's So Heavy)." Side 2: "Here Comes the Sun"; "Because"; "You Never Give Me Your Money"; "Sun King"; "Mean Mr. Mustard"; "Polythene Pam"; "She Came in through the Bathroom Window"; "Golden Slumbers"; "Carry That Weight"; "The End"; "Her Majesty" [unlisted].

Let It Be, May 8, 1970, Apple [Parlophone] PCS 7096 (stereo)

Side 1: "Two of Us"; "Dig a Pony"; "Across the Universe"; "I Me Mine"; "Dig It"; "Let It Be"; "Maggie Mae." Side 2: "I've Got a Feeling"; "One after 909"; "The Long and Winding Road"; "For You Blue"; "Get Back."

US Singles releases

"My Bonnie"/"The Saints"; April 23, 1962, Decca 31382 (as Tony Sheridan and the Beat Brothers)

"Please Please Me"/"Ask Me Why"; February 25, 1963, Vee-Jay VJ 498

"From Me to You"/"Thank You Girl"; May 27, 1963, Vee-Jay VJ 522

"She Loves You"/"I'll Get You"; September 16, 1963, Swan 4152

"I Want to Hold Your Hand"/"I Saw Her Standing There"; December 26, 1963, Capitol 5112

"Please Please Me"/"From Me to You"; January 30, 1964, Vee-Jay VJ 581

"Twist and Shout"/"There's a Place"; March 2, 1964, Tollie 9001

"Can't Buy Me Love"/"You Can't Do That"; March 16, 1964, Capitol 5150

"Do You Want to Know a Secret"/"Thank You Girl"; March 23, 1964, Vee-Jay VJ 587

"Love Me Do"/"P.S. I Love You"; April 27, 1964, Tollie 9008

"Sie Liebt Dich" ["She Loves You"]/"I'll Get You"; May 21, 1964, Swan 4182

"A Hard Day's Night"/"I Should Have Known Better"; July 13, 1964, Capitol 5122

"I'll Cry Instead"/"I'm Happy Just to Dance with You"; July 20, 1964, Capitol 5234

"And I Love Her"/"If I Fell"; July 20, 1964, Capitol 5235

"Matchbox"/"Slow Down"; August 24, 1964, Capitol 5255

"I Feel Fine"/"She's a Woman"; November 23, 1964, Capitol 5327

"Eight Days a Week"/"I Don't Want to Spoil the Party"; February 15, 1965, Capitol 5371

"Ticket to Ride"/"Yes It Is"; April 19, 1965, Capitol 5407

"Help!"/"I'm Down"; July 19, 1965, Capitol 5476

"Yesterday"/"Act Naturally"; September 13, 1965, Capitol 5498

"We Can Work It Out"/"Day Tripper"; December 6, 1965, Capitol 5555

"Nowhere Man"/"What Goes On"; February 21, 1966, Capitol 5587

"Paperback Writer"/"Rain"; May 30, 1966, Capitol 5651

"Eleanor Rigby"/"Yellow Submarine"; August 8, 1966, Capitol 5715

"Strawberry Fields Forever"/"Penny Lane"; February 13, 1967, Capitol 5810

"All You Need Is Love"/"Baby, You're a Rich Man"; July 17, 1967, Capitol 5964

"Hello Goodbye"/"I Am the Walrus"; November 27, 1967, Capitol 2056

"Lady Madonna"/"The Inner Light"; March 18, 1968, Capitol 2138

"Hey Jude"/"Revolution"; August 26, 1968, Apple [Capitol] 2276

"Get Back"/"Don't Let Me Down"; May 5, 1969, Apple [Capitol] 2490 (as the Beatles with Billy Preston)

"The Ballad of John and Yoko"/"Old Brown Shoe"; June 4, 1969, Apple [Capitol] 2531

"Something"/"Come Together"; October 6, 1969, Apple [Capitol] 2654

"Let It Be"/"You Know My Name (Look Up the Number)"; March 11, 1970, Apple [Capitol] 2764

"The Long and Winding Road"/"For You Blue"; May 11, 1970, Apple [Capitol] 2832

US EP Releases

The Beatles, March 23, 1964, Vee-Jay VJEP 1–903 (mono)

A: "Misery"; "A Taste of Honey." B: "Ask Me Why"; "Anna (Go to Him)."

Four by the Beatles, May 11, 1964, Capitol EAP 1–2121 (mono)

A: "Roll over Beethoven"; "All My Loving." B: "This Boy"; "Please Mister Postman."

4 by the Beatles, February 1, 1965, Capitol R 5365 (mono)

A: "Honey Don't"; "I'm a Loser." B: "Mr. Moonlight"; "Everybody's Trying to Be My Baby."

US Album releases

Introducing the Beatles [first issue], July 22, 1963, Vee-Jay VJLP 1062 (mono) / SR 1062 (stereo)

Side 1: "I Saw Her Standing There"; "Misery"; "Anna (Go to Him)"; "Chains"; "Boys"; "Love Me Do." Side 2: "P.S. I Love You"; "Baby It's You"; "Do You Want to Know a Secret"; "A Taste of Honey"; "There's a Place"; "Twist and Shout."

Meet the Beatles!, January 20, 1964, Capitol T 2047 (mono) / ST 2047 (stereo)

Side 1: "I Want to Hold Your Hand"; "I Saw Her Standing There"; "This Boy"; "It Won't Be Long"; "All I've Got to Do"; "All My Loving." Side 2: "Don't Bother Me"; "Little Child"; "Till There Was You"; "Hold Me Tight"; "I Wanna Be Your Man"; "Not a Second Time."

Introducing the Beatles [second issue], January 27, 1964, Vee-Jay VJLP 1062 (mono)

Side 1: "I Saw Her Standing There"; "Misery"; "Anna (Go to Him)"; "Chains"; "Boys"; "Ask Me Why." Side 2: "Please Please Me"; "Baby It's You"; "Do You Want to Know a Secret"; "A Taste of Honey"; "There's a Place"; "Twist and Shout."

The Beatles' Second Album, April 10, 1964, Capitol T 2080 (mono) / ST 2080 (stereo)

Side 1: "Roll over Beethoven"; "Thank You Girl"; "You Really Got a Hold on Me"; "Devil in Her Heart"; "Money (That's What I Want)"; "You Can't Do That." Side 2: "Long Tall Sally"; "I Call Your Name"; "Please Mister Postman"; "I'll Get You"; "She Loves You."

A Hard Day's Night, June 26, 1964, United Artists UA 6366 (mono) / UAS 6366 (stereo)

Side 1: "A Hard Day's Night"; "Tell Me Why"; "I'll Cry Instead"; "I Should Have Known Better" (instrumental); "I'm Happy Just to Dance with You"; "And I Love Her" (instrumental). Side 2: "I Should Have Known Better"; "If I Fell"; "And I Love Her"; "Ringo's Theme (This Boy)" (instrumental); "Can't Buy Me Love"; "A Hard Day's Night" (instrumental).

Something New, July 20, 1964, Capitol T 2108 (mono) / ST 2108 (stereo)

Side 1: "I'll Cry Instead"; "Things We Said Today"; "Any Time at All"; "When I Get Home"; "Slow Down"; "Matchbox." Side 2: "Tell Me Why"; "And I Love Her"; "I'm Happy Just to Dance with You"; "If I Fell"; "Komm, Gib Mir Deine Hand" ["I Want to Hold Your Hand"].

The Beatles' Story, November 23, 1964, Capitol TBO 2222 (mono) / STBO 2222 (stereo)

Side 1: Interviews plus extracts from "I Want to Hold Your Hand"; "Slow Down"; "This Boy." Side 2: Interviews plus extracts from "You Can't Do That"; "If I Fell"; "And I Love Her." Side 3: Interviews plus extracts from "A Hard Day's Night"; "And I Love Her." Side 4: Interviews plus extracts from "Twist and Shout" (live); "Things We Said Today"; "I'm Happy Just to Dance with You"; "Long Tall Sally"; "She Loves You"; "Boys."

Beatles '65, December 15, 1964, Capitol T 2228 (mono) / ST 2228 (stereo)

Side 1: "No Reply"; "I'm a Loser"; "Baby's in Black"; "Rock and Roll Music"; "I'll Follow the Sun"; "Mr. Moonlight." Side 2: "Honey Don't"; "I'll Be Back"; "She's a Woman"; "I Feel Fine"; "Everybody's Trying to Be My Baby."

The Early Beatles, March 22, 1965, Capitol T 2309 (mono) / ST 2309 (stereo)

Side 1: "Love Me Do"; "Twist and Shout"; "Anna (Go to Him)"; "Chains"; "Boys"; "Ask Me Why." Side 2: "Please Please Me"; "P.S. I Love You"; "Baby It's You"; "A Taste of Honey"; "Do You Want to Know a Secret."

Beatles VI, June 14, 1965, Capitol T 2358 (mono) / ST 2358 (stereo)

Side 1: "Kansas City"/"Hey! Hey! Hey! Hey!"; "Eight Days a Week"; "You Like Me Too Much"; "Bad Boy"; "I Don't Want to Spoil the Party"; "Words of Love." Side 2: "What You're Doing"; "Yes It Is"; "Dizzy Miss Lizzy"; "Tell Me What You See"; "Every Little Thing."

Help!, August 13, 1965, Capitol MAS 2386 (mono) / SMAS 2386 (stereo)

Side 1: "James Bond Theme" [unlisted]; "Help!"; "The Night Before"; "From Me to You Fantasy" (instrumental); "You've Got to Hide Your Love Away";

"I Need You"; "In the Tyrol" (instrumental). Side 2: "Another Girl"; "Another Hard Day's Night" (instrumental); "Ticket to Ride"; "The Bitter End"/"You Can't Do That" (instrumental); "You're Going to Lose That Girl"; "The Chase" (instrumental).

Rubber Soul, December 6, 1965, Capitol T 2442 (mono) / ST 2442 (stereo)

Side 1: "I've Just Seen a Face"; "Norwegian Wood (This Bird Has Flown)"; "You Won't See Me"; "Think for Yourself"; "The Word"; "Michelle." Side 2: "It's Only Love"; "Girl"; "I'm Looking through You"; "In My Life"; "Wait"; "Run for Your Life."

Yesterday . . . and Today, June 20, 1966, Capitol T 2553 (mono) / ST 2553 (stereo)

Side 1: "Drive My Car"; "I'm Only Sleeping"; "Nowhere Man"; "Doctor Robert"; "Yesterday"; "Act Naturally." Side 2: "And Your Bird Can Sing"; "If I Needed Someone"; "We Can Work It Out"; "What Goes On"; "Day Tripper."

Revolver, August 8, 1966, Capitol T 2576 (mono) / ST 2576 (stereo)

Side 1: "Taxman"; "Eleanor Rigby"; "Love You To"; "Here, There, and Everywhere"; "Yellow Submarine"; "She Said She Said." Side 2: "Good Day Sunshine"; "For No One"; "I Want to Tell You"; "Got to Get You into My Life"; "Tomorrow Never Knows."

Sgt. Pepper's Lonely Hearts Club Band, June 2, 1967, Capitol MAS 2653 (mono) / SMAS 2653 (stereo)

Side 1: "Sgt. Pepper's Lonely Hearts Club Band"/"With a Little Help from My Friends"; "Lucy in the Sky with Diamonds"; "Getting Better"; "Fixing a Hole"; "She's Leaving Home"; "Being for the Benefit of Mr. Kite!" Side 2: "Within You Without You"; "When I'm Sixty-Four"; "Lovely Rita"; "Good Morning, Good Morning"; "Sgt. Pepper's Lonely Hearts Club Band (Reprise)"; "A Day in the Life."

Magical Mystery Tour, November 27, 1967, Capitol MAL 2835 (mono) / SMAL 2835 (stereo)

Side 1: "Magical Mystery Tour"; "The Fool on the Hill"; "Flying"; "Blue Jay Way"; "Your Mother Should Know"; "I Am the Walrus." Side 2: "Hello Goodbye"; "Strawberry Fields Forever"; "Penny Lane"; "Baby, You're a Rich Man"; "All You Need Is Love."

The Beatles [the "White Album"], November 25, 1968, Apple [Capitol] SWBO 101 (stereo)

Side 1: "Back in the USSR"; "Dear Prudence"; "Glass Onion"; "Ob-La-Di, Ob-La-Da"; "Wild Honey Pie"; "The Continuing Story of Bungalow Bill"; "While My Guitar Gently Weeps"; "Happiness Is a Warm Gun." Side 2: "Martha My Dear"; "I'm So Tired"; "Blackbird"; "Piggies"; "Rocky Raccoon"; "Don't Pass Me By"; "Why Don't We Do It in the Road"; "I Will"; "Julia." Side 3: "Birthday"; "Yer Blues"; "Mother Nature's Son"; "Everybody's Got Something to Hide Except Me and My Monkey"; "Sexy Sadie"; "Helter Skelter"; "Long Long Long." Side 4: "Revolution 1"; "Honey Pie"; "Savoy Truffle"; "Cry Baby Cry"; "Can You Take Me Back" [unlisted]; "Revolution 9"; "Good Night."

Yellow Submarine, January 13, 1969, Apple [Capitol] SW 153 (stereo)

Side 1: "Yellow Submarine"; "Only a Northern Song"; "All Together Now"; "Hey Bulldog"; "It's All Too Much"; "All You Need Is Love." Side 2: "Pepperland" (instrumental); "Sea of Time"/"Sea of Holes" (instrumental); "Sea of Monsters" (instrumental); "March of the Meanies" (instrumental); "Pepperland Laid Waste" (instrumental); "Yellow Submarine in Pepperland" (instrumental).

Abbey Road, October 1, 1969, Apple [Capitol] SO 383 (stereo)

Side 1: "Come Together"; "Something"; "Maxwell's Silver Hammer"; "Oh! Darling"; "Octopus's Garden"; "I Want You (She's So Heavy)." Side 2: "Here Comes the Sun"; "Because"; "You Never Give Me Your Money"; "Sun King"; "Mean Mr. Mustard"; "Polythene Pam"; "She Came in through the Bathroom Window"; "Golden Slumbers"; "Carry That Weight"; "The End"; "Her Majesty" [unlisted].

Hey Jude, February 26, 1970, Apple [Capitol] SW 385 (stereo)

Side 1: "Can't Buy Me Love"; "I Should Have Known Better"; "Paperback Writer"; "Rain"; "Lady Madonna"; "Revolution." Side 2: "Hey Jude"; "Old Brown Shoe"; "Don't Let Me Down"; "The Ballad of John and Yoko."

Let It Be, May 18, 1970, Apple [Capitol] AR 34001 (stereo)

Side 1: "Two of Us"; "Dig a Pony"; "Across the Universe"; "I Me Mine"; "Dig It"; "Let It Be"; "Maggie May." Side 2: "I've Got a Feeling"; "One after 909"; "The Long and Winding Road"; "For You Blue"; "Get Back."

Select bibliography

"101 Greatest Beatle Songs," *MOJO* 146, January 2006.

Abraham, Mark, *The Teenage Consumer* (London: London Press Exchange, 1959).

Adler, Renata, "Screen: 'Candy', Compromises Galore," review of *Candy* (Cinerama Releasing Corporation movie), *New York Times*, December 18, 1968, 54.

Adorno, Theodor, "The Aging of the New Music," *Essays on Music*, in Richard Leppert (ed.), *Essays on Music* (Berkeley: University of California Press, 2002), 181–202.

——— "On the Contemporary Relationship of Philosophy and Music," in Richard Leppert (ed.), *Essays on Music* (Berkeley: University of California Press, 2002), 135–61.

——— "On Popular Music," in Richard Leppert (ed.), *Essays on Music* (Berkeley: University of California Press, 2002), 437–69.

——— "Why Is the New Art so Hard to Understand?," in Richard Leppert (ed.), *Essays on Music* (Berkeley: University of California Press, 2002), 127–34.

"Albums: Some Time in New York City," review of *Some Time in New York City* (Apple LP), by John Lennon and Yoko Ono, with the Plastic Ono Band, *Melody Maker*, October 7, 1972, 25.

Aldridge, Alan (ed.), *The Beatles Illustrated Lyrics* (London: Macdonald, 1969).

Alexander, Marsha, *The Sexual Paradise of LSD* (North Hollywood: Brandon House, 1967).

Alterman, Loraine, "Pop: Paul's Grooves Will Grab You," review of *Band on the Run* (Apple LP), by Paul McCartney and Wings, *New York Times*, December 2, 1973, 208.

——— "Ringo Dishes Up a 'Hot Fudge Sundae,'" review of *Mind Games* (Apple LP), by John Lennon, and *Ringo* (Apple LP), by Ringo Starr, *New York Times*, November 25, 1973, 188.

Anson, Robert Sam, "At the Garden," *New Yorker*, January 13, 1975, 30.

——— *Gone Crazy and Back Again: The Rise and Fall of the Rolling Stone Generation* (Garden City: Doubleday, 1981).

Axelrod, Mitchell, *BeatleToons: The Real Story Behind the Cartoon Beatles* (Pickens, SC: Wynn Publishing, 1999).

Babiuk, Andy, *Beatles Gear: All the Fab Four's Instruments, from Stage to Studio* (San Francisco: Backbeat, 2001).

Badman, Keith, *The Beatles: Off the Record* (New York: Omnibus, 2000), reissued as *The Beatles: Off the Record: The Dream Is Over* (New York: Omnibus, 2002).

——— *The Beatles Diary*, II: *After the Breakup, 1970–2001* (London: Omnibus Press, 2001).

Baird, Julia, with Guiliano, Geoffrey, *John Lennon: My Brother* (New York: Henry Holt, 1988).

Barthes, Roland, "The Death of the Author," in Roland Barthes, *Image–Music–Text*, trans. Stephen Heath (London: Fontana; New York: Noonday Press, 1977), 142–8.

_____ "Musica practica," in Roland Barthes, *Image–Music–Text*, trans. Stephen Heath (London: Fontana; New York: Noonday Press, 1977), 149–54.

Baur, Steven, "Ringo Round *Revolver*: Rhythm, Timbre, and Tempo in Rock Drumming," in Russell Reising (ed.), *"Every Sound There Is": The Beatles' Revolver and the Transformation of Rock and Roll* (Aldershot: Ashgate, 2002), 171–82.

"Beatle George Harrison Dies," Cable News Network (CNN), December 1, 2001, at http://archives.cnn.com/2001/SHOWBIZ/Music/11/30/harrison.obit (accessed August 26, 2005).

Beatles, The, *The Beatles Anthology* (London: Cassell; San Francisco: Chronicle, 2000).

_____ *The Beatles Anthology* (television series), directed by Geoff Wonfor (Apple, 1996).

Beatles Ultimate Experience website: www.beatlesinterviews.org.

_____ *"The Beatles," Television Chronicles* 3 (1995), 8–15.

_____ *The Beatles Complete Scores* (Milwaukee: Hal Leonard Corporation, 1989).

Bender, William, "Let George Do It," review of *All Things Must Pass* (Apple LP), by George Harrison, *Time*, November 30, 1970, 57.

Bernstein, Adam, "George Harrison Dies, 58, Pushed Fab Four in New Directions," *Washington Post*, December 1, 2001, A01.

Best, Pete, and Doncaster, Patrick, *Beatle! The Pete Best Story* (London: Plexus, 1985).

Bird, Brian, *Skiffle: The Story of Folk-Song with a Jazz Beat* (London: Robert Hale, 1958).

Bird, Donald Alport, Holder, Stephen C., and Sears, Diane, "Walrus Is Greek for Corpse: Rumor and the Death of Paul McCartney," *Journal of Popular Culture* 10 (1976), 110–21.

Bisbort, Alan, and Puterbaugh, Parke, *Rhino's Psychedelic Trip* (San Francisco: Miller Freeman, 2000).

Bishop, Malden Grange, *The Discovery of Love: A Psychedelic Experience with LSD-25* (New York: Dodd, Mead & Co., 1963).

Blaney, John, *Lennon and McCartney: Together Alone* (London: Jawbone Press, 2007), 31–2.

Booker, Christopher, *The Neophiliacs: The Revolution in English Life in the Fifties and Sixties* (London: Collins, 1969).

Bowen, Phil, *A Gallery To Play To: The Story of the Mersey Poets* (Exeter: Stride Publications, 1999).

Bradby, Barbara, "She Told Me What to Say: The Beatles and Girl-Group Discourse," *Popular Music and Society* 28/3 (2005), 359–90.

Bresler, Fenton, *The Murder of John Lennon* (London: Sidgwick & Jackson, 1989).

Brewer-Giorgio, Gail, *Is Elvis Alive?* (New York: Tudor, 1988).

Brocken, Michael, "Was It Really Like That?: *Rock Island Line* and the Instabilities of Causational Popular Music Histories," *Popular Music History* 1/2 (2006), 147–66.

Brookhiser, Richard, "John Lennon, RIP," *National Review*, December 31, 1980, 1555.

Brown, Peter, with Gaines, Steven, *The Love You Make: An Insider's Story of the Beatles* (London: Macmillan, 1983).

Burns, Gary, "Refab Four: Beatles for Sale in the Age of Music Video," in Ian Inglis (ed.), *The Beatles, Popular Music and Society: A Thousand Voices* (Basingstoke: Macmillan, 2000), 176–88.

———— "The Myth of the Beatles," *South Atlantic Quarterly* 86 (1987), 169–80.

Byatt, A. S., *Babel Tower* (London: Vintage, 1997).

Carr, Roy, and Tyler, Tony, *The Beatles: An Illustrated Record* (New York: Harmony, 1975).

Carson, Tom, "Bad Boy," review of *Bad Boy* (Polidor/Portrait LP), by Ringo Starr, *Rolling Stone*, July 12, 1978, 52.

Charlesworth, Chris, "Mutton Dressed as Ram?," review of *Ram* (Apple LP), by Paul and Linda McCartney, *Melody Maker*, May 27, 1971, 11.

Christgau, Robert, "Symbolic Comrades," *Village Voice*, January 14, 1981, 31–2.

Clayson, Alan, *George Harrison: The Quiet One* (London: Sidgwick & Jackson, 1989).

———— *Ringo Starr* (1996; London: Sanctuary, 2003).

Clayson, Alan, and Sutcliffe, Pauline, *Backbeat: Stuart Sutcliffe – The Lost Beatle* (London: Pan, 1994).

Cloud, Cam, *The Little Book of Acid* (Berkeley: Ronin, 1999).

Clydesdale, Greg, "Creativity and Competition: The Beatles," *Creativity Research Journal* 18 (2006), 129–39.

Cohen, Mitchell, "John Lennon's Last," review of *Double Fantasy* (Geffen LP), by John Lennon and Yoko Ono, *High Fidelity*, February 1981, 92.

Cohen, Sidney, *The Beyond Within: The LSD Story* (New York: Atheneum, 1966).

Coleman, Ray, *Brian Epstein* (Harmondsworth: Penguin, 1990).

———— *Lennon* (New York: McGraw-Hill, 1986), revised and updated as *Lennon: The Definitive Biography* (London: Pan, 1995).

———— "George Harrison: Somewhere in England," review of *Somewhere in England* (Dark Horse LP), by George Harrison, *Melody Maker*, June 6, 1981, 27.

Cone, Edward T., *Musical Form and Musical Performance* (New York: Norton, 1968).

Connolly, Ray, *John Lennon 1940–1980: A Biography* (London: Fontana, 1981).

Cooper, Grosvenor W., and Meyer, Leonard B., *The Rhythmic Structure of Music* (Chicago: University of Chicago Press, 1956).

Cording, Robert, Jankowski-Smith, Shelli, and Miller Laino, E. J. (eds.), *In My Life: Encounters with the Beatles* (New York: Fromm International, 1998).

Coren, Alan, "James Paul McCartney," review of *James Paul McCartney* (ATV television program), *The Times*, May 11, 1973, 11.

Cott, Jonathan, "Two Virgins," review of *Two Virgins* (Apple LP), by John Lennon and Yoko Ono, *Rolling Stone*, March 1, 1969, 20.

"Dark Horse," review of *Dark Horse* (Apple LP), by George Harrison, *High Fidelity*, April 1975, 101.

Davies, Hunter, *The Beatles* (New York: McGraw-Hill, 1968; rev. edns., New York: Norton, 1985, 1996).

Davis, Evan, "Psychological Characteristics of Beatle Mania," *Journal of the History of Ideas* 30 (1969), 273–80.

DeRogatis, Jim, *Kaleidoscope Eyes: Psychedelic Rock from the '60s to the '90s* (Secaucus, NJ: Carol Publishing Group, 1996).

Dickinson, Emily, Poem 745, in Thomas H. Johnson (ed.), *Final Harvest: Emily Dickinson's Poems* (Boston, MA: Little, Brown, 1961).

Doggett, Peter, *Let It Be / Abbey Road* (New York: Schirmer; London: Prentice Hall International, 1998).

Doney, Malcolm, *Lennon and McCartney* (New York: Hippocrene, 1981).

Dove, Ian, "Records: Harrison's Turn," review of *Living in the Material World* (Apple LP), by George Harrison, *New York Times*, June 6, 1973, 37.

_____ "Records by McCartney," review of *Red Rose Speedway* (Apple LP), by Paul McCartney and Wings, *New York Times*, May 2, 1973, 37.

Dowlding, William J., *Beatlesongs* (New York: Fireside, 1989).

Draper, Robert, *Rolling Stone Magazine: The Uncensored History* (New York: Doubleday, 1990).

Duncan, Amy, "Soundtakes: George Harrison, *Cloud Nine*," review of *Cloud Nine* (Dark Horse LP), by George Harrison, November 18, 1987, 21.

Dyer, Richard, *Stars*, new edn., with a supplementary chapter by Paul McDonald (London: British Film Institute, 1998; 1st edn. 1980).

Dylan, Bob, "Love Minus Zero / No Limit," *Bringing It All Back Home* (Columbia, 1965).

Eastland, Terry, "In Defense of Religious America," *Commentary*, June 1981, 39–45.

Ebert, Roger, "Cinema: Two Virgins and Number Five, by Yoko Ono and John Lennon," *Rolling Stone*, December 21, 1968, 15, 30.

Edera, Bruno, *Full Length Animated Feature Films* (London: Focal Press, 1977).

Edwards, Henry, "Mind Games," review of *Mind Games* (Apple LP), by John Lennon, *High Fidelity*, March 1974, 109.

_____ "The Provocative Lennon–Ono Marriage," review of *Imagine* (Apple LP), by John Lennon, *High Fidelity*, January 1972, 77.

Elliott, Anthony, *The Mourning of John Lennon* (Berkeley: University of California Press, 1999).

Ellis, Royston, *Rave* (Northwood: Scorpion Press, 1960).

Ellson, R. N., *Sex-Happy Hippy* (San Diego: Corinth, 1968).

Emerick, Geoff, and Massey, Howard, *Here, There, and Everywhere: My Life Recording the Music of the Beatles* (New York: Gotham, 2006).

Epstein, Brian, *A Cellarful of Noise* (London: Souvenir Press, 1964).

Everett, Walter, *The Beatles as Musicians: The Quarry Men Through* Rubber Soul (New York: Oxford University Press, 2001).

_____ *The Beatles as Musicians:* Revolver *Through the* Anthology (New York: Oxford University Press, 1999).

"Fellow Traveling with Jesus," *Time*, September 6, 1971, 54–5.

Fletcher, Colin, "Beat and Gangs on Merseyside," *New Society*, February 20, 1964.

Flippo, Chet, *Yesterday: The Unauthorized Autobiography of Paul McCartney* (New York: Doubleday, 1989).

Fogo, Fred, *"I Read the News Today": The Social Drama of John Lennon's Death* (Lanham, MD: Rowman & Littlefield, 1994).

Fraenkel, Michael, *"Passing of Body" in Death Is Not Enough: Essays in Active Negation* (London: C. W. Daniel, 1939).

Friedan, Betty, *The Feminine Mystique* (New York: Norton, 1963).

Frith, Simon, "Introduction: Everything Counts," in Simon Frith, *Music for Pleasure: Essays in the Sociology of Pop* (New York: Routledge, 1988), 1–10.

Frith, Simon, and Goodwin, Andrew (eds.), *On Record: Rock, Pop and the Written Word* (New York: Pantheon, 1990).

Frith, Simon, and Horne, Howard, *Art Into Pop* (London and New York: Methuen, 1987).

Frontani, Michael, *The Beatles: Image and the Media* (Jackson: University Press of Mississippi, 2007).

Gaitskill, Mary, *Veronica* (New York: Vintage, 2005).

Garbarini, Vic, Cullman, Brian, and Graustark, Barbara, *Strawberry Fields Forever: John Lennon Remembered* (New York: Bantam Books, 1980).

Geller, Debbie, and Wall, Anthony (eds.), *The Brian Epstein Story* (London: Faber & Faber, 2000).

"George Harrison," review of *George Harrison* (Dark Horse LP), by George Harrison, *High Fidelity*, May 1979, 124–5.

"George Harrison: Thirty-Three & 1/3," review of *Thirty-Three & 1/3* (Dark Horse LP), by George Harrison, *High Fidelity*, March 1977, 140.

Gerson, Ben, "Records: All Things Must Pass," review of *All Things Must Pass* (Apple LP), by George Harrison, *Rolling Stone*, January 7, 1971, 46.

———— "Records: Imagine," review of *Imagine* (Apple LP), by John Lennon, *Rolling Stone*, October 28, 1971, 48.

———— "Records: Ringo," review of *Ringo* (Apple LP), by Ringo Starr, *Rolling Stone*, December 20, 1973, 73.

———— "Walls and Bridges," review of Walls and Bridges (Apple LP), by John Lennon, *Rolling Stone*, November 21, 1974, 72, 74, 76.

Gillett, Charlie, *The Sound of the City* (London: Souvenir Press, 1970).

Gitlin, Todd, "John Lennon Speaking . . . " *Commonweal*, September 22, 1972, 500–3.

———— "The Lennon Legacy," *The Center Magazine*, May/June 1981, 2–4.

Giuliano, Geoffrey, *The Lost Beatles Interviews* (New York: Plume Books, 1994).

———— *Two Of Us: John Lennon and Paul McCartney Behind the Myth* (New York: Penguin, 1999).

Gledhill, Christine, *Stardom: Industry of Desire* (London: Routledge, 1991).

Goldman, Albert, *The Lives of John Lennon* (New York: William Morrow, 1988).

Goldstein, Toby, "London Town: So What's Wrong with Silly Love Songs?," review of *London Town* (Capitol LP), by Paul McCartney, *High Fidelity*, July 1978, 120.

Golson, G. Barry (ed.), *John Lennon and Yoko Ono: The Final Testament* (New York: Berkeley Books, 1981).

_____ *The* Playboy *Interviews with John Lennon and Yoko Ono: The Final Testament* (New York: Berkeley, 1981).

Goodwin, Andrew, *Dancing in the Distraction Factory: Music, Television and Popular Culture* (Minneapolis: University of Minnesota Press, 1992).

Gorman, P., "Badly Drawn Boys," *MOJO* (July 2000), 20–1.

Gould, Jonathan, *Can't Buy Me Love: The Beatles, Britain, and America* (New York: Harmony, 2007).

Gramsci, Antonio, *Selections from the Prison Notebooks*, ed. and trans. Quintin Hoare and Geoffrey Nowell-Smith (London: Lawrence & Wishart, 1971).

Granados, Stefan, *Those Were the Days: An Unofficial History of the Beatles Apple Organization 1967–2002* (London: Cherry Red Books, 2002).

Graustark, Barbara, "The Real John Lennon," *Newsweek*, September 29, 1980, 76–7.

Greenspun, Roger, "Screen: Satirical 'Magic Christian,'" review of *The Magic Christian* (Commonwealth United movie), *New York Times*, February 12, 1970, 29.

Grof, Stanislav, MD, *LSD Psychotherapy: Exploring the Frontiers of the Hidden Mind* (Alameda, CA: Hunter House, 1980).

Grossberg, Lawrence, *We Gotta Get Out of This Place: Popular Conservatism and Postmodern Culture* (New York: Routledge, 1992).

Harrington, Richard, "McCartney & Sinatra: The Past Is Still Best," review of *McCartney II* (Parlophone/EMI LP), by Paul McCartney, *Washington Post*, June 15, 1980, A1.

Harrington, Richard, "Pap from John and Yoko," review of *Double Fantasy* (Geffen LP), by John Lennon and Yoko Ono, *Washington Post*, November 26, 1980, A1.

Harris, John, "Sgt. Pepper, *the Day the World Turned Day-Glo*," *MOJO* 160 (March 2007), 72–89.

Harrison, George, *I Me Mine* (London: W. H. Allen, 1982; San Francisco: Chronicle Books, 2002).

"Harrison: Eastern Promise," review of *Dark Horse* (Apple LP), by George Harrison, December 21, 1974, 36.

"Harrison Regains His Rubber Soul," review of *Thirty-Three & 1/3* (Dark Horse LP), by George Harrison, *Melody Maker*, November 27, 1976, 23.

Harry, Bill, *The Book of Beatle Lists* (Poole: Javelin, 1985).

Heckman, Don, "Pop: Two and a Half Beatles on Their Own," review of *All Things Must Pass* (Apple LP), by George Harrison, and *Plastic Ono Band* (Apple LP), by John Lennon, *New York Times*, December 20, 1970, 104.

_____ "Recordings: Making a Star of Starr," review of *Beaucoups of Blues* (Apple LP), *New York Times*, November 22, 1970, 133.

Henderson, Leigh, "About LSD," in *LSD: Still with Us after All These Years* (New York: Lexington Books, 1994).

Hennessey, Peter, *Having It So Good: Britain in the Fifties* (London: Allen Lane, 2006).

Hertsgaard, Mark, *A Day in the Life: The Music and Artistry of the Beatles* (New York: Delacorte, 1995).

Hieronimus, Robert R., *Inside the Yellow Submarine: The Making of the Beatles'
Animated Classic*, editing and compilation assistance by Laura Cortner (Iola, WI:
Krause Publications, 2002).

Hofmann, Albert, *LSD: My Problem Child* (Los Angeles: Tarcher, 1983).

Holden, Stephen, "George Harrison," review of *George Harrison* (Dark Horse LP),
by George Harrison, *Rolling Stone*, April 19, 1979, 90.

———— "Lennon's Music: A Range of Genius," *Rolling Stone*, January 22, 1981, 64–7,
70.

———— "Living in the Material World," review of *Living in the Material World*
(Apple LP), by George Harrison, *Rolling Stone*, July 19, 1973, 54.

———— "*McCartney II*," review of *McCartney II* (Parlophone/EMI LP), by Paul
McCartney, *Rolling Stone*, July 24, 1980, 54.

———— "On the Wings of Silly Love Songs," review of *Wings at the Speed of Sound*
(Capitol LP), by Wings, *Rolling Stone*, May 20, 1976, 67, 69.

———— "Pop View: Rock Grows Up, Gracefully and Otherwise," review of *Cloud
Nine* (Dark Horse LP), by George Harrison, *New York Times*, November 8, 1987,
H29.

———— "Records: Sometime in New York City," review of *Some Time in New York
City* (Apple LP), by John Lennon and Yoko Ono, with Elephant's Memory,
Rolling Stone, July 20, 1972, 48.

———— "Ringo the 4th," review of *Ringo the 4th* (Polydor/Atlantic LP), by Ringo
Starr, *Rolling Stone*, November 17, 1977, 94.

———— "Songs of Innocence and Experience for the Pop Fan of a Certain Age,"
review of *Flaming Pie* (Capitol CD), by Paul McCartney, *New York Times*,
November 28, 1997, E1, 33.

Hollingsworth, Roy, "Albums: Some Time in New York City," review of *Some Time
in New York City* (Apple LP), by John Lennon and Yoko Ono, with the Plastic
Ono Band, *Melody Maker*, June 10, 1972, 9.

———— "Pop Albums: 'Imagine,'" review of *Imagine* (Apple LP), by John Lennon,
Melody Maker, October 9, 1971, 21.

Howlett, Kevin, *The Beatles at the Beeb 1962–65: The Story of Their Radio Career*
(London: BBC Publications, 1982).

———— "The Beatles' Radio Sessions 1962–65," in CD booklet, *The Beatles Live at
the BBC* (Apple, 1994), 7–12.

Hudson, Winthrop S., *Religion in America*, 3rd edn. (New York: Charles Scribner's
Sons, 1981).

Inglis, Ian (ed.), *The Beatles, Popular Music, and Society: A Thousand Voices* (New
York: St. Martin's, 2000).

———— "Conformity, Status and Innovation: The Accumulation and Utilization of
Idiosyncrasy Credits in the Career of the Beatles," *Popular Music and Society* 19/3
(1995), 41–74.

Irvin, Jim, "The *MOJO* Interview: George Martin," *MOJO* 160 (March 2007), 37–40.

Jarrett, Michael, "Authenticity," in Michael Jarrett, *Sound Tracks: A Musical ABC*, 3
vols. (Philadelphia: Temple University Press, 1998), I, 189–201.

Johnston, Laurie, "Women's Group to Observe Rights Day Here Today," *New York
Times*, August 25, 1972, 40.

"Jolly Nice, Ringo," *Melody Maker*, October 23, 1976, 27.

Jonas, Oswald, *Introduction to the Theory of Heinrich Schenker*, trans. and ed. John Rothgeb (1934; New York: Longman, 1982).

Jones, Jack, *Let Me Take You Down: Inside the Mind of Mark David Chapman, the Man Who Killed John Lennon* (New York: Villard Books, 1992).

Jones, Nick, "The Rolling Stone Interview: George Harrison," *Rolling Stone*, February 24, 1968, 16.

Joyce, Mike, "Records: Traveling Wilburys Vol. 1," review of *The Traveling Wilburys: Volume One* (Warner Brothers LP), by the Traveling Wilburys, *Washington Post*, November 16, 1988, D7.

Judt, Tony, *Postwar: A History of Europe since 1945* (London: Heinemann, 2005).

Kaye, Lenny, "Red Rose Speedway," review of *Red Rose Speedway* (Apple LP), by Paul McCartney and Wings, *Rolling Stone*, July 5, 1973, 68.

Kernis, Mark, "McCartney and Wings Just Won't Fly," review of *London Town* (Parlophone/EMI LP), by Wings, *Washington Post*, April 16, 1978, A1.

Kinsey, Alfred C., *Sexual Behavior in the Human Female* (Philadelphia: W. B. Saunders, 1953).

_____ *Sexual Behavior in the Human Male* (Philadelphia: W. B. Saunders, 1948).

Kot, Greg, "Toppermost of the Poppermost," in June Skinner Sawyers (ed.), *Read the Beatles* (New York: Penguin, 2006), 322–6.

Kozinn, Allan, *The Beatles* (London: Phaidon, 1995).

_____ "Music of a Beatle Who Never Stopped," review of *Brainwashed* (Dark Horse CD), by George Harrison, *New York Times*, November 17, 2002, A27.

_____ "'Ram,'" review of *Ram* (Apple LP), by Paul and Linda McCartney, *Rolling Stone*, July 8, 1971, 42.

_____ "Ringo Outdistances His Past, Finally," review of *Vertical Man* (Mercury LP), by Ringo Starr, *New York Times*, June 21, 1998, AR28.

_____ "Ringo Starr, a 60's [*sic*] Relic? Not if He Can Help It," *New York Times*, May 31, 1992, H24.

Laing, R. D., *The Politics of Experience* (New York: Ballantine, 1967).

Lambert, Philip, *Inside the Music of Brian Wilson* (New York: Continuum, 2007).

Landau, Jon, "Band on the Run," review of *Band on the Run* (Apple LP), by Paul McCartney and Wings, *Rolling Stone*, January 31, 1974, 48, 50.

_____ "Mind Games," review of *Mind Games*, by John Lennon, *Rolling Stone*, January 3, 1974, 61.

_____ "Singles: 'My Sweet Lord' / 'Isn't It a Pity,'" review of "My Sweet Lord" / "Isn't It a Pity" (Apple single), by George Harrison, *Rolling Stone*, December 24, 1970, 56.

Lasch, Christopher, *The Culture of Narcissism: American Life in an Age of Diminishing Expectations* (New York: Norton, 1978).

Leary, Timothy, *Flashbacks: An Autobiography – A Personal and Cultural History of an Era* (New York: Putnam, 1983).

_____ *High Priest* (Berkeley: Ronin, 1995).

Leary, Timothy, Metzner, Ralph, and Alpert, Richard, *The Psychedelic Experience: A Manual Based on "The Tibetan Book of the Dead"* (New Hyde Park, NY: University Books, 1964).

Lee, Martin A., and Shlain, Bruce, *Acid Dreams: The Complete Social History of LSD: The CIA, the Sixties, and Beyond* (New York: Grove Press, 1985).

Lerdahl, Fred, and Jackendoff, Ray, *A Generative Theory of Tonal Music* (Cambridge, MA: MIT Press, 1983).

Leng, Simon, *While My Guitar Gently Weeps: The Music of George Harrison* (New York: Hal Leonard, 2006).

"Lennon Has a Legacy," *Nation*, December 20, 1980, 657.

"Lennon Returns MBE," *Variety*, November 26, 1969, 2.

Lennon, Cynthia, *A Twist of Lennon* (London: Star Books, 1978).

Lennon, John, *The Penguin John Lennon* (Harmondsworth: Penguin, 1965).

_____ *Skywriting by Word of Mouth and Other Writings, Including The Ballad of John and Yoko* (New York: Harper & Row, 1986).

Lennon, John, and Ono, Yoko, "A Love Letter From John and Yoko, To People Who Ask Us What, When and Why," *New York Times*, May 27, 1979, E20.

Lewis, J., "'Over My Dead Body!,'" *Uncut*, May 2007, 74–6.

Lewisohn, Mark, liner notes, *The Beatles Anthology Volume 2*, CD (Apple Corps Ltd. / EMI Ltd., 1996), 4–45.

_____ *The Beatles Day by Day: A Chronology 1962–1989* (New York: Harmony, 1990).

_____ *The Beatles Recording Sessions* (New York: Harmony, 1988).

_____ *The Complete Beatles Chronicle* (New York: Harmony, 1992; London: Hamlyn, 2000).

_____ *The Complete Beatles Recording Sessions: The Official Story of the Abbey Road Years* (London: Hamlyn, 1988).

Liddy, G. Gordon, *Will: The Autobiography of G. Gordon Liddy* (New York: St. Martin's, 1996).

Luke, Timothy, *Museum Politics: Power Plays at the Exhibition* (Minneapolis: University of Minneapolis Press, 2002).

Lyon, G. W., Jr., "More on Beatles Textual Problems," *Journal of Popular Culture 4* (1970), 549–52.

Mabey, Richard, *The Pop Process* (London: Hutchinson Educational, 1965).

Madow, Stuart, and Sobul, Jeff, *The Colour of Your Dreams: The Beatles' Psychedelic Music* (Pittsburgh: Dorrance Publishing, 1992),

McCabe, Peter, and Schonfeld, Robert D., *Apple to the Core: The Unmaking of the Beatles* (New York: Pocket Books, 1972).

McCartney, Paul, *Blackbird Singing: Poems and Lyrics 1965–1999*, ed. A. Mitchell (New York: Norton, 2001).

_____ *Paintings* (Boston: Little, Brown, 2000).

McCartney, Paul, Dunbar, Geoff, and Ardagh, Philip, *High in the Clouds* (New York: Dutton Children's Books, 2005).

McDevitt, Chas, *Skiffle: The Definitive Inside Story* (London: Robson, 1997).

MacDonald, Ian, *Revolution in the Head: The Beatles' Records and the Sixties* (London: Fourth Estate; New York: Henry Holt, 1994; fully updated edn., London: Pimlico, 1998).

McDonald, Kari, and Kaufman, Sarah Hudson, "'Tomorrow Never Knows': The Contributions of George Martin and His Production Team to the Beatles' New

Sound," in Russell Reising (ed.), *"Every Sound There Is": The Beatles'* Revolver *and the Transformation of Rock and Roll* (Aldershot: Ashgate, 2002), 139–57.

McGregor, Craig, "Rock's 'We Are One' Myth," *New York Times*, May 9, 1971, D15.

McKinney, Devin, *Magic Circles: The Beatles in Dream and History* (Cambridge, MA: Harvard University Press, 2003).

McRobbie, Angela, "*Jackie* Magazine: Romantic Individualism and the Teenage Girl," in Angela McRobbie, *Feminism and Youth Culture* (London: Macmillan, 1991), 135–88 (first published as "*Jackie*: An Ideology of Adolescent Femininity," Stencilled Occasional Paper 53, Women's Series [Birmingham: Centre for Contemporary Cultural Studies, 1978]).

Maraschin, Donatella, "The Swinging 60s," *In London: Summer Living* (London: Morris Visitor Publications, June–July 2006), 29–32.

Marcus, Greil, "The Beatles," in Jim Miller (ed.), *The* Rolling Stone *Illustrated History of Rock and Roll*, revised and updated edn. (New York: Random House, 1980; London: Picador, 1981), 177–89.

———— *Dead Elvis: A Chronicle of a Cultural Obsession* (New York: Doubleday, 1991).

Marsh, Dave, "Extra Texture," review of *Extra Texture (Read All About It)* (Apple LP), by George Harrison, *Rolling Stone*, November 20, 1975, 75.

———— "An Open Letter to John Lennon," *Rolling Stone*, November 3, 1977, 50.

Marshall, Geoffrey, "Taking the Beatles Seriously: Problems of Text," *Journal of Popular Culture* 3 (1969), 28–34.

Martin, George, with Jeremy Hornsby, *All You Need Is Ears* (New York: St. Martin's, 1979).

Martin, George, with William Pearson, *Summer of Love: The Making of* Sgt. Pepper (London: Macmillan, 1994; London: Pan Books, 1995).

Martin, Linda, and Segrave, Kerry, *Anti-Rock: The Opposition to Rock 'n' Roll* (New York: Da Capo, 1993).

Maslin, Janet, "London Town," review of *London Town* (Parlophone/EMI LP), by Wings, *Rolling Stone*, June 15, 1978, 89, 91–2.

Matteo, Steve, *33 1/3: Let It Be* (New York: Continuum, 2004).

———— *Let It Be* (New York and London: Continuum, 2004).

Mellers, Wilfrid, *Twilight of the Gods: The Beatles in Retrospect* (London: Faber & Faber, 1973).

Meltzer, Richard, "George Harrison Surrenders to Goodies," review of *Thirty Three & 1/3* (Dark Horse LP), by George Harrison, *Village Voice*, December 20, 1976, 87–9.

Mendelsohn, John, "'Wild Life,'" review of *Wild Life* (Apple LP), by Wings, *Rolling Stone*, January 20, 1972, 48.

"Method in Their Fabness," *MOJO*, May 2007, 14.

Miles, Barry, *The Beatles: A Diary – An Intimate Day by Day History* (New York: Barnes & Noble, 2004).

———— *Paul McCartney: Many Years From Now* (London: Secker & Warburg; New York: Henry Holt, 1997).

Miller, Jim, "Dark Horse: Transcendental Mediocrity," review of *Dark Horse* (Apple LP), by George Harrison, *Rolling Stone*, February 13, 1975, 75–6.

Moore, Allan F., *The Beatles:* Sgt. Pepper's Lonely Hearts Club Band (Cambridge: Cambridge University Press, 1997).

"Music: 'Hello, Goodbye, Hello,'" review of *McCartney* (Apple LP), by Paul McCartney, *Time*, April 20, 1970, 57.

Mutsaers, Lutgard, "Indorock: An Early Eurorock Style," in *Popular Music* 9/3 (1990), 307–20.

Neaverson, Bob, *The Beatles Movies* (London: Cassell, 1997).

Negus, Keith, "Popular Music: Between Celebration and Despair," in John Downing and Annabelle Sreberny-Mohammadi (eds.), *Questioning the Media*, 2nd edn. (London: Sage, 1995).

Nolan, Tom, "Goodnight Vienna," review of *Goodnight Vienna* (Apple LP), by Ringo Starr, *Rolling Stone*, April 24, 1975, 62.

Norman, Philip, *Shout! The Beatles in Their Generation* (New York: MJF, 1981) = *Shout! The True Story of the Beatles* (London: Hamish Hamilton, 1981; revised and updated edn., London: Sidgwick & Jackson, 2003).

Northcutt, William M., "The Spectacle of Alienation: Death, Loss, and the Crowd in *Sgt. Pepper's Lonely Hearts Club Band*," in Kenneth Womack and Todd F. Davis (eds.), *Reading the Beatles: Cultural Studies, Literary Criticism, and the Fab Four* (Albany: State University of New York Press, 2006), 129–46.

O'Connor, John J., "TV: McCartney and His Group on ABC Tonight," review of *James Paul McCartney* (ABC television program), *New York Times*, April 16, 1973, 75.

O'Dell, Denis, and Neaverson, Bob, *At The Apple's Core: The Beatles from the Inside* (London: Peter Owen, 2002).

O'Grady, T. J., *The Beatles: A Musical Evolution* (Boston: Twayne, 1983).

O'Neill, William L., *Coming Apart: An Informal History of America in the 1960s* (Chicago: Quadrangle Books, 1971).

Palmer, Robert, "Paul McCartney's Latest is Exquisite but Flawed," *New York Times*, April 25, 1982, Section 2, pp. 1, 19.

———— "The Pop Life: Did Ringo Starr Alone Escape Trap of Beatles?," review of *Stop and Smell the Roses* (RCA LP), by Ringo Starr, November 11, 1981, C26.

———— "The Pop Life: '(Just Like) Starting Over,'" review of "Just Like Starting Over"/"Kiss Kiss Kiss," by John Lennon and Yoko Ono, October 24, 1980, C15.

———— "Two Icons of Rock Music," review of *Somewhere in England* (Dark Horse LP), by George Harrison, *New York Times*, May 31, 1981, D23.

Patterson, R. Gary, *"The Walrus Was Paul": The Great Beatle Death Clues of 1969* (Oak Ridge, TN: Excursion Productions and Publications, 1994).

"Paul McCartney: Band on the Run," review of *Band on the Run* (Apple LP), by Paul McCartney and Wings, *High Fidelity*, April 1974, 124.

Pawlowski, Gareth, *How They Became the Beatles* (New York: Dutton, 1989).

Peel, Mark, "McCartney and Friends," review of *Tug of War* (Columbia LP), by Paul McCartney, *Stereo Review*, June 1982, 76.

Peterson, R. A., "Taking Popular Music Too Seriously," *Journal of Popular Culture* 4 (1971), 590–4.

Petigny, Alan, "Illegitimacy, Postwar Psychology, and the Reperiodization of the Sexual Revolution," *Journal of Social History* 38/1 (2004), 63–79.

Pichaske, David R., *The Poetry of Rock: The Golden Years* (Peoria, IL: Ellis Press, 1981).

Pichaske, David R. (ed.), *Beowulf to Beatles: Approaches to Poetry* (New York: Free Press, 1972).

Plasketes, George, *Images of Elvis Presley in American Culture, 1977–1997: The Mystery Terrain* (New York: Haworth Press, 1997).

Pleasants, Henry, "Taking the Beatles Seriously," *Stereo Review*, November 1967, 52–4.

Pollack, Alan W., "Notes on . . . " series of online analyses of Beatles songs, the "Official" rec.music.beatles home page (1989–2001), at www.recmusicbeatles.com.

Porter, Alan J., *Before They Were Beatles: The Early Years 1956–60* (Bloomington, IN: Xlibris, 2003).

Pye, Ian, "Double Fantasy," review of *Double Fantasy* (Geffen LP), by John Lennon and Yoko Ono, *Melody Maker*, November 22, 1980, 26.

Quantick, David, *Revolution: The Making of the Beatles' White Album* (London: Unanimous; Chicago: A Cappella, 2002).

Rabinowitz, Dorothy, "John Lennon's Mourners," *Commentary*, February 1981, 58–61.

Reece, G. L., *Elvis Religion: The Cult of the King* (London and New York: Tauris, 2006).

Reeve, A. J., *Turn Me On, Dead Man: The Complete Story of the Paul McCartney Death Hoax* (Ann Arbor, MI: Popular Culture Ink, 1994).

Reising, Russell, *"Every Sound There Is": The Beatles' Revolver and the Transformation of Rock and Roll* (Aldershot: Ashgate, 2002).

Reising, Russell, and LeBlanc, Jim, "The Whatchamucallit in the Garden: *Sgt. Pepper* and Fables of Interference," in Olivier Julien (ed.), *Sgt. Pepper and the Beatles: "It Was Forty Years Ago"* (Aldershot: Ashgate, 2009).

Riley, Tim, *Tell Me Why: A Beatles Commentary* (New York: Knopf, 1988; Vintage, 1989), revised as *Tell Me Why: The Beatles – Album by Album, Song by Song, the Sixties and After* (Cambridge, MA: Da Capo, 2002).

Rockwell, John, "Music: George Harrison," *New York Times*, December 21, 1974, 19.

———— "Old Timers Out for a Spin Cut a Couple of Disks," review of *The Traveling Wilburys: Volume One* (Warner Brothers LP), by the Traveling Wilburys, *New York Times*, November 13, 1988, H27.

———— "The Pop Life," review of *Back to the Egg* (EMI/Columbia LP), by Wings, *New York Times*, June 29, 1979, C24.

———— "The Pop Life," review of *The Best of George Harrison* (Capitol/EMI LP), by George Harrison, *New York Times*, December 24, 1976, 44.

———— "The Pop Life," review of *McCartney II* (Parlophone/EMI LP), by Paul McCartney, *New York Times*, July 11, 1980, C14.

———— "The Pop Life," review of *Thirty Three & 1/3* (Dark Horse LP), by George Harrison, *New York Times*, December 24, 1976, 44.

Rodman, G. B., *Elvis After Elvis: The Posthumous Career of a Living Legend* (London and New York: Routledge, 1996).

Rohter, Larry, "Dear Santa: All I Want for Christmas is No. 11578," review of *The Best of George Harrison* (Capitol/EMI LP), by George Harrison, *Washington Post*, December 19, 1976, 147.

———— "For Harrison, Some Things Must Pass," *Washington Post*, December 14, 1974, C1.

Roos, M. E., "The Walrus and the Deacon: John Lennon's Debt to Lewis Carroll," *Journal of Popular Culture* 18/1 (1984), 19–29.

Rosen, R. D., *Psychobabble: Fast Talk and Quick Cure in the Era of Feeling* (New York: Atheneum, 1977).

Rosenberg, N. V., "Taking Popular Culture Seriously: The Beatles," *Journal of Popular Culture* 4 (1970), 53–6.

Roszak, Theodor, *The Making of a Counter Culture: Reflections on the Technocratic Society and its Youthful Opposition* (Garden City, NY: Doubleday, 1969; New York: Faber & Faber, 1971).

Rothstein, William, *Phrase Rhythm in Tonal Music* (New York: Schirmer, 1989).

Russell, Jeff, *The Beatles Album File and Complete Discography*, rev. edn. (London: Blandford, 1989).

———— *The Beatles Complete Discography* (New York: Universe Publishing, 2006).

Ryan, Kevin, and Kehew, Brian, *Recording the Beatles: The Studio Equipment and Techniques Used to Create Their Classic Albums* (Houston: Curvebender, 2006).

Saal, Hubert, "The Beatles Minus One," review of *McCartney* (Apple LP), by Paul McCartney, *Newsweek*, April 20, 1970, 95.

Salewicz, Chris, *McCartney: The Biography* (London: Queen Anne Press, 1986).

Sandbrook, Dominic, *Never Had It So Good: A History of Britain from Suez to the Beatles* (London: Abacus, 2000).

Santiago, L. P. R., "The Lyrical Expression of Adolescent Conflict in the Beatles' Songs," *Adolescence* 4 (1969), 199–210.

Sauceda, James, *The Literary Lennon: A Comedy of Letters – The First Study of All the Major and Minor Writings of John Lennon* (Ann Arbor, MI: Pierian Press, 1983).

Savage, Jon, "100 Greatest Psychedelic Classics," *MOJO* 43 (June 1997), 56–67.

Sawyers, June Skinner (ed.), *Read the Beatles: Classic and New Writings on the Beatles, Their Legacy, and Why They Still Matter* (New York: Penguin, 2006).

Schaffner, Nicholas, *The Beatles Forever* (New York: McGraw Hill; Harrisburg, PA: Cameron House, 1977).

Schmalfeldt, Janet, "Cadential Processes: The Evaded Cadence and the 'One More Time' Technique," *Journal of Musicological Research* 12 (1992), 1–52.

Schofield, Carey, *Jagger* (London: Methuen, 1983).

Sedgwick, Eve Kosofsky, *Between Men: English Literature and Male Homosexual Desire* (New York: Columbia University Press, 1985).

Shames, Laurence, "John Lennon, Where Are You?," *Esquire*, November 1980, 31–8, 40, 42.

Sheff, David, "John Lennon and Yoko Ono: Candid Conversation," *Playboy* 28/1 (January 1981), 75–114, 144.

———— *The* Playboy *Interviews with John Lennon and Yoko Ono*, ed. G. Barry Golson (New York: Playboy Press, 1981; New York: St. Martins, 2000).

Shepherd, Billy, *The True Story of the Beatles* (London: Beat Publications, 1964).

Sigerson, Davitt, "Paul Carries That Weight," review of *Tug of War* (Parlophone/EMI LP), by Paul McCartney, *Village Voice*, May 11, 1982, 64.

Simons, David, *Studio Stories* (San Francisco: Backbeat Books, 2004).

"Somewhere in England," review of *Somewhere in England* (Dark Horse LP), by George Harrison, *Rolling Stone*, August 6, 1981, 44.

Smith, Larry R., "The Beatles as Act: A Study of Control in a Musical Group," PhD thesis, University of Illinois at Urbana-Champaign (1970).

Southall, Brian, *Abbey Road* (Wellingborough: Patrick Stephens, 1985).

Spitz, Bob, *The Beatles: The Biography* (New York: Little, Brown, 2005; 2nd edn., 2007).

Spitz, Robert S., "George Harrison on the Move," review of *George Harrison* (Dark Horse LP), by George Harrison, *Washington Post*, March 4, 1979, A1.

Spizer, Bruce, *The Beatles on Apple Records* (New Orleans: 498 Productions, 2003), reissued as *The Beatles Solo on Apple Records* (New Orleans: 498 Productions, 2005).

Spock, Benjamin McLane, *The Common Sense Book of Baby and Child Care* (New York: Pocket Books, 1946).

Sterritt, David, "Discs: Hello, Paul – Bye-bye Beatles," *Christian Science Monitor*, June 29, 1970, 8.

———— "Latest from ex-Beatles McCartney, Harrison," review of *Red Rose Speedway* (Apple LP), by Paul McCartney and Wings, and *Living in the Material World* (Apple LP), by George Harrison, *Christian Science Monitor*, June 29, 1973, 12.

———— "On the Disc Scene: 'Ram,'" review of *Ram* (Apple LP), by Paul and Linda McCartney, *Christian Science Monitor*, July 7, 1971, 4.

———— "Plastic Ono Band," review of *Plastic Ono Band* (Apple LP), by John Lennon, *Christian Science Monitor*, March 19, 1971, 4.

———— "Will the Real Beatle Please Sing Out?," *Christian Science Monitor*, January 28, 1972, 13.

Stevens, Jay, *Storming Heaven: LSD and the American Dream* (New York: Atlantic Monthly Press, 1987).

Storey, John, "The Politics of the Popular," in John Storey (ed.), *An Introductory Guide to Cultural Theory and Popular Culture* (Athens, GA: University of Georgia Press, 1993), 181–202.

Suczek, Barbara, "The Curious Case of the 'Death' of Paul McCartney," *Urban Life and Culture* 1 (1972), 61–76.

Sullivan, Henry W., *The Beatles with Lacan: Rock 'n' Roll as Requiem for the Modern Age* (New York: Peter Lang, 1995).

Sulpy, Doug, and Schweighhardt, Ray, *Get Back: The Unauthorized Chronicle of the Beatles' "Let It Be" Disaster* (New York: St. Martin's, 1997).

Sumrall, Harry, "Paul McCartney's Scrambled 'Egg,'" review of *Back to the Egg* (EMI/Columbia LP), by Wings, *Washington Post*, July 22, 1979, A1.

Sutcliffe, Pauline, and Thompson, Douglas, *Stuart Sutcliffe: The Beatles' Shadow and His Lonely Hearts Club* (London: Sidgwick & Jackson, 2001).

Taylor, A. J. W., "Beatlemania – A Study in Adolescent Enthusiasm," *British Journal of Social and Clinical Psychology* 5 (1966), 81–8.

Taylor, Alistair, with Roberts, Martin, *Yesterday: The Beatles Remembered* (London: Sidgwick & Jackson, 1988).

Terry, Sara, "George Harrison," review of *George Harrison* (Dark Horse LP), by George Harrison, *Christian Science Monitor*, March 22, 1979, 22.

Thompson, Edward, *The Making of the English Working Class* (1963; New York: Penguin, 1975).

Thomson, Elizabeth, and Gutman, David (eds.), *The Lennon Companion: Twenty-five Years of Comment* (Basingstoke and London: Macmillan, 1987).

Thribb, E. J., "George Harrison: *George Harrison*," review of *George Harrison* (Dark Horse / Warner Brothers LP), by George Harrison, *Melody Maker*, February 24, 1979, 29.

Tillikens, Ger, "A Flood of Flat-Sevenths," in Russell Reising (ed)., *"Every Sound There Is": The Beatles'* Revolver *and the Transformation of Rock and Roll* (Aldershot: Ashgate, 2002), 121–36.

Townsend, Ken, "Preface" to Mark Lewisohn, *The Complete Beatles Recording Sessions: The Official Story of the Abbey Road Years* (London: Hamlyn, 1988).

Townshend, Peter, *The Family Life of Old People* (London: Routledge & Kegan Paul, 1957).

Turner, Steve, *The Gospel According to the Beatles* (London: Westminster John Knox Press, 2006).

———— *A Hard Day's Write: The Stories Behind Every Beatles Song* (New York: HarperCollins, 1999; London: Carlton, 2000).

Vachon, Brian, "Jesus Movement is Upon Us," *Look*, February 9, 1971, 5–21.

Ward, Ed, "Unfinished Music No. 2: Life with the Lions," review of *Unfinished Music No. 2: Life with the Lions* (Apple LP), by John Lennon and Yoko Ono, *Rolling Stone*, August 9, 1969, 37.

Warwick, Neil, Kutner, Jon, and Brown, Tony, *The Complete Book of the British Charts: Singles and Albums*, 3rd edn. (London: Omnibus, 2004).

Watts, Michael, "*Living in the Material World*," review of *Living in the Material World* (Apple LP), by George Harrison, *Melody Maker*, June 9, 1973, 3.

Weinberg, Max, *The Big Beat: Conversations with Rock's Great Drummers* (Chicago: Contemporary Books, 1984).

Welch, Chris, "Albums: Ringo Starr: Ringo the 4th," review of *Ringo the 4th* (Polydor/Atlantic LP), by Ringo Starr, *Melody Maker*, February 11, 1978, 20.

Wenner, Jann, *Lennon Remembers: The* Rolling Stone *Interviews* (New York: Fawcett Popular Library; London: Verso; and Harmondsworth: Penguin, 1971; New York: Verso, 2000).

———— "Man of the Year: John Lennon," *Rolling Stone*, February 7, 1970, 24–5.

West, Alan, and Martindale, Colin, "Creative Trends in the Content of Beatles Lyrics," *Popular Music and Society* 20/4 (1996), 103–25.

"What Songs the Beatles Sang...," *The Times*, December 27, 1963, Arts section, 4 (uncredited article "From Our Music Critic," who was William Mann).

Whitburn, Joel, *Joel Whitburn Presents Billboard's Top 10 Charts, 1958–1988* (Menomonee Falls, WI: Record Research, 1988).

Whitburn, Joel (ed.), *Billboard Top Pop Singles, 1955–2002*, 10th edn. (Menomonee Falls, WI: Record Research, 2004).

White, Timothy, "Back to the Egg," review of *Back to the Egg* (EMI/Columbia LP), by Wings, *Rolling Stone*, August 23, 1979, 55–6.

Whiteclay, John (ed.), *The Oxford Companion to American Military History* (Oxford: Oxford University Press, 1999).

Whiteley, Sheila, *The Space Between the Notes: Rock and the Counter-Culture* (London: Routledge, 1992), 39–60.

———— "Love, Love, Love: Representations of Gender and Sexuality in Selected Songs by the Beatles," in Kenneth Womack and Todd F. Davis (eds.), *Reading the Beatles: Cultural Studies, Literary Criticism, and the Fab Four* (Albany: State University of New York Press, 2006), 55–70.

Whitley, Ed, "The Postmodern White Album," in Ian Inglis (ed.), *The Beatles, Popular Music and Society: A Thousand Voices* (London: Macmillan, 2000), 105–25.

Wiener, Jon, *Come Together: John Lennon in His Time* (New York: Random House, 1984; Chicago: University of Illinois Press, 1991).

———— *Gimme Some Truth: The John Lennon FBI Files* (Berkeley: University of California Press, 1999).

———— "The Last Lennon File," *The Nation*, January 8–15, 2007, 4–5.

Wild, David, "'The Lives of John Lennon,'" review of Albert Goldman, *The Lives of John Lennon* (New York: William Morrow, 1988), *Rolling Stone*, October 6, 1988, 21.

Wild, David, "Cloud Nine," review of *Cloud Nine* (Dark Horse LP), by George Harrison, *Rolling Stone*, December 3, 1987, 80.

Williams, Richard, "Solo Beatles," review of *All Things Must Pass* (Apple LP), by George Harrison, and *Plastic Ono Band* (Apple LP), by John Lennon, *The Times Saturday Review*, January 23, 1971, 17.

Willis, Ellen, "Rock, etc.: George and John," review of *All Things Must Pass* (Apple LP), by George Harrison, and *John Lennon / Plastic Ono Band* (Apple LP), by John Lennon, *New Yorker*, February 27, 1971, 95–7.

Wimsatt, William K., Jr., and Beardsley, Monroe C., "The Intentional Fallacy," in Vincent B. Leitch (ed.), *The Norton Anthology of Theory and Criticism* (New York: Norton, 2001), 1374–87.

"Wings: Shooting Stars!," review of *Venus and Mars* (Capitol/EMI LP), by Wings, *Melody Maker*, May 31, 1975, 22.

Winner, Langdon, "Records: Instant Karma," review of "Instant Karma" (Apple single), *Rolling Stone*, April 16, 1970, 48, 50.

———— "Records: McCartney," review of *McCartney* (Apple LP), by George Harrison, *Rolling Stone*, May 14, 1970, 50.

Wolfe, T., "The 'Me' Decade and the Third Great Awakening," *New York*, August 23, 1976, 26–40.

Womack, Kenneth, *Long and Winding Roads: The Evolving Artistry of the Beatles* (New York: Continuum, 2007).

Womack, Kenneth, and Davis, Todd F. (eds.), *Reading the Beatles: Cultural Studies, Literary Criticism, and the Fab Four* (Albany: State University of New York Press, 2006).

Wood, Andy, *The Politics of Social Conflict: The Peak Country, 1520–1770*
(Cambridge: Cambridge University Press, 1999).

Wood, Michael, "John Lennon's Schooldays," in Elizabeth Thomson and David
Gutman (eds.), *The Lennon Companion: Twenty-Five Years of Comment* (London:
Macmillan, 1987), 145–9 (originally published in *New Society*, June 27, 1968).

Woods, William C., "Ringo Goes it Solo, Pleasantly Enough," review of *Sentimental
Journey* (Apple LP), *Washington Post*, May 17, 1970, 142.

Young, Michael, and Willmott, Peter, *Family and Kinship in East London* (London:
Routledge and Kegan Paul, 1957).

Young, Warren, and Hixson, Joseph, *LSD on Campus* (New York: Dell, 1966).

Zito, Tom, "The Beatles: Looking Back Ten Years," *Washington Post*, February 17,
1974, P1, P8.

——— "Christmas Records," review of *Imagine* (Apple LP), by John Lennon,
Washington Post, November 28, 1971, 128.

——— "Hamming and Homage," review of *James Paul McCartney* (ABC television
program), *Washington Post*, April 17, 1973, B6.

——— "Hey, Venus, Could That Be a New Beatles Album?," review of *Venus and
Mars* (Capitol LP), by Wings, *Washington Post*, July 6, 1975, 71.

——— "Peace, Love, Art, and Yoko," *Washington Post*, October 9, 1971, C1.

——— "Within Him, Without Them: The Consciousness of George Harrison,"
Washington Post, January 3, 1971, F1–F2.

Index

Abbey Road, 56, 58–60, 83, 125, 132–6, 146, 149, 153, 167, 199, 215, 233
Adorno, Theodor, 77, 82, 88, 225
ADT (Artificial Double Tracking), 51
Aguilera, Christina, 243
Alexander, George, 143
All Things Must Pass, 128, 130, 149, 154, 156, 157–8, 159, 163, 170, 179
Alpert, Richard, 90, 103
Andrew, Sam, 93
Animals, the, 41, 73, 108, 226
Antonioni, Michelangelo, 207
Apple Records, 128, 142–52, 222, 250
Ardagh, Philip, 225
Armstrong, Louis, 34, 230
Asher, Jane, 113, 145
Asher, Peter, 144, 145, 151
Aspinall, Neil, 13, 143, 237, 238, 250, 251
Astaire, Fred, 122
Axton, Hoyt, 157
Ayckbourn, Alan, 207

Bach, Barbara, 178
Back in the US, 239
Back to the Egg, 168
Bad Boy, 157
Badfinger, 150, 159, 222
Bailey, David, 206, 207
Baird, Julia, 21
Baker, Ginger, 149
Band on the Run, 147, 157, 167
Band, the, 130, 156
Barham, John, 158
Barrett, John, 231
Barthes, Roland, 19
Beach Boys, the, 35, 36, 41, 55, 93, 226, 228, 233, 249
Beachles, the, 249, 253
Beatles Anthology, the, 218, 221, 222, 232, 233, 235, 236–9, 251
Beatles for Sale, 41, 74, 135, 230, 233
Beatles, The (the "White Album"), 55–6, 117–24, 125, 146, 153, 167, 214, 228, 233
Beaucoups of Blues, 150, 156, 162
Beethoven, Ludwig van, 59, 186
Belew, Adrian, 237
Berio, Luciano, 93
Bernstein, Elmer, 156
Berry, Chuck, 25, 40, 55, 75, 133, 172, 174, 205, 206
Best of George Harrison, the, 161

Best, Mona, 23
Best, Pete, 9, 10, 11, 13, 22, 24, 26, 33, 34
Big 3, the, 22
Billy J. Kramer and the Dakotas, 70, 73
Bishop, Malden Grange, 110–11
Black Dyke Mills Band, 118, 146
Black, Cilla, 20
Blackbird, 225
Blake, Peter, 98, 180
Bonzo Dog Band, the, 105, 118
Bowie, David, 175
Bradby, Barbara, 228–9
Brahms, Johannes, 186
Braine, John, 207
Brainwashed, 179
Brecht, Bertolt, 78
Brodax, Al, 116
Bromberg, David, 156
Brookhiser, Richard, 176
Brown, Peter, 12
Burdon, Eric, 108
Burnett, Johnny, 156
Burroughs, William, 209
Byrds, the, 75, 93, 104, 130, 226, 233

Caine, Michael, 206, 207
Caldwell, Alan, 22
Candy, 155, 221
Carlos, John, 112
Carroll, Lewis, 51
Carter, Jimmy, 175, 177
Caveman, 178
Cavern Club, 25, 26, 33, 50, 66, 67, 70, 134
Chaos and Creation in the Back Yard, 249
Chaplin, Charlie, 218
Chapman, Norman, 12
Charles, Ray, 24
Chiffons, the, 161
Chipperfield, Chips, 237
Choose Love, 182
Christie, Julie, 206
Churchill, Winston, 10, 208
Cirque du Soleil, 105, 179, 218, 247
Clapton, Eric, 41, 55, 119, 123, 135, 147, 148, 149, 150, 157, 160, 178, 247
Clarke, Allan, 23
Clash, the, 168
Cleave, Maureen, 208
Clinton, William J. (Bill), 230
Cloud Nine, 178, 181
Cloud, Cam, 105

Coasters, the, 21
Cochran, Eddie, 21
Cockburn, Bruce, 108
Cohen, Sidney, 103, 105
Concert for Bangladesh, 149, 158
Connolly, Ray, 9
Cookies, the, 23, 68
Corday, Charlotte, 209
Costello, Elvis, 180
Cox, Kyoko Chan, 169, 172
Cream, 118, 217
Crompton, Richmal, 19
Crosby, Bing, 34

Danger Mouse, 222, 249, 253
Dark Horse, 159
Dave Clark Five, the, 41, 73, 226,
    228
Davies, Hunter, 9, 33, 177
Davies, Ray, 77
Davis, Carl, 180
Davis, Miles, 251
Davis, Rod, 21
Dekker, Thomas, 135
Delaney and Bonnie and Friends, 158
Dell-Vikings, the, 21
DeRogatis, Jim, 92
Dickinson, Emily, 139
Doggett, Peter, 228
Domino, Fats, 115, 121, 134
Donegan, Lonnie, 18, 20, 21, 206
Donovan, 105
Doors, the, 93
Doran, Terry, 143
Double Fantasy, 175
Douglas-Home, Alec, 207
Dowlding, William J., 228
Drake, Pete, 156
Drifters, the, 73
Driving Rain, 181
Dubček, Alexander, 112
Dunbar, Geoff, 225
Dylan, Bob, 41, 75, 93, 117, 130, 158, 159, 161,
    170, 171, 179, 218, 225, 228, 234

Eastman, Linda, *see* McCartney, Linda
Ecce Cor Meum, 180
Ed Sullivan Show, the, 42, 206
Edison, Thomas, 34
Eisenberg, Evan, 232
Electronic Sound, 148
Elephant's Memory, 148, 172
Elliott, Anthony, 240
Ellis, Royston, 17
Ellmann, Richard, 1–2
Emerick, Geoff, 38, 39–40, 41, 45, 46, 48, 49, 50,
    51, 52, 53, 55, 57, 58, 59, 60, 94, 98, 119, 136,
    177, 178, 242, 249

Epstein, Brian, 9, 25–6, 56, 66, 70, 71, 77, 113,
    117, 119, 143, 223
Esquivel, Juan Garcia, 36
Evans, Allan, 73
Evans, Mal, 53
Everett, Walter, 95, 125, 228, 245
Everly Brothers, the, 21, 22, 68
Ewing, Marsha, 244
Extra Texture, 161

Fairport Convention, 105, 130
Family Way, The, 221
Farrow, Prudence, 122
Fenton, Shane, 68
Ferry, Bryan, 150
Fireman, the, 180
Flaming Pie, 179
Fletcher, Colin, 19
Flowers in the Dirt, 180
Fonda, Peter, 90
Fool, the, 144
Ford, Mary, 36
Formby, George, 22
Frampton, Peter, 157, 168
Frankael, Michael, 81
Freelance Hellraiser, the, 180
Freeman, Robert, 71
Frith, Simon, 17, 232
Fury, Billy, 68

Gaitskill, Mary, 75
Garry, Len, 22
Gaye, Marvin, 224
Geffen, David, 175
Geller, Debbie, 26
Gentle, Johnny, 23, 24
George Harrison, 162
Gerry and the Pacemakers, 25, 41,
    70
Gerson, Ben, 158, 171
Get Back Project, 58, 149, 242
Gibb, Maurice, 156
Ginsberg, Allen, 206, 239
Gitlin, Todd, 171, 176
Give My Regards to Broad Street, 180
Goffin, Gerry, 130
Goldman, Albert, 9, 177
Goodnight Vienna, 151, 156, 175
Goon Show, 12, 23
Goons, the, 22
Grade, Lew, 175
Gramsci, Antonio, 9
Grant, Cary, 103
Green, Al, 230
Griffiths, Eric, 11, 19, 22
Grof, Stanislav, 90, 100
Gustafson, Johnny, 22
Guthrie, Woody, 18

Hain, Peter, 212
Hamilton, Richard, 117
Hanton, Colin, 20, 21, 65
Hard Day's Night, A (album), 40, 65, 73, 75, 76, 230, 233
Hard Day's Night, A (film), 73, 113, 221, 230
Harrison, Dhani, 162, 179
Harrison, George, early years, 12–13, 16; solo years, 157–62, 177, 178
Harrison, Olivia Trinidad Arias, 162, 247, 248
Harrison, Pattie Boyd, 159, 160
Harry, Bill, 9, 17
Hayakawa, S. I., 225
Help! (album), 77, 88, 135, 233, 234, 237
Help! (film), 41, 113, 220, 221
Hendrix, Jimi, 95, 104, 237
Henke, James, 244
Herman's Hermits, 41, 73, 226
Hertsgaard, Mark, 228, 232, 254
Hicks, Paul, 242
Higginbotham, Daryl, 151
Hodge, Chris, 151
Hoffman, Abbie, 172, 239
Hofmann, Albert, 92, 104
Holiday, Billie, 34
Hollies, the, 23, 41
Holly, Buddy, 22, 23, 25, 65, 205
Hooper-Greenhill, Eileen, 246
Hopkin, Mary, 116, 118, 132, 146, 222
Hopkins, Nicky, 147, 170
Horne, Howard, 17
Hot Chocolate Band, the, 148
How I Won the War, 221
Howlett, Kevin, 242
Hudson, Mark, 182
Huxley, Aldous, 91, 110

Idle, Eric, 161
Imagine, 147, 154, 157, 163, 170, 173
In His Own Write, 221
Incredible String Band, the, 105
Inglis, Ian, 218
Isley Brothers, the, 68

Jackson, Glenda, 209
Jackson, Michael, 179
Jagger, Mick, 44, 45, 165, 206, 207, 212, 216
James Paul McCartney, 166
James, Dick, 129
Janov, Arthur, 169
Jay-Z, 222, 249
Jefferson Airplane, 89, 93, 107, 222
Jenkins, Roy, 211
John Lennon/Plastic Ono Band, 130, 147, 154, 156, 157, 163, 167, 169, 170, 173, 174
John, Elton, 175
Johnny and the Moondogs, 23
Johns, Glyn, 58, 132

Johnson, Lyndon Baines, 212
Jones, Brian, 45
Jones, Jeff, 251
Jones, Quincy, 156
Jones, Raymond, 66
Jones, Spike, 36, 37
Jowell, Tessa, 212
Judt, Tony, 14

Kaempfert, Bert, 65, 66
Kaleidoscope, 104
Kantner, Paul, 239
Kass, Ron, 144, 151
Kaye, Lenny, 9
Keeler, Christine, 209
Keightley, Keir, 252
Keltner, Jim, 147
Kennedy, John F., 168, 224
Kennedy, Robert F., 112, 214
Kesey, Ken, 98
King Crimson, 237
King, Carole, 130
King, Larry, 240
King, Martin Luther, Jr., 112, 214, 243
King, Tony, 151
Kinks, the, 73, 89, 93, 226, 253
Klein, Allen, 58, 127, 128, 129, 147, 151
Kozinn, Allan, 121, 179
Kyd, Thomas, 133

Laing, R. D., 100
Laliberté, Guy, 179, 247
Landau, Jon, 164, 167
Laozi, 115
Lavigne, Emma, 246
Lawrence, D. H., 209
Leadbelly (Huddie William Ledbetter), 18
Leary, Timothy, 90, 91, 100, 103, 106, 110, 133
Lennon, Alfred "Freddie," 12
Lennon, Cynthia Powell, 9, 20, 116, 209, 215
Lennon, John Winston Ono, early years, 12, 13, 16, 17; solo years, 168–77
Lennon, Julia Stanley, 12, 18
Lennon, Julian, 52, 116, 122, 217
Les Stewart Quartet, the, 22
Lester, Richard, 73
Let It Be (album), 60–1, 125, 130–2, 136–41, 146, 157, 162, 215, 222, 228, 233, 242
Let It Be (film), 153, 221
Let It Be . . . Naked (album), 140, 222, 242–3
Levy, Morris, 174
Lewisohn, Mark, 39, 40, 41, 44, 45, 46, 60, 68, 77, 129, 131, 231, 232
Liddy, G. Gordon, 106
Lindisfarne, 105
Lindsay-Hogg, Michael, 242
Little Richard, 21, 25, 55, 68, 73, 75, 121, 206
Live at the BBC, 235–6

Live in Red Square, 181
Liverpool 8, 182
Liverpool Oratorio, 155, 180
Liverpool Sound Collage, 180, 240
Living in the Material World, 159, 218, 247
Livingston, Alan, 71
Lomax, Jackie, 116, 118, 132, 144, 146, 147, 149, 151
London Town, 168
Love, 89, 105, 179, 218, 222, 246–9, 250, 251
Love, Mike, 42, 122
Lowe, Duff, 65
Luke, Timothy, 246
Lush, Richard, 51
Lynne, Jeff, 179
Lyttleton, Humphrey, 115

McBean, Angus, 71
McCartney II, 168
McCartney, 126, 130, 147, 164
McCartney, Beatrice, 181
McCartney, Heather (née Mills), 166, 181, 218
McCartney, James Paul, early years, 12, 13, 15–16; solo years, 162–8, 177–8
McCartney, Jim, 11, 18, 22
McCartney, Linda (née Eastman), 113, 120, 123, 128, 129, 162, 171, 180, 181, 215
McCartney, Mary Mohin, 22, 139
McCartney, Mary, 166
McCullough, Henry, 165
MacDonald, Ian, 14, 109, 133, 228, 231, 232, 238, 241, 245, 253
McGuinn, Roger, 210
McKinney, Devin, 82, 86, 218
McLuhan, Marshall, 246
Macmillan, Harold, 204, 207
McNamara, Robert, 212
McRobbie, Angela, 210
Madow, Stuart, 106
Magic Christian, The, 128, 132, 155, 221
Magical Mystery Tour (album), 97–111, 112, 143, 233
Magical Mystery Tour (film), 125, 221
Maharishi Mahesh Yogi, 99, 113, 118, 122, 223
Mann, Manfred, 73
Mann, William, 239
Mansfield, Ken, 145
Manson, Charles, 55, 215
Mao Zedong, 168, 173
Marcos, Ferdinand, 43, 238
Mardas, Alexis, "Magic Alex," 131, 144
Martin, George, 22, 25, 26, 33, 34, 36, 37, 38, 39, 41, 46, 49, 50, 52, 57, 58, 59, 65, 66, 68, 76, 88, 92, 94, 98, 105, 115, 119, 123, 131, 132, 133, 156, 164, 167, 177, 178, 181, 210, 214, 218, 228, 233, 238, 242, 248–9
Martin, Giles, 105, 218, 248–9
Marvelettes, the, 40, 41

Marvin, Hank, 11
Maslow, Abraham, 81
Mason, Barry, 67
Massey, Gary, 242
Matteo, Steve, 131, 228
MC5, 172
Mellers, Wilfred, 116, 228, 239
Meltzer, Richard, 161
Memory Almost Full, 181, 249
Mendelsohn, John, 165
Merseybeat, 19
Metzner, Ralph, 90, 103
Michael X, 169
Michael, George, 243
Mickey Mouse, 230
Mike Douglas Show, The, 172
Miles, Barry, 9, 10, 13, 14, 239, 241
Milk and Honey, 155
Miller, Henry, 209
Miller, Steve, 132
Mills, Heather, *see* McCartney, Heather
Mind Games, 173
Mintz, Elliot, 240
Mirror, the, 104
Mitchell, Mitch, 119
Moby Grape, 93
Modern Jazz Quartet, the, 151
Monkees, the, 227
Monroe, Marilyn, 218, 230
Monty Python, 161, 162, 247
Moody Blues, the, 222
Moon, Keith, 173
Moore, Allan F., 228
Moore, Tommy, 24
Most, Mickie, 148
Mozart, Wolfgang Amadeus, 139, 192
Murray, Mitch, 25, 67
Mutsaers, Lutgard, 25

Nash, Graham, 23
Nerk Twins, the, 23
Newman, Randy, 156
Newmark, Andy, 160
Newton, Huey, 172
Nilsson, Harry, 156, 173, 175, 177, 178
Nixon, Richard M., 112, 173
Norman, Philip, 126, 205
Northcutt, William, 208

O'Grady, Terence, 121, 228
Off the Ground, 180
Old Wave, 155
1, 220, 230, 248, 251
Ono, Yoko, 10, 56, 58, 113, 117, 119, 120, 123, 127, 133, 143, 148, 151, 169, 171, 172, 173, 174, 175, 215, 221, 238, 240, 241, 243, 244, 245, 246, 247, 248
Orbison, Roy, 67, 73, 75, 179

Osborne, John, 207
Osmond, Humphrey, 91
Owen, Alun, 73
Owens, Buck, 150

Pang, May, 174
Parks, Van Dyke, 35–6, 37, 43
Parnes, Larry, 23, 68
Past Masters, 233
Paul, Les, 36
Peel, David, 148
Pentangle, 105
Perkins, Carl, 73, 178, 206
Pet Sounds, 35, 36, 37, 235
PETA (People for the Ethical Treatment of
    Animals), 181
Peter and Gordon, 41
Petty, Tom, 179
Philby, Kim, 207
Phillips, Michelle, 239
Photograph: The Very Best of Ringo Starr, 182
Pichaske, David R., 225
Pink Floyd, 41, 104, 226
Pinter, Harold, 207
Pipes of Peace, 179
Plastic Ono Band, the, 147, 148, 169, 224
Platters, the, 157
Please Please Me, 25, 38, 39, 65, 68–9, 233, 234
Polanski, Roman, 215
Police, the, 217
Pollack, Alan W., 228
Powell, Enoch, 112
Presley, Elvis, 21, 25, 65, 70, 71, 76, 88, 205, 217,
    218, 224, 230, 238
Presley, Lisa Marie, 217
Press to Play, 180
Preston, Billy, 59, 131, 135, 137, 140, 149, 150,
    151, 156, 158, 159, 160, 161, 222

Quant, Mary, 206
Quantick, David, 228
Quarrymen, the, 9, 11, 18, 19, 20–3, 65

Ram, 147, 163, 164, 170
Raskin, Gene, 146
Raynsford, Nick, 212
Reagan, Ronald W., 176
Rebels, the, 20
Red Rose Speedway, 166
Redding, Otis, 104
Rees-Mogg, William, 214, 239
Revolver, 41, 43, 44, 45–8, 75, 76, 77, 79, 82, 83,
    88, 93–6, 98, 101, 104, 106, 109, 110, 205, 226,
    228, 233, 234, 241
Rice, Tim, 158
Richard, Cliff, 11, 67, 70, 181, 204
Richards, Keith, 119, 149, 165, 204
Richards, Ron, 67

Ricky and Dave, 23
Riddle, Nelson, 150
Riley, Tim, 78, 80, 85, 131, 228
Ringo, 151, 156, 175
Ringo Rama, 182
Ringo the 4th, 157
Ringo's Rotogravure, 157, 175
Rock 'n' Roll, 174
Rockwell, John, 168
Roeg, Nicolas, 207
Rolling Stones, the, 41, 73, 104, 130, 138, 178,
    205, 214, 216, 222, 226, 228, 253
Ronettes, the, 150
Roosevelt, Franklin D., 176
Rory Storm and the Hurricanes, 12, 22, 24, 26
Roszak, Theodor, 211
Rothko, Mark, 139
Rothstein, William, 190
Rouse, Allan, 242
Rowling, J. K., 230
Rubber Soul, 41, 43, 44–5, 73, 75–89, 167, 205,
    226, 233, 235
Rubin, Jerry, 148, 172
Run Devil Run, 180
Rushdie, Salman, 230
Russell, Leon, 150, 159

Sandbrook, Dominic, 14
Sauceda, James, 225
Scaggs, Boz, 150
Schweighhardt, Ray, 126
Scott, Jack, 65
Scott, Tom, 161
Seales, Bobby, 172
Sedgwick, Eve Kosofsky, 20
Sentimental Journey, 128, 137, 150, 155
Sex Pistols, the, 168
Sgt. Pepper's Lonely Hearts Club Band, 35, 47,
    48–54, 88, 91, 97–111, 112, 143, 171, 180, 213,
    214, 223, 225, 226, 228, 231, 233, 234, 235,
    237, 239
Sgt. Pet Sounds' Lonely Hearts Club Band, 249
Shadows, the, 11
Shakespeare, William, 133
Shankar, Ravi, 149, 160, 179, 247
Shapiro, Helen, 69
Shepherd, Billy, 9
Sheridan, Tony, 24, 33, 65, 219
Sherrin, Ned, 208
Shirelles, the, 23, 68
Shotton, Pete, 19, 20
Silver Beetles, the, 23, 205
Simon, Paul, 161
Sinatra, Frank, 134
Sinclair, John, 172
Sitwell, Edith, 209
Skiffle, 18–23
Smile, 37, 43, 163

Smith, Alan, 137
Smith, Bessie, 34
Smith, James Russell, 253
Smith, Larry, 228
Smith, Norman, 41
Smith, Patti, 166
Smith, Tommie, 112
Sobul, Jeff, 106
Some Time in New York City, 171, 172, 173
Somewhere in England, 177, 178
Spaniard in the Works, A, 221
Spector, Phil, 35, 37, 60–1, 137, 138, 140, 150,
    157, 170, 172, 173, 174, 222, 242
Spizer, Bruce, 72
Spock, Benjamin, 209
Standing Stone, 180
Starr, Ringo (Richard Starkey), early years, 13,
    16; solo years, 155–7
Steppenwolf, 104
Stewart, Rod, 150
Stills, Stephen, 178
Stockhausen, Karlheinz, 93
Stooges, the, 217
Stop and Smell the Roses, 155, 178
Sullivan, Henry, 9, 14
Sulpy, Doug, 126
Sundown Playboys, the, 151
Supremes, the, 73
Sutcliffe, Pauline, 9
Sutcliffe, Stuart, 9, 10, 11, 13, 16, 23, 24

13th Floor Elevators, 104
33 & 1/3, 161
Tate, Sharon, 215
Tavener, John, 151
Taylor, Alistair, 143, 145
Taylor, Alvin, 161
Taylor, Derek, 43, 147, 230, 238, 239, 254
Taylor, James, 116, 145, 147, 151, 222
Tepper, Ron, 43
Texans, the, 22
Thomas the Tank Engine and Friends, 178
Thoreau, Henry David, 101
Thurmond, Strom, 172
Time Takes Time, 155, 182
Titelman, Russ, 162
Townsend, Ken, 40, 45, 51, 231
Townshend, Pete, 77, 206
Townshend, Peter, 12, 13
Toynbee, Polly, 211
Traveling Wilburys, the, 179
Troggs, the, 41
Troy, Doris, 149, 151, 158
Tug of War, 177, 178, 180
Twiggy, 206
Twin Freaks, 180

U2, 243
Unfinished Music No. 1: Two Virgins, 147
Unfinished Music No. 2: Life with the Lions, 132
Unterberger, Ritchie, 253
U.S. vs. John Lennon, The, 218, 244

Van der Graaf Generator, 217
Van Eaton, Lon and Derek, 150, 151
Vartan, Sylvie, 72
Vaughan, Ivan, 21
Velvet Underground, the, 77
Venus and Mars, 167
Vertical Man, 182
Vincent, Gene, 65
Voormann, Klaus, 137, 147, 148, 149, 151, 156,
    170

Wall, Anthony, 26
Walls and Bridges, 174
Webber, Andrew Lloyd, 158
Weeks, Willie, 160, 161
Wenner, Jann, 154, 163, 164, 170, 241
Wertheimer, Alfred, 71
Wesker, Arnold, 207
Whalley, Nigel, 21
White, Alan, 137, 170
White, Andy, 67
Whitehead, Peter, 206
Whiteley, Sheila, 92
Who, the, 41, 122, 217, 226
Wiener, Jon, 172, 218
Wild Life, 9, 165
Williams, Larry, 73, 121
Wilson, Brian, 35, 36–7, 43, 77, 235
Wilson, Carl, 42
Wilson, Harold, 204, 207, 208, 209 .
Wings, 165–8
Wings at the Speed of Sound, 167
Wings over America, 168
Wingspan: Hits and History, 181
With the Beatles, 25, 40, 65, 70–1, 220, 233
Womack, Kenneth, 59, 84
Wonder, Stevie, 178
Wonderwall Music, 221
Wood, Ron, 178
Working Classical, 180
Wright, Gary, 161

Yardbirds, the, 41, 93, 226
Yellow Submarine (album), 56
Yellow Submarine (film), 98, 105, 113–14, 220,
    221
Yes, 103
Young, Neil, 104

Zappa, Frank, 173

Cambridge Companions to Music

Topics

The Cambridge Companion to Ballet
Edited by Marion Kant

The Cambridge Companion to Blues and Gospel Music
Edited by Allan Moore

The Cambridge Companion to the Concerto
Edited by Simon P. Keefe

The Cambridge Companion to Conducting
Edited by José Antonio Bowen

The Cambridge Companion to Eighteenth-Century Music
Edited by Anthony R. DelDonna and Pierpaolo Polzonetti

The Cambridge Companion to Electronic Music
Edited by Nick Collins and Julio D'Escriván

The Cambridge Companion to Grand Opera
Edited by David Charlton

The Cambridge Companion to Jazz
Edited by Mervyn Cooke and David Horn

The Cambridge Companion to the Lied
Edited by James Parsons

The Cambridge Companion to the Musical, second edition
Edited by William Everett and Paul Laird

The Cambridge Companion to the Orchestra
Edited by Colin Lawson

The Cambridge Companion to Pop and Rock
Edited by Simon Frith, Will Straw and John Street

The Cambridge Companion to Recorded Music
Edited by Eric Clarke, Nicholas Cook, Daniel Leech-Wilkinson and John Rink

The Cambridge Companion to the String Quartet
Edited by Robin Stowell

The Cambridge Companion to Twentieth-Century Opera
Edited by Mervyn Cooke

Composers

The Cambridge Companion to Bach
Edited by John Butt

The Cambridge Companion to Bartók
Edited by Amanda Bayley

The Cambridge Companion to the Beatles
Edited by Kenneth Womack

The Cambridge Companion to Beethoven
Edited by Glenn Stanley

The Cambridge Companion to Berg
Edited by Anthony Pople

The Cambridge Companion to Berlioz
Edited by Peter Bloom

The Cambridge Companion to Brahms
Edited by Michael Musgrave

The Cambridge Companion to Benjamin Britten
Edited by Mervyn Cooke

The Cambridge Companion to Bruckner
Edited by John Williamson

The Cambridge Companion to John Cage
Edited by David Nicholls

The Cambridge Companion to Chopin
Edited by Jim Samson

The Cambridge Companion to Debussy
Edited by Simon Trezise

The Cambridge Companion to Elgar
Edited by Daniel M. Grimley and Julian Rushton

The Cambridge Companion to Gilbert and Sullivan
Edited by David Eden and Meinhard Saremba

The Cambridge Companion to Handel
Edited by Donald Burrows

The Cambridge Companion to Haydn
Edited by Caryl Clark

The Cambridge Companion to Liszt
Edited by Kenneth Hamilton

The Cambridge Companion to Mahler
Edited by Jeremy Barham

The Cambridge Companion to Mendelssohn
Edited by Peter Mercer-Taylor

The Cambridge Companion to Monteverdi
Edited by John Whenham and Richard Wistreich

The Cambridge Companion to Mozart
Edited by Simon P. Keefe

The Cambridge Companion to Ravel
Edited by Deborah Mawer

The Cambridge Companion to Rossini
Edited by Emanuele Senici

The Cambridge Companion to Schubert
Edited by Christopher Gibbs

The Cambridge Companion to Schumann
Edited by Beate Perrey

The Cambridge Companion to Shostakovich
Edited by Pauline Fairclough and David Fanning

The Cambridge Companion to Sibelius
Edited by Daniel M. Grimley

The Cambridge Companion to Verdi
Edited by Scott L. Balthazar

Instruments

The Cambridge Companion to Brass Instruments
Edited by Trevor Herbert and John Wallace

The Cambridge Companion to the Cello
Edited by Robin Stowell

The Cambridge Companion to the Clarinet
Edited by Colin Lawson

The Cambridge Companion to the Guitar
Edited by Victor Coelho

The Cambridge Companion to the Organ
Edited by Nicholas Thistlethwaite and Geoffrey Webber

The Cambridge Companion to the Piano
Edited by David Rowland

The Cambridge Companion to the Recorder
Edited by John Mansfield Thomson

The Cambridge Companion to the Saxophone
Edited by Richard Ingham

The Cambridge Companion to Singing
Edited by John Potter

The Cambridge Companion to the Violin
Edited by Robin Stowell